D0367784

Viva la Libertà!

Viva la Libertà!

Politics in Opera

ANTHONY ARBLASTER

VERSO

London · New York

First published by Verso 1992
© Anthony Arblaster 1992
All rights reserved

Verso
UK: 6 Meard Street, London W1V 3HR
USA: 29 West 35th Street, New York, NY 10001-2291

Verso is the imprint of New Left Books

ISBN 0-86091-391-0

British Library Cataloguing in Publication Data
A catalogue record for this book is available from the British Library

Library of Congress Cataloging-in-Publication Data
A catalogue record for this book is available from the Library of Congress

Typeset in Bembo by York House Typographic Ltd, London
Printed in Great Britain by Bookcraft (Bath) Ltd

Contents

Preface
and Acknowledgements

What I am up to in this book is explained in the Introduction. It was always a rather ambitious project, and I am grateful to the many friends who showed an interest in it, and encouraged me to persevere. I am especially grateful to all those tolerant and encouraging editors who gave me the opportunity to air some of these ideas in pithier formats. I must thank in particular Antony Peattie who, as Publications Editor at Welsh National Opera, gave me my first break as a contributor to that company's generally excellent programme books. Thanks too to his successor, Simon Rees, who has been comparably encouraging. At Opera North, Nicholas Payne and Keith Cooper provided similar opportunities, and I am grateful also to Anthony Whitworth-Jones, formerly of Glyndebourne Touring Opera, and Stewart Spencer, editor of *Wagner* magazine. Nothing written for them has been reprinted here *in toto*, but odd paragraphs and sentences have been incorporated into the text.

A special word of thanks is due to Tom Sutcliffe of the *Guardian*, who enabled me to publish a number of articles on opera and music in that newspaper some years ago, and who has been a source of encouragement and ideas ever since. Malcolm Imrie, my editor at Verso, has been admirably supportive and helpful, and Liz Heron, who read the manuscript at his request, made some acute critical observations and suggestions, several of which I have adopted. I owe thanks also to Margaret Smith of Bexhill, whose faith in this project was unflagging, and who made available to me a number of Glyndebourne programme books that I would not otherwise have seen. I made extensive use of the library of the Sheffield University Music Department, and must thank the Librarian, Tom McCanna, for his tolerance of my heavy borrowings.

Opera is expensive to stage, and it is an expensive interest for the individual to pursue, especially when he or she has family commitments as well. So it is worth adding that this project has been financed, in effect, by myself and my family. An application for a modest sum (£200) to the British Academy was turned down, and with some honourable exceptions, such as the Leverhulme Trust, there are not many bodies that are interested in supporting a non-utilitarian cultural project of this kind – such is the philistine climate of the age.

Finally, I give love and thanks above all to Lynda Snowden. She has read and re-read the pages that follow, typed some of them, corrected most of them, and made innumerable suggestions for improvements of style and expression, nearly all of which turned out to be right. It would be difficult for me to achieve anything on this scale without her constant help and support. It is to her that this book is dedicated.

Anthony Arblaster
Sheffield, March 1992

Introduction

Politics in opera: one can already hear the groans of despair and cries of outrage that the very idea will evoke in some quarters. Is even music, the purest of the arts, to be pawed over by politicians in search of hidden meanings or sinister significances? Cannot these ideologists leave anything alone?

It is hard to think of any sentiment more likely to raise an easy round of applause in Britain than the appeal 'let's keep politics out of this'. Even professional politicians often seem unwilling to defend their occupation. They are forever telling us that this or that issue 'transcends' politics, or should be 'taken out' of politics. Politics, in short, is a dirty word, and we want as little to do with the reality of it as possible.

This hostility, or distaste, rests upon a particular understanding (or misunderstanding) of what politics is, or rather a set of images of it. One is of the petty squabbling and unscrupulous feuding of men and women who are hungry for one thing only – power. Or there is the equation of politics with *party* politics, which provokes resistance since many people are neither members nor supporters of political parties. Or there is the perception of politics as a straitjacket or Procrustean bed into which awkward realities are forcibly fitted, but only at a cost to reality itself. None of these images and impressions is without substance, but none of them corresponds entirely to what I

I

understand by the term 'politics', or consequently to what is meant by it in the context of this book.

Traditionally, politics has been centred on the question of government or rule: what persons or institutions govern and should govern society. Discussion of politics can then become a discussion of the forms that government takes: monarchy, oligarchy, democracy, dictatorship, and so on. Discussion is not usually the essence of opera, yet there is more exploration of these questions in opera than might be supposed. *Idomeneo* and, even more explicitly, *La clemenza di Tito* are among other things meditations or homilies on the virtues appropriate to a good ruler; as such they stand at the end of a long tradition in *opera seria* of fables about good kings and queens – or sometimes bad ones – fables that are many of them blatantly sycophantic in character. *Simon Boccanegra* and *Don Carlos*, *Boris Godunov* and *Khovanschina*, and more recently *Gloriana* and *King Priam* are all operas that are at one level about government, its problems and responsibilities.

More widely, politics is indeed about power, meaning not only the struggles of individuals to achieve it or hold onto it, but also the distribution of power in society between various groups and individuals, and the relations between the (relatively) powerful and the (relatively) powerless. Everyone is familiar with power relationships: within families, within groups, within institutions of every size and type. These structures of power are political not only because of their power dimension, but because these products of human societies and human activities can be changed by human action, if we so wish. This is something that feminism in particular has shown us, or at least reminded us of. Relations between men and women are likely also to be in part power relations, with the balance of power usually lying with men. In so far as opera explores or exposes these relations – as it so often does – it is dealing with what must now be acknowledged to be political issues, that is, matters of controversy in society about which there is considerable agitation for change.

To extrapolate, we can say that politics is about how we live and how we might live – to borrow a phrase from William Morris – when these are treated as collective as well as individual questions. Politics is not only about how we are governed, or who governs us, but also about the collective values and purposes of our societies, and what they might be, or should be. In this broad sense at least, virtually everyone is interested in politics, and has political views or convictions. Nearly everyone has views about the proper pattern of relations between men and women, or husbands and wives. Nearly everyone has an opinion, usually strongly held, about what loyalty to one's country implies or requires, or about what freedom is, or fairness, and why and to what extent they are to be valued.

It is clear that politics in Morris's broad sense is bound to be woven into the texture of opera simply because the large questions of politics are not separate from the other large questions that have always preoccupied dramatic composers. The great issues of politics affect and stir us all at one time or another. In so far as opera at its greatest aims to present as profound and comprehensive an interpretation of human life as do drama or fiction or poetry, it is bound to incorporate a political dimension. Hence many, if not all, of the recent complaints about the 'politicization' of operas by producers, often from central or eastern Europe, seem to me misplaced. These producers are often drawing attention to aspects of opera that have simply been ignored or neglected by producers and designers who have too readily accepted Samuel Johnson's famous description of it as an 'exotic and irrational entertainment', in which ideas of any kind have no place.

Politics can and does reach into many kinds of music, but opera, as a form that is essentially both public and dramatic, could hardly avoid it. A piano sonata or a string quartet or a song cycle may treat of essentially personal and intimate themes and experiences, though they may often reach out beyond them. But opera is not in that sense an intimate form. Once it moved beyond its courtly beginnings, as it very soon did, it became a form of public entertainment for substantial audiences. It therefore had to address themes that would be the common property of those audiences. It was pushed in the direction of public and political themes by its own nature as a form. Opera is more like drama than it is like the novel: the stage is naturally a public arena, and opera, like drama, tends to happen in public places. The purely domestic play or opera, despite the modern 'drawing-room' or 'kitchen-sink' play, is the exception rather than the rule. Nevertheless it is this domestic exception that has tended to dominate the modern stage, and it may be that the special fondness that operas like *The Marriage of Figaro*, *La traviata* and *Eugene Onegin* inspire in contemporary audiences derives in part from their rough approximation to this familiar domestic model.

One special feature that pushes opera in the direction of politics is the chorus. It plays a minimal role in Mozart's collaborations with da Ponte and in a good many other eighteenth-century operas, representing marginal groups of well-wishers, hangers-on, and so forth. But post-1789 is another matter. In comedy the chorus is still often marginal and dispensable. But in serious opera it plays an increasingly prominent and integral part, and certain nineteenth-century operas might be thought of as primarily choral works, such as Rossini's *Mosè in Egitto*, or contain whole scenes and episodes that are essentially choral, such as *Guillaume Tell, Nabucco, Lohengrin, Boris Godunov, Aida, Parsifal*, and many others. The collective voice of the chorus takes us at once into the public realm, and very often it represents that new actor on the political scene the people – or 'the masses', as some would have it. It is through the chorus in *Nabucco, I lombardi, Macbeth* and other works that Verdi gave expression to the patriotic sentiments of Italians in the period of the Risorgimento. Mussorgsky uses the chorus in *Boris Godunov* and in *Khovanschina* as the voice of the suffering, waiting Russian people. The positive role of the chorus is one way in which opera adjusts to the more democratic politics of the post-1789 era.

It does not follow from any of this that audiences will welcome or accept the presence of politics in opera. If they go to opera in search of uncomplicated entertainment, or pure musical delight (whatever that might be), they may well resent being invited to construct more complex and even ambivalent responses to what they hear and see. But I would argue that this approach simply does not take opera seriously enough. No one goes to *King Lear* or *The Three Sisters* looking for uncomplicated entertainment. It is accepted that drama at its most ambitious seeks to explore the human condition in all its depth and complexity. Why are some people reluctant to recognize that the same is true of opera? The great composers of opera are not less serious or ambitious artists than Shakespeare, Schiller, Büchner, Pushkin, Melville and Henry James, who are, of course, some of the writers on whose texts these composers based their operas. Critics have no difficulty in identifying the political dimension in Shakespeare or Schiller or Pushkin. Why should we assume, without further

4

evidence, that this dimension of their work was of no interest to Verdi or Mussorgsky or Alban Berg?

To be sure, it is sometimes the case that a political text is depoliticized to some degree when it is turned into an opera: comparison between Ostrovsky's play *The Storm* and the opera Janáček based on it, *Katya Kabanova*, is a case in point, as is, to a lesser extent, the adaptation by Mozart/da Ponte of Beaumarchais's *La folle journée ou le mariage de Figaro*. But on the other hand Rossini and his librettists make of *William Tell* a more explicit and unambiguous political drama than Schiller had done, and Verdi enhances and underlines the topical political elements in *Macbeth*. Beethoven's transformation of *Leonore* into *Fidelio* also involved developing its general political elements at the expense of the personal drama around which the opera is built. The notion that musicians, or composers, are by their very nature apolitical, uninterested in anything but pure music and the processes of composition, is a cosy piece of mythology; more precisely, it is a generalization that fits a few composers no doubt, but not all by any means, and particularly not most opera composers.

It seems to be more true of critics and musicologists. It is they who disregard the political views and involvements of composers, and who then complain of the 'politicization' of their works. But composers must make their music out of something: a something that in some sense lies outside or beyond the music itself.

It is true that poetry and prose are composed of words, and that music is composed of notes. Because notes, unlike words, make no direct reference to the world beyond notes, it is always possible for musicians to argue that music consists in the notes alone – although this argument does not apply to opera or any vocal music that combines music with words. But in many cases we know, from the composers themselves, that their apparently 'pure' music is actually 'about' something beyond the music itself. When we respond to it most fully, we do not experience it as something totally separate from the rest of our lives, but as something that illuminates, deepens and extends our responses to and understanding of life as a whole.

Of course this is not necessarily or always the way in which we experience music. Just as politics can be compartmentalized and kept separate from daily life, so it is perfectly possible to make no connection between what music might have to teach us and our behaviour at work or in the home. George Steiner has insisted on this point often enough, pointing to the capacity of those directly involved in or responsible for the mass killing of Jews in World War Two to listen with apparent equanimity to Bach or Beethoven after a day's work in the bureaucracy of cruelty and mass murder. Religion is often confined to the weekend; in a similar way some people turn to music as an escape from the stresses and contradictions of everyday life, and hence do not connect it, or want to have it connected, with difficult daily dilemmas. From this escapism springs resentment at opera productions that insist on making those kind of connections, and the associated demand that opera should offer us entertainment, enchantment, but nothing deeper or more disturbing. This reaction, understandable as it is, simply does not do justice to the scope and complexity of music or opera.

If we respond to music as fully as we are able, then we have to accept that it cannot be fully understood without a knowledge of its historical and political context. Moreover, the very word 'context' is misleading if it is taken to mean something extraneous to the music. Beethoven's passionate response to the ideals of 1789 and to Napoleon is written into the *Eroica* Symphony, into the *Egmont* music, into *Fidelio* and its overtures, into the Ninth Symphony, and much else. Smetana's ardent nationalism is the very essence of *Ma Vlast* and *Libuse*. Sir Michael Tippett's lifelong pacifism is a thread that runs through many of his works from *A Child of Our Time* to his most recent opera, *New Year*. Examples could be multiplied – and will be in the pages that follow.

But it may be asked whether we could know this context from the music alone. In opera and other vocal music the words are at least a clue to the composer's concerns. But does the music itself contain a political meaning? I would and will argue that it does. Let us consider one or two examples. I think it would be hard for a listener with a reasonable comparative knowledge of classical music to listen to the *Egmont* Overture and not hear it as a piece of music that is essentially about public heroism and its ultimate triumph. The music, the notes, do not tell us who the hero is or what his or her cause is. Nor does the *Eroica*, if we know nothing of its cancelled dedication. But that this is music of public, political struggle rather than of subjective, private agonies seems to be part of the character of the music itself. Or suppose that we heard the famous 'Va pensiero' chorus from *Nabucco* without knowing who precisely was singing, or what about. The long unison line of the vocal melody would be enough in itself, I think, to tell us that this is the voice of a group lamenting its own collective plight, not mourning the death of a king or an individual. So much, at least, is inherent in the music itself.

Still, we are brought back to the non-specificity of music. Richard Strauss is probably the most brilliant of all orchestral illustrators and mimics, but we still need his titles and synopses to guide us through the episodes of *Don Quixote* or *Ein Heldenleben*. The music does not completely speak for itself. Yet with that minimal guidance, we can hear how apt the music is for its chosen programme. In the same way, Janáček's Piano Sonata needs its subtitle 'I.X. 1905, From the Street', and the note that explains that it was composed to commemorate a man who was killed while taking part in a demonstration calling for a Czech university in Brno. Given this help, we can hear this as a work of protest and political grief.

In dealing specifically with opera my task is made easier by the presence of words, and it will be apparent throughout this study how dependent I am upon a close study of libretti. This is not, I hope, to treat opera as mere word-setting. Opera is not the setting to music of a pre-existing drama: it is the creation of drama through the music – *dramma per musica*, as the old Italian phrase had it; the phrase that forms the basis for the title of Joseph Kerman's classic study, *Opera as Drama*. Sometimes the words in their plainness barely hint at what the composer may make of them. The final lines of *The Marriage of Figaro* provide a classic instance. Out of da Ponte's perfunctory 'Contessa perdono! Perdono, perdono!' from the Count, and the Countess's brief reply – 'Piu docile io sono / e dico di si', Mozart creates one of the supreme resolutionary moments in opera. Then again, what looks politically interesting in a libretto may be treated musically as gabbled recitative: the composer's interests lie elsewhere. I have tried, no doubt not entirely successfully, not to rely too heavily on the words alone.

Nevertheless, opera is words as well as music, and *prima facie* we must assume that the words form a part of the meaning of the whole. Only the most benighted canary-fanciers persist in treating opera as if it were one long wordless *vocalise*. And in fact it is the rule rather than the exception that composers involve themselves in the production of the text of the opera. Mozart's letters in relation to both *Idomeneo* and *Die Entführung aus dem Serail* exemplify this. Verdi would clearly have written his own texts had he felt competent to do so, so detailed are his instructions to his various long-suffering librettists, and so persistent is his interference with their work. Puccini, Strauss and Britten show a similar concern to get the exact text they want. And above all it is striking how many composers have written or compiled their own texts. There is a tendency to think of this as a Wagnerian, or Tippettian, eccentricity. This is a misapprehension. Berlioz, Mussorgsky, Boito, Borodin, Tchaikovsky, Rimsky-Korsakov, Janáček, Strauss, Busoni, Schoenberg, Berg, Prokofiev, Dallapiccola, Zimmermann and Stockhausen are among those who have either written their own texts or made their own adaptations of existing texts. In these cases at least, we can be reasonably sure that attention to the words will tell us a good deal about the composer's preoccupations and intentions, even though it is still possible that his musical instincts will lead him in other directions.

A comparison of the libretto with its sources will also often tell us something about the composer's concerns. What he or she selects or focuses on will be a clue to the nature of the completed work. The differences between Pushkin's *Eugene Onegin* and Tchaikovsky's, for example, tell us much about the composer and his opera.

Given the attention that so many opera composers have devoted to getting the words right, it seems to me that the libretto has been unduly neglected by many musical commentators. Indeed I am struck by the number of musical writers who seem indifferent to anything that lies beyond a 'purely' musical analysis (assuming such a thing to be possible at all); moreover, many of those who do attend to words and ideas as well as music seem automatically suspicious of any attempt to connect music with politics or ideology, or to 'read politics into' the music itself, even when connections, or the presence of the political element, seem obvious and undeniable. There is a perverse, wilful determination in some quarters to deny the political dimension of opera, as of much other music, as if to admit its existence was to allow the exalted realm of pure music to be contaminated by contact with sordid reality.

I am not a trained or professional musician or student of music, and that is an obvious disadvantage as far as this book is concerned. But I was educated as an historian, and having taught politics, in particular political theories and ideologies, for more than twenty years, I do have some understanding of the historical, political and cultural context in which opera has been produced over the past two hundred years. And given that so many excellent musical commentators approach the subject of this book with reluctance or even distaste, or simply disregard it altogether, my own venture into this relatively un-explored territory does not, I think, require any very elaborate justification.

Probably the ideal form of this study would be a comprehensive history of opera, properly informed by an understanding not only of political developments and ideas, but also of the way in which cultural and musical forms and styles reflect or embody in their development significant political, social and economic changes. Such a history is beyond my capacity. What I have written is a selective study of various composers, operas and operatic developments of the past two hundred years, which will simply illustrate the usefulness, and, no doubt, the limitations, of a politically aware approach to the form.

By way of an example, let us consider an opera by a composer who is rarely associated by commentators with politics or ideology of any kind: Delius's *A Village Romeo and Juliet*. What little comment there has been on what is probably Delius's most successful opera has concentrated, understandably enough, on its adaptation of the Shakes-pearian story and its Wagnerian echoes. But a closer look at the text and structure of the opera reveals that it has an interesting and very characteristic social dimension: characteristic, that is, of Delius and the culture he belonged to.

The strange figure of the Dark Fiddler is sometimes treated as an excrescence or oddity. In fact he is central to the story and its themes. He represents, like the Rhinemaidens, the original wronged victim; from the crime against him all the evil and tragedy of the story follows quite inevitably. The two farmers, Manz and Marti, struggle like Wotan and Alberich for control of the land that rightfully belongs to the Fiddler; the dispute ruins them both and leaves their children, the young lovers Sali and Vrenchen, destitute. The farmers' robbery of the Fiddler's land, like Alberich's theft of the gold, is a crime against nature, an act of despoliation. Both in the first and last scenes of the opera, the Fiddler celebrates the land that is rightfully his in its wild, unploughed state. So long as it remains wild, 'As long as the wind thro' the tangled thicket sings,' he tells the children, 'no harm shall come to you.' But the farmers are determined to exploit the wilderness, and their greed ruins their children as well as themselves.

Once Sali has accidentally killed Vrenchen's father Marti, the lovers have no choice but to flee from respectable society. But the social alternative that is available to them, to join a band of carefree vagabonds, is not one they can accept. They are wholly committed to each other and therefore to monogamy, the vagabonds to promiscuity, or the absence of lasting ties. One of them scoffs at Vrenchen, 'Silly goose! our gay life would never do for you, you're far too prudish!' and Vrenchen accepts that 'We could not live as they do, their way of life could never be ours.' And so the lovers accept the inevitability of death. There is no other way out of their dilemma. What dooms them is not some kind of unspecific, metaphysical fate, but their inability to find a place in the available social groupings.

That this is at least a part of what Delius, and his source, Gottfried Keller, intended is, I think, likely. For one thing the vagabonds are sympathetically portrayed. They stand for a kind of freedom, from conventions, ties and property, which clearly represents a positive alternative to the property obsession that has destroyed the two farmers. For another, the gypsies represent the kind of bohemian revolt against the nineteenth century with which Delius himself enthusiastically identified, especially in the 1890s.

So one way of responding to this pastoral tragedy is to see it as a critique of property-centred materialism, and especially of the alienated and exploitative attitude to nature that it generates, by contrast with the passionate identification *with* nature that is so central to Delius's philosophy. It is also a hymn to the anti-bourgeois bohemianism that meant far more to Delius than it ever did to Puccini. So much, then, by way of example. Those who are uninterested, or unconvinced, need read no further.

My interest is essentially in the period since 1789, or perhaps 1776. Those are the dates that mark the beginning of modern politics, politics as we know it. That is to say, they mark the beginning of a politics in which the issues, the ideologies and the forces at work are all familiar to us because they have remained much the same throughout the subsequent period. In this book I am concerned to discover what impact these ideologies and issues have made upon opera, and how the forms and nature of opera have changed to encompass these new, demanding and often perplexing realities.

So I have confined myself to opera from Mozart onwards, simply as a matter of convenience and personal interest (it has still left me plenty to write about). I have no doubt that an excellent study could be written about the politics of *opera seria*, and the different treatments of the themes of kingship and good government that are central to so much eighteenth-century opera. But that is another task for another writer.

Some major composers get chapters to themselves. Others are grouped together thematically, and this sometimes means that a single composer – Janáček, for example – appears in more than one chapter. This is awkward, but I do not see how it could have been avoided. I was anxious not to provide simply a catalogue of the relevant operas, a kind of political *Kobbé*, but instead to construct something a little more coherent and argued.

I have had to be selective, in any case. Opera in performance is now much more widely available in Britain than it was twenty years ago, and records can partially compensate for the absence of a staging. Quite a number of the more than eighty operas I discuss I have heard but not seen. They include some works by Rossini, a number of Verdi's early operas, Auber's *La muette de Portici*, Glinka's two operas, Vaughan Williams's operas, Dallapiccola's *Il prigioniero*, and several others. There are a few operas I have not even managed to hear, including Cherubini's *Lodoiska* and *Les deux journées*, Smetana's *Dalibor*, Britten's *Owen Wingrave* and some others. Perhaps one day we shall be able to see as well as hear *Riders to the Sea*, *Il prigioniero*, *Die Soldaten* and the neglected operas of Glinka and Smetana. Meanwhile, these gaps only underline the selective character of this current project. It will have been worth undertaking if its readers find that it casts some additional and even unexpected light on the operas that they do see and hear.

1

Mozart: Class Conflict and Enlightenment

Mozart, who is generally agreed to have been the most phenomenally gifted composer who ever lived, is likely to remain also the most enigmatic. Like Shakespeare, like Homer, but unlike, say, Michelangelo or Milton, the person, the creator, remains hidden behind the work. Whereas with some creative artists the work is clearly felt to be an expression of the artist's personality, and self-expression may even be a conscious purpose of the work, with Mozart there is the sense of a gap between the man and the work. Indeed, it is more than that. The disjunction between the human being, who seems in some way coarse and immature to the point of childishness, and the extraordinary maturity of understanding of human feelings and social relations displayed in the operas is so acute as to be paradoxical and puzzling. This was what, in my view, gave Peter Shaffer's much-derided play *Amadeus* its validity: it raised the question of the perennially problematic relationship between artistic creation and human personality, which is posed almost as acutely in the cases of Beethoven and Wagner.

As with Shakespeare, it is hard to know or to be sure what Mozart believed and, even where there is relevant evidence, it is hard to know at what level he believed what he believed, and how far it may or may not be embodied in the music. With Beethoven or Verdi or Mussorgsky or Tippett there is not the same problem. We do not doubt that there is a consonance between Verdi's personal patriotism and anti-clericalism and the rendering of such sentiments in his operas. But how far does Mozart identify himself with the anti-aristocratic sentiments of *The Marriage of Figaro*, or the Masonic Enlightenment of *The Magic Flute*? It may be in part a question of a musical style, the classical idiom of the late eighteenth century, which was sustained in the early nineteenth century by Schubert in his symphonies and by Rossini. For I think the same question arises with *Guillaume Tell*, an opera in which a national and popular struggle against an occupying foreign power is depicted with vividness and sympathy. As in the case of Mozart, Rossini's command of his musical resources may have enabled him to express feelings and attitudes with which, ultimately, he did not wholly or deeply identify.

These points need to be made by way of a caution, because the thrust of my argument is that Mozart was in fact a more politically aware composer than is usually supposed, and that the more overtly political operas do in fact harmonize with what we know of his attitudes and experiences outside the music itself.

The two dimensions of his work that concern us here are, first, his awareness of social class, class distinctions and class conflict; and, second, his sympathy with the rational humanism of the Enlightenment. In both respects Mozart can be seen as a pre-revolutionary composer, one who belonged, necessarily and essentially, to the moment at which modern politics, with its awareness of class and its sense of hope generated by the new possibilities of progress, was born.

Just as the modern world begins with the French Revolution, or perhaps with the American Declaration of Independence in 1776, so modern opera begins with *Le nozze di Figaro*, first performed just three years before the storming of the Bastille. Opera audiences today can see a far wider repertory than was the case, say, thirty years ago, so they may well be familiar with operas by Monteverdi, Handel, Gluck and others. Nevertheless, it is probably still true that *Figaro* is the earliest opera that every opera-goer knows and that no opera company would dream of omitting from its repertory. And this is no accident. *Figaro* is truly the first modern opera, the first in which the characters, their sentiments and their dilemmas seem to belong to our world, the first opera where we do not have to make a special effort of one kind or another to grasp the conventions and significance of what is going on:

'The complexity and ambiguity of sentiment in *The Marriage of Figaro* made it possible for Mozart to put on stage, for the first time in the history of opera, really human, three-dimensional, individual characters,' Charles Rosen has written.[1] Even in the hands of Mozart, in *Idomeneo* and especially in *La clemenza di Tito*, the conventions of *opera seria* are still, from a modern audience's point of view, a straitjacket, imposing a degree of aloofness and formality, a statuesque quality, which the producer and performers will strive to counteract but cannot wholly abolish, because they are inherent in the designs of the works themselves. *Opera buffa*, on the other hand, had developed from the start as an alternative to the aristocratic and absolutist classicism of *opera seria*. It was always intended to be more popular and more topical. And so it was. Yet the *buffo* operas of the eighteenth century have not survived as part of the standard repertory. What makes *Figaro* different?

To say 'Mozart's genius' is hardly an answer. By the time he came to compose *Figaro* Mozart was nearly thirty, and an experienced opera composer. Of his earlier works only *Idomeneo* and *Die Entführung aus dem Serail* are now regularly performed. Neither is a *buffo* work, although *Die Entführung* has some *buffo* characteristics and characters. It was an inspired choice for Mozart to decide that he wished to use Beaumarchais's recent and scandalous play *Le mariage de Figaro* as the basis for an Italian opera; he was equally fortunate in securing the services of Lorenzo da Ponte to make the necessary adaptation. It was Beaumarchais's comedy that enabled Mozart to realize to the full for the first time his genius for the depiction of three-dimensional characters, seen in interaction with each other and placed firmly within a clearly depicted social context. Rosen has even gone so far as to say that 'Beaumarchais invented modern opera with some help from Mozart.'[2] With *Figaro*, *opera buffa* moves beyond stereotype and caricature to achieve characters who are both individual and typical, realistic and representative. We may contrast *Figaro* in this respect with Pergolesi's entertaining *buffo* piece *La serva padrona*.

As its title ('The maid as mistress') suggests, Pergolesi's intermezzo is also a comedy of class. It hinges on the reversal of the normal relations between servant and master, and promotes the pleasing myth that the servant, especially the female servant, can, by cunning and the exploitation of sex appeal, lord it over her nominal master and actual employer. In any kind of class society, the subordinate majority always enjoys seeing the tables turned in this manner. And, as with all really durable myths, there is a degree of truth in it. There *are* situations in which the tables can be turned. Economic power is not the only form of power. Nevertheless 'the tables turned' is a myth, much in the same way that 'rags-to-riches' is a myth: meaning not that it never happens, but that it does not and cannot offer a general solution to the problem of class inequality and exploitation. Both myths serve the function of cheering up the lower orders, by assuring them that there is always a way out or a possibility of revenge, if only they have the wit to find it.

It is of course true that *La serva padrona*, when it was brought to Paris in 1752, nearly twenty years after it was first performed, became the spark that ignited a famous controversy over the relative merits of Italian and French opera. And undoubtedly the wit and topicality of Pergolesi's comedy were part of what recommended it to French champions of musical reform and renewal, including Jean-Jacques Rousseau. But I doubt that even Rousseau saw anything subversive in *La serva padrona*. It is a mild joke, which all but the most pompous bourgeois could enjoy without misgiving. And it ends with foolish old Uberto admitting defeat and marrying his own maidservant. The classes are reconciled.

Figaro is a very different matter. Here within the household of Count Almaviva at Aguas Frescas near Seville, we witness a significant episode in the struggle against aristocratic privilege, in which the Count's sexual designs are comprehensively frustrated by the ingenious resistance of Figaro and Susanna, and he is in the end compelled to accept defeat and seek forgiveness from his long-suffering wife. Whereas in the earlier Figaro play, *Le barbier de Seville*, Figaro and his master Almaviva combined to outwit Bartholo and win Rosine for the Count, in *Figaro* master and servants are pitted against each other, and victory goes to the quick-witted servants.

This was something new for Mozart too. In *Die Entführung* the role of the servants Blonde and Pedrillo is to support their mistress and master, Constanze and Belmonte, and to assist the rescue of the former by the latter. Their only real enemy is not the Pasha Selim, who is finally a model of magnanimity, but his cruel steward Osmin. He is the servant who abuses his delegated powers, and is in the end rebuked if not punished for it. So traditional relations between the classes are respected, and the prestige of the nobility, including the 'heathen' Pasha, remains in the end unimpaired.

Not so in *Figaro*. Here as in *Le barbier de Seville* Figaro is the quintessence of the man or woman who must needs live by his or her wits because (s)he was not born with any other advantages (much like Beaumarchais himself). And, like the so-called self-made man through the ages, Figaro despises the aristocrat who has merely inherited his advantages:

> Because you are a great nobleman, you think you are a great genius. . . . Nobility, fortune, rank, position! How proud they make a man feel! What have you done to deserve such advantages? Put yourself to the trouble of being born – nothing more! For the rest – a very ordinary man! Whereas I, lost among the obscure crowd, have had to deploy more knowledge, more calculation and skill merely to survive than has sufficed to rule all the provinces of Spain for a century! Yet you would measure yourself against me . . .[3]

It is true that this insubordinate railing appears only in Beaumarchais's play, and not in the opera libretto, and that Figaro is left in Act Four to reflect bitterly only on the relations between men and women. But the omitted words are in no way inconsistent with the character of Figaro as he appears in the opera.

The essence of the class war in the opera is contained in the duel between Figaro and the Count, and each has a recitative and aria in which he issues a challenge to the other. Necessarily, the declaration of war comes from below. 'Bravo, Signor padrone', says Figaro angrily early in the first act, when Susanna has explained to her slightly naïve fiancé just why the Count has allocated them a room so close to his own. And then Figaro goes on to sing, 'Se vuol ballare, Signor Contino', a mocking, yet menacing minuet which asserts that if the Count wishes to dance – very well, but it will be Figaro who will be the dancing teacher. It is often said that da Ponte and Mozart played down or even eliminated the element of social satire in *Figaro*. It is therefore worth noting that this openly challenging song of Figaro's is one of their additions to Beaumarchais's text, the only cue for it in the play being Figaro's exit line 'et puis, dansez, Monseigneur' in Act

Two, the moment when Mozart offers a miniature reprise of 'Se vuol ballare'.

In Act Three the Count responds with a soliloquy recitative and aria ('Hai gia vinto la causa') full of anger and violence, in which it is clear that it is his pride and sense of status as much as his lust that are offended by the plan to keep Susanna out of his clutches. Why should I sigh with frustration while a servant of mine is happy? he asks:

> Vedro, mentrio sospiro,
> Felice un servo mio?

Almaviva, wrote Joseph Kerman, 'is Mozart's most savage creation'.[4] Behind his suave manners and charm, which Beaumarchais in his guidance to the actor insisted should always be sustained, he hides a brutality that surfaces in his private behaviour towards his wife in Act Two, when he suspects that she is concealing something or someone from him, and in this aria, which as Basil Deane observed, 'reminds us of the underlying current of intolerance and violence, barely held in check, in the opera'.[5]

At first sight it might appear that the unhappy Countess, who plays a vital role in the plot to expose her husband's philandering, stands outside this pattern of antagonistic class relations. But she, like her husband, has a strong sense of what is proper to her social position, and her saddest aria, 'Dove sono', springs directly out of a double sense of humiliation: first, at being insulted and betrayed by her husband, but, second, at having to stoop to seek the help of her servant Susanna:

> O cielo! A quale
> Umil stato fatale io son ridotta
> Da un consorte crudel . . .
> Fammi or cercar da una mia serva aita!

(Heavens, to what a humiliating condition I have been reduced by a cruel husband . . . that I am forced to seek the help of one of my servants!)

All this comes at the climax of the very eloquent accompanied recitative that leads directly into the aria itself. Her sadness and isolation are an expression both of her class position and of her dependence on an aristocratic husband who, despite his public renunciation of the infamous *droit de seigneur*, still intends to take full advantage of his social and economic position in relation to the women he employs – Barberina as well as Susanna.

For *Figaro* is an episode in the sex war as well as the class war. As we have seen, Susanna is quicker than Figaro to detect the Count's real purposes behind his apparent benevolence. It is Susanna who draws the Countess into the conspiracy, and it is Susanna who uses it to teach her fiancé a lesson in trust. For in the final act Figaro as well as the Count has to learn to respect women, rather than assuming in the age-old chauvinist way that it is they rather than men who are to be mistrusted in matters of love and sex – *così fan tutte*. Marcellina, once she has discovered her true relationship to Figaro, joins the Countess and Susanna in their alliance of women against men, and it is she who issues the call for female solidarity in her Act Four recitative and aria:

> Ogni donna è portata alla difesa del suo povero sesso,
> Da questi uomini ingrati a torto oppresso.

(All women ought to come to the defence of their unhappy sex, so wrongly oppressed by these ungrateful men.)

This is often cut in performance for quite plausible reasons. Marcellina is not a major character, and the first part of the act, if complete, includes a sequence of five arias, not all of which do much to advance the action. Nevertheless, its omission detracts from the radical character of the opera, and reinforces the misleading impression that Mozart and da Ponte converted Beaumarchais's challenging comedy into an anodyne country-house romp.

The other last-act aria that is usually dropped is Basilio's, and this cut too is a significant loss to the social meaning of the opera. For while Bartolo questions whether Figaro ought to put up with his master's pursuit of Susanna, Basilio says that it is unwise to confront the great, for nine times out of ten you'll be defeated:

> Nel mondo, amico,
> L'accozzarla co'grandi
> Fu pericolo ognora:
> Dan novanta percento, e vien vinto ancora.

Wear an ass's skin, is his advice. It is thick enough to resist every insult and humiliation.

This is certainly not advice that would have appealed to Mozart, who had far too strong a sense of his own worth meekly to accept put-downs from aristocrats or employers. For he had been a servant, and had been ostentatiously treated as one by the Archbishop of Salzburg. He wrote with bitterness about this to his father:

> We lunch about twelve o'clock, unfortunately somewhat too early for me – Our party consists of the two valets, . . . the contrôleur, Herr Zetti, the confectioner, the two cooks, . . . and my insignificant self. By the way, the two valets sit at the top of the table, but at least I have the honour of being placed above the cooks. . . . The Archbishop is so kind as to add to his lustre by his household, robs them of their chance of earning and pays them nothing. . . . If I get nothing, I shall go to the Archbishop and tell him with absolute frankness that if he will not allow me to earn anything, then he must pay me, for I cannot live at my own expense.[6]

Mozart and his father were undoubtedly tiresome employees from the Archbishop's point of view. In the end their frequent and prolonged absences from Salzburg, and the younger Mozart's minimal compliance with the requirements of service in the Prince-Archbishop's household, led to the famous showdown in the summer of 1781, when Mozart, to his father's dismay, resigned from the Archbishop's service, and was literally kicked out of the Archbishop's residence by Count Arco.

That kick was not forgotten or forgiven by the composer, and provoked him to a memorable expression of his sense of human worth and dignity:

> It is the heart that ennobles a man; and though I am no count, yet I have probably more honour in me than many a count. Whether a man be a count or a valet, the moment he insults me, he is a scoundrel.[7]

As Hugh Ottaway pointed out, these are 'sentiments indistinguishable from those of Beethoven'.[8] What is more, they recall the moment in *Die Zauberflöte* when the priestly order is considering Tamino's application to become a member. When the Speaker says 'he is a prince', Sarastro responds, 'More than that, he is a man.'

As with Beethoven, the sense of equality and the indifference to titles are mingled with a powerful sense of self-esteem and of the respect due to individual genius. Thus Leopold Mozart wrote approvingly of Paris: 'There the nobility treat men of genius with the greatest deference, respect and courtesy.'[9] But the idea of respect being due to genius was at odds, the young Mozart was to find, with the principle he had been taught of respect for the aristocratic and the titled.

Thus Mozart's personal experience of employment by 'the great', coupled with his belief in his own abilities, would predispose him to sympathize with Figaro's outbursts against aristocracy, and we should remember that it was not da Ponte but Mozart who chose Beaumarchais's play as a possible basis for an opera. He must have known what he was doing. Beaumarchais had had a struggle to get the play performed at all in Paris, and in the domains of the Austrian emperor it was banned completely. If the composer had not had some sympathy with the themes and attitudes of the play, it seems unlikely that he would have made such a risky choice of subject on purely musical grounds. Perhaps Mozart hoped, in choosing *Figaro*, to rival or eclipse Paisiello's version of *Il barbiere di Siviglia*, which had been premiered in 1782 and was the most popular opera of the period. But if so, he either underestimated the novelty and complexity of what he created in *Figaro*, or overestimated the responsiveness of the Viennese audience. *Figaro* was not a great success in Vienna. It had had 20 performances up to January 1790, and *Don Giovanni* 15. This total of 35 Mozart performances compares with 166 of works by Paisiello, 138 of Salieri, 124 of Cimarosa, and 105 of Soler in the period 1783–90. *Figaro* was 'much too clever to succeed in Vienna', said Joseph Kerman.[10]

It is undoubtedly the case that da Ponte's version of *Figaro* is less forthright, less aggressively anti-aristocratic than the original play. But too much has been made of this, even to the point of suggesting that the opera is essentially a 'refined, courtly rococo comedy' devoid of 'social satire', in which 'everything is transformed into an enchanting atmosphere of unreality'.[11] Those who argue thus have failed to note how closely, for the most part, the opera follows the play; or to ask themselves why such an unreal and courtly entertainment so signally failed to enchant its first aristocratic audiences.

Structurally, the striking thing about *Figaro* is the great number of ensembles – fourteen out of twenty-eight listed musical 'numbers' – and the relative unimportance of individual arias: except, perhaps, in the case of that rather isolated and lonely figure, the Countess. And, unlike the beautiful but statuesque quartet in *Idomeneo*, for instance, or even the more varied and dramatic quartet in *Die Entführung*, which is nevertheless strictly superfluous to the action, in *Figaro* it is through the ensembles that the action is advanced and played out, and characters are filled in. The most spectacular example of this is the immensely extended and cumulative finale to Act Two.

The other great advance registered by Mozart's wonderfully varied use of ensembles is the sense of a complex, structured society which is conveyed through them. Consider just two of the duets involving Susanna. In 'Crudel! Perche finora' the Count arranges to meet Susanna in the garden in the evening. The duet is basically an interrogation: the Count wants to be sure of her compliance. Susanna is preoccupied with the plot of which this assignment is a part, and cannot always remember whether to say yes or no to the Count's questions. But as a servant, and also to further the plot, she must appear compliant. Later in the same act, the Countess tells her to confirm the arrangement by writing him a note, which she then dictates – *sull'aria*. This provides a perfect model of (literally) harmonious employer–secretary relations. The Countess dictates, and Susanna repeats the end of each phrase as she finishes writing it; then she reads the whole letter back to the Countess. The rest he will understand – 'Ei gia il resto capira' – on this they are agreed, and sing together in thirds and echoing phrases. All of this is contained in a brief duet (sixty-two bars) of musical perfection. It is through such brilliant musical patterns that the social relations of this household are conveyed.

Beaumarchais's original play and da Ponte's extremely skilful adaptation of it are both so important to the success of *Figaro* that it is worth adding a word or two about the political sympathies of these two writers. Both led the kind of lives that has resulted in them often being referred to as 'adventurers'. But this verdict only reflects the stability of a society in which job specialization and a lifelong career are the norm. For the talented and enterprising, bourgeois specialization meant frustration.

Beaumarchais began, under the auspices of his father, as a clock- and watchmaker, and by his early twenties had become the royal watchmaker. Like other talented and self-confident bourgeois, like Voltaire for example, he came into conflict with the privileged nobility, touchy and jealous of their increasingly threatened social superiority. He made a name as a polemicist in these disputes, and also as a dramatist, but also acted as a secret agent for Louis XVI. In the mid 1770s he became convinced that France ought to be helping the Americans in their struggle for independence from Britain. Louis was unwilling to quarrel openly with Britain, but the French and Spanish governments agreed to fund the front company that Beaumarchais invented and presided over, which traded in supplies to the Americans. Another of Beaumarchais's projects was the publication, after Voltaire's death, of a collected edition of the great man's works. His direct operatic collaboration with Mozart's jealous rival, Salieri, was on *Tartare*, a story in which a cruel despot was pitted against an ordinary citizen of extraordinary virtue. Virtue triumphed in the end, and this edifying legend enjoyed popularity after the Revolution, especially as Beaumarchais was willing to alter the ending to suit the changing political circumstances of the post-revolutionary years. Beaumarchais was thus a radical, but also an opportunist and an entrepreneur, not unwilling to serve the king, and keen to make money out of his political projects if the two could be conveniently combined.

Lorenzo da Ponte was another young man whose radical sympathies got him into trouble. As Professor of Rhetoric at the seminary of Treviso, in 1776 he produced a sequence of verses on the Rousseau-esque theme 'whether the happiness of mankind is increased within the social system, or whether he would be happier in a simple state of nature'. These verses were subversive enough to lose him his job, and he was forbidden to teach anywhere in the Venetian Republic. The personal scandal that finally forced him to leave Venice in 1782 may also have had a political dimension. He moved to Vienna, hoping to make a living there as a literary figure.[12]

Neither Beaumarchais nor da Ponte could be considered respectable people. They were raffish and radical, though not so radical that they were unwilling to flatter the aristocratic and powerful when the need arose. They belonged to a recognizably bohemian and insecure stratum of literary and artistic people who, eighteenth-century society being what it was, needed patronage and approval from above, yet were unwilling to tie themselves to the aristocracy in a long-term manner. Mozart himself, though probably more socially conventional than either of them, had effectively joined that stratum when he left the employment of Archbishop Colloredo in 1781. This was the decisive move in his career as a professional musician. From then on he had to make a living in the musical market, as both composer and performer, and as is well known this turned out to be a desperately difficult and precarious business.

But his move was not simply an individual gesture. The era of stable patronage was coming to an end. In 1790 Haydn left the employment of the Esterhazys after nearly thirty years. Two years later the young Beethoven moved from Bonn to Vienna, and after his contract with the Elector of Cologne expired in 1794, he too had to earn his living as a performing and composing musician. The dodges and subterfuges for which he and other composers were notorious – selling the same piece of music to more than one publisher or promoter – reflect the insecurity of the freelance composer's position in a still rather primitive market society.

This then was the social and economic position from which Mozart and da Ponte launched their three great masterpieces. It was a position of some freedom but also of great insecurity. They needed success, but Mozart was too great and original a creator to be content to repeat the winning recipes of Paisiello or Cimarosa, and so they ran risks both in their choice of subjects and their treatment of those subjects. In the short term, which was all that was available to Mozart, those risks were too great. The operas did not give him the commercial success he needed. All three were too original and too adventurous to win immediate popularity. However elegant and orderly they have seemed to some later commentators and audiences, at the time they appeared to be dangerously radical and overburdened with seriousness. Those used to opera as lightweight entertainment did not know how to cope with such weight and substance.

After *Figaro* came *Don Giovanni*, premiered this time in Prague, a city whose more liberal atmosphere had ensured a greater success for *Figaro* there than it had enjoyed in Vienna. With *Figaro* it is always possible to prise open a gap between Beaumarchais on the one hand

24

and Mozart and da Ponte on the other, blaming the French playwright for the radical or subversive elements from which some commentators have always been anxious to dissociate 'the divine Mozart'. With *Don Giovanni* no such strategy is available, In this case there could be no question of simply adapting a single extant text. There had been seven operas based on the Don Juan theme in the previous ten years alone, and there were, of course, famous dramatic treatments by Molière and Goldoni. From all these, da Ponte and Mozart had to fashion their version, and the emphases and balance of the work that emerged have to be taken as what they intended.

There is no doubt that da Ponte was exactly the librettist Mozart needed and was looking for. As he wrote to his father at the time of *Die Entführung*, 'The best thing of all is when a good composer, who understands the stage and is talented enough to make sound suggestions, meets an able poet, that true Pheonix . . .' Mozart, like nearly all opera composers, allotted the dominant and initiating role to the composer, with 'the words written solely for the music and not shoved in here and there to suit some miserable rhyme . . .'[13] We know from the correspondence relating to *Idomeneo*, as well as from the many changes Mozart made to that opera when it was in rehearsal and performance, how positive were his ideas about the needs of drama, how thorough was his understanding of the nature of opera and of the essentially dramatic singing that it required. We may assume, therefore, that da Ponte's libretti are the product of close collaboration with Mozart, and reflect what Mozart wanted as much as what da Ponte himself may have had in mind.

Le nozze di Figaro was manifestly a social comedy, with a clear narrative and explicit themes. *Don Giovanni*, by the nature of its tale, could never be so straightforward. Some commentators have stressed its *buffo* character,[14] and the work is subtitled *dramma giocoso*, but a 'comedy' that begins with the murder of an old man who is trying to protect his daughter against seduction or rape, and ends with the same man's statue visiting the hero for supper and dragging him down into the flames of hell, is clearly something more than a bundle of uncomplicated laughs.

However we react to it, the figure of Don Juan is one of the key myths of post-Renaissance Europe. It is not simply the male-invented, self-congratulatory myth of the irresistibly attractive man, but the more ambiguous conception of a man who is fatally attractive to women, even though he is known to be a faithless, restless philanderer – so that even when his servant reads out to one infatuated or obsessed woman a list of his 'conquests', it fails to repel her. This is a very potent image, and not only for men. Juan/Giovanni is a dream figure, the person who indulges his or her sexual appetites entirely without restraint, inhibition or guilt. The reader of Freud will have no difficulty in understanding the profound appeal of this fantasy. Giovanni simply ignores the conventional restraints on desire or libido, the repression or self-discipline on which, according to Freud, all civilized life depends. The final outcome of following Giovanni's course of self-indulgence is to be found in the exactly contemporary lurid sexual fantasies of the Marquis de Sade, which Sade explicitly justifies in terms of following the dictates of nature and disregarding the restraints imposed by conventional society. That Sade's sexual tastes were less orthodox than Giovanni's is irrelevant. The same philosophy of the uninhibited pursuit of personal pleasure is basic to both fictions.

Following Rousseau, the idea of obedience to nature rather than convention was usually turned into a radical or even revolutionary political and social challenge to existing society. The idea of the 'natural rights' of men – and sometimes women too – provided a moral measure by which the actual rights conceded by actual governments could be tested, and usually found wanting. But Sade's idea of following nature and defying convention, which he certainly associated with the revolutionary project of 1789 and after, was ultimately not political at all, but destructive of any conceivable community or social structure. It is doubtful that it is even compatible with anarchism, since it explicitly rejects the principle of respect for the autonomy and rights of others. 'Others' are simply objects to be used for the individual's own (sexual) convenience. This is Giovanni's philosophy too. Courageous and true to his own self, as he shows when, on the brink of damnation, he defies the statue's exhortations to repent, he is nevertheless an egoist; and this is undoubtedly part of his fascination. A part of each of us perhaps longs secretly to be equally ruthless, and guilt-free, in pursuit of our own gratification. But unlike Sade, unlike Giovanni, we dare not.

Don Giovanni is also, however, a social comedy, and one embracing a wider range of social types than *Figaro*, even if the interplay of classes is less clearly focused than in the earlier work. Giovanni's licentiousness is class-based. Like Almaviva, only with far less circumspection, he takes advantage of his aristocratic position to seduce women of the lower classes as well as of his own class. When it comes to sex, he is not a snob, but he knows how to exploit both his position and its economic and social attractions, as we can hear in his brazen wooing of Zerlina. You were not born to be a peasant, he tells her. To which she replies that it is only rarely that you gentlemen (*cavalieri*) are honest and sincere with women. That is a slander put about by the common people, he retorts. Zerlina is not a fool, but she finds it hard to resist Giovanni's social as well as sexual appeal. But when he thinks that his rank might prove a disadvantage in seduction, as with Elvira's maid, he employs his servant Leporello to do the wooing on his behalf.

Zerlina and Masetto represent the lower orders in this opera, and they make a striking pair. Neither of them really belongs to the gullible country booby type who often appears in opera. Although Masetto is outwitted twice, by Giovanni and Leporello, he is under no illusions about what is happening, and on the first occasion he submits only to *force majeure*. The whole of his brief aria 'Ho capito, signor, si!' is an exercise in heavy sarcasm that makes it abundantly clear that he neither trusts nor respects this lecherous, bullying aristocrat. Throughout the Act One finale Masetto is in a state of rage at what is going on between his fiancée and Don Giovanni, uttering against the latter dire threats whose fierce resentment against aristocratic presumption might well be seen as pre-revolutionary. These are not altogether empty threats either, for when he reappears in Act Two, it is with a band of armed peasants, and with the decided intention of killing Giovanni. Zerlina rebukes him for his jealousy, but more than jealousy is involved. Under the normal circumstances of feudal society, peasants did not set out to murder aristocrats who seduced their fiancées: it was far too common an occurrence, and all the sanctions of class society and class-based law were stacked against such rashness. Masetto's impetuosity is an indication that traditional deference is crumbling.

Zerlina is a more ambivalent figure. She seems to be flattered by the Don's attentions, but not really deceived. Like Susanna, like Despina, though less positively, she is capable of looking after herself. Theodor

Adorno's characterization of her, summarized by Welsh National Opera, is shrewd: 'neither shepherdess nor citoyenne, she belongs to that historical moment between rococo and revolution . . .'[15] Interestingly, in some extra scenes which Mozart and da Ponte added for the Vienna production in 1788, Zerlina acts rather more like the citoyenne. She enters 'with a knife in her hand, and leading Leporello out by the hair', still under the illusion that it is he who has beaten Masetto. These scenes suggest, as the usual performing version does not, that she shares Masetto's anger at what has happened to them both.

The third representative of the lower orders is Don Giovanni's servant and accomplice, Leporello. Servant–master or servant–mistress relations are a recurring feature of opera as they are of spoken drama, but the relationship between Giovanni and Leporello is surely the most detailed and subtle of all such portraits. This is more than a cash connection. There is mutual dependence here, partly because Giovanni knows that no ordinary employee could be expected to perform some of the outrageous tasks that he demands of Leporello. Leporello knows this too, and it gives him a certain licence to criticize and cheek his master. But in this respect he plays the part of jester, all-licensed fool, at Giovanni's court. More than once he resolves to leave his dissolute master, but is easily dissuaded by money. He is particularly active in the constant baiting and tormenting of Elvira. In the last analysis he is the epitome of the abject servility that such perpetual personal availability to an employer has always required.

Of the remaining four characters, three – Donna Anna, her father the Commendatore and her lover Don Ottavio – represent the respectable upper classes; appropriately both Anna and Ottavio seem almost like refugees from *opera seria*: repetitive, fixed characters whose music usually has a formality very different from Elvira's more personal outbursts, or from the songs of Giovanni on the one hand and Zerlina on the other. When Donna Anna reveals her conviction that Giovanni was the man who tried, unsuccessfully by her own account, to rape her, Ottavio is shocked to think that a gentleman (*un cavaliero*) could behave so badly. Is it anachronistic to suggest that the formality of relations between this pair is meant to be contrasted unfavourably with the spontaneity, the relaxation and the real, if shallow, feelings that characterize Giovanni's relationships and brief liaisons with Elvira and Zerlina? And is not Anna more deeply disturbed by her encounter with Giovanni than she cares or dares to admit? Her account of what happened may not be truthful, and the excuse of her father's death as a reason to delay further her wedding to Ottavio seems thin. She can be seen as the epitome of that repression of powerful feelings by convention that is the exact antithesis of Giovanni himself; her music, powerful yet formalized, reflects this.

Elvira is a different matter. She is decidedly an independent and unconventional woman. For – whether she genuinely regards Giovanni as her husband, or whether she is simply infatuated with him and determined to hold him to his promises and avenge her desertion – her action in pursuing him across Spain is not that of an ordinarily respectable woman. Perhaps she belongs to a different social stratum from Anna and Ottavio. At all events she is spirited and resourceful enough to belong in spirit to the age of Mary Wollstonecraft, who showed a similar independence in her personal life, and whose *Vindication of the Rights of Woman* appeared five years after this opera.

What *Don Giovanni* depicts is a traditional stratified society still in full operation at the formal level, but substantially in serious decay: subverted both by challenge from below (Masetto and his armed peasants) and by the irresponsible abuse of wealth and privilege by the aristocracy itself. We can see this class society musically in operation at Don Giovanni's ball. In a virtuoso display Mozart brings three separate instrumental ensembles on stage, each playing simultaneously a different dance with different social connotations: a minuet for the gentry, a contradanza for the middling folk, and a Deutscher or fast waltz for the peasantry (this is danced by Leporello and Masetto).

But this display is a symbol of disorder as well as order, for the mix of dances is more or less what Giovanni ordered in 'Fin ch'han dal vino':

> Senza alcun ordine
> La danza sia
> Ch'il minuetto,
> Chi la follia,
> Chi l'alemanna
> Farai ballar . . .

Giovanni has in any case arranged the celebration simply as an opportunity for licentiousness, and specifically to facilitate the seduction of Zerlina. So the formality and grandeur of the occasion barely conceal dissipation and indulgence. And when the three masked avengers arrive as uninvited guests, Giovanni is hospitality itself:

> E aperto a tutti quanti:
> Viva la libertà!

Or, in modern parlance, this is liberty hall. It is doubtful that he means much by this except that he is keeping open house. But Mozart makes much of these words: they become a grand climax to this section of the finale, being sung no fewer than thirteen times by the guests and their host, and it seems likely that the composer was adding a political meaning to an ostensibly social flourish. At all events that is how it must have been perceived by the Austrian authorities, since the words were altered to 'Viva la società' in the Viennese libretto.[16] Giovanni's ball, in the responses it evokes, becomes the focus of all the forces that are gnawing away at the fabric of the old order: upper-class irresponsibility, bourgeois militancy and the anger and resentment of the lower orders.

A final word must be said about the opera's extraordinary denouement. The opera's subtitle, *Il dissoluto punito*, sometimes came to dominate advertising for the work, as if to reassure potential audiences of its moral character. The trouble is that the dissolute man is only punished as a result of the unlikely intervention of a statue which invites itself to supper and then drags his host down to hell. As Bernard Shaw sensibly pointed out, 'Gentlemen who break through the ordinary categories of good and evil . . . do not, as a matter of fact, get called on by statues, and taken straight down through the floor to eternal torments; and to pretend that they do is to shirk the social problem they present.'[17] This penultimate scene is one of the most powerful in all opera. The Commendatore as the angel and messenger of death is a terrifying figure, and Don Giovanni's fearless defiance, contrasted with Leporello's comic terror, gives him at the last a nearly heroic stature.

But Shaw is right. Considered as a device for dealing with the challenge presented by Giovanni to the established social order and conventional morality, the statue's intervention is no more than an

evasion. And this is in itself revealing. *Figaro* ended with a reconciliation of the conflicting parties, however fragile. When we come to
Giovanni, the disruption caused by this entirely egoistic figure is so
damaging, so disturbing, that no reconciliation, no truce with those he
has wronged and abused, is possible. But nor, within pre-revolutionary society, is there any possibility that society will be able to check,
contain or punish him. Aristocratic privilege was of the essence of that
social order. Hence only supernatural intervention can override its
abuse. The sheer unreality of that solution indicates the depths of the
crisis posed by Giovanni's challenge. The Commendatore's arrival can
be seen as a mythical picturesque parallel to the Revolution itself,
which only two years later was to bring upon the aristocracy of France
their long-expected, long-delayed retribution.

The last of the three collaborations between Mozart and da Ponte, *Così
fan tutte*, is the least political of the three operas in the ordinary sense,
and the most restricted in its social scope. Yet it is in some ways the
most original and the most disturbing of the three works, and a central
work for any study of opera's treatment of women, sexual politics and
the relations between men and women. These are questions that will
be raised more than once in this book, but the subject as a whole
requires a separate study and so *Così*, along with a number of other
works of primary importance for any study of the presentation of
women in opera, will not receive here more than glancing attention.
   The ostensible lesson of *Così* is summed up in its title, which Don
Alfonso, the instigator of the plot, compels his two pupils to sing to
the musical phrase with which the opera's overture begins. 'That's the
way all women behave.' This apparently cynical old bachelor sets out
to prove to two young men, Ferrando and Guglielmo, that their
supposedly devoted girlfriends, Dorabella and Fiordiligi, are no more
constant than any other women. To prove it, he has the two men
disguise themselves and each pay court to each other's fiancée. In the
end both sisters agree to marry these new lovers, at which point the
deception is revealed and Alfonso has proved his point.
   The narrative is so blatantly sexist, and the trick played so utterly
cruel, that it is not surprising that this opera has always provoked
mixed reactions; its apparent cynicism and frivolity were condemned
by Beethoven and Wagner among others. On the whole, nineteenth-

century taste found *Così* too sour, and it was either neglected or bowdlerized. Only in the twentieth century was it rediscovered. And even then it seems to me that an undercurrent of unease is indicated by the insistence of many writers that this is not an opera to be taken seriously. Thus Dent claimed, 'In *Così fan tutte* nothing is serious,' and Sacheverell Sitwell wrote, 'There are no fine sentiments in *Così fan tutte* and its purpose is only to amuse.' Sir Thomas Beecham, who did so much to restore the opera to circulation in Britain, compared it to 'a long summer day spent in a cloudless land by a Southern sea, and its motto might be that of Hazlitt's sundial: *Horas non numero nisi serenas*'.[18]

Much of the music is indeed of astonishing poise and beauty, but in some ways nineteenth-century unease showed a deeper understanding of *Così* than that of Dent and the others. Cloudless serenity, let alone total frivolity, is not what this opera is about. One way of understanding *Così*, and of coping with its sexist narrative, is to see that ultimately it is not important that the trick is played by men upon women: it could equally well be the other way round. For what is explored is the difficulty in knowing our own feelings, in distinguishing a short-term infatuation from a deeper attachment, in distinguishing being in love from being in love with the idea of being in love. *Così* is a study of illusion and reality in human relations, and it seems clear, from the music as much as from the words, that by the end the men are as uncertain about their true feelings as the woman are about theirs. For each man has entered so fervently into his role as wooer of the other's sweetheart that his own detachment from this supposedly artificial affair is thrown into doubt. Thus in his recitative in Scene Nine of Act Two Ferrando confesses the confusion of his thoughts and feelings on having discovered that Dorabella has surrendered to Guglielmo:

> In qual fiero contrasto, in qual disordine
> Di pensieri e di affetti io mi ritrovo?

(In what fierce contrast, in what a disorder of thoughts and feelings do I find myself.)

He cannot decide whether to abandon Dorabella or not, and it seems likely that a developing attraction to Fiordiligi is part of the reason. A little later Guglielmo's refusal to participate in the celebratory quartet and his muttered curses on them all indicate how profoundly he has been upset by the whole misguided escapade.

But it is the two sisters from Ferrara who stand at the heart of the opera, and it is on them that Mozart lavishes his deepest sympathy, even to the point where the music sometimes subverts the verbal text, as in the quintet of farewell at the opening of the opera: 'Di scrivermi ogni giorno'. No doubt the protestations and demands of the women are exaggerated – Dorabella demands two letters a day from Ferrando – and beneath their lamentations Don Alfonso keeps repeating 'Io crepo, se no rido!' ('I'll burst if I don't laugh'). Nevertheless the music is full of genuine sorrow, and so is the equally lovely trio that follows: 'Soave sia il vento'. Mozart makes it impossible for us to respond to these as mere pastiche, shallow expressions of shallow feelings. On the contrary, 'The first deception is now completed, and, as if to underline the betrayal of the two girls, Mozart writes music of peculiarly searching depth.'[19] When he wishes to show exaggerated or faked emotions he does it by parodying *opera seria*: in Fiordiligi's 'Come scoglio' ('Like a rock'), and Dorabella's 'Smanie implacabili' ('Implacable longings'), which is prefaced by melodramatic cries of 'Fuggi per pietà' ('Fly, for pity's sake'), and so forth. Here we are left in no doubt that the ladies protest too much, in high-flown language and elaborate references to classical mythology. When the sisters declare to Despina that they are likely to die without the company of their men, she retorts that it has never been known for a woman to die of love. But this need not be taken as a comment on women only since, after all, consciously or not it echoes Rosalind's lines in *As You Like It*:

. . . men have died from time to time, and worms have eaten them, but not for love. (Act IV, Scene 1)

We might consider also the character of Despina, the sisters' maid. It could be thought that her advice to her employers, to enjoy themselves and make the most of their lovers' absence, is a prime example of the opera's alleged cynicism. But Despina, like Figaro and Leporello, is a servant without illusions about those who employ her. She is also a woman who has learnt how to survive and hold her own against men, like Don Alfonso, who try to take advantage of their maleness and their social superiority in relation to her. Despina is scornful of the idea that men are faithful: 'In uomini, in soldati, sperare fedeltà?' ('You hope for constancy in men or soldiers? The idea is too ridiculous.') Despina is an element in the way in which the substance of the opera itself subverts its title.

In the end, though, *Così* is certainly not a romantic work, even if it is not a cynical one. Its alternative title, *La scuola degli amanti* ('The school for lovers'), indicates that far from being an amoral or frivolous work, it is actually a didactic comedy; like *Don Giovanni*, it ends with the cast pointing out the moral to the audience:

> Fortunato l'uom che previde
> Ogni cosa pel buon verso,
> E tra i casi e le vicende
> Da ragion guidar si fa.

(Happy is the man who calmly takes life strictly as he finds it. And with humour and patience only lets sweet reason be his guide.)

In this school Don Alfonso is the tutor and Ferrando and Guglielmo are the pupils. But we could see Despina, Alfonso's accomplice, as tutor to the sisters, and of course the lesson is one that both sexes are meant to learn. They should not entertain illusions about their partners, or form impossible expectations of fallible human beings. Human weakness is unflinchingly exposed, but not condemned. Finally the work is a plea, in Virgil Thompson's words, 'for an enlightened and philosophic toleration of human weakness'. Clear-sighted realism and tolerance are what are required to make human relationships work. *Così* is decidedly a work of the Enlightenment.

With *The Magic Flute*, we come to the work in which Mozart's identification not simply with the Enlightenment, but with the radical utopian humanism of the Enlightenment is most clearly revealed. At first sight, this seems surprising, for *Die Zauberflöte* was written for and with Emmanuel Schikaneder for the large popular music theatre he was running on the outskirts of Vienna. Schikaneder was clearly aiming to add yet another popular success to the run of spectacular, magical fairytales he had been putting on at the Theater auf der Wieden over the previous two years. Mozart, who had little hope of presenting another opera at the court theatre, needed a success for financial reasons. There was therefore every reason to expect that *The Magic Flute* would turn out to be one of Mozart's more superficially charming but ultimately not very memorable works.

In the event he bequeathed us a musical miracle: a work that certainly contains popular elements, and can appeal at the level of a touching and picturesque fable, but which is also profound, enigmatic, moving and sublime. It has charm and comedy, yet it is also a work of ethical grandeur and vision. Mozart himself complained of those who laughed too much at some of its early performances, but he also wrote appreciatively of the 'silent applause' with which much of the music was received. It is clear that from the start the opera was understood by some at least of its hearers and viewers to be something more than an enchanting and exotic fairytale. Its popularity outlived Mozart himself, and Schikaneder claimed, probably with some exaggeration, that by the beginning of 1798 it had received 300 performances in Vienna alone.

Die Zauberflöte is a German *Singspiel*, as was *Die Entführung*. That is to say that it was presented in the vernacular rather than in the Italian favoured by the court and the upper classes, and the music is interspersed with spoken dialogue rather than being through-composed (although it is noticeable in *Die Zauberflöte* as in *Fidelio* and other *Singspiels* that as the drama intensifies music takes over altogether and the spoken element fades away). It is an open question at what point a *Singspiel*, or an *opéra comique*, ceases to be an opera and becomes a play with incidental music. Lord Harewood excludes *The Threepenny Opera* – despite its title – from Kobbé's *Complete Opera Guide*, presumably on the grounds that it is actually a play with music. There is a tendency in some quarters to think that opera *ought* to be continuous music, and this has led to the re-composing of some works originally written in the *opéra comique* form, such as Cherubini's *Medée*, *Carmen* and *Les contes d'Hoffmann*, with sung recitative replacing the original spoken dialogue. Whether this tampering produces any improvement is debatable, but it is notable that no one has dared to interfere with *Die Zauberflöte* or *Fidelio* in this way. Nor has anyone denied them the title 'opera'.

The relevant point here is that since no one actually insists that opera has to be continuous music, the boundaries between opera and more inherently approachable and popular forms such as, today, the musical, are always fluid and uncertain. Less sophisticated or less trained audiences tend to prefer music in the form of songs, whose form and function are clear, and which are often strophic. And the musical, unlike opera, is always performed in the language of its audience: there is a premium on verbal communication. The composer, such as in this century Kurt Weill, who seeks to reach a large popular audience may therefore prefer to use the mixed form of the *Singspiel* or the musical, and, as we shall see, *The Threepenny Opera* contains a number of explicit references to *Die Zauberflöte*, the supreme model of the popular yet musically substantial *Singspiel*.

Mozart was working in a popular genre, and as usual he understood how to respect the genre while using it for his own musical and dramatic purposes. *Die Zauberflöte* includes quite a few brief, clearly defined musical numbers, some of which, such as Papageno's two strophic songs, are instantly appealing. The opera's popularity is not hard to understand. But it seems likely that this popularity owed something to that other dimension of the work: the ethical and political idealism, which is rather too readily assumed to be of concern only to the more educated minority. This was, after all, the decade of the French Revolution, an event or series of events whose impact was felt all over Europe and beyond; so it does not seem wholly fanciful to suppose that the humane idealism that appealed so strongly to French audiences in, for example, Cherubini's *Les deux journées* might also win a response from popular audiences in Vienna. It is possible, too, although this is also conjectural, that both Mozart and Schikaneder saw their *Singspiel* as a work of propaganda, not only for Freemasonry, but also for the wider ideals of the Enlightenment and for the dream of a new or better world which many believed the Revolution in France had made a possibility for the first time in human history. One of Mozart's biographers, Alfred Einstein, is positive about this: 'Its sensational success with its first audience in Vienna arose from political reasons, based on the subject-matter.'[20]

There is and has been some argument as to whether *Die Zauberflöte* is properly regarded as a Masonic opera. I think this discussion can be ignored, since it seems to hang on whether those with most internal knowledge of Freemasonry regard the opera as conforming in every detail to Masonic rituals, codes and orthodoxies. This is unimportant. Mozart and Schikaneder clearly intended the work as a celebration and assertion of Masonic ideas, and they filled it with Masonic emblems and details, some of them easily recognized, others not.

It is very common for writers on Mozart to assert that he was not a political person, and no doubt in a rather narrow sense that is true. There are very few observations on specific political events in his letters, and we know of no comment by Mozart on the French Revolution, even though two and a half years passed between its outbreak and his sudden death. On the other hand we have seen that he had some egalitarian instincts and seems to have shared some of the class resentments and class confidence of Beaumarchais and those for whom and to whom Beaumarchais spoke so successfully. He was also a committed and enthusiastic Mason from the time he joined the Viennese lodge, Zur Wohltätigkeit (Beneficence) in December 1784 until his death seven years later. There is a substantial body of Masonic music in Mozart's catalogue, including the magnificent Masonic Funeral Music composed in 1785 for the burial service of two fellow Masons; he even interrupted the composition of the Requiem in the final month of his life to write *Eine Kleine Freymaurer Kantate*, which despite its name is a quite substantial work for soloists, chorus and orchestra lasting more than thirteen minutes.

At that time Freemasonry was far from being the businessmen's and establishment's mutual aid society into which it has since degenerated. It was one of the important organized forces of the Enlightenment itself. Like all secret societies it aroused suspicion, not least from state authorities, who saw it as a prime source of political subversion, and even of the Revolution itself. In *Mozart's Last Year*, H.C. Robbins Landon quotes a memorandum from the Austrian Minister of Police, written in the same year as *Die Zauberflöte*:

> . . . many of these secret societies . . . are not – as they pretend – simply there for the purpose of sensible enlightenment and active philanthropy, but . . . their intention is none other than slowly to undermine the reputation and power of the monarchs, to excite the sense of freedom among the nations, to change the processes of thought among the people, and to guide them according to their principles by means of a secret ruling elite. The defection of the English colonies in America was the first operation of this secret ruling elite . . . and there can be no doubt that the overthrow of the French monarchy is the work of such a secret society.[21]

Like police and secret services in all times and places, the Count von
Pergen was apt to see subversion lurking in every corner of society,
and hugely to exaggerate the role and effectiveness of organized
political groups. Nevertheless this revelation of official attitudes towards the Masons (who are mentioned specifically later in the report)
has a double significance. First, it suggests that Mozart and Schikaneder showed some courage in mounting an opera that openly celebrated the values and rituals of an organization so suspect to the state
authorities, and which was in fact banned in Austria only five years
later; just as Mozart had shown courage in choosing to make an opera
out of Beaumarchais's banned play. Second, although the authorities
exaggerated the influence and the subversive intentions of the Masons,
they were not wrong to see that the values of Masonry did in some
ways constitute a challenge to the existing social and political order.

There was, for example, that streak of egalitarianism that asserted
that a prince was no more remarkable than other men. The basis of this
egalitarianism lay in the ideas of brotherly love and of the unity of the
human race that were central to Masonry. 'By the exercise of Brotherly Love we are taught to regard the whole human species as one
family, the high and the low, the rich and the poor, created by one
Almighty Being,' wrote Lessing in his *Masonic Dialogues*.[22] Such
sentiments did not have to be interpreted in a radical manner: the idea
of the family is not incompatible with the idea of a hierarchy of status
and power within it. But the contrast between wealth and poverty *was*
very often seen as incompatible with the cohesion of the family of
humankind, as, for example, by Johann Caspar Riesbak, a member of
Mozart's own lodge, who wrote in 1787: 'The clearest proof that a
country is unhappy is the confrontation between the greatest magnifi-
cence and the most wretched poverty, and the greater the confrontation, the unhappier the country.'[23]

There were, of course, more and less radical strands within Freemasonry. One of the most radical was the Illuminati. The leader of the
Illuminati was Adam Weishaupt, who in 1776 founded a secret order
called the Perfectibilists. They aimed to convert humanity into a
'masterpiece of reason and, thus, to attain the highest perfection in the
art of government'. The way of achieving this was through 'Illumi-
nation, enlightening the understanding by the sun of reason, which
will dispel the clouds of superstition and prejudice'.[24] Illuminati led

Mozart's lodge. One of their leaders was Ignaz von Born, who has often been thought to have provided the model for Sarastro. Altogether Mozart seems to have been in close contact with some of the more radical Viennese Masons.

Although *Die Zauberflöte* is the work of Mozart that most fully and clearly expresses the utopian hopes of Masonic Enlightenment, it is not the only such work. In earlier operas too, including *Così* as we have seen, Enlightenment ideals often find expression. In *Die Entführung* it is the Pasha Selim who embodies the virtues of the humane, rational ruler. It was a challenging characterization, since in Vienna the Turks were popularly perceived as the principal threat, non-European and non-Christian, to the Austrian Empire; it was, moreover, a distinctive feature of the opera, since in Christoph Friedrich Bretzner's libretto for *Belmont und Constanze*, on which *Die Entführung* is based, the Pasha is finally revealed as Belmonte's father! But in Gottlieb Stephanie's adaptation the Pasha's final act of generosity and clemency in forgiving and releasing his European captives is that of a statesman rather than a father, so that 'Ultimately, he is a ruler of the opera seria stamp' – a modern Titus, in fact.[25] This gives the cue for the moral sentiments of the vaudeville finale to the opera:

> Nichts ist so hasslich wie die Rache;
> Grossmutig, menschlich, gutig sein.
> Und ohne Eigennutz verzeihn,
> Ist nur der grossen Seelen Sache!

(Nothing is as hateful as revenge. To be generous, merciful, kind, and selflessly to forgive is the mark of a noble soul.)

Sarastro says, or sings, much the same to Pamina, when he tells her that her mother deserves to be punished, but that:

> In diesen heil'gen Hallen
> Kennt man die Rache nicht . . .

(In these sacred halls, vengeance is unknown.)

And in *La clemenza di Tito*, which was mostly composed after *Die Zauberflöte*, the Emperor Titus shows his greatness of spirit by refusing to take revenge on Sextus, the friend who has tried to assassinate him. In the marvellous quartet for the two pairs of lovers which ends Act Two of *Die Entführung* the most central and typical metaphor of the Enlightenment is employed, when all four join to sing

> Endlich scheint die Hoffnungs sonne
> Hell durchs trube Firmament!

(At last the sun of hope is shining brightly through the gloomy sky.)

But these elements are not central to the earlier *Singspiel*, or to *La clemenza*, as they are to *Die Zauberflöte*. This is an opera that combines the old story of the lover who has to undergo various trials, tests or ordeals before he can win the hand of the beloved, with the idea of initiation into a select society or order, which similarly involves tests and trials. In the end Tamino wins Pamina, and Pamina wins Tamino, but both also win admission to the order of the enlightened over which Sarastro presides. It is a quest opera, and the quest is not only for love and personal happiness, but also for virtue and enlightenment. And these are not merely personal qualities or assets, but the key to a better and happier world: indeed, to the transformation of human life. Twice at focal points in the score these words are sung:

> Dann ist die Erd ein Himmelreich,
> Und sterbliche den Gottern gleich.

(Then earth becomes a heavenly realm, and mortals become godlike.)

They are the concluding words of Act One, and they are repeated when the Three Boys open the finale to Act Two, predicting that the sun (of reason) will soon rise, superstition will vanish, and the wise man will be victorious. The image of the sun banishing darkness and shadows of superstition and prejudice is the key image of the Enlightenment. We can find it in Thomas Paine's *Rights of Man*, for example, a work exactly contemporary with *Die Zauberflöte*:

> But such is the irresistible nature of the truth, that all it asks, and all it wants, is the liberty of appearing. The sun needs no inscription to distinguish him from darkness; and no sooner did the American governments display themselves to the world, than despotism felt a shock, and man began to contemplate redress.

It occurs too in the chorus 'O, Isis und Osiris – Die dustre Nacht verschencht der Glanz der Sonne', as it did in the incidental music Mozart composed in 1773 for *Thamos, König in Ägypten*, in which the Egyptians are portrayed as sun-worshippers. Its most splendid musical expression, however, occurs not in an opera but in Haydn's *The Creation* when, after the graphic depiction of chaos in the orchestral introduction, the chorus sings 'And God said, Let there be light, and there was light'; on that last decisive word, the chorus sweeps away all musical uncertainty and confusion with a sustained *fortissimo* shout in affirmative C major. Haydn was a devout Catholic, but in celebrating the original act whereby light overcame darkness and disorder, he was aligning Christianity with the (usually secular) spirit of the Enlightenment.

Die Zauberflöte is one of the great achievements of the eighteenth-century Enlightenment, and one of the greatest ethical works of art ever created. This is not, of course, a matter simply of the sentiments expressed in words, but of the way in which words and music combine to give those sentiments their power and beauty. One example must suffice. Pamina, with Papageno's help, is trying to escape from Sarastro's control, since her appointed guardian, Monostatos, has tried to rape her, when they hear fanfares and a chorus which announces Sarastro's arrival. Papageno scurries fearfully about, wishing he were a mouse with somewhere to hide. What are we going to say to him, he asks. To which Pamina replies, with inspired moral courage, 'Die Wahrheit, wär sie auch verbrechen' – the truth, even if it were a crime. It is Mozart's music that transforms this sentence into a thrilling gesture of moral commitment: this is the key that opens up the music to the grandly direct dialogue between her and Sarastro which then follows, leading to the first encounter between Pamina and Tamino, and the idealistic assertion with which the first act closes.

Among other things, *The Magic Flute* accurately reflects the strain of misogyny that was characteristic of Freemasonry as of other all-male organizations. The Speaker is the principal spokes*man* for anti-woman sentiments, but even Sarastro, who proposes that Pamina should be admitted to the order along with Tamino, tells her that she needs a man's leadership, rather than trusting in her mother: 'Ein Mann muss eure Herzen leiten.' ('A man must guide your heart.') But the work itself subverts these patronizing attitudes, mainly through Pamina herself. It is she who undergoes the more severe trials, which push her to the point of contemplating suicide, and it is she who says to Tamino that she will lead him through the trials of fire and water:

> Ich selbsten fuhre dich,
> Die Liebe leitet mich.

('I myself will lead you; love guides me' – a meaning which is lost, incidentally, in Anthony Besch's widely used translation.) She emerges as the more positive and determined of the two lovers. And in her sublimely simple duet with Papageno they sing of the love of man and wife, and also of wife and man, repeating the phrases but reversing the key words in a way surely intended to stress the equality of man and woman in marriage.

Similar observations can be made about the opera's treatment of race. Monostatos, the most villainous figure in the story, is black, which is crudely invidious. But Monostatos is very much aware of his blackness. He understands that it may be his colour that frightens or repels Pamina, and this naturally angers him. In his aria he sings bitterly that whilst everyone experiences love, he apparently must forswear it because a black man is hateful (*hasslich*). And then, in a line which recalls Shylock, he asks, 'Bin ich nicht von Fleisch und Blut?' ('Am I not flesh and blood?') Hath not a Jew eyes? As with Shakespeare, the casual racism of the story is at least to a degree questioned by the way in which the character is presented.

The Magic Flute is not tightly coherent in the manner of *Così fan tutte* or even *Figaro*. It is a hybrid work, designed to appeal to small children like Mozart's seven-year-old son Karl as well as to Masonic initiates and political sophisticates. It needs all of Mozart's skills to hold together its disparate parts: Papageno's songs, the Queen of the Night's coloratura displays, the bare simplicities of the trial march, and the baroque counterpoint beneath the solemn chorale of the Two Armed Men. And even Mozart, it seems to me, could not overcome all the contradictions, or at least obscurities, of the plot. The story begins with Tamino being commissioned by the grieving Queen to rescue her daughter Pamina, with whose portrait he has already fallen in love, from the control of Sarastro. When he arrives in Sarastro's realm he learns that he has been misled by the Queen, and that Sarastro is concerned to rescue Pamina from her mother's malevolent designs.

But this leaves us with several puzzles. It is extraordinary that Sarastro, *der göttliche Weise* (the divinely wise), should entrust Pamina to the unreliable, lustful Monostatos. It is equally extraordinary that Tamino and Papageno should obtain from the Queen's Three Ladies the magical instruments, flute and bells, through which they can obtain protection and guidance at moments of crisis.

It is sometimes said that the Queen and her ladies only appear to be good to Tamino. But this does not explain the magical gifts, nor yet that it is the Three Ladies who tell Tamino and Papageno about the Three Boys who will guide them on their way (for the Three Boys play a positive role throughout the story). Nor does this explain why it is the Three Ladies who, when they remove the (Masonic) golden padlock from Papageno's mouth, utter some of the first Masonic sentiments to be heard in the opera:

> Bekamen doch die Lugner alle
> Ein solchess Schloss vor ihren Mund:
> Statt Hass, Verleumdung, schwarzer Galle
> Bestunde Lieb' under Bruderbund.

(If all liars received a lock like this on their mouths instead of hatred, calumny and black gall, love and brotherhood would flourish.)

Rather than attempt to iron out these paradoxes, as some devotees of the work feel impelled to do, it seems better to admit that the libretto shows signs of haste and confusion. For all its beauties and grandeur, *Die Zauberflöte* is not a perfect work.

It was, however, in its originality a vastly influential one. The theme of initiation through trials into a brotherhood of the elect is one that much preoccupied Wagner. It is present in *Tannhäuser*, *Lohengrin*, *Die Meistersinger*, and above all in *Parsifal*, the work closest to the Mozartian prototype. Beethoven's *Singspiel Fidelio* owes much to Mozart's example, particularly in its use of the same symbolism of darkness and light, although in Beethoven's prison it is, of course, far less of a metaphor. 'Under the cloak of symbolism, *Die Zauberflöte* was a work of rebellion, consolation and hope. Sarastro and his priests represent hope in the victory of light, of humanity, of the brotherhood of man,' wrote Alfred Einstein.[26] *The Magic Flute*, even more than *Figaro* or *Don Giovanni*, belongs to its time, that moment of hope and optimism after 1789 that was shared so widely and so memorably expressed in literature as well as in music. At the time of the American revolt against Britain, Thomas Paine had written, 'We have it in our power to begin the world over again. . . . The birthday of a new world is at hand . . .'[27] This is exactly the exalted and confident mood of idealism that Mozart captures in his last great masterpiece for the stage. Its only true successor, as an expression of that faith in humanity and its future, was *Fidelio*.

2
Opera and the Revolution

That opera should have flourished in France during the decade of the Revolution may at first sight seem surprising. Thinking of it, knowing it, as essentially an expensive and exclusive form of museum culture, it seems out of place in the years of fierce egalitarianism and struggle on the streets. But revolutions by their very nature are not narrowly political events, but great transformations that leave no aspect of society quite untouched. Every revolution also aspires to create a culture that will both embody and nourish the vision and values of the revolution itself. The line between art and propaganda, never clear in any case, is swept aside, and people look to the arts to commemorate, celebrate and sometimes even explore the momentous events they are living through.

So it was with opera in revolutionary France and especially, of course, in Paris. In 1789 there were only three officially licensed theatres in Paris, and their output was carefully controlled by the state. In 1791 a law proclaimed the freedom of the theatre, and this led to a profuse flowering of dramatic and operatic performances of every kind. 'By 1793, there were 63 theatres in Paris alone . . .'[1] Composers were expected to provide music for revolutionary occasions, and operas were expected to have suitably inspiring and celebratory themes. But although the calendar was reconstituted, and Year One of a new era was proclaimed, music like other arts could not wipe the

45

slate entirely clean, could not start altogether from scratch. In fact the themes and ideals of the Revolution had been adumbrated in much pre-revolutionary art. The neo-classical movement in painting had signalled a strong reaction against the luxurious, court-supported prettiness of Boucher and Fragonard. It made a cult of the severe republican virtues of ancient, pre-imperial Rome and classical Athens, as epitomized in such paintings as David's *The Oath of the Horatii* of 1783, or his *Socrates Drinking the Hemlock*, or his *The Lictors Bringing Brutus the Bodies of his Sons*, which he painted in 1789. This cult had its counterpart in Gluck's celebrated operatic reforms, and his choice of serious classical subjects in *Alceste* and the two Iphigénie operas.

But *opera seria*, though perhaps not irredeemably aristocratic, was too deeply rooted in the old world of court and aristocracy to survive long in the new bourgeois climate. Hence even a very serious composer like Cherubini, who undoubtedly learned and profited from the example of Gluck, did not adopt the conventions of *opera seria*, but based even so intense and unremitting a tragedy as *Medée* (1797) on the conventions of *opéra comique*, using spoken dialogue between set numbers. There was nothing remotely *comique* about *Medée*, but it was *opéra comique* that flourished in the revolutionary period, and it is significant that the two German works in which Enlightenment and revolutionary ideals are most clearly expressed, *Die Zauberflöte* and *Fidelio*, are both in *Singspiel* form, *opéra comique*'s German equivalent.

Rescue Opera: Cherubini and Auber

One genre of opera that was established before the Revolution, but lent itself readily to revolutionary purposes, was the so-called rescue opera. The best-known and most popular pre-revolutionary example was Grétry's *Richard Coeur-de-Lion* of 1784, which has a plot with obvious similarities to that of *Fidelio*. Richard is imprisoned, and is rescued, primarily by his faithful troubadour Blondel, but also by his devoted lover Marguerite, who has to disguise herself as a man in the final battle to rescue the king. The opera actually includes a character called Florestan, but he is Richard's jailor! Much is made of the fact that it is a king who is rescued, and Blondel's role is that of an ultra-faithful subject, so the radical implications would seem to be few. Blondel's song of devotion to his king

O Richard! O mon roi!
L'univers t'abandonne.

was, as one might expect, taken up by royalists after 1789; and in fact the royalist potentialities of the piece led to it being more or less banned from 1791 onwards, until it came back into fashion under the Emperor Napoleon. Nevertheless in the 1780s it was received as a fable about liberty; Beethoven was sufficiently interested in it to compose in 1796 a set of variations on its best-known melody, the 'Romance', 'Une Fièvre brulante'.

But if *Richard Coeur-de-Lion* is typical of pre-revolutionary rescue opera (or operetta), then it is clear that the Revolution itself and the dramatic talents of Cherubini were needed to convert the genre into something truly serious. For, as Basil Deane has written, 'Grétry's easy-going approach precludes penetration of character'.[2] And, one might add, any strong sense of drama as well. The two most durable and influential examples of the revolutionary 'rescue' operas – David Charlton has suggested that 'Bastille opera' would be a better label – are both the work of Luigi Cherubini, the Italian-born composer who settled in Paris in 1786 and was for the next forty years a major figure in French musical life. *Lodoiska* (1791) was by all accounts something new in opera – romantic, intense and powerful – and it made an immediate impact, receiving two hundred performances straightaway. We can imagine something of its qualities from listening to *Medée* (or *Medea*, in the Italian adaptation in which it has been performed and recorded), the only opera by Cherubini that is still regularly revived. Its power and intensity might well be thought to owe something to the composer's response to the overwhelming public events he had lived through in the previous eight years. *Les deux journées* is another story of rescue, but altogether lighter and more cheerful in tone and character, as was perhaps possible by 1800; it had not been earlier.

Les deux journées is set in seventeenth-century France. Cardinal Mazarin, the all-powerful minister of Louis XIV, has ordered the arrest of an aristocratic couple, Count Armand and his wife (symbolically named Constance), because they have dared to defy his power

and denounce him to the Queen. The gates of Paris are being watched
and people are searched as they pass in and out. There is something of
the atmosphere of a reign of terror. Mikeli, a water-carrier, hides the
innocent couple in his house, and eventually smuggles them out of the
city in his water-waggon. They escape to Switzerland, where Mikeli's
son Antonio is preparing for his marriage to Angelina. Armand is still
in hiding, but when soldiers threaten Constance, he emerges to
protect her. He is recognized and arrested. But then Mikeli arrives
with a pardon from the Queen for Armand and all others unjustly
threatened by Mazarin. All ends happily.

The text, by Jean-Nicolas Bouilly (also the author of *Léonore*), is full
of humane and noble sentiments, and the mainspring of the action is
disinterested idealism. Mikeli, for example, sings of the joy of being
able to save 'deux époux, deux Français', and declares that no memory
is sweeter than being able to recall 'j'ai secouru, j'sauvé l'innocent' ('I
have helped, I have saved an innocent person'). The voice of nature
tells him constantly to help his brother and save the innocent: 'aide ton
frère, et sauve l'innocent'. In the finale everyone sings that 'le premier
charme de la vie, c'est de servir l'humanité'. All this reflects clearly the
humane and principled idealism of that revolutionary period, and it is
not surprising to find that *Les deux journées* was the first opera to be
staged in Prague's Provisional Theatre in 1862: its idealism must have
appealed to the champions of Czech nationalism and independence.
Beethoven considered that *Les deux journées* had one of the two best
libretti he knew – the other being Etienne de Jouy's for Spontini's *La
vestale*.

The music is in a suitably democratic or populist vein as well. There
are only two solo numbers. Otherwise it consists of ensembles and a
quite striking use of melodrama: spoken dialogue against musical
background or interjections. The opera was a great popular success,
and it is not hard to see why. Not only is the music appealing and
tuneful. The story is equally attractive, and is sufficiently ambiguous
to appeal to a broad audience. Thus it is possible to see it as a story of
class reconciliation. Not only does the 'humble' water-carrier gladly
rescue two aristocrats; it also turns out that Antonio was once rescued
from destitution by Armand. So there is a reciprocal benevolence
between the classes. But it is also possible to interpret the opera in a
more egalitarian way: aristocrats need the common people to protect

them; and the ties and obligations of common humanity override social divisions.

It was possible also to interpret the persecution of the innocent aristocrats Armand and Constance in an anti-Jacobin way. When Mikeli sings of the importance of protecting the innocent, many people's thoughts must have gone back to the Terror and its many innocent victims. So although *Les deux journées* certainly embodies much of the idealism and moral seriousness of the revolutionary moment, it does so at a level of generality that allowed its audiences to draw a variety of different political lessons from its story.

Cherubini was not a genius of the highest order, and it may be that those commentators are right who wrote, 'If Cherubini's melodic invention had matched his other musical gifts, his operas would surely still hold the stage today.'[3] Nevertheless, on the basis of what little of his work is readily available – *Medée*, the requiems and a little more – it is surely clear that his music is unjustly neglected, and that *Lodoiska* and *Les deux journées* both deserve the occasional revival (quite as much as the more routine works of Donizetti, for instance). But it is true that they are not works for the canary-fancier, and perhaps need an audience with some sympathy for their ethical content.

The vicissitudes of opera in France from the 1790s onwards reflected the vicissitudes of politics. With the exception of the occasional revival of *Medée* and of Spontini's *La vestale*, little of this work is seen or heard today. But in the later 1820s the revival of liberal and revolutionary sentiment that was to culminate in the Revolution of 1830 and the final expulsion of the Bourbons was reflected in and nourished by the reappearance on the stage of the Paris Opéra of operas with a radical political message. A principal contributor to this trend was Rossini. But Rossini's last and most overtly political opera, *Guillaume Tell*, which was designed especially for the Opéra, had been anticipated and inspired by the work of Daniel Auber.

Auber's grand opera *La muette de Portici*, which had its premiere in Paris on 29 February 1828, would deserve a place in this survey if only because it is one of the few operas that directly inspired significant political action. A performance at the Théâtre de la Monnaie in Brussels on 25 August 1830 so excited its audience that they rushed out to storm the courthouse, and so began the national revolution that finally established Belgian political independence. *La muette* has a place in the history of opera, too, since it is the work that links the revolutionary tradition with that of Parisian grand opera. It is constructed in the conventional five acts of grand opera, complete with ballet music, large-scale ensembles and lavish spectacle, which culminates with the dumb heroine apparently hurling herself into the crater of an erupting Vesuvius. These were doubtless some of the ingredients that helped to ensure the opera's Parisian popularity. It had clocked up 100 performances at the Opéra by 1840, and 500 by 1880. But its political content probably did it no harm either.

Auber's opera is based around the uprising that took place in Naples in 1647 – one of many popular revolts in mid-seventeenth-century Europe – led by the fisherman called Masaniello. The two dimensions of conflict in the opera are class and nationality. It is a revolt of the native Italians or Neapolitans against their Spanish Bourbon rulers, and by the common people against the ruling class. Auber's opera was composed to a libretto provided by Eugene Scribe and G. Delavigue. There had been a play on the same subject not long before at the Opéra-Comique, which had run into difficulties with the censors but had nevertheless proved popular; Auber and the Opéra authorities can thus hardly have misunderstood the political significance of mounting an opera on this subject.

Masaniello's dumb sister Fenella has been seduced, or possibly raped, by Alfonse, the son of the Spanish viceroy. This is revealed to Alfonse's prospective bride Elvire on their wedding day. Meanwhile Masaniello, his friend Pietro and the fishermen of Naples reflect on their unhappy lot. When Masaniello hears the fate of his sister, it is the final straw that pushes him into rebellion: 'Mieux vaut mourir que rester misérable.' ('It is better to die than to remain wretched.') He and Pietro sing a patriotic duet, 'Amour sacre de la patrie', of a suitably rousing character. This was the piece that particularly stirred the Belgian audience in 1830. But musically more striking is the lilting but sinister *barcarolle* that dominates Act Two. Ostensibly an innocent fishing song, it contains an ominous political message. This is both musically effective and politically plausible. The oppressed under a tyranny always have to find coded ways of expressing their opposition.

In Act Three the attempt to find Fenella and bring her to the Bourbon palace, benevolently inspired by the compassionate Elvire but understandably misconstrued by the people, is what finally sparks

off the popular uprising. By Act Four, however, Masaniello, ostensibly the leader of the revolt, is reacting with disgust and horror to the
brutal excesses of the 'mob'. When he expresses these feelings to Pietro
– 'Trop de sang, de carnage' ('Too much blood, too much carnage') –
Pietro denounces him as a traitor, a suspicion apparently confirmed
when Masaniello unknowingly gives refuge to Alfonse and Elvire as
they flee from the vengeful crowd, and then refuses to hand them
over. Pietro and the crowd denounce him as a new tyrant. 'N'avons-
nous que changer d'oppresseur?' ('What have we done but change our
oppressor?') they ask.

In the final act Masaniello is poisoned by Pietro, and this deprives
the revolution of the leader it needs, although the dying Masaniello is
still able to lead the people against Alfonse and his followers. But in
trying to protect Elvire once again, Masaniello is cut down by one of
his own followers. 'Il en était l'idole', says one of the fishermen, to
which Alfonse succinctly replies 'Il en est la victime.' Fenella's suicide
follows, and the collapse of the revolt.

La muette enshrines some of the more sombre lessons that were
learnt from the revolutionary experience: that revolution is a bloody
and brutal affair in which the moderation and generosity of such as
Masaniello are likely to be swept aside by the popular thirst for
vengeance; that the revolution devours its own leaders; and that it may
fail in the end. But it is not a one-sided work. Masaniello's clemency
towards Alfonse may be noble, but it is also misplaced: the Spaniard
returns to the battle as soon as he can. And it is the revolutionaries who
have the best and most exciting music. Hence its impact in Brussels.
Otherwise, it is musically rather humdrum. Auber has a gift for
popular melody, but does not rise to the lyrical moments and is a dull
harmonist. The device of a mute heroine, acted by a dancer, is now
more likely to embarrass than to enchant us. If the enthusiasm this
opera once aroused is now difficult to comprehend, it would nevertheless be worth the occasional revival.

Beethoven, *Leonore* and *Fidelio*

It was not until 1802 that the operas of revolutionary France reached
Vienna. In March of that year Schikaneder put on Cherubini's *Lodoiska*

at the Theater an der Wien, with immediate success. A craze for these operas began. Later in that same year there were two productions of *Les deux journées*, as well as productions of *Medée* and *Elisa*. Thus all Cherubini's major operas of the revolutionary period had been staged within ten months. Many works by Méhul, Dalayrac, Berton and others followed, including Lesueur's *La caverne*.[4] These provided the exemplars that Beethoven needed for *Leonore*, or *Fidelio*. Beethoven frequently expressed his admiration for Cherubini and met him when he came to Vienna in 1805. It was during that visit that Cherubini attended the premiere of *Leonore*, on 20 November 1805.

It is entirely appropriate that it was Beethoven who provided the operatic masterpiece in which the values and vision of the revolutionary age are expressed in their most inspiring and overwhelming form. For Beethoven was not only the greatest composer of the revolutionary age; he was also a musical revolutionary, and the revolutionary changes and expansion he achieved in music are intimately tied to his lifelong identification with the spirit of the political and social revolution inaugurated by the fall of the Bastille.

'. . . to us, Beethoven *is* the Revolution', wrote Hugh Ottaway.[5] It is not hard to see what this means. Beethoven inherited the Viennese classical tradition and its forms from Haydn and Mozart, but to meet his own expressive needs he had to undertake a vast expansion and even reconstruction of many of the classical forms and conventions. Thus, for example, while it would be an exaggeration to say that Beethoven invented the scherzo, it was in Beethoven's hands that the old-style courtly minuet and trio ceased to be the norm for the brisker of the two internal movements in the four-movement symphony or sonata, and was replaced by the more dynamic and dramatic scherzo (although the ABA pattern, with a usually more relaxed trio section sandwiched between two renderings of the scherzo, was normally retained). The fading of the minuet was in itself a sign of the changing social and economic circumstances within which the composer worked. Beethoven's symphonies were not aristocratic commissions; nor were they written for performance at the royal or archiepiscopal court, as were Mozart's *Linz* or *Prague* symphonies, or Haydn's set of six symphonies, numbers 82 to 87. The Viennese musical public of the 1800s might even have found the minuet and trio somewhat old-fashioned.

On the other hand, audiences must have been astonished by the sheer scale and weight of Beethoven's works, beginning with the Third Symphony in 1806. The scale of the *Eroica*, as it became known, and especially of its first two movements, was something absolutely new in Western music. The vast structure of the first movement and its insistent, tramping dynamic were unprecedented. Even more so was the transformation of the second, slow movement into a gigantic funeral march – the two movements together lasting more than half an hour – longer than many a complete symphony by his predecessors. Even if we knew nothing of the background of this symphony, or of Beethoven's intentions, its momentous character would still be apparent. Here, and in the Fifth, Sixth, Seventh and Ninth symphonies particularly, the sense of historical–musical forces bursting into established forms, taking them over and dominating them, is surely unmistakable. As it is, we know – for once the picturesque story is not apocryphal – that Beethoven originally intended to dedicate this symphony to Napoleon, and tore out the title page when he heard that the erstwhile First Consul had had himself crowned emperor. (Beethoven's dislike of such titles makes the nickname of his Piano Concerto No. Five – the 'Emperor' – especially inappropriate.) But the title *Eroica* remained, and the shadow of the world-historical figure whom Hegel dubbed 'the spirit of the age on horseback' and was so portrayed by Jacques-Louis David looms over the whole work. It is consciously a work of the revolutionary era and its spirit. A model for the second movement may have been Cherubini's *Hymne funèbre sur la mort du Général Hoche* of 1797 – as Basil Deane has suggested – which would add a further link connecting the symphony with the revolutionary culture of the 1790s.[6]

Even more explicitly expressive of the revolutionary spirit is the Ninth Symphony, with its setting of Schiller's celebrated 'Ode to Joy'. It is possible that Schiller's ode was originally, in 1785, dedicated not to Joy (*Freude*) but to freedom (*Freiheit*), and was altered partly in order to pass the Austrian censorship. Its similarity to the idealistic poems set by French composers in the 1790s is striking. 'It was . . . the nearest German equivalent to the hymns and odes to brotherhood, liberty and humanity set to music by the revolutionary composers in France.'[7] Beethoven had first contemplated setting the words to music in the early 1790s; that it took him thirty years to do so is testimony to the consistency with which he adhered to his early radical convictions. The Choral Symphony is a product of the composer's last years, the years of withdrawal, which are usually associated with the isolation imposed by his deafness and a growing misanthropy. But, as Ottaway argued, this withdrawal should also be seen as a response to the era of resurgent political reaction that followed the downfall of Napoleon and the Battle of Waterloo, a reaction with which Beethoven was wholly out of sympathy.[8] He might have echoed Shelley's 'Feelings of a Republican on the Fall of Bonaparte': 'I hated thee, fallen tyrant!' (although as late as 1820 he was defending Napoleon's role in replacing the feudal system with 'right and law'), but like Shelley he found no pleasure or comfort in the illiberal climate established by the Emperor's defeat. For Beethoven to set Schiller's poem, with its ringing affirmation of human brotherhood, in this political context, was an act of profound faith and even political defiance.

Some commentators nevertheless seem anxious to play down Beethoven's political radicalism. He was not a genuine egalitarian, they suggest. His resentment of monarchs and aristocrats was inspired by egoistical *amour propre* rather than by democratic principles. It is true that Beethoven, like Mozart, was sure of his own genius, and expected others to recognize it. But to reduce his political outlook to personal pique does him less than justice. The sentiments he inscribed in a friend's autograph album as a young man were ones we have no reason to suppose he ever discarded:

> To help wherever one can,
> Love liberty above all things,
> Never deny the truth
> Even at the foot of the throne![9]

Or there is the song he set as a teenager, 'Der freie Mann', with words by G.C. Pfeffel that express the same egalitarian and fraternal sentiments as attracted Beethoven to Schiller's 'Ode to Joy':

> Wer ist ein freier Mann?
> Dem nicht Geburt noch Titel
> Nicht Samtrock oder Kittel
> Den Bruder bergen kann.

(Who is a free man? He from whom neither birth nor title, peasant smock nor uniform, hides his brother man.)[10]

This theme of human brotherhood, overriding and breaking down conventional social distinctions, is one of Beethoven's recurring pre-occupations. In *Fidelio* the Minister announces, 'Es sucht der Bruder seine Bruder' ('A brother comes to seek his brothers'); a note of 1811 shows that Beethoven was still thinking of setting words from the first version of the 'Ode' in which instead of 'Alle Menschen werden Bruder' Schiller had written, 'Bettler werden Furstenbruder' ('beggars become the brothers of princes'), a phrase that lodged itself firmly in the composer's mind.

Above all, we have as evidence of Beethoven's political radicalism the music itself. Even if we knew nothing of the stage works with which they are connected, we could hardly miss the sense of grand public conflict and ultimate triumphant idealism in the Overture to *Egmont*, or *Leonore* No. 3. Nothing like them had been heard before, and if they have antecedents these lie in the intensely dramatic works of Cherubini, which were themselves the product of that composer's involvement in the great public issues of revolutionary and Napoleonic France.

The theme of freedom is thus a recurring one in Beethoven's life and work, and it is the leitmotif of his one opera, *Fidelio*, or *Leonore* as it was called in its original form. The entire opera is set in a prison, and to grasp the full significance of that we need to remember that the fall of the Bastille in 1789 was what, at a single epochal stroke, had established the prison as the symbol of oppression and injustice, of the denial of that very liberty which became the battle-cry of the new age:

. . . the prison haunted the mind of the nineteenth century, which may be said to have had its birth at the fall of the Bastille. The genius of the age, conceiving itself as creative will, naturally thought of the prisons from which it must be freed, and the trumpet call of the 'Leonore' overture sounds through the century, the signal for the opening of gates, for a general deliverance . . .[11]

It was not for nothing that the workhouses introduced in England by the infamous New Poor Law of 1834 were known as Bastilles. Prisons feature prominently in the operas of Verdi, such as *I due Foscari*, *Il trovatore*, *Don Carlos* and *Aida*, and even in some works of the *verismo* school, such as *Tosca* and *Andrea Chénier*, both, as it happens, set in the revolutionary period. They provide the setting for some of the darkest operas of the twentieth century, Janáček's *From the House of the Dead*, and Dallapiccola's *Il prigioniero*. The gloomy but fantastic prisons of Piranesi and the dark sketches of Goya provide a contemporary visual counterpart to Beethoven's opera, and especially to the vision of darkness, set in F minor and full of discords and rhythmic dislocations, with which Beethoven opens the second act, in the 'dark subterranean dungeon' where Florestan is kept in solitary confinement. *Fidelio* is the supreme version of the 'Bastille opera', in which the experience of imprisonment features as prominently as the 'rescue' with which such works usually conclude, if not more so.

Fidelio is based on a libretto written by Jean-Nicolas Bouilly for an opera by Pierre Gaveaux called *Léonore, ou l'amour conjugal*, which was first performed in Paris on 19 February 1798. Bouilly based his plot on an actual episode of the Revolution in which he had been involved. An aristocratic opponent of the Revolution in the Vendée was imprisoned, but his jailor smuggled his wife into prison in disguise. The radical Carrier, leading the revolutionary terror in the Vendée, entered the prison determined to kill the imprisoned count, but was opposed by the countess brandishing a pistol. According to John Warrack, Bouilly's autobiography makes it clear that other episodes of the 1790s supplied him with further source material for his *Léonore*.[12] The topicality of the story was thinly masked by transferring it to sixteenth-century Spain.

Fidelio or *Leonore*: either title properly directs our attention to the heroic and devoted woman who is at the centre of the action. Her imprisoned husband remains unseen, though the object of much discussion and planning, until the opening of the second act. The focus is on the heroism and loyalty of a woman and wife. This in itself is characteristic of the revolutionary era, which like other such historical moments was a time when women emerged from the shadows of private life to take an active part in public affairs. But Leonore also belies the argument of some feminists, such as Catherine Clément, that woman's role in opera is always, or at least usually, that of victim.

Leonore's disguise as a man is certainly not the implausible piece of theatricality that some commentators take it to be. There are well-documented cases from the same period of women successfully disguising themselves as soldiers, either to pursue an active life or to be near their husbands or lovers. Leonore's involvement in the family affairs of Rocco the jailor and his daughter Marzelline is therefore not a distracting piece of near-farce, but a plausibly embarrassing entanglement, with obvious comic undertones, which Leonore can only view as an absurd diversion from her self-appointed mission of rescue. It adds a note of realism as well as humour, and also highlights the contrast between Leonore's selfless conjugal devotion and Rocco's firm conviction that money is the true foundation of a successful marriage.

Steadily, though, the perspective of the opera broadens out. Her husband's plight is not all that moves Leonore. She is joined by Marzelline and Jaquino in pleading with Rocco to allow the prisoners out of their cells to enjoy the fresh air and sunlight of early spring, and when Leonore finally arrives with Rocco in the cell of the man whose grave they are to dig, she resolves – not yet knowing whether or not the prisoner is Florestan – that she will try to save this man whoever he is. Rocco mutters obsessively about the need to get the work done before Pizarro arrives, while Leonore's voice soars above him in grand phrases of courage and compassion:

> Wer du auch seist, ich will dich retten
> Bei Gott, du sollst Rein opfer sein!
> Gewiss, ich lose deine Ketten,
> Ich will, du Amer, dich befrei'n

> (Who you may be, I'm here to save you, I vow you shall not perish here!
> No more shall cruel chains enslave you, You shall be rescued, that I
> swear.)

In the final scene it is not only Florestan who is released, but all the state prisoners, although we should note that the final chorus is a hymn not to liberty or to monarchical benevolence and justice, but to Leonore and her constant love.

The common criticism of *Fidelio* is that it is not really an opera but an uneasy mixture of forms in which the ethical message ultimately and unfortunately comes to dominate all else. David Cairns, a defender of the work, summed up the case against: 'an opera which begins as a singspiel, then turns into a heroic melodrama, only to end as a cantata . . .'[13] There is more than a hint of this view in Winton Dean's chapter entitled 'Beethoven and Opera' in *The Beethoven Companion*: Dean suggests that in the final, 1814 version of *Fidelio* Beethoven 'drains his characters of individuality and smudges the portrait of the hero and heroine so movingly drawn in 1805. They become personifications . . .' In the earlier versions 'the moral is not emphasized, but allowed to emerge through the action' whereas in 1814 Treitschke and Beethoven 'ram it home so hard that the hollow reverberations of a thumped tub are all but discernible'.[14]

Dean is certainly correct in identifying the general direction of the changes made to the work for its final version, and this direction is summed up in his observation that 'The more Beethoven revised the opera the more deeply he impregnated it with the spirit of 1789.'[15] But we may debate whether these changes detract from *Fidelio* as an opera, as he clearly believes. Comparison between *Fidelio* and its first incarnation as *Leonore* is certainly instructive. The original version was in three acts, and was longer than the final version by nearly half an hour (to judge from the recorded version made under the direction of Herbert Blomstedt). To listen to *Leonore* with the score of *Fidelio* in front of you makes clear how much more concise and concentrated, and therefore dramatically more effective, the final version is. Everywhere redundant bars, unnecessary repetitions, whether orchestral or vocal, have been eliminated. Some important music is added, including the dramatic recitative 'Abscheulicher', which leads into Leonore's aria 'Komm Hoffnung', and the *poco allegro* finale to Florestan's prison aria in which he imagines, or hallucinates, a vision of Leonore as an angel leading him out to freedom. This replaces a weaker, more pathos-laden concluding section. But a trio for Marzelline, Jaquino and Rocco, and a duet for Marzelline and Leonore are cut from what becomes Act One.

In the 1805 version, the denouement of the drama is handled at far greater length, and much more care is taken to tie up all the potential loose ends of the plot (though the unfortunate Marzelline gets her brief moment of embarrassed understanding only in the later version). Time is allowed for Leonore and Florestan to explain matters to each other, for Rocco to explain his role to the Minister, and for Pizarro's fate to be more or less clearly resolved. In the familiar final version, the exaltation and excitement of the triumph of good over evil sweep all before them; there is no time for anxieties or explanations, and Pizarro is bundled off the stage without it being at all clear what will happen to him.

Dean obviously regrets these changes; but it is clear that Beethoven did not. By 1814 he was no longer interested in a conventionally tidy and plausible ending to the story. It is the universal meaning that he wishes finally to leave with us, and the apparent move from opera to cantata or oratorio, as it is often seen, is an expression of this. Otto Klemperer related that both Richard Strauss and Hans Pfitzner used to omit the chorus that opens the last scene because 'it was too four-square'. Klemperer's perceptive comment was that 'It is just because it is foursquare that it is so beautiful, and it is so beautiful because it must be foursquare.'[16] Klemperer, who was perhaps the supreme inter-preter of this opera, understood that Beethoven here as in the Ninth Symphony places his rejoicings firmly in this world, and gives them a strongly popular character. By the final scene 'the drama is finished – yes. But then Beethoven raises this story of an individual, who lives in chains and is rescued by a loving woman, to a universal level. The destiny of the individual becomes the destiny of the human race.'[17]

In fact the submergence, or integration, of the individual characters into a final act of common rejoicing is not unoperatic at all. It is the usual form of the operatic happy ending, in which a community rejoices collectively and the leading figures rejoice as part of that community. *Figaro* and *Die Zauberflöte* offer condensed examples; *Die Meistersinger*, *Parsifal* and *Falstaff* have finales on a more Beethovenian scale. What Dean and other commentators cling to is a belief that opera must be about the fate of particular individuals. But opera is often about general or collective fates and themes, and it was Beetho-ven's plain intention in this finale to link the fate of Leonore and Florestan with the wider themes of liberty and mutual love. More-over, the central pair are not forgotten or obliterated in the general rejoicing: as I noted, the final chorus is in praise of Leonore herself. And one alteration made to the 1814 version enhanced the focus on Leonore and Florestan. In the original version the sublime ensemble that follows the moment when Don Fernando, the Minister, who is about to release Florestan from his manacles, by an inspired second thought hands the key to Leonore, was an ensemble piece from the start. In the final version it is inaugurated by Leonore herself, joined by Florestan and then by the rest of the company.

This ensemble forms a further link between the early and the later Beethoven, since its melody is one he used first in his *Cantata on the Death of Joseph II*, composed in 1790. In that, it was used to set words beginning 'Mankind rose up to the light'. The author of these words was the poet Eulogius Schneider, Professor of Literature at Bonn University. Beethoven had been a subscriber to a book of poems he had published in 1790, which included one celebrating the fall of the Bastille. (Schneider nevertheless fell victim to the Terror and was executed in Paris on 10 April 1794.)[18] The words to which the melody is set in *Fidelio* similarly employ the Enlightenment image of light dispersing darkness and fanaticism.

Beethoven's amalgamation and reconstruction of the first two acts is all of a piece with the changes he made in the last act. Originally Act One ended with the trio 'Gut, Söhnchen, gut', thus hardly taking the story beyond the domestic comedy in Rocco's household. Act Two was effectively dominated by Pizarro; the prisoners' chorus was set apart from the main action, merely their routine daily exercise, not the exceptional event it becomes in the revision; and Pizarro ended the act with a solo supported by a chorus of sentries. But Beethoven reorders these events, so that the prisoners' chorus opens the finale to Act One, and the fate of the prisoners, including the unseen solitary prisoner below, dominates it. Beethoven thus shifts the balance decisively away from the individual villain to the collective plight of the prisoners. They enjoy their brief taste of sunlight and express their yearning for freedom before they descend once more into the darkness that will be so intensely conveyed in the opening scene of the act that follows.

In some ways, though, *Fidelio* is a less revolutionary work than it may appear. It is not a drama of popular liberation or struggle. Heroism belongs only to its central couple. They are isolated in a conformist, collaborationist environment represented by the kind-hearted but cringeing chief jailor Rocco. He is the reluctant but nevertheless compliant agent of oppression: the accommodating, subservient underling that all regimes depend on, especially cruel and unjust ones. The prison is not stormed by a revolutionary crowd, nor do the prisoners themselves rebel. They are liberated from above by the minister of an enlightened ruler, who is very cautious as to what he can do: 'Und kann er helfen, hilft er gern' ('If he can help, he gladly will'). And at the moment of thanksgiving, it is to God they turn. Thus the story of *Fidelio* belongs in some ways to the eighteenth century, and looks to the just ruler for salvation rather than to revolution or popular upheaval (though the dynamism of the music belies this pattern to some extent).

Fidelio, with its overwhelmingly affirmative conclusion, is expressive not only of Beethoven's humanism but also of the optimism of its particular historical moment, as is the similarly exultant conclusion to the Ninth Symphony. It is hard for us, at the end of a century that has disappointed so many hopes of progress, to share that optimism. Michael Tippett, a modern humanist composer much influenced by Beethoven, has offered a musical comment on that optimism by quoting the opening of the finale of the Ninth Symphony in his own Third Symphony, following it with words very different from Schiller's; some modern producers of *Fidelio*, such as Joachim Herz and Harry Kupfer, have tried to embody this awareness in their productions.

But Beethoven, finally, needs no special pleading or defence. For some people the word 'optimism' is always accompanied by the word 'facile', but there is nothing facile about Beethoven's optimism. His victories are always hard won. *Fidelio*, like many of the symphonies and sonatas, is suffused with Beethoven's characteristic sense of struggle against the odds. Leonore constantly has to revive her fading hopes of success, and the sense of terror is present not only in her passionate response to Pizarro's cruel threats, but also in the darkness of the cell where Florestan lies and to which she, of all people, comes to help dig his grave, in preparation for his murder. As Herz has pointed out, the very moment of salvation is the potential moment of absolute tragedy.[19] Without that delivering trumpet call, she and Florestan, and Rocco too, would be doomed to failure and death.

Leonore does triumph. As in the Third and Fifth symphonies, and the *Egmont* Overture, heroic struggle against the odds brings victory in the end. And we can identify with this, not as a fairytale conclusion, but as a triumph that has been earned. As E.M. Forster wrote in the famous passage on Beethoven's Fifth Symphony in *Howards End*, it is because the composer brings back the ominous music of the scherzo trio in the midst of the final movement – the walking goblins with their music of 'panic and emptiness' – that we can trust Beethoven when he celebrates triumph and victory. Such events are not unknown in real life. Prisoners are released – some, like Nelson Mandela, after decades behind bars; dictators and torturers are overthrown – not always, and not without struggle, but often enough for us to know what it is that Beethoven is telling us: we need not, should not, despair, because heroism and humanity do sometimes achieve their victories. *Komm Hoffnung*, and sustain us as you sustained Leonore and Florestan through their years of separation and darkness.

3

Patria Oppressa:
Rossini, Bellini, Donizetti and the Risorgimento
(NATIONALISM I)

Of the political changes that followed, and to some extent followed from, the French Revolution, none was more important than the rise of nationalism, first within Europe, later beyond. The idea of self-government for nations was a catalyst that dissolved the old imperial order in Europe, in South America, and subsequently in Asia and Africa as well.

But what was and is a nation? There cannot be any definitive answer to that question, one reason being the crucial role of consciousness in any kind of nationhood. If a group claims to be a nation, and does so with sufficient fervour, determination and unanimity, there is no known way in which outsiders can prove to that group that it is not. Conversely, it would be odd to say that a group constituted a nation if none of its members felt that it was so. To be a nation without being conscious of the fact is very nearly a contradiction in terms. Yet under the right conditions, that consciousness can be created and nourished, so that nations appear to come into being where none existed before.

To be a nation is a matter of having or believing that you have a distinct and separate collective identity. If the claim to such an identity is to be plausible, it is necessary to argue that history and culture prove the existence of the nation. So the creation of a national movement has usually involved the rediscovery and rewriting of the nation's history, and the revival and assertive celebration of the national culture and language (if there is such a language). If necessary a distinctively national culture must be invented, or re-created. In these processes music has frequently played a central role. 'Music is the least political of the arts,' Professor Norman Stone wrote recently.[1] I am sometimes inclined to think that this is the reverse of the truth. In relation to European nationalist movements, music played a central role in creating a sense of national identity and rallying people to the national cause.

It is impossible to think of any other ideological force or creed that has had a more profound and lasting impact on music in the past two centuries than nationalism. From Weber to Vaughan Williams, from Berlioz to Bartók, from Chopin to Shostakovich, there is a long list of composers whose musical achievement is bound up with their involvement with nationalism. The musical development of some composers suggests that only when they discovered or turned to the music of their own nation did they discover their own authentic voice and musical identity. This is clear in the cases of Glinka, Mussorgsky, Smetana and Vaughan Williams, all of whom began by composing competent but rather anonymous music within the dominant Austro-German idiom, but then in discovering their nation and its music discovered their musical selves.

First in Germany and Italy, a little later in Russia and Czechoslovakia, opera played a major role in the creation of both a national music and a national consciousness. Often, because explicitly political activities were prohibited, the opera house became a forum for the expression of subversive political sentiments, and the encoring of patriotic arias or choruses became a form of political demonstration, which was then forbidden by law. The idea that you could or should keep politics out of the opera house would have struck nineteenth-century Italians or Czechs as absurd.

In Italy, especially as far as opera was concerned, the musical situation was different from elsewhere. Italy had never been dominated musically by the Austro-German tradition, and opera was of course an Italian invention which, by the time of Rossini, had a continuous history of two hundred years. The centrality of music, and especially opera, in Italian social and political life was remarked on by many contemporary observers. Both Stendhal and Heine suggested that the repression of political life, of the press and of the written word under the various Italian regimes – the Bourbon kingdom of Naples, the Papal States, the Austrian provinces – compelled Italians to turn to music as an outlet for frustrated national and political feelings. Heine wrote:

> Even the use of speech is forbidden to poor enslaved Italy, and she can only express by music the feelings of her heart. All her resentment against foreign domination, her inspiration of liberty, her rage at the consciousness of weakness, her sorrow at the memories of past greatness, her faint hopes, her watching and waiting in silence, her yearning for aid: – all is marked in those melodies which glide from an intense intoxication of animal life into elegiac weakness, and in those pantomimes which dart from flattering caresses into threatening rage.[2]

Stendhal had made similar observations in his famous *Life of Rossini*, published just four years earlier.[3]

On the other hand, the opera house had its convenience from the point of view of the authorities as well, as John Rosselli has pointed out. '. . . it attracts to a place open to observation during the hours of darkness a large part of the educated population', noted the Chief Minister of Lombardy-Venetia in 1825.[4] Opera was sometimes seen as a means of keeping people quiet and distracting them from more serious political activities. It may have been, but that did not prevent either the production of political operas or operas including significant political gestures, or the use of the opera house for what were in effect political demonstrations.

Rosselli refers loftily to 'the old clichés about opera as a carrier of Risorgimento nationalism'.[5] But whilst it is doubtless easy, especially for non-specialists, to underestimate the complexity of early-nineteenth-century Italian opera, it seems to me that outside Italy at least the political dimension of pre-Verdian opera is still underappreciated and ignored. Moreover, there is a pleasing irony in the fact that in the process of adapting Italian opera to the spirit of the age, and particularly to the ethos of patriotism and heroism that was the ideal of the Risorgimento, it was one of the least 'committed' of composers, Rossini, who almost unwittingly played the leading role.

Rossini

The bare facts of Rossini's occasional political involvements can be easily summarized. In 1815, when Murat declared Italy's independence from Austria, he composed an 'Inno dell'Indipendenza'. This was played in Bologna, but unfortunately the next day the Austrians reconquered the city. From 1816 to 1822 he was court composer to the Bourbon king Ferdinand I of Naples, and in that capacity he composed a lot of music for royal occasions. In 1822, at the specific request of Metternich, he composed cantatas for the congress of the dominant European powers at Verona; when he visited Vienna in the same year, Metternich staged a banquet in his honour. At the same time, however, Rossini was under police surveillance, and was said by the police in 1821 to be 'strongly infected by revolutionary principles'.[6]

After Rossini settled in Paris in 1824, he showed some sympathy for the cause of Greek independence, which then attracted support from liberals all over Europe. He wrote a cantata commemorating the death of Byron, and in 1826 he conducted a charity concert to raise money for the Greek cause. At the same time, to mark the coronation of Charles X in Rheims Cathedral, he composed the delightful if sycophantic *Il viaggio a Reims*. But his next opera, *Le siège de Corinthe*, which was adapted from an earlier Neapolitan opera, *Maometto Secondo*, was also a tribute to the Greek cause.

Rossini's final opera was *Guillaume Tell*, a thoroughly political work which was interpreted as a gesture of support for Greek and also Italian independence. Later, when living again in Bologna, he was drawn into the political ferment that seized Italy between 1846 and 1848. In 1846 he signed a petition addressed to Pope Pio Nono in support of political reforms, and in the year of revolutions, 1848, he provided music for a patriotic hymn which was performed in Bologna to great enthusiasm. This was not enough to convince everyone of Rossini's devotion to the national cause, and a hostile demonstration prompted him to leave the city in haste. He spent his last years in Paris; among his last compositions was a hymn to Napoleon III 'and his valiant people'. Rossini was upset, though, by suggestions that he was an unpatriotic reactionary, and in a letter of 1864 he drew attention to the 'Hymn to Independence' he had composed nearly fifty years before.

Obviously, this is not the record of an ardently committed patriot. But though Rossini was clearly ready to accommodate the powers that be, it is harsh to indict this as 'craven', as does Nicholas Till.[7] Especially in Italy, it was still difficult for composers to survive without the patronage of rulers. As Richard Osborne writes, Rossini may have become 'ultra-conservative' in his middle years. But he resented the idea that he was not a patriotic Italian, and it looks as if, when occasion afforded, he showed his nationalist colours.[8] Francis Toye's summary, in one of the first studies written in English to treat the composer seriously, seems fair:

> . . . he always remained first and foremost a musician; a musician, too, who liked his life to be as easy and free from disturbance as possible, [so] he was naturally inclined to favour the established order of things. Which is not to assume, as some have done, that he had no feeling for the legitimate aspirations of his native land. He had; but music and a tranquil existence came first. . . .[9]

When we turn to Rossini's operas we are faced with more than one puzzle. The first is that Rossini's popular reputation is sharply at odds with the facts of his career as an opera composer. That career was highly productive but strikingly short. It lasted from 1810 to 1829, and all but one of the comic operas for which he is still best known date from the period up to 1817. After that he devoted himself to dramatic and tragic opera. Most, though not all, of these later works have been persistently neglected, and it is only comparatively recently that they have been rediscovered, thanks to the enterprise of some record companies and to the annual Rossini Festival at the composer's birthplace, Pesaro. It is unlikely that even the finest of these works will ever be as popular as the perennial *Barber of Seville*. But even if we were to conclude, with Beethoven, that Rossini's genius was for comedy, we would still have to explain why this apparently light-hearted composer turned away from the genres that had brought him such fame and success and instead ventured into the much more risky territory of *opera seria*. In fact, as the later works are rescued from their long oblivion, it is becoming clear that they contain music of great power and beauty; in their sustained seriousness and grand architectural designs, culminating in the spacious layout of *Guillaume Tell*, they reveal aspects of Rossini's genius of which most people were unaware.

But these discoveries exacerbate a further problem, which is that of commitment, of deciding what, on the evidence of the music, Rossini really believed in and cared for. In works like *Mosè in Egitto*, or *Maometto Secondo* or *Guillaume Tell*, it becomes an inescapable subject of speculation. All three are operas about national oppression, a subject stirringly and frequently dealt with by Rossini. But in contrast to the works of, let us say, Beethoven or Verdi, we cannot be so sure that there is a personal charge of emotion behind Rossini's notes and words. There is a sense of detachment, of a creator effacing himself behind his creation. It is hard to infer Rossini's own feelings from the music he composed. This is by no means a criticism of the music, but wider knowledge of his music confirms the judgement of the Italian critic who described him as 'the most enigmatic and misunderstood composer of the nineteenth century'.[10] Or rather, even as we know him better, he becomes more rather than less enigmatic.

Despite Toye's judicious verdict, I think it is possible to argue that Rossini was more touched by the great issue of national liberation than perhaps he realized or cared to admit, and that his patriotic audiences were not mistaken in their enthusiasm for such works as *Mosè*, *Tell*, or the stirring martial finale to Act One of *La donna del lago*. But even the earlier works, including some of the *buffo* operas, are not without their patriotic gestures. One of Rossini's earliest successes was *Tancredi*, first seen in Venice in 1813, a drama whose essential ingredients are love, patriotism and the possible conflicts between them. *Tancredi* is one of the first of many such dramas placed in the supposedly picturesque context of the Crusades, during which patriotic loyalty conveniently coincided with religious duty. Amenaide loves the exiled Tancredi, but agrees to the marriage her father Argirio has arranged for her because it is the means of healing the old family feud and binding the city together in its fight against the Saracens. When it seems that she has pledged herself to the 'heathen' Solamir, there is natural outrage among her compatriots, and she is condemned to die. Her own father has to sign the death warrant, and he is torn between his love for his daughter and his sense of duty to his country. Later, when Tancredi appears to avenge Orbanazzo's insult to Amenaide, he and Argirio sing one of those rousing, tramping duets that form a

regular feature of early-nineteenth-century Italian opera: at once gestures of male solidarity or brotherhood and of defiance against an
enemy who is usually also an enemy of the brothers' country. 'We find
no sign of martial vigour in Italian music until the appearance of
Tancredi,' wrote Stendhal, who saw the opera as a first echo of the
defeats Napoleon had inflicted on the Austrians in 1796. In this duet,
he writes, 'Rossini bursts forth into a heroic vision of *modern national
idealism*, in the best sense of the term . . . '[11]

Even the *buffo* operas that followed *Tancredi* are not without their
patriotic notes. They are heard in *L'italiana in Algeri*, premiered less
than four months after *Tancredi*. Isabella, who is *l'italiana*, is rallying
her compatriots for the planned escape from the bey, Mustafa, and it is
to their patriotism that she appeals in a relatively serious aria, 'Pensa
alla patria', during which she reminds them that throughout Italy
examples of daring and courage are being reborn:

> Vedi per tutta Italia
> Rinescere gli esempi
> D'ardire e di valor.

The chorus responds in martial style that this test will show what
Italians are worth:

> Quanto vaglian gl'Italiani
> Al cimento si vedra.

Stendhal thought this gesture towards reviving patriotic sentiments
was a shrewd move on Rossini's part: 'Rossini knew his audience, read
into its secret heart, and feasted its imagination on the delights which it
craved.'[12] *L'italiana in Algeri* celebrates the triumph of a resourceful
woman over gullible men, but also of an Italian woman over foolish
foreigners.

In 1814 *Il turco in Italia* was not initially a success at La Scala, where
the Milanese fancied themselves insulted by the obvious similarity of
title and theme with the Venetian opera of the previous year. But
whereas Isabella and the Italians were eager to leave Algiers as soon as
possible, the Turkish pasha Selim is, as one would expect in an Italian
opera, enchanted by Italy; even if, by the end of the opera, he is
disenchanted with Italian women, he leaves their country with real
regret:

Cara Italia io t'abbandono
Ma per sempre in cor t'avro:
Che per te felice io sono,
Ogni ai rammentero.

Philip Gossett, who today is probably the leading authority on Rossini, has written, 'Superb as the *buffo* operas are, Rossini is historically more important as a composer of *opera seria*.'[13] Given the ostensibly by then outdated character of *opera seria*, which not even Mozart could rescue from ossification, this looks an extraordinary claim. But it is probably correct. In *Mosè in Egitto*, for example, Rossini creates a new kind of serious opera in which not arias and solo individual singers dominate the score, but ensemble pieces and choruses; some of the central figures, including Moses himself, are emblematic figures rather than individuals. This may make an opera of this kind less interesting to today's audiences and singers, but such indifference rests on a misunderstanding of the work itself. *Mosè* is not primarily about individuals but about peoples, just as was *Israel in Egypt*, Handel's oratorio on the same subject. The chorus and individuals who represent forces larger than themselves must dominate the work (although Rossini avoids monotony by creating dramatic contrast between the big choral ensembles and more intimate and reflective arias and duets, inserting a duet for Elcia and her friend Amenophis into the grand Act One finale, for example). Moses is the voice both of the enslaved Israelites and of God Himself. He possesses God's power to bring down every kind of misfortune upon the Egyptians, so that when he sings, on the first occasion accompanied only by trombones, horns and woodwind, it is not surprising that it is in the accents of Mozart's Commendatore.

But Rossini and his librettist, Andrea Tottola, do make some concessions to conventional taste by incorporating the story of the love of Osiris, the Pharaoh's son and heir, for the Hebrew woman Elcia. Osiris therefore has his own reasons for wanting to prevent the Israelites from leaving Egypt. But he is punished for his hostility to Moses and the Jews, being struck dead by a bolt of lightning at the end of Act Two. This decidedly unsentimental treatment of the romantic tenor is typical of this severe work.

The brief third act – it lasts barely fifteen minutes – is in the nature of an epilogue in which the Israelites are miraculously conveyed over the Red Sea to safety, while the pursuing Egyptians are drowned. Musically it is distinguished by the famous Prayer, in which Moses, Aaron, Elcia and the chorus all in turn beseech God to have mercy on his people ('del popol' tua pietà'). This became one of Rossini's most popular compositions, and it is not hard to see why. It has a simple memorable melody with that grandly swaying motion we shall meet again in certain choruses in Verdi's earliest operas. It is the prototype for such choruses, which are the arias (songs) not of individuals, but of whole nations. Balzac in his story 'Massimilla Doni' has the heroine explain to her companion the response the Prayer evokes from Italian audiences:

> Moses is the liberator of a people in slavery. Remember that idea, and you will see with what religious hope the entire audience will hear the prayer of the liberated Hebrews, and with what thunderous applause they will respond to it.[14]

Mention should also be made of the opening scene of *Mosè*, which Wagner so much admired. We are used to associating Rossini's name with operatic overtures, whether witty or grand. But in *Mosè* as in others of his serious operas, he dispenses entirely with the overture. Three bare unison Cs and a brief transition lead straight into an opening scene in which the Egyptians, led by the Pharaoh and his family, lament the darkness Moses has called down on them. The scene is underpinned by a simple figuration which gains in effectiveness from its repetition. Pharaoh has no choice but to summon Moses and promise release for the Israelites. Moses then invokes the power of God, and darkness is transformed into C major light in a splendid passage that recalls the similar effect in Haydn's *The Creation*, a work with which Rossini was familiar. Stendhal gives a vivid account of the effect of this magnificent opening scene on one hearer who went to the Teatro San Carlo 'feeling rather like a man who has been offered a front seat at an *auto-da-fé*', but was overwhelmed once the music started:

> . . . before I had heard twenty bars of this superb *introduzione*, I could see nothing less profoundly moving than a whole population plunged into deep misery; it might have been the people of Marseilles in prayer at the outbreak of the plague in 1720.[15]

It is precisely this sense of *Mosè* as an opera of peoples, of collective experience, that makes it so powerful, and so much in tune with the developing consciousness of Risorgimento Italy, which found in history and the Old Testament some rather extravagant parallels to its own oppression by Austria and the Bourbons.

In the revised version which Rossini produced for the Paris Opéra in 1827, this scene loses much of its impact by being transferred to the beginning of Act Two, and in general the second and longer version lacks the concentration and directness of the original. Rossini's revision of *Mosè* achieves the opposite of what Beethoven did to *Leonore*. While Beethoven compressed, sacrificing good music and some dramatic cogency as a result, Rossini expanded and elaborated; whilst some good music was added, the impact of the earlier version was diffused and blurred.

Another Neapolitan opera which underwent a similar revision was *Maometto Secondo* of 1820, which reappeared in an enlarged Parisian form as *Le siège de Corinthe* in 1826. In the first version Venice and Italy are opposed by the Turkish ruler Mahomet, whose aim is the conquest of all Italy. In the Paris version it is Greece that is at war with Turkey, an obvious reference to the Greek war for independence then in progress. But the earlier version made a direct appeal to Italian patriotism, with a narrative that could be considered either as a serious version of *L'italiana in Algeri* or as an anticipation of *Norma*, in so far as it focuses on a woman who finally puts patriotic duty before her love for a foreigner who is also an enemy.

Maometto Secondo consists of only two long acts, each lasting around an hour and a half. These extended spans are not mosaics of many small scenes, but are constructed from a small number of greatly extended musical numbers. What is more, some of these do not reach a full close, but run directly into the next. Rossini's concern with forward momentum and dramatic continuity is evident, although the libretto has neither the drive nor the tension he really needs. But the grandeur of the musical structure matches the largeness of his chosen themes: patriotic duty, personal courage and self-sacrifice.

Like *Mosè*, the opera opens magnificently with a brief and sombre orchestral introduction, which leads straight into a choral scene in which the Venetians, besieged by the Turks in Negroponte, meet to discuss how to respond to this crisis. Erisso, the governor, is in two minds as to what to do. The first speaker, Condulmiero, advises surrender, but he is repudiated by Calbo, who urges a fight to the finish. Calbo's stirring appeal revives the general morale, and Erisso calls on his followers to swear on their swords to fight for their country to the end, to which they respond with one of those patriotic marching choruses so typical of the period. Negroponte will, if necessary, be the tomb and monument of the Venetian forces:

> Negroponte alla veneta schiera
> monumento e sepolcro sara.

This sets the scene for the tragic, patriotic struggle that dominates the opera, and especially Act One. Act Two focuses on Erisso's daughter Anna, who fell in love with Maometto without knowing who he was, and is now, along with her father and other Venetians, his captive. Despite her personal emotions, she resolves upon suicide, and fulfils her intention when there seems no alternative but submission to the Turks. Like Norma, she is a 'sublime donna'. Perhaps *Maometto* and *Mosè* are a little too unrelentingly exalted, or serious, ever to achieve vast popularity, but they are grand and powerful works that hardly deserved the neglect they fell into, and from which they are only now being slowly rescued.

A little better known than either *Mosè* or *Maometto* is *La donna del lago*, in which Rossini, courtesy of Sir Walter Scott, undertakes a first venture into the territory of pastoral romanticism that he was to explore more fully, but finally, in *Guillaume Tell*. In Act One the evocation of landscape and atmosphere, with echoing horn calls, a gentle *barcarolle* for Ellen as she rows herself across the lake, and some lovely writing for women's chorus, is particularly fresh and touching. But at the end of this act the note of patriotism, and indeed militarism, is sounded once again. This is hard to understand simply in terms of the opera itself, since Tottola's libretto is so scanty in setting out motivations: a group of rebels against the Scottish king invoke *la patria* and *la Scozia oppressa*, but why is unclear unless we refer back to Scott, who presents the Highlanders as resisting the domination of lowland Scotland as represented by James V. But none of this is likely to have worried an Italian audience in 1819. King James, who turns out to be a remarkably, even foolishly, forgiving oppressor, is the tyrant against whom the people must arm and defend themselves, putting aside private trouble ('privato affano') in favour of patriotism ('patrio amor'). Every man is called on to swear an oath either to conquer or die, and then a chorus of bards, appropriately accompanied by harps and pizzicato lower strings, urges the sons of heroes ('figli d'Eroi') to slaughter their oppressor. And so with cries of 'Marciamo, struggiamo!' ('let us march and destroy'), the act ends on a fiercely martial note. Like the prayer from *Mosè*, the Bardic hymn became 'a favourite with patriots for the next fifty years'.[16] Edward Dent shrewdly noted that 'Rossini's style is chiefly a product of the warlike age in which he lived', although it was unfair of him to add that Rossini seemed 'to compose everything with the military band in view'.[17] If these patriotic and martial displays were indeed merely a calculated bid for popularity on Rossini's part, then he was at least extraordinarily successful in gauging the mood and likely responses of his audiences. It seems more reasonable to believe that if he had not shared those feelings to some degree, he could not have given them such memorable expression.

In 1824 Rossini settled in Paris, and it was there and for Parisian audiences that he composed, or re-composed, his last five operas. One of these, *Il viaggio a Reims*, was a unique occasional piece, which he refused to allow to be repeated after its original performances; instead he adapted much of the music for his last comic opera, *Le Comte Ory*. Finally there were the three grand operas, written specifically for the Paris Opéra, of which, as we have seen, only *Guillaume Tell* was wholly new. Nevertheless, it is striking that all three of these serious works, written for the fairly conservative audience which came to the Opéra, are 'operas of rebellion against oppression' in which 'the political aspect is far more important than the love story, which, like the ballet, remains secondary and conventional'.[18] All three, in short, belong in theme and atmosphere to the tradition of militant liberal nationalism, which was by no means the officially approved ideology of post-Napoleonic France.

The last of these three operas, *Guillaume Tell*, is the most explicitly political and partisan of all. Not surprisingly, it had only a moderate success at the Opéra, and this may have contributed to Rossini's decision to compose no more operas. Be this as it may, *Guillaume Tell* remains not only a stirring but also a profound and challenging work in its portrayal of the nature and the ethics of a classic national struggle. It would be unreasonable to expect the opera to encompass the range of characters, the complexities and ambiguities that are so conspicuous in Schiller's play. For example, it would be impossible for an opera to parallel the play's introduction in its final act of the figure of Duke Johann, the murderer of the Emperor himself, to provide a counterpoint and a challenge to Tell, whose murder of Gessler, the Austrian governor, has been hailed by the Swiss as an act of liberation. Again, given the conventions of Italian opera – or most opera, for that matter – it would be unthinkable to have an operatic hero who appears briefly in only two scenes in the first two acts, and is conspicuously absent from the decisive gathering that resolves on a campaign of resistance. Schiller's Tell is a man who is drawn almost accidentally and reluctantly into the national struggle, who at first counsels quietism, and when he acts, acts as an individual, in the spirit of his own dictum 'The strong man's strongest when he acts alone', rather than accepting the disciplines of a collective struggle.

The opera simplifies Tell. He is a discontented patriot from the very beginning. While at the opening the villagers rejoice in chorus, and the fisherman sings an amorous *barcarolle*, Tell bursts in with a bitter comparison between this contentment and his own unhappiness:

> Pour nous plus de patrie!
> Il chante, et l'Helvétie
> Pleure, pleure sa liberté.

The ambiguity with which Schiller invests Tell is in the opera confined to the character of Arnold von Melchthal. Arnold is a skilful blend of two of Schiller's characters, Arnold and Ulrich von Rudenz. The play's Arnold has an impetuousness that is retained in the opera character, who derives rather different qualities from Ulrich, who is disposed to collaborate with the occupiers, and is rebuked for his lack of patriotism by the aristocratic Bertha (who in the opera is transmuted into Mathilde, a Habsburg princess).

The opera nevertheless faithfully re-creates some of the principal features and themes of Schiller's splendid play: the free and simple existence of a mountain people whose lives are lived in intimate relation with the natural world; the importance of family affections and loyalties; the exploration of the ethics of resistance to oppression.

The opera's simplifications make it more partisan than the play, and place Tell firmly at the centre of the collective national struggle; even his shooting of Gessler is done in public, rather than being the lonely act of assassination it is in the play.

Above all, the opera is about collective action and collective forces rather than individuals, using chorus and orchestra for its purpose and thus achieving something that the individualist tradition of post-Renaissance drama put largely beyond Schiller's reach. As Bernard Shaw put it, 'it is an opera not of heros and heroines, but of crowds and armies'.[19] Tell, in spite of his large role in the opera, has no solo aria except at the terrible moment before he has to shoot at the apple on his son's head. Arias and duets belong to Arnold and Mathilde, the only characters with any significant private emotions. Even the family feelings of the Tells are given expression only in so far as the central narrative of the conflict with the Austrians allows (although because of Gessler's infamous command to Tell to shoot the apple, family ties and feelings are numbered among the values the Swiss are defending).

Tell is an outdoor opera. Its epigraph could be Blake's couplet:

> Great things are done when Men & Mountains meet;
> This is not done by Jostling in the Street.

Only a single short scene, at the beginning of Act Four, takes place indoors. Otherwise everything happens in an environment of lakes, mountains, woods and valley pastures. Rossini constantly evokes a sense of space, with distant horn calls, bells, and choral groups answering one another from a distance in the great gathering of cantons that ends Act Two. There is a Rousseauesque dimension to this version of the Tell legend. The freedom that is invoked is not simply political and national freedom, but the traditional independence of those who till their own fields, hunt their own food, and live according to the moods and cycles of nature. This pastoral life, with its simple but dignified ceremonies, its celebration of home and family, is evoked in the rather leisurely processes of Act One. The magnificent final chorus is a hymn both to nature and to liberty, and its vast crescendo simulates the clearing of the clouds and the emergence of the sun (which the stage directions call for). Perhaps to evade censorship, regrettably the Italian translation made for the first performance in

Italy by Calisto Bassi, and still in use, wholly eliminates the references to liberty in this chorus, with which the opera properly ends:

A nos accents religieux,
Liberté, redescends des cieux,
Et que ton reigne recommence,
Liberté, redescends des cieux!

In the opera, the heroism of Tell and the Swiss is not hedged about with the doubts and qualifications Schiller weaves into the play. The opera is clear that resistance to national and personal oppression and injustice justifies what might otherwise be morally questionable. In the very first dramatic episode, Leuthold is pursued by Gessler's soldiers, having killed one of their number who had tried to abduct, in effect rape, his daughter. No one is in any doubt that Leuthold's action was justified. 'Il eut le courage d'un père,' says Melchthal, adding, 'we would all have done the same'. But to the pursuing soldiers Leuthold's act was murder, and requires payment in kind.

When Gessler's lieutenant Rodolphe arrives, he demands to know who has helped the murderer to escape. No one volunteers any information, and Melchthal has the nerve to say that 'this country harbours no informers'. He is immediately arrested (and later killed), and Rodolphe orders the indiscriminate destruction and pillage of the community. Everything conforms to the now all-too-familiar pattern of relations between an occupying power and an indigenous resistance. What is seen by the occupiers as murder or, nowadays, as terrorism, appears as legitimate self-defence to the resistance. The resisters are protected by a wall of silence and non-cooperation among even those not actively engaged in opposition; the occupiers have only one response: indiscriminate punishment of entire communities. This makes them even more hated than before. It is a classic sequence which, with variations, has been observable in recent years in Vietnam, Tibet, Northern Ireland, the Israeli-occupied territories, Kurdistan . . . *Guillaume Tell* is a very topical opera.

The national liberation struggle, for that is what it is, requires organization and self-discipline. This is the message of Act Two in particular. In the course of the splendid trio for Arnold, Tell and Walter, Arnold discovers that his father, Melchthal, has been killed; this resolves him to throw in his lot with the patriots, his love for

Mathilde having caused him to hold back before. Almost delirious with grief, he is all for an immediate attack on Gessler, but Tell has to restrain his impetuousness as he did in Act One, and integrate him into the collective struggle. He sees in Arnold the rashness and unsteadiness of someone whose motives for action are immediate personal feelings rather than more durable and principled commitments. Arnold, an ardent high tenor, is a foil to the wisdom and steadfastness of the baritone Tell.

The trio is followed by the gathering of the three cantons, which solemnly pledge to help each other when in danger. The whole act, rightly admired by so many other composers, moves steadily towards this climax. Beginning with scene-setting choruses for hunters and shepherds, we move from an aria by Mathilde ('Sombres forêts'), to a duet for Mathilde and Arnold, to the trio and then to the great choral finale. Gradually, steadily, the musical perspective broadens, and individuals are absorbed into the community and its struggle. The grand, clear structure of the act is itself a demonstration of the moral and political perspective of national struggle which the opera so wholeheartedly endorses.

By contrast with the play, Tell kills Gessler at the end of the opera, and engages in no kind of self-searching post-mortem. The assassination is hailed immediately as an occasion for rejoicing, an act of liberation. Once we have learnt that the tyrant's castle is in Swiss hands, the way is open for the final chorus of celebration and thanksgiving.

Like its predecessor at the Opéra, *La muette de Portici*, the success and example of which certainly influenced Rossini, *Tell* when it was new certainly had the capacity to generate political excitement. A rehearsal of the opera on 26 July 1830 broke off abruptly when those involved found themselves so stirred by the cry, in the trio, of 'ou l'indépendance ou la mort!' that they felt compelled to rush out into the street and join the crowds who were making the 1830 revolution that toppled Charles X. The tenor who sang Arnold was the famous Adolphe Nourrit, who had already sung the leading role in *La muette*. He threw himself into the revolutionary movement with particular enthusiasm, and nine days after that interrupted rehearsal he returned to the Opéra to preface the evening's performance by singing the Marseillaise, attired as a National Guard and holding a tricolour.[20]

The neglect of this great work in Britain is something of a scandal. It had no professional production between the Welsh National Opera's version of 1961 and the Covent Garden production of 1990. Neither its length nor the scarcity of tenors willing and able to sing Arnold wholly explains this. After all, the opera is no longer than *Der Rosenkavalier*, which every self-respecting company stages, and its musical merits are not obviously less. But modern Western audiences, with their appetite for escapism, are always more likely to warm to an exercise in romantic nostalgia than to a celebration of heroic struggle.

I cannot leave Rossini without a mention of his most recently recovered work, the brilliant *Journey to Rheims* (*Il viaggio a Reims*). It is essentially a *divertissement*, with only the slenderest of plots. A diverse group of travellers on their way to the very event that the opera is celebrating, the coronation of Charles X, find themselves stranded at the Golden Lily hotel in Plombières. Unable to reach Rheims, they are compelled to improvise their own entertainment for the occasion, which concludes with a notably effusive, not to say obsequious, tribute to Charles X.

Charles X was a dim figure, and the regime he presided over was central to the counter-revolutionary order set up in Europe after the final defeat of Napoleon. Perhaps it is necessary to forget all this in order to enjoy Rossini's extravaganza of vocalism, just as we have to overlook the grovelling doggerel verses for which Purcell provided such magnificent music in more than one of his birthday odes for Queen Mary. Even a convinced republican could hardly resist the radiance and serene high spirits of this superb entertainment.

Yet there is a little more to it than that. What Rossini and his librettist Luigi Balochi have managed to do, against the odds, is to invest this essentially trivial and reactionary event with an aura of genuine liberal idealism. They even manage to introduce a reference to good news about the progress of the Greek War of Independence, although the reference is musically insignificant (it is in any case cut from the marvellous recording of the work made at Pesaro in 1984). More central is the Ossianic song, to harp accompaniment, which Rossini inserts into the sextet, in which Corinna expresses a yearning for the return of the Golden Age in which brotherly love will reign for ever in human hearts, a sentiment that is taken up by the other participants:

> Che un di rinasca io spero
> Dell'aurea eta l'albore;
> Che degli umani in core
> Regni fraterno amor.

(I hope that one day the dawn of the golden age will reappear, and brotherly love will reign in human hearts.)

Once again Rossini, the political accommodator, manages partially to belie his established reputation as a political cynic and reactionary.

Vincenzo Bellini

By 1829 Rossini's triumphant reign in the opera house was over, and Vincenzo Bellini's brilliant but tragically brief career as an opera composer was getting into its stride. It lasted until his death in September 1835 at the age of thirty-three. Bellini belongs to the 1830s. His music, like that of Chopin and Berlioz, has the freshness, the unforced lyricism and elegance of early romanticism, which is still not too far from the classicism of Mozart and Haydn. But Bellini is not, as Rossini always was, a composer with one foot in the eighteenth century. In Bellini the expression of feeling and the pressure of personal involvement are not repressed or restrained. Those famous long-drawn-out melodies, so much admired by composers as different as Wagner and Stravinsky, have a melancholy, yearning quality that is of the essence of early romanticism. If Bellini had been a poet, he could have written Wordsworth's 'The Solitary Reaper':

> Alone she cuts and binds the grain,
> And sings a melancholy strain;
> O listen! for the Vale profound
> Is overflowing with the sound. . . .
>
> Will no one tell me what she sings? –
> Perhaps the plaintive numbers flow
> For old, unhappy, far-off things,
> And battles long ago.

As we have seen, Heine heard in these elegiac, languishing melodies the music of a nation rather than of a purely individual sensibility, a nation lamenting its past glories and longing for revival.

This may be fanciful, but what is beyond dispute is that two of the three Bellini operas most frequently performed today have political themes and settings that carry strong Risorgimento overtones and allusions. *Norma* is a story of national resistance to imperial occupation, while *I puritani* revolves around a conflict of political with personal loyalties, and is full of the rhetoric of *patria* and *libertà*. Only *La sonnambula*, a pastoral comedy with tragic overtones, makes no reference to the patriotic theme. Lesley Orrey has pointed out that two of Bellini's earliest operas, *Bianca e Gernando* and *Il pirata*, had political dimensions, and his 1830 decision to make an opera out of Victor Hugo's play *Ernani* was only abandoned when the composer realized that the authorities in Italy would make performance of it impossible.[21]

Even in *I Capuletti e i Montecchi*, which is Bellini's and Felice Romani's highly simplified version of the Romeo and Juliet story, we are occasionally reminded of the Italian dimension of this quarrel between families. Lorenzo, who in the opera is a doctor not a friar, is consistently an advocate of peace and an end to feuding; Romeo comes to the Capulets urging the same course in a notably conciliatory style. Their response is to call with one voice for renewed war ('Guerra, guerra, guerra'). Romeo warns that the fatherland will pay in blood for their intransigence:

> E su voi ricada il sangue
> Che alla patria costera.

When he urges Juliet to flee Verona with him, he speaks – like Radames to Aida – of finding a better homeland ('Miglior patria avrem di questa'). It is clear that in this version of the story Verona stands for an Italy torn apart by strife, as of course it had been so often; the love of the young pair is doomed from the start by the context of violence and intolerance in which it struggles to survive.

If *Norma* is Bellini's greatest achievement – and it is certainly his most powerful and single-minded opera – then that certainly owes a good deal to Romani's sensitive and thoughtful libretto, which enabled Bellini, who paid great attention to the words he had to set, to convey the complexities of the conflicting forces, loyalties and emotions of the drama. As in Spontini's *La vestale*, an opera that must have been in the minds of both Bellini and Romani, there is a central conflict between love and public duty which is also experienced by both Norma and Adalgisa as a conflict between love and religion. More interesting, and more central to the drama, is the way in which Norma, this always fully human and deeply flawed heroine, allows her public judgements to be corrupted by her personal feelings for Pollione, the Roman consul. So long as she has some hope of reconciliation with him, she uses her priestly authority to restrain the Gauls' impatient desire for an uprising against the occupying Romans. But when in her anger she finally turns against him, she uses her public position to reverse her previous advice and call for war, slaughter and extermination.

True, she redeems herself in the end by her public confession and her readiness to sacrifice herself. But her earlier action in holding the Gauls in check could plausibly be regarded as that of a collaborator with an occupying power. It is worthwhile imagining how *Norma* might have been received in France or in the Netherlands or Czechoslovakia during World War Two. There would have been much enthusiasm for the Gauls' desire to attack the Romans, but Norma, despite the eloquence with which Bellini pleads her cause, might have met with rather a cool response. Her dilemma might not have seemed like a dilemma at all. Either she should resign her office and throw in her lot with the Romans, or else she should do her patriotic and religious duty.

To a peacetime Western audience, the Gauls are bound to appear an unattractive lot: filled with bloodlust, cruel and unforgiving towards Norma right up to the last words of the opera. A chorus that shouts for war, and glories in the prospect of slaughter, extermination and vengeance, is more likely to evoke a shudder of horror than of eager excitement – at least, if we pay attention to the words. 'The oppressed', Simon Meecham Jones has written sardonically, 'live in a bloodthirsty claustrophobic world centred on the altar.'[22] True, but is not this rigid, unbending claustrophobia the understandable response of groups and cultures that feel threatened, and struggle to survive in a basically hostile environment? Unqualified distaste cannot be our considered response to the Gauls, for the simple reason that it is dangerously close to the response that Romani and Bellini attribute to Pollione, who is, in effect, the Roman colonial governor. Pollione refers to the Gauls casually as 'barbari', and shows no respect for their religion. He refers to their god as a god of blood, and because of Norma's commitment to this religion he threatens, in the best imperial style, to burn down the sacred groves of the Druids and destroy their altars.

As for peace, that peace for which Norma prays to the chaste goddess of the moon, for all the serene beauty of her famous prayer, we are bound to feel ambiguous about it, not only because of what we know about Norma's motives for recommending non-resistance, but also because that is precisely what peace means to the Gauls: accepting occupation. The chorus sings early on of this peace that is fatal to us ('pace per noi mortal'), and Oroveso confesses in his last-act aria that he too chafes beneath the Roman yoke, but God is against them, and so they must simulate docility:

> Ma nemico e sempre il cielo,
> Ma consiglio e il simular.

The topical meaning of all this would have been only too clear to contemporary Italian audiences. When Norma suddenly reverses her position and calls for war, massacre and extermination, the Gauls respond enthusiastically with cries of 'Guerra! guerra!', 'Sangue! sangue!' This fierce chorus, with its surprisingly peaceful conclusion, which so exactly corresponds to Romani's words, was sometimes called the Italian Marseillaise, 'and attracted to performances of *Norma* more than a few political demonstrations', according to John Deathridge.[23]

Certainly Norma herself is the heart of the opera, and we see her in a range of situations and relationships, wrestling with her mixed feelings towards her children, responding with extraordinary generosity to the discovery of Adalgisa's passion, treating Pollione with the anger and contempt he deserves. The structure is such that the two central acts are given over entirely to individual voices: Norma, Adalgisa, Pollione and Clotilde. They are framed by the two outer acts, both of which are public events in which Oroveso and the chorus play leading roles. Thus individual dilemmas and destinies are placed firmly within their political and public context. That context is a colonial situation in which resistance is being held in check by a leader whose attitude towards the occupying power is conditioned by a personal relationship that is in breach of both her political and her religious duties. Some commentators give the impression that the adoption of *Norma*, and especially of its 'war' chorus, by the Risorgimento was a kind of accident, unrelated to the character of the opera.[24] Their arguments seem to me to be strained attempts to depoliticize an opera with a manifest political dimension, whose authors could hardly have been unaware of how it would be interpreted and received in their native land. As we shall see when we come to *I puritani*, Bellini knew very well what were the political implications of operatic gestures towards patriotism.

After *Norma* came *Beatrice di Tenda*, the last opera Bellini composed to a libretto by Felice Romani and the first, it is said, to take actual events in Italian history as its basis. It was not a success when first performed, and it remains a rarity, certainly in Britain.

Those unfamiliar with it might be surprised at its sternness, particularly in Act Two, though their reaction might suggest only that they had forgotten what a severe and public work *Norma* is in many ways. *Beatrice* has rather similar preoccupations, although its focus is much more uncertain. Through much of the opera, Beatrice herself is less the centre of attention than her vicious husband, Filippo Visconti; her tenor lover, Orombello, is an even less effective figure than Pollione. Nor is there any aspect of conflict or ambiguity to her personality. She is the heroic victim of her husband's malevolence: he accuses her of the unfaithfulness of which he is in fact guilty.

But despite these personal concerns, the political dimension, and specifically the patriotic ingredient, is there: because Beatrice represents not simply herself, but also the people over whom she ruled with her first husband, Facino Cane. Her sufferings are paralleled by those of her people, as she makes plain in her opening scena. In Act Two, with Beatrice on trial, it becomes clear that her fate is a matter of politics as well as personal vengeance on Filippo's part. For it is when he hears that Beatrice's supporters are rising against him that he finally banishes any thoughts of clemency and resolves that she must die. 'Her murder is a political one.'[25]

The conclusion of the opera with a conventionally pathetic *cavatina* prayer followed by an equally conventional and exhilarating *cabaletta*

for the condemned Beatrice may seem like an inappropriate conces-
sion to operatic convention and vocal display. But it may also be seen
as an assertion of the ultimate triumph of good over the evil represented by Filippo, containing thus both a moral and a patriotic
message. As Beatrice is led away to the scaffold we hear the chorus
singing mournfully, 'Unhappy we to witness such a crime! How
afflicted the land that permits the death of such a woman!'

'O patria, o amore, omnipossenti nomi!' ('Oh fatherland, Oh love,
all-powerful words'), sings Arturo when, at the opening of the last act
of *I puritani*, he returns from exile to seek his beloved Elvira. Love and
patriotism are indeed the conflicting themes of this opera, and the
greater of these is love. The patriotic theme revolves around Arturo
but, until the last act at least, it is Elvira, her love and her madness that
provide the principal focus of the opera. In *I puritani* love and politics,
love and duty, conflict in a familiar way, even if the twists given to this
commonplace theme are somewhat bizarre.

The opera is set in a Puritan fortress near Plymouth around the year
1650; Charles I is dead, but the Civil War is still raging (historical
accuracy is not the forte of *bel canto* operas based on English history).
Elvira, daughter of the commander of the fortress, is to marry the man
she loves, Lord Arthur Talbot, a Royalist. But when Arturo arrives he
discovers that Queen Henrietta Maria is a prisoner in the fortress.
Even though it is the eve of his wedding he resolves to help her escape
to safety. They are discovered by Riccardo, who is Arturo's rival for
Elvira's love. Riccardo lets them escape, hoping thus to wreck the
planned marriage. When Elvira learns that Arturo has fled with an
unidentified woman, she falls into madness. Not until Arturo's return
is her sanity restored. A general pardon from Cromwell saves him and
enables the opera to end happily.

The improbabilities of the plot place an obvious strain on our
credulity. It is Bellini's triumph, despite the clumsiness of the libretto,
that he makes Elvira's plight not merely believable but painfully
touching. Is there any music more heartbreaking than that of her
madness in Act Two? Did even Bellini ever write anything more
beautiful than 'Qui la voce'?

Elvira seems to exist in a world of her own, oblivious of the harsh
demands made by the political conflict which surrounds her. She is

one of the few women in Bellini's operas who does conform to Peter Conrad's characterization of them as 'self-hypnotized lyrical dreamers'.[26] Perhaps this is what explains her mental instability. The male figures who surround her accept their involvement in the war. The partial exception is Riccardo, who allows his infatuation with Elvira and his jealousy of Arturo to interfere with his patriotic obligations. For this he is rebuked by Bruno in the opera's first scene. Bruno is shocked by Riccardo's indifference to his duties, but Riccardo is Elvira's dark shadow, taken up with his passions to the exclusion of all else. That is why he allows the Queen to escape.

But Elvira's uncle, Giorgio, suspects Riccardo, and confronts him: if he fails to save Arturo, he will be forever haunted by two spectres, those of Arturo and Elvira. Riccardo is eventually softened, and the two men join in a resounding duet in which they reaffirm their devotion to their country, freedom and victory:

> Bello e affrontar la morte,
> Gridando: 'Libertà!'

(It is beautiful to face death, crying 'Liberty'.)

This section was originally planned as a chorus, a *coro di libertà*, for the opening scene, but Bellini decided that it would be more effective placed later in the opera, and converted it into a duet for baritone and bass. It is one of the more blatant pieces in the score, but it was predictably popular with audiences; equally predictably, Bellini knew that it would prove unacceptable to Italian state authorities, since 'love of one's native land and Liberty enter into it'. He therefore omitted it from the version of the opera that was to be performed in Naples.[27]

A more intimate note of patriotism is sounded by Arturo at the opening of Act Three when, still hunted by Parliamentarians, he returns from exile. The spirit is that of Walter Scott's lines:

> Breathes there the man, with soul so dead,
> Who never to himself hath said,
> This is my own, my native land!
> Whose heart hath ne'er within him burned,
> As home his footsteps he hath turned,
> From wandering on a foreign strand!

And Count Carlo Pepoli's libretto here must surely have expressed his own heartfelt emotions. For he himself was a political exile. Having been involved in the revolution in the Romagna in 1831, he had been imprisoned in Venice by the Austrians and then exiled to France (it was in Paris that he met Bellini). The scene of Arturo's return is the moment at which we begin to feel sympathy for him; his earlier behaviour having seemed at best ludicrous, at worst cruel.

Despite its improbabilities and weaknesses of construction, *I puritani* is a wonderful opera. It shows a widening of Bellini's scope, and is richly varied in its musical elements. I hear no evidence of that falling off in melodic invention that Orrey claimed to detect. The production by Andrei Serban that was staged by Welsh National Opera and Opera North in the 1980s showed how real and touching it can be if it is taken seriously as a piece of musical drama.

Bellini's copious letters do not suggest that politics or patriotism preoccupied him in the way that they did Verdi. Like Rossini, he was primarily concerned with music, with being a composer and having his work performed. But like Rossini again, he was probably more touched by rising Italian nationalism than he recognized – hence its large role in his operas. We have noted his collaboration with Pepoli on *I puritani*, and Lesley Orrey wrote perceptively about his many contacts with individuals actively involved in Risorgimento politics.[28] Lady Morgan, one of those who welcomed the composer to London in 1833, reported an occasion when Bellini and a friend sang a patriotic song:

> O bella Italia che porte tre color
> Sei bianca e rose e verde co'un fiore![29]

The colours of the future Italian flag were already a symbol of the national struggle, it seems. On the other hand, he had no qualms about dedicating *I puritani* to the Bourbon Queen of France, a gesture which annoyed many Neapolitans, including his lifelong friend Francesco Florimo. It was with Florimo that Bellini, as a young man, joined the secret society of nationalists known as the Carbonari, during the revolution of 1820–21 in Naples. When that revolt was put down the two of them were saved by the kindly protection of the Rector of the Collegio di Musica.[30] But doubtless the danger of imprisonment or even execution had been frightening enough.

Gaetano Donizetti – A Note

Of the three Italian opera composers who dominated the thirty years before the appearance of Verdi, Donizetti would seem to be the one least affected by the political context within which he was working. But any judgement about a composer who produced around sixty-seven operas, only three of which are regularly performed and many of which are completely unknown to the ordinary opera-goer and opera-listener, must be tentative. And although, according to William Ashbrook, 'His letters reveal no interest in the political events of his time,' and there is no evidence of his ever having been involved in nationalist politics, it is also the case that 'some of his close associates were political activists or exiles'.[31] These associates included the Ruffini brothers, Giovanni, Agostino and Jacopo, all three of them followers of the nationalist leader Mazzini. Giovanni and Jacopo were imprisoned for their revolutionary activities, and Jacopo committed suicide in prison. Giovanni escaped to France, and later wrote the libretto for *Don Pasquale*. To be in close touch with such people, who had had such experiences, could hardly leave anyone wholly unaffected.

Several of Donizetti's operas were political enough to run into trouble with the Neapolitan censors, and two, *Maria Stuarda* and *Poliuto*, were banned outright on the orders of King Ferdinand II. But the serious and overtly patriotic *L'assedio di Calais* was passed for performance in 1836 with only a single line amended. *Anna Bolena*, composed to a fine libretto by Felice Romani, is usually treated simply as a vehicle for a dramatic *bel canto* soprano; but it could also be considered, as Mazzini himself observed, a perceptive study of the nature and effects of tyranny. The theme of political exile which we have noted in Bellini's works appears here too, and Mazzini's enthusiasm for much of Donizetti's music suggests that, like Rossini, he soaked up more of the spirit of the Risorgimento than he perhaps realized.[32] Against the composer's declared indifference to politics, we must as always set the evidence of the music itself. Rossini, Bellini, Donizetti: all three, despite themselves to some extent, responded to the political concerns and ethos of their time and their country.

4

Verdi: the Liberal Patriot

The achievement of modern opera, the opera of the past two centuries, is crowned by three great composers, Mozart, Verdi and Wagner. The reputations of all three are surely now secure, but it was not always so. All have been the victims of fashion and neglect to an extent which must now seem remarkable. Verdi, born in 1813, began his operatic career at the end of the 1830s, produced his final operatic masterpiece, *Falstaff*, in 1893, and died in 1901. Although his death was the occasion for national mourning in Italy, and his funeral was attended by more than 200,000 people, much of his music was by then already falling into neglect, and its future was by no means certain. George Bernard Shaw's quasi-obituary made this clear:

> It may be that, as with Handel, his operas will pass out of fashion and be forgotten while the Manzoni Requiem remains his imperishable monument. Even so, that alone, like Messiah, will make his place safe among the immortals.

Shaw was healthily sceptical about those obituarists who claimed a knowledge of *Oberto* and *Un giorno di regno*; the list of those operas he knew 'honestly right through' included only eight out of the twenty-six (or twenty-eight, if you count second versions).[1] It included *Ernani* and *Un ballo in maschera*, but not *Simon Boccanegra, La forza del destino* or *Don Carlos*. Shaw could hardly be blamed for that. *Boccanegra* was not staged in Britain until 1948, and did not reach Covent Garden until 1965. *Don Carlos* was not seen in Britain between its first performances in 1868 and its revival by Sir Thomas Beecham at Covent Garden in 1933. *La forza del destino* has fared better, at least since the 1920s, but in the fifty years from 1877 to 1928 it was produced only once at La Scala: in 1908 under Toscanini's direction. The neglect of so much of Verdi's work, which set in well before his death, has only slowly been remedied. Most of the early (pre-*Rigoletto*) operas were not recorded until the 1970s, and several have not been professionally performed in Britain within living memory. As with certain other great and productive composers – Handel and Haydn are two outstanding examples – we are still in the process of discovering the full range of Verdi's work and achievement.

That Verdi had strong political convictions, took a constant interest in political events, and even allowed himself at one period to be drawn into active politics are all beyond contention. His life, his letters and recorded opinions are the testimony. That his politics and his involvements in politics feed into his music is more disputed; but in Verdi's case there seems to me to be one simple reason for believing that they do: Verdi himself was all of a piece, a direct, integrated if complex personality, not divided or compartmentalized in the way that some creative personalities seem to be. With Verdi, as with Beethoven, we sense the pressure of a powerful personality behind the music: there is not that feeling of distance between creator and creation that we may find with Mozart or Rossini or Stravinsky.

Commentators have often remarked on the sympathy with which Verdi treats parent–child relations in his operas, and especially father–child relations; this is often related to the terrible tragedy of his early adulthood, when within two years (August 1838 to June 1840) his two infant children died, to be followed by their mother Margherita. Setting down his memories of those griefs some forty years later, Verdi remembered these three deaths as occurring within two months – a mistake that has puzzled some biographers, but surely shows how for Verdi these three deaths made up a single cumulative tragedy. There were no more children to replace the lost ones, and it does not seem fanciful to think that the composer poured his frustrated fatherly feelings into scenes such as those between Rigoletto and Gilda, and between Boccanegra and Amelia. But if this is plausible, why should critics baulk at the comparable suggestion that Verdi's political feelings and commitments also found their way into his operas?

Verdi was generally reticent about his personal life and feelings. But about his political views he was always candid and, without wishing to oversimplify, it seems to me that his politics were as clear and consistent as one would expect from a person of such strong and open character. Verdi was a nationalist liberal of a classic nineteenth-century kind. He was a fervent patriot who identified himself unhesitatingly with the Italian struggle for independence and unity, and he was known to do so. So much so, indeed, that in 1859 the apparently innocent slogan VIVA VERDI was used as an acronym for the more subversive Viva Vittorio Emmanuele, Re d'Italia. In fact Verdi was a republican, though not an inflexible one: in the 1850s he came round to the idea that the most realistic prospect for Italian unification lay in supporting the King of Piedmont. He was also strongly anti-clerical. Although he was not a pacifist, being prepared to be actively involved in the armed struggle against Austria and the Bourbons, he viewed war with horror and detested those who gloried in it. He despised mere conventionality and claimed the right to live his personal life as he pleased, free from the pressure or censure of conventional opinion. If he had read John Stuart Mill's *On Liberty* of 1859, he would, I think, have found little to disagree with, allowing for its Anglocentric bias.

In all these respects he was quintessentially liberal in his attitudes. And that is how he described himself, according to Giuseppina Strepponi, his second wife:

> I am a Liberal to the utmost degree, without being a Red. I respect the liberty of others and I demand respect for my own. The town [he was referring to his home town of Busseto] is anything but Liberal. It makes a show of being so, perhaps out of fear, but is of clerical tendencies.[2]

That liberalism's chief enemy in Italy was the power of the Catholic Church was something he took for granted. When in the 1830s he had been involved in a lively rivalry for the post of Maestro di Musica in Busseto, he was already identified as the candidate of the liberals, whilst his competitor, Ferrari, had the support of the Church.

As for conformity to orthodox morality and behaviour, Verdi made his position abundantly clear in a famous letter to his one-time father-in-law and long-time friend, Antonio Barezzi, written in January 1852. By then Verdi had been living for some years with Strepponi, whom he married in 1859, and who was his constant companion until her death in 1897. It was a relationship that lasted longer and better than many a sanctified marriage. Inevitably, though, there was gossip, and worse. The pair were more or less ostracized in Busseto, and whilst Verdi cared little about such behaviour, the situation was much more difficult and painful for Strepponi. She was 'ignored in the street and no one sat near her in church'[3] (she attended this alone: Verdi would drive her there, but refused to go inside). Eventually Barezzi must have raised the subject (his letter does not survive), provoking an indignant response from the composer:

> I do not believe that, of your own accord, you would have written a letter which you knew could only cause me displeasure. But you live in a district that has the bad habit of continually interfering in other people's affairs, and disapproving of everything which does not conform to its own ideas. It has never been my habit to interfere in other people's business unless asked to, precisely because I require that no one should interfere in mine. . . . This liberty of action, which is respected even in less civilized communities, I claim as a right in my own vicinity. . . . With this long chatter, all I have meant to say is that I claim my right to freedom of action, because all men have a right to it, and because my nature rebels against mere conformity.[4]

Both Verdi's liberalism and his anti-clericalism are exemplified in his reaction to the momentous events of 1870, when almost simultaneously France was defeated by the Prussians at Sedan, and the Italian army took over the Papal States, thus completing the unification of Italy. In a letter to Clarina Maffei Verdi lamented the French defeat, because 'France gave liberty and civilization to the modern world; and, if she falls, let us not delude ourselves, the liberty and civilization of us all will fall.' The Prussians he deeply mistrusted: 'a strong race but uncivilized'. As for the annexation of the Papal States:

> The business in Rome is a great event, but it leaves me cold: . . . because I cannot reconcile Parliament with the College of Cardinals, liberty of press with the Inquisition, civil law with the Syllabus . . . Pope and King of Italy: I cannot envisage them together even in this letter.[5]

This was written when he was working on *Aida*, and these themes and sentiments found their way into the opera, as we shall see.

The annexation of Rome took place essentially because the French garrison protecting papal authority had been removed and France had been defeated. It was not a glorious or even a very honourable finale to the process of unification, and Verdi's disillusion is understandable. He had lived through the entire period of the Risorgimento, and had identified himself wholeheartedly with its heroic spirit. He was in Paris in early 1848 when the revolution broke out in Milan. As soon as he heard about it, he hurried home:

> You can imagine whether I wanted to remain in Paris, after hearing there was a revolution in Milan. I left the moment I heard the news, but I could see nothing but these stupendous barricades. Honour to these heroes! Honour to all Italy, which in this moment is truly great! The hour of her liberation has sounded.

Verdi was writing to his librettist, Francesco Piave, but music was the least of his concerns at that moment:

> You speak to me of music!! What's got into you? . . . Do you believe I want to concern myself now with notes, with sounds? . . . There must be only one music welcome to the ears of Italians in 1848. The music of the cannon![6]

Later that year, at Mazzini's request, Verdi composed a patriotic hymn, 'Suona la tromba', and started work on his most overtly patriotic opera, *La battaglia di Legnano*. This had its premiere, appropriately enough, in Rome in January 1849, at a time when the Pope had been expelled from the city, and a republic was about to be proclaimed. But in July the Pope and his power were restored through the agency of French troops, and hopes of an independent and united Italy were set back for a decade. Verdi was in despair:

> Let us not talk of Rome!! What would be the use!! Force still rules the world! And justice? What good is it against bayonets!! We can only weep over our misfortunes and curse the authors of so much disaster![7]

After this Verdi turned away from politics to compose some of his most intimate and least public operas. They include *Luisa Miller*, *Stiffelio*, and *La traviata*.

When the prospect of unity opened up once more in 1859, Verdi was again much involved: raising money for those wounded at the Battle of Magenta, buying arms for the local militia in his home state of Parma (from which the Austrians had fled), acting as one of the delegates sent from Parma to Turin with the results of the plebiscite on union with Piedmont. Verdi was excited by Garibaldi's stunning conquest, in 1860, of Sicily and Naples – 'By God, there truly is a man to kneel to!' – and by the concerted advance of the Piedmontese and Garibaldian troops on Rome later that year: 'Those are composers,' he wrote of Garibaldi and Cialdini, the Piedmontese general. 'And what operas! What finales! To the sound of guns!'[8] That Verdi should see life as opera seems natural enough. But the metaphor also indicates, I think, Verdi's desire to bring opera closer to life.

In 1861, in response to pressure from Cavour, Verdi agreed to stand for election to the new national parliament, and was duly elected. He attended dutifully, but after Cavour's death in June of that year Verdi's commitment declined, and he did not stand for re-election when his term expired in 1865. He continued to follow events closely, but the heroic period of the Risorgimento was over, and Verdi became disillusioned with the politics of manoeuvrings and compromises that replaced it. He had had high hopes for a united and independent Italy, but by 1870 it was already apparent that these hopes were not being realized.

Luigi Dallapiccola wrote, 'The Verdi phenomenon is inconceivable without the Risorgimento. It makes little or no difference, for our discussion, whether or not Verdi played an active role in the movement. He absorbed its atmosphere and tone.'[9] This is certainly true: and it is in the operas themselves that we find the most eloquent expressions of his involvement and commitment.

In different forms, politics enters into many of Verdi's operas; they bear witness to his extraordinary grasp of social dynamics as well as to his feeling for large public issues and his ability to understand and express collective emotions. But among his more thoroughly political operas a rough and ready division can be made between the patriotic operas, which belong mainly to the 1840s (the early part of his career), and the political operas of his maturity, from *Les vêpres siciliennes* to

Aida, which generally cover a wider canvas and dig deeper into the complexities of power and public life, Church and State, war and peace.

Verdi's first real success as an opera composer was also his first venture into the territory of heroic patriotic opera. *Nabucco* had its premiere at La Scala, Milan, in March 1842. It had a further 50 productions in Italy in the next two years.

Verdi had prudently chosen a biblical subject, the captivity of the Jews in Babylon. It is almost a sequel to *Mosè in Egitto*, and the Moses figure in this opera, the High Priest Zaccaria, reminds the Israelites in his very first utterance of how God had previously brought Moses out of Egypt. Who, trusting Him in time of adversity, has ever perished? he asks. In *Nabucco* the Israelites must struggle against the persecution of Nebuchadnezzar (Nabucco) to preserve their identity and their religion. But Nabucco's blasphemous proclamation of himself as God proves his undoing; he is turned mad by a divine thunderbolt. His resentful and ambitious supposed daughter Abigaille assumes the throne, but is subverted by the opposition of her father and his supporters. In the end both Nabucco and Abigaille, who has poisoned herself, acknowledge the supremacy of the Hebrew god.

The opera has a double focus: on the collective resistance of the Israelites, led by their High Priest, Zaccaria; and on the relations between Nabucco and his two daughters, the illegitimate Abigaille and the legitimate Fenena, who is in love with Ismaele, an Israelite prince, and has been converted to the Jewish religion. Verdi finds it almost impossible to give us outright villains as black as Pizarro in *Fidelio*, or Gessler in *Tell*. Here, the two most flamboyantly wicked characters are the most fully drawn as individuals, and have the largest individual parts. Nabucco the arrogant blasphemer learns wisdom and humility after his fall, and is genuinely moving in his pleas to Abigaille for mercy. We notice in particular the tenderness with which the stricken king appeals to his daughter for help immediately after the thunderbolt (the music moves from F minor to A flat, the relative major), and the deep feeling with which he pleads with Abigaille for her sister's life.

Abigaille is a splendid figure: cruel and vengeful certainly, but her motivation is interestingly depicted. Her resentment is like that of Edmund, the illegitimate son of Gloucester in *King Lear*. Her discovery that she is actually the daughter of slaves, not of the king, only fuels her anger and ambition; in her long duet with her father in Act Three, she harps constantly on the fact that she, a slave, now reigns as queen over her royal sister and father. She exemplifies the malevolent passions nourished by a society in which birth and rank are the absolute arbiters of power and success.

It is surely not accidental that the fierce and brilliant *cabaletta* of vengeance that ends Abigaille's aria in Act Two is followed immediately by the serene sound of six unaccompanied cellos setting the scene for Zaccaria's beautiful prayer 'Tu sul labbro', in which he asks God to speak through his mouth to heathen Assyria. This is the contrast at the heart of the drama, between the cruel and egoistical rulers of Babylon and the patient, oppressed Israelites, keeping their national faith alive even in the darkest hours of persecution and exile:

> . . . at the point where the prayer actually begins . . . the bass voice is supported by a single cello. Like the solitary candle that burns on stage, the orchestral scoring is a vivid symbol of the old priest's loneliness in Israel's darkest hour.[10]

Zaccaria is not an individual in the mould of Nabucco and his daughter. As leader of an oppressed people, he cannot afford their vanities and excesses. He is wholly absorbed in his public role. That role is to speak to the Hebrews as the voice of God, and to the Babylonians as the voice of the Hebrews and their God. His prayer, like so many others in Italian opera from *Mosè* onwards, is not so much a religious act as a gesture of personal or collective dedication to a cause. And Verdi depicts two faces of religion in *Nabucco*. For while Zaccaria is a dedicated, spiritual figure, the High Priest of Baal is Verdi's first in a long line of bloodthirsty, vengeful clerics which culminates with the Grand Inquisitor in *Don Carlos* and the Egyptian priests in *Aida*. It is the High Priest of Baal who encourages Abigaille in her ambitions, and who then demands the extermination of the Jews once she is on the throne.

But Zaccaria himself is almost dwarfed by the chorus of the Israelites, who express with unforgettable eloquence their resistance to persecution, their determination to survive as a community and, in the famous chorus 'Va pensiero', their nostalgia and longing for the land they may never see again:

Oh, mia patria si bella e perduta!
Oh, membranza si cara e fatal!

(Oh my country so lovely and lost! Oh memory so precious and ill-fated!)

This is the first of Verdi's great choruses, the one that was spontaneously sung by the vast crowd at his funeral sixty years later, and it remains the best known of all. In it we hear the collective voice of a people, a nation, a community. As Julian Budden has written: 'The great swing, the sense of a thousand voices is something inherent in the melody even if it is sung as a solo or played on an instrument.'[11] The main melody is sung in unison, which makes the break into harmony at the climax, 'arpa d'or', all the more splendid and imposing. But the use of unison here, in the first scene of the opera – and elsewhere – is itself indicative that what Verdi was trying to do was to express a feeling in which all were united: 'the choral texture becomes a musical metaphor of the democratic ideal'.[12]

In some later operas Verdi focused more strongly upon individuals, with the chorus playing only an incidental role. But in *Nabucco* and several of the works that followed it the chorus is more strongly present. It is sometimes suggested that Verdi was unaware of the political significance that would be read into this story of national resistance and this chorus of patriotic yearning, and that he thus 'inadvertently became the composer of the Risorgimento'.[13] This seems perverse. Why should Verdi, of all people, be the one person not to see the significance or make the connection perceived by everyone else? But whether or not he was fully aware of what he had done in *Nabucco*, it is wholly implausible to suppose, as Charles Osborne does, that he could have continued to compose operas on themes of national struggle, exile and patriotism without realizing what he was doing or how his music would be received.[14] On the contrary, it seems much more likely that, having discovered that he could voice the patriotic feelings of his fellow Italians, he should try to go on doing so. For one thing it offered a potential recipe for success in the opera house. And that is exactly what he attempted to follow in his next opera, *I lombardi alla Prima Crociata*, which was first performed at La Scala just under a year after *Nabucco*.

Budden has observed rightly that *Nabucco* is a 'triumph of the whole over the parts': weak sections are saved by the dynamism and coherence of the work as a whole. The problem with *I lombardi* is, simply, its lack of that coherence. Some of its individual numbers are warmer, more characteristically Verdian than almost anything in *Nabucco*. But a ludicrously convoluted plot and layout of the drama prevent Verdi from achieving the dramatic tightness and momentum that could have unified this often very attractive work. Once again the importance of a good libretto and scenario are demonstrated by their absence.

For *I lombardi* Verdi chose an Italian subject but retained, as the political situation required, the device of historical remoteness, placing events at the time of the first Christian crusade to recover the Holy Land from Moslems in 1095. Within this context is set a complicated story of sibling rivalry, parricide and penitence, and a love affair that, as so often in Verdi, transgresses the boundaries of political and national loyalties, and is consequently doomed (the happy ending of *Nabucco* is very much the exception to the general rule).

Verdi was working once again with the young patriot Temistocle Solera, who provided the libretti for most of his most nationalist operas of the 1840s: *Nabucco, Giovanna d'Arco* and *Attila* as well as *I lombardi*. In 1839 Verdi had set Solera's poem 'L'esule' ('The exile') to music in the form of a two-part aria preceded by recitative. It is as if Verdi saw exile from the first as a theme for opera. The exile amongst the beauties of nature in countries not his own sighs for his native land. The sentiment is much the same as that of 'Va pensiero', and of the chorus the crusaders and pilgrims sing in the final act of *I lombardi*, when amid the arid sands near Jerusalem, they wistfully recall the fresh breezes, the meadows and vineyards of their native Lombardy ('O Signore, dal tetto natio'). Their longing has been anticipated by the heroine Giselda in her Act Three duet with Oronte, when in its most eloquent section ('O belle a questa misera') she too bids farewell to her homeland, knowing that she and Oronte are both forever outcasts from their warring communities.

In *Nabucco*, the Jews, as an oppressed nation, were treated with unhesitating sympathy. Verdi's and Solera's treatment of the Christian crusaders is decidedly more ambivalent. On the one hand the crusaders may appear as dedicated people fighting for an ideal, which in the 1840s it was easy to identify with the goal of national independence. Arvino's proclamation, before the final battle, 'La santa terra oggi nostra sara' ('Today the Holy Land will be ours') was liable to provoke nationalist demonstrations. The chorus 'O Signore', which is clearly modelled on 'Va pensiero' and is hardly less successful, was for long as popular as its predecessor. And when, in the other great chorus for the pilgrims as they come in sight of the Holy City, they sing 'Oh, sangue bene sparso' ('Oh blood well shed'), we are not, I think, meant to shudder but to accept, as the Italian nationalists did, that if it was necessary to fight and die in the struggle for independence, then that was indeed blood well shed.

But in its other dimension *I lombardi* is a tragedy, in which both Oronte and the penitent Pagano die as a result of the crusade. Verdi does not allow us to think that struggle and heroism, courage and self-sacrifice, are without their high human costs. This is the difference between Verdi's treatment of Risorgimento themes and that of Rossini in *Guillaume Tell*, where the general rejoicing finally blots out all else. Perhaps because Verdi was closer to the struggle, he found it harder to be wholly optimistic about it. Tragic heroism is the core of much of his work.[15]

In *I lombardi* Verdi pushes this dialectic a stage further by having Giselda denounce the crusade to her father's face at the moment when he has come to rescue her from captivity. Appalled by the news that her lover Oronte has apparently been killed, she denounces the bloodshed in vehement terms:

> No! No! giusta causa non e d'Iddio
> La terra spargere di sangue umano.

(No, no! It is not the just cause of God to soak the earth with human blood.)

And her *cabaletta* finale to Act Two is a deliberate denial of the motto of the crusade – 'Dio lo vuole' ('God wills it') – earlier mentioned by Pagano. 'No, Dio nol vuole', she sings repeatedly, words her father interprets as blasphemy and sacrilege. Her hearers conclude that she has gone mad, but the passion with which Verdi invests her outburst suggests that it was a sentiment he shared. At any rate this is the first of several moments in the opera when he reminds us of the horror and cruelty of war. The complexities of *I lombardi*, an opera of splendours as well as some crudities, extend well beyond the convolutions of the plot.

The rest of Verdi's operas of the 1840s can be roughly divided into those that are primarily dramas of individuals and those which are primarily political, public and patriotic. Into the first category fall *Ernani, I due Foscari, Il corsaro, I masnadieri* and *Luisa Miller*, with *Alzira* and *Macbeth* as borderline cases. Into the second fall *Giovanna d'Arco, Attila* and *La battaglia di Legnano*.

Having made this distinction, it must be said at once that it is both approximate and debatable. *Ernani, I due Foscari* and *Macbeth* are all to some extent public dramas, in which kings, doges and other eminences play leading roles, in which a struggle for power is taking place, and in which political issues matter. This is also true of some later operas such as *Il trovatore, Un ballo in maschera*, and even *Otello*. It is also true that a distillation of the spirit of the Risorgimento, that spirit of tragic, self-sacrificing heroism about which George Martin has written so perceptively, is to be found in many of these latter works, and perhaps in none more powerfully than *Il trovatore*. But it *is* a distillation. *Il trovatore*, like *Ernani*, channels public passions and energies into individuals. The individuals can be seen as representative of different and conflicting social forces and groups, but that is not a dimension that is insisted on. Groups, as represented by the chorus, become shadowy, or at best picturesque, as in *Il trovatore*.

Nevertheless, much that in these dramas may appear to us romantic, or merely colourful, undoubtedly had a more substantial intention and a greater political resonance when the operas first made their appearance. We should notice, for example, how often the theme of exile, and sometimes happy return, features in these operas: glancingly in *Ernani*, but importantly in *I due Foscari, Attila* and *Macbeth*. Imprisonment is another recurring theme: even before we reach the final scene of *Il trovatore*, Verdi is writing sombre and evocative prison scenes in *I due Foscari* and *Il corsaro*.

However, it is difficult, at this distance in time, to grasp exactly what it was about Victor Hugo's play *Hernani* which caused so great a political furore that Bellini was deterred from turning it into an opera in 1830, and Verdi's version could only be performed in the kingdom of Naples under a different title. No doubt part of the trouble was that the play depicts a band of largely aristocratic conspirators plotting to assassinate a king, and takes as its hero a bandit who claims equality with the king when it comes to competing for a woman's love. *Ernani* is an intensely exciting opera, and most of that excitement derives from the clash of three figures who can also be felt to represent different social groups and forces: Silva, the traditional nobleman with his strict code of honour, who in his conflict with the king makes a temporary alliance with his rival, the aristocratic outlaw Ernani, and the king himself, the Emperor Charles V, whose attempt to impose centralized monarchy on Spain stirs up furious resentments among the established nobility. This conflict can be sensed, but is not dwelt upon, until we reach Act Three, in which the malcontents gather together in an effort to prevent Carlo (Charles) becoming emperor. It is a scene of muttering conspiracy and dramatic oath-swearing, which climaxes in the famous chorus 'Si ridesti il Leon di Castiglia'. In this characteristically rousing Risorgimento chorus, the plotters present themselves as the gallant resisters of oppression, looking forward to the day when

> Spain will be rich in heroes,
> she will be liberated from bondage.

Since this opera was written for Venice, it would not have been surprising if its first audiences had mentally substituted the lion of St Mark for the lion of Castille, and heard in it 'a battle hymn of the Venetian republic'.[16] But Carlo hardly fits the role of oppressor, since in response to Elvira's pleas he agrees both to pardon the conspirators and to allow her to marry Ernani. It is the relentless Silva who destroys their happiness in the last act.

Of the other mainly 'non-political' dramas, *Alzira* is discussed later in relation to *La forza del destino*; but Verdi's treatment of *Macbeth* must be considered here, if only because of the striking way in which the composer enhanced the work's political dimension. Of course *Macbeth* is not in any case a plain tale of crime and punishment, of wrongdoers who are finally destroyed, morally and psychologically as well as physically, by their crimes and their guilt. The horror of their crimes is that they are political crimes to which they are driven by the logic of their ruthless pursuit of power; their effect is inevitably felt not only by individuals, but by a whole society. This is why the chorus, although not so central to the drama as in *Nabucco* or *I lombardi*, is nevertheless vital to the story, which cannot, or should not, be presented as an essentially private or domestic tragedy.

At the end of both Acts One and Two the chorus is there to express its anxiety and horror at what is happening to the country. Of course, in Italian opera exclamations of 'orrore' and 'terrore' are a stock choral response to tragic or terrible events; choral finales were entirely conventional, too. But at each of these points in *Macbeth* it is the function of the chorus to express the sense of moral outrage among ordinary people at political events. In the finale to Act One the chorus, horror-stricken at the murder of King Duncan, prays to God to punish the murderer. Act Two concludes with the feast at which the ghost of Banquo appears to Macbeth. Macduff decides to flee to England, while the chorus exclaims with disgust that the country has become a den of robbers:

> Uno speco di ladroni
> Questa terra divento.

It is not until the opening of Act Four that we are made fully aware of the plight of the people under Macbeth's rule in the great chorus of exiles, 'Patria oppressa'. It is worth noting that the version that we know now was the product of Verdi's extensive revision of the score for the Paris production of 1865. The words received a quite different and far more pedestrian setting in the 1847 version. Verdi's feeling for national and popular oppression, far from being only an aspect of his nationalist feelings in the Risorgimentale 1840s, actually deepened and intensified as part of his growth in maturity and subtlety as a composer. There is no grand melody such as that in 'Va pensiero', which inevitably gave that lament a collective power which counteracted the grief itself. Here the atmosphere is far bleaker and darker. There is an affinity with the depiction of popular misery at the opening of *Don Carlos*, Verdi's next project after the revision of *Macbeth*.

So intense is this chorus that the following aria of Macduff, and even more the rousing duet and chorus in which Malcolm and Macduff together summon the people to take up arms to rescue the oppressed, inevitably strike a jarringly crude note. Yet the *cavatina/cabaletta* duality is not inappropriate here, for this is the turning point of the whole drama. 'Patria oppressa' is the opera's darkest moment, but it is the darkest moment before the dawn. Once the tyrant's opponents have been rallied, he is doomed. Whilst the original version ended effectively with Macbeth's death, in the 1865 version it is the chorus which, with Macduff and Malcolm, has the last word. Quite apart from its wonderful portrayal of the terrible, tortured pair of evildoers, the popularity of *Macbeth* in Italy and elsewhere owed something to its clear political message: tyrants do not last for ever. They can be overthrown. This message was reinforced in the revised version.

If *Macbeth* lies on the border between my two rough categories, the same might be said of *Giovanna d'Arco*, better known to English-speakers as *Joan of Arc*, for despite its patriotic theme it is also a study in conflicting personal loyalties and emotions, and it is these that increasingly dominate the opera. This was the first of four operas Verdi based on plays by Schiller. It revolves around a number of Verdi's most constant preoccupations: the anguished love of a father, Giacomo, for his daughter, Giovanna, in which he anticipates *Rigoletto* and *Boccanegra*; a woman's guilty, repressed love for a man who is forbidden to her (Giovanna is in a similar position to Amelia in *Un ballo in maschera*); and the consequent conflict between patriotic duty and personal emotions, or rather between love of country and love of one person, which Giovanna shares most clearly with Aida. In fact she sometimes sounds like a less accomplished, less assured version of the Ethiopian princess, particularly in her Act One aria; this takes place on the eve of the coronation of Charles VII, whom she has rescued from military disaster and guiltily loves; she wanders away from the crowds into a garden, and resolves to return to her father, her cottage and the forest full of prophetic voices. She is a case of the reluctant warrior who, like Garibaldi, will retire modestly to her or his home when duty has been done.

The opera begins strikingly with the harried and desperate French prepared to accept that their plight is a punishment for having tried to conquer 'other shores'. The king accepts that it is better to end the bloodshed by surrender than to prolong the war. Hence he absolves his followers from their allegiance. This is an early example of that horror of bloodshed that is as strong a Verdian theme as straightforward patriotism. Meanwhile Giovanna yearns to take up arms to end the miserable fate of oppressed France. Angels appear to grant her wish, but on condition that she renounces worldly love. She then assumes her new role of reviving the king's flagging determination, and prays that her country may be her only thought: 'Or sia patria il mio solo pensiero', a prayer that perhaps betrays her uneasiness about her love for the king. It is her guilt about that love that prevents her from denying her father's angry accusations, and leads ineluctably to the final tragedy. But we know that her guilt is excessive, and is in itself a sign of her purity and dedication. She has not allowed love to come before duty. Hence, although the opera ends with her death, it is a glorious, redemptive death. She has saved France and is taken up into heaven.

Strangely perhaps, a woman warrior is prominent in Verdi's next patriotic opera. *Attila* is one of the most fiercely and insistently patriotic of Verdi's early operas, even though it was adapted from a German play that had quite different themes and implications. It is also one of the most ambivalent, whether intentionally or not. This is already indicated by its title. Attila was the barbarian leader who around AD 450 invaded and overran Italy and came near to capturing Rome. The opera tells of how he was deterred from attacking the Holy City and how he was finally killed by the Italians. Attila's name is still a byword for brutality and barbarism, and this image is partially sustained by the opera, at least in relation to his followers, who sing cheerfully about feasting all night on limbs and severed heads.

All this combines to make Attila the villain of the piece. But Verdi was not in the habit of naming operas after their villains, if that is all they are. Hence his treatment of the Macbeths rivals Shakespeare's in insight and complexity. *Attila* is the opera Verdi composed immediately before *Macbeth,* so it is not surprising to find that the bass Attila, like the baritone Macbeth, is a guilty and haunted figure who is losing his appetite for slaughter and power, rather than the elemental brute of popular myth. Having been persuaded to withdraw from Rome by the majestic appearance before him of the Pope, Attila could presumably have been given a penitent death of the kind that Verdi often uses to end a tragedy. But then, of course, he would cease to be seen as the enemy of Italian independence. So, instead of having that kind of finale, to which the opera seems to be moving at the end of Act One, the Italian protagonists vie with each other to stab him to death, and the curtain finally comes down on this crude act of vengeance, which by then seems only half deserved. Solera, who had left the libretto unfinished, was justifiably indignant at the way in which Piave, under Verdi's guidance, had wound up the drama.

The consequence of the ambiguity with which Attila is treated is that the Italian patriots emerge in a less than heroic or even honourable light. All three of them seem motivated less by disinterested patriotism than by personal motives of ambition or vengeance. Ezio, the Roman general, pursues his vendetta against Attila even after a truce has been declared and the latter has withdrawn from Rome. Foresto, who is in love with Odabella, is obsessed with the jealous fear that she will succumb to Attila's wish to marry her, whilst she is equally obsessed with avenging her father's death, and casts herself in the biblical role of Judith, who drove a tent peg through the head of the sleeping Holofernes. In the end it is she who successfully claims the 'privilege' of stabbing Attila to death. Attila's final reproaches to all three seem not at all misplaced.

Nevertheless, all three also appear as Italian patriots, champions of their country and its capital against the barbarian invaders. In the first scene a band of captured Italian warrior women are brought before Attila. The latter, a conventional man beneath the savagery, is amazed. 'Whoever inspired unwarlike women with bravery?' he asks. Their leader, Odabella, replies with a splendid dramatic flourish spread over more than two octaves: 'Santo di patria indefinito amor' ('the unbounded holy love of our country'). This opening line sets the mood for the rest of the Prologue. She goes on to boast that while Attila's women stay weeping in the waggons, Italian women fight on the battlefield; this boast forms the fine melodic and structural climax of her aria: 'Ma noi, donne italiche'. Attila is bewitched by this heroic woman.

Ezio is called in, and offers Attila a deal: he would gladly cede the whole world to the conqueror, he sings, but leave Italy to me:

> Avrai tu l'universo,
> Resti l'Italia a me.

These lines form the musical as well as textual climax of his stanza in the duet with Attila. It is a characteristically Verdian melodic arch, warm in its use of the F major arpeggio. Budden has referred to these lines, which evoked huge enthusiasm from Italian audiences of the

1840s, as 'the eternal cry of small patriotic nations'.[17] This seems unduly patronizing. What they express is the ideal essence of liberal nationalism, a nationalism that is not expansionist, nor aggressive nor overweening, but demands simply independence, self-determination for the nation in question, be it large or small. This was the spirit of Mazzini's principled nationalism.

When Foresto makes his first appearance in a scene evidently intended as a piece of flattery to Venice and its opera house, he too establishes his patriotic credentials, by lamenting the lot of the exile and prophesying that his *cara patria* will rise once again like a new phoenix and become the wonder of both sea and land.

This is the substance of the Prologue, in which different aspects of patriotism are portrayed: the warlike, the political and the prophetic. Fancifully, each character could be compared to the great triumvirate of Italian nationalism: Garibaldi the inspired general, Cavour the politician, and Mazzini the visionary and philosopher. This comparison of course could not have been intended in 1846, but it would not have been surprising if Italian audiences a few years later had made analogies of this kind.

After the Prologue things do not go simply. The final act of assassination has to be justified by each of the three patriots reminding Attila and us of their reasons for killing him. 'Ezio', writes Budden, 'embodies all the more squalid aspects of resistance warfare.'[18] His behaviour is too individualistic for that comment to be quite accurate, I think. But it may be that behaviour that repels us did not strike nineteenth-century Italians in the same way. Assassination of political leaders is not, after all, always greeted with universal horror. It depends on the particular political circumstance. Charlotte Corday, who murdered Marat in his bath, became a hero to counter-revolutionaries all over Europe. So if Benjamin Lumley was right in saying that 'None, perhaps of Verdi's works has kindled more enthusiasm in Italy', a different response to Attila's murder and murderers may constitute part of the explanation.

'Viva Italia!' The very first words of *La battaglia di Legnano* establish its mood and theme. Even before that, the march that dominates the Prelude, and is the theme of the Lombard League, has ended with a clear echo of the Marseillaise. The chorus goes on to rejoice that a holy pact has united all Italy's sons, and at last made out of so many a single people of heroes. Composed in 1848, the opera had its premiere in republican Rome in January 1849. It is Verdi's chief contribution to the nationalist uprisings of those stirring years.

Set in the year 1175, when the Lombard League combined to defeat Frederick Barbarossa, the text is nevertheless full of references to recent events and contemporary hopes and emotions. It is Milan that, as in 1848, is at the heart of the resistance to the foreign invader, and it is Milan that the hero, Arrigo, hails in his first utterance:

> O magnanima, e prima delle città Lombarde,
> O Milan valorosa, io ti saluto . . .

This first scene culminates in another of those oath-swearing ceremonies that were so important to nineteenth-century resistance movements. The Italians all swear to defend Milan, the doom of 'the Austrian', that is, Barbarossa, is prophesied, and everyone sings enthusiastically of chasing this fierce nation back to the Danube. Let our cities be ours and free, they cry.

Verdi's most explicitly patriotic opera is fervent, but also moving, and far from simplistic in its treatment of its theme. The first celebratory scene is immediately followed by a scene in which Lida, the woman at the core of the usual love triangle, grieves over her dead parents and brothers and also over another unnamed grief, the apparent death of her old love, Arrigo. We are at once reminded of the costs of commitment and courage, and the balance between cause and cost, between public and personal, is finely sustained throughout this unfairly neglected work. Only in the figure of Arrigo is there an ambiguity that vitiates the overall pattern. When Arrigo reappears and discovers that Lida has married his close friend and comrade in arms Rolando, he rushes off to join the Knights of Death, those ready to die for the patriotic cause. As Budden aptly puts it: 'Is his heroism prompted by patriotic ideals, or is it that of the jilted lover who goes to Africa to hunt big game?'[19]

That uncertainty apart, private and public are balanced and interwoven in a most skilful manner. Thus in Act Three, after the second oath-swearing scene, in which Arrigo joins the Knights and they swear to put an end to Italy's injuries and chase her oppressors beyond the Alps (another obvious anti-Austrian gesture), the scene shifts again to

Lida's apartments. In a short but superb scene she confesses to Imelda her love for Arrigo; this is immediately followed by the arrival of Rolando, who like Hector in *The Iliad* has come to bid her and their child farewell on the eve of battle. He knows that he may never return. The price of victory is blood. If it is mine that is shed, tell my son that he is of Italian blood, and teach him to respect, after God, his country ('E dopo Dio la patria'). The music tenderly dwells on these words, before Arrigo arrives and Rolando appoints him guardian to his wife and child should he fail to return. Both these scenes were suggested by Verdi himself. But it is Arrigo's death that brings the opera to an end. He dies rejoicing that Italy is saved. As in *I lombardi* and *Giovanna d' Arco*, tragedy and rejoicing are combined.

One of the great achievements of this opera is the short but powerful Act Two, entitled 'Barbarossa'. This is entirely political and demonstrates what is sometimes doubted: the capacity of opera to deal with public issues even when they are not personified in individuals. Arrigo and Rolando come as emissaries to Como to appeal to the Comaschi to forget their ancient feud with Milan and join forces against Barbarossa. 'We have one enemy and one fatherland', they plead. The Comaschi reply that they are bound by a pact with Barbarossa. The Lombards denounce them, but are suddenly confronted by the enemy himself. They are ready to defy him, for only with the sword can the oppressed argue with the oppressor. They are confident that a mercenary army cannot conquer a people that rises up for its liberty. Italy will be great and free ('Grande e libera Italia sara!'). The aptness of all this to the situation in Italy in 1848–49 needs no stressing (this whole act too was suggested by Verdi to his librettist, Salvatore Cammarano). And musically, it is splendid. A muttering chorus by the Comaschi is followed by the entry of Arrigo and Rolando to the strains of the Lombard march. They then sing a duet that is a harangue full of scorn, more an act of abuse than persuasion. When Frederick Barbarossa appears and reveals that his troops surround the town, the two ambassadors continue to express their defiance in a stormy and complex ensemble that forms one long crescendo to the end of the act. The whole sequence lasts less than fifteen minutes. It is masterly in its speed and compression.

Of course, *La battaglia di Legnano* was received with great enthusiasm when first performed, but after Austria, the Papacy and the

Bourbons had reasserted their authority it inevitably fell foul of the censors and the location of the story had to be transferred to Holland. The new title was *L'assedio di Haarlem* ('The Siege of Haarlem'), and Barbarossa became the Spanish governor, the Duke of Alva. Verdi must have recalled all this when he returned to the theme of the revolt of the Netherlands when composing *Don Carlos* in the mid 1860s.

The defeat of the Italian uprisings of 1848–49, culminating in the fall of the Roman republic in July 1849, threw Verdi into despair. Passing through Rome, then under French occupation, late that year, Verdi wrote to Leon Escudier, 'The affairs of our country are desolating! Italy is now only a vast and beautiful prison!'[20] It is not surprising that in these depressing political circumstances Verdi turned away from public and political subjects to compose a series of operas set mainly in intimate, domestic contexts, in which personal dilemmas are searchingly explored, and large public issues only glanced at. These operas include *Luisa Miller, Stiffelio, La traviata* and, more ambiguously, *Rigoletto*. *Il trovatore* is more difficult to categorize, but whilst being in no way domestic, it does focus primarily on the strong passions of its protagonists. All these operas were composed in the years 1849–53.

The first of these operas, *Luisa Miller*, was composed for Naples and premiered there in December 1849. It is another of Verdi's adaptations of Schiller, this time of the play *Kabale und Liebe* (Love and Intrigue), and the opinion of most commentators is that Verdi's librettist, Salvatore Cammarano, converted a play full of harsh social criticism into a romantic mixture of pastoral idyll and conventional tragedy. Certainly he was mindful of the constraints placed upon any opera destined for performance in Bourbon Naples. The atmosphere of the opening scene, a gentle pastoral chorus, does indeed put us in mind of *La sonnambula*, as has often been pointed out. But what has been less remarked on is the similarity of social theme and pattern: there is the same contrast between honest and straightforward villagers (epitomized by Miller and his daughter) and a devious, corrupt and tyrannical aristocracy (represented by Count Walter and his adviser, Wurm). Bellini's opera being a relatively light work in touch and tone, this contrast is not treated there too weightily. But it is central to *Luisa Miller*, which is not as empty of social content as is sometimes supposed.

Verdi, with his perennial concern with parent–child relations, draws a sharp contrast between Luisa's relationship with her father, and Rodolfo's with his, the Count Walter. This contrast is established in the first two scenes of the opera. Miller is visited by Wurm, who suggests that Miller should compel Luisa to marry him; Miller replies that the choice of a husband is a sacred matter and must be freely made. In the final climactic lines of his aria Miller asserts that a father should resemble God in His kindness rather than His severity. In the very next scene Walter brusquely informs Rodolfo that he has arranged for him to marry the Duchess Frederica d'Ostheim. Like many tyrannical parents, he does love his son in his way, and in his aria he laments with some tenderness that fatherly affection has not brought him the consolation he had hoped for. He has convinced himself that he knows what is best for Rodolfo, and that Luisa is a scheming girl who has seduced his son in order to marry into the aristocracy.

Miller, for his part, once he knows who Rodolfo really is, is sure that it is the young aristocrat who is the seducer, if anyone is. When the Count insults Luisa to her face, calling her a 'vendutta sedutrice', Miller is outraged. The aristocracy can no longer get away with such abuse. He forbids her to kneel before the Count. Kneel before God, but not before a man with the heart of a beast, he tells her. The villagers are not so bold. They pity Luisa, but say that the Count must be obeyed, for he is their father and lord: 'egli e padre, egli e signore!', they sing with unconscious irony. The Millers stand for the bourgeois principle of love as the basis for marriage, whilst Walter the aristocrat clings to the manifestly cynical, wealth and property-based principle of arranged marriages. The idea of romantic love, so central to nineteenth-century opera, was always an anti-feudal, individualist aspiration.

Miller is arrested, and Wurm tells Luisa that he can only be saved from execution and freed if she writes a letter confessing that she loves Wurm, not Rodolfo. He mocks both her and the principle of freedom by telling her that she is free to choose whether or not to write the letter. Of course she does so, and her apparent betrayal of Rodolfo and his credulity (so like that of Alfredo in La traviata, but with even less justification) lead to the final tragedy. Although it is not insisted on overmuch, this is a tragedy in which conflict between classes and their different ethics plays an important part.

Of Verdi's next opera, *Stiffelio*, there is less to say in this context. Apart from *La traviata*, whose originality and boldness have been obscured by familiarity, this is Verdi's most original choice of subject. Based, like *La traviata*, on a recent play, it concerns a Protestant clergyman, Stiffelio, who discovers that his wife Lida has committed adultery; he is torn by conflicting emotions and pressures in deciding how to respond. In the end it is Lida's father who murders her lover, a deed that so shocks Stiffelio that he publicly forgives his wife by reading in church the story of Christ and the woman taken in adultery.

The opera ran into trouble with the censors, not so much over particular lines and sentiments as because of its basic premise: that a priest could be married. Since this notion could not be portrayed on an Italian stage, *Stiffelio* was mangled even at its premiere, and was rendered almost unintelligible when the entire final act was omitted, as it sometimes was. These difficulties led Verdi, who rightly believed in the qualities of his score, to transmute *Stiffelio* into *Aroldo*, which had its premiere in 1857, a tale of medieval crusaders which, although it contains some excellent additional music, lacks the coherence and power to shock of the original. *Stiffelio* shows Verdi trying to push back the boundaries of opera to take in serious and contemporary moral issues, issues that lie at the core of relations between marital and sexual partners. It was too much for Catholic Italy in the 1850s to cope with, and *Stiffelio* was only rediscovered in the 1960s.

Rigoletto is the work that is generally recognized as marking a turning point in Verdi's musical and dramatic development – although the better we know the once neglected works that immediately preceded it, especially *Luisa Miller* and *Stiffelio*, the more clearly can we see Verdi's operatic art steadily growing in confidence, subtlety and flexibility. But *Rigoletto* is the triumphant outcome of this evolution, a dramatic masterpiece of exceptional power and conviction. Its popularity hardly needs explanation. The drama is clear, swift and exciting, the music magnificent, especially in the assurance and clarity of the characterization.

Yet there is something puzzling. This is an exceptionally grim tale, even by Verdi's standards. The censors inevitably found it subversive: the notion of a court jester trying to kill a king, the king who employs him, was quite unacceptable, and hence Victor Hugo's King of France becomes the Duke of Mantua. But it is also sordid. As David Kimbell has written, 'we have a story pivoting on a curse, a seduction, and an assassination', in which the principal characters are, with one exception, 'a libertine monarch, a hunchback buffoon, a professional assassin and his harlot sister'.[21] *Rigoletto* is not exactly family entertainment. What is more, it is very clearly a tale in which class antagonism and class hatred feature prominently. And they are hardly favourite themes of the average opera audience. Conflict in Verdi is usually between individuals, often within the same family, between nations and between Church and State. The dimension of class is not usually of great significance. But in *Rigoletto* it is the key to everything that happens.

The Duke himself bears an obvious resemblance to Don Giovanni. Like Mozart's aristocrat, he abuses his power and position in pursuit of pleasure. He is not malevolent and destructive by intent so much as by carelessness and egoism. Like Don Giovanni he hardly seems to notice how he is disrupting the world around him. This insouciance or arrogance, expressed in both his songs – 'Questa o quella' and 'La donna è mobile' – is not so much a personal quirk as an attitude that comes naturally to an aristocrat and an absolute ruler. Like Giovanni, he sees the world, and especially its women, as entirely at his disposal. It is a view shared by his court, and it is the Duke and his court who determine the whole course of events.

Rigoletto is a member of that court, and under normal circumstances he aids and abets his master's arrogance and licentiousness, as Leporello does Giovanni's. But when the court jester discovers that his own daughter is not exempt from the general licence, he turns into a more angry and determined Masetto: he is consumed with grief and rage, and inexorably bent on revenge.

His revenge is inspired above all by his protective and indeed possessive love for his daughter. His wife is dead, and Gilda is all he has. 'Il mio universo è in te,' he tells her. So he confines her to his household, to be watched over by the supposedly trustworthy Giovanna. This is necessary because of the lawless and predatory behaviour of the Duke and his associates. But inevitably she yearns to escape, and is easily bowled over by the charming 'student' who pays court to her.

Rigoletto's attachment to Gilda, and his rage when she is abducted and seduced (or raped?), also reflects his self-disgust, the shame he feels at his own involvement in the Duke's court, and the hatred he feels for the courtiers whom it is his job to amuse and abuse. 'Pari siamo' ('We are alike'), he says, after meeting Sparafucile, the hired assassin. 'Odio a voi, cortigiani schernitori! . . . Se iniquo son, per cagion vostra e solo.' ('I loathe you, you sneering courtiers. . . . If I am evil, you alone are the cause.') He has always concealed from Gilda the truth about where he works and what he does. He hates the servility that is forced upon him by his employment. Gilda's kidnapping opens the flood-gates through which rush all the bitterness and fury held back during the long years of toadying and humiliation. So when he goes to the court in search of his daughter, he is not afraid to attack the courtiers directly: 'Cortigiani, vil razza dannata. . . .' This is the nearest that Verdi and Piave get to the celebrated outburst in the original play in which Triboulet attacks the aristocracy and their pretensions: 'Your mothers gave themselves to their lackeys. You are all bastards.' At the solitary performance of *Le Roi s'amuse* that was allowed in 1832, this line stopped the show. The aristocrats in the boxes were furious, while the bourgeoisie and intellectuals in the pit shouted their approval.

Fatherly feeling is all that sets Rigoletto apart from the court he serves. As he says, when he reaches home in the second scene, 'Ma in altr'uom qui mi cangio!' ('Here I become another person.') All his humanity is invested in Gilda and in his relationship with her. Hence her infatuation with, or devotion to, the Duke represents the collapse of his only refuge from the taint and corruption of the Duke's court. His response, to arrange for the assassination of the Duke, is tragically in tune with the cruel and ruthless ethos of the society he belongs to. The law of the court, and of the wider society in which Sparafucile can make a living, is the law of the jungle. Rigoletto shows that he is as dangerous as any of the animals of the jungle, and perhaps more so, because of the bitter resentment that he as a servant and an outsider feels towards those who dominate this dreadful world. So Rigoletto, though Verdi ensures that he wins our sympathy, can hardly be the hero of this opera. He is too much a part of the evil of which he is also a victim.

Only his daughter Gilda brings a ray of moral light and gentleness into the darkness of this sordid society. She alone is capable of selfless, self-sacrificing love, thus contradicting the cynical view of women as fickle that is held by the very man for whom she gives her life. Her very goodness had made her survival unlikely. Her love, placed in conjunction with her father's remorseless pursuit of vengeance, both destroys her and frustrates his purpose. The intrusion of something so unexpected as self-sacrificing love in so cruel and cynical a world brings about a catastrophe far worse than the business murder her father has paid for.

Rigoletto, unlike Stiffelio, was not fatally mutilated by the changes the Austrian authorities required. Despite many departures from the original play, the disturbing and subversive content of the work remains intact. The notion that there could be a moral justification for a wronged subject seeking revenge upon his ruler is still clearly present. So is the thoroughly anti-aristocratic tone of the piece, and the strong current of class resentment embodied in Rigoletto himself.

The last of these generally more intimate operas, which deal with social rather than political issues, is of course La traviata, and although it is musically and structurally less original than Rigoletto, its choice of theme and its central figure make it a work of exceptional boldness, even in Verdi's output. But I have chosen, however awkwardly, to consider it in Chapter Seven, in the wider context of the portrayal of women in modern opera.

After La traviata Verdi's career underwent another important change of direction. Of the six operas he composed in the next eighteen years, only two were for Italian theatres. The other four were variations on the pattern of grand opera, particularly as it had been established at the Paris Opéra. Indeed two of the four were written specifically for the Opéra, including his next opera, Les vêpres siciliennes, which had its premiere there in June 1855. This was not Verdi's first experience of the Opéra. He had converted I lombardi into Jerusalem for Paris in 1847, so he knew what was required of him. Paris, as Verdi himself said, had 'the world's leading opera house'; it was only natural that, like Wagner some years earlier, he should want to achieve a success there.

The established conventions of grand opera were in many ways the exact opposite of what Verdi had so successfully achieved in operas like Il trovatore and Rigoletto. These had been works of speed and compression. Verdi's concern with drama had led him increasingly to break with the stale conventions of Italian opera. Rigoletto, for example, has no formal arias to sing; Gilda's one aria, 'Caro nome', has no *cabaletta* and almost dispenses with a formal ending, and so on. Grand opera, by contrast, was by its very nature lengthy and discursive. Its four or five acts were expected to include a ballet, substantial choral episodes and, of course, arias and duets for the leading singers. If Verdi's career had ended with *Les vêpres*, critics would probably have concluded that, for all the magnificent music it contains, he had taken a wrong turning, away from his 'natural' aptitude for fast-moving, economical musical drama. But when we look ahead to *La forza del destino* and *Don Carlos*, we can see that Verdi became a master of this more expansive type of opera too, and in fact needed it to achieve the Shakespearian breadth and richness that were precluded by the more compressed and single-minded forms he had worked with in earlier years. As early as 1853 he was writing: 'Today I would refuse subjects of the kind of *Nabucco*, *Foscari* etc. . . . They harp on one chord, elevated, if you like, but monotonous. . . . I prefer Shakespeare to all other dramatists, the Greeks not excepted. . . .'[22]

Grand opera, whose patterns were partly fixed by Auber's *La muette de Portici* and Rossini's *Guillaume Tell*, dealt with historical subjects, but they often had a strong political dimension. This was by no means uncongenial to Verdi, and the years after *La traviata* mark his return to treating public and political issues in his operas, but now with the public matters and private agonies interwoven, and the balance between them sustained, with far more assurance and imagination.

Les vêpres siciliennes or *I vespri siciliani* (it is more often performed and recorded in Italian and in Italy) is another tale of foreign occupation and national resistance, focusing on a famous episode in Palermo in 1282 during which the Sicilians slaughtered numbers of the French who were then occupying their island, under the rule of Charles of Anjou. The libretto originally suggested by the leading French librettist of the period, Eugène Scribe, was *Le Duc d'Albe*, a plot based on the sixteenth-century revolt of the Netherlands, which had been previously offered to Halévy and Donizetti, and had been partially set by the latter. Verdi, however, was insistent that the setting should be in 'a climate less cold than that of the Low Countries; a climate full of warmth and music such as Naples or Sicily'.[23] The libretto was accordingly adapted, but its generic, all-purpose character did lasting damage to the opera. The project was a difficult one in any case. *Les vêpres* was intended for a French audience, but the French appeared in it as a typically crass, much-loathed army of occupation. And Verdi, who was certainly not anti-French (he was living in Paris at this time), was nevertheless quite determined not to slander his compatriots: 'In any event I am Italian above all and come what may I will never be an accessory to any injury done to my country.' He was particularly dismayed by Scribe's portrayal of the Sicilian patriot Procida, whom according to Verdi he had made 'according to his favourite system – a common conspirator with a dagger in his hand'.[24]

The worst of it was that Scribe proved to be the least accessible and cooperative of librettists. He failed to attend rehearsals and he seemed deaf to Verdi's pleas for revisions. The result was that the composer found himself working with a scenario and libretto that he could see had many faults, but which he could not get amended. Not surprisingly, the end result has serious weaknesses. It is undeniable that the work is too long. There is neither plot nor character interest enough to sustain the five-act structure, and the fault lies, not with Verdi, but with Scribe and his hackwork.

The wonder is that Verdi does so much with such arid material. The score is extraordinarily inventive, varied and brilliant. Verdi's harmonic language is richer and more adventurous than ever before, and the orchestration is almost everywhere subtle, original and imaginative. The basic political conflict is presented with characteristic complexity, even if some of the ambiguities are not quite what Verdi intended. The most fully drawn character, and in some ways the most sympathetic, is Montfort, the French governor whose love for his son Henri (Arrigo) is complicated by the latter's commitment to the Sicilian resistance and his love for the even more strongly committed Hélène (Elena). As Budden has said, he is 'a King Philip who has not yet become old and bitter'[25] – another of Verdi's unhappy fathers whose paternal love comes into conflict with their public roles and duties. His Act Three scena and aria is splendid, as are his two difficult emotional dialogues with his son.

The revelation to Henri that he is the governor's son means that he can no longer behave as a wholehearted member of the resistance led by Procida, since it is plotting to assassinate his father. This revelation should produce classic agonies of conscience and choice, but the libretto makes far too little of them, and even the dilemma it produces for him and Hélène is not very effectively explored or exploited. Henri is a one-dimensional tenor lead. The same, alas, is true of the patriot bass, Procida. His opening scene of arrival from exile, with its famous address to Palermo ('Et toi, Palerme'), establishes his credentials as a genuine, deep-feeling patriot. But thereafter his single-minded obsession with plotting and assassination does indeed, as Verdi feared, make him seem like a cardboard conspirator.

The most interesting and impressive member of the resistance is Hélène, the Austrian duchess whose brother Frederick has been executed by the French along with Conradin, the German claimant to the Sicilian throne. She is a more bold and brilliant figure than the dour Procida, as she shows in the opera's very first scene. The French soldiery compel her to sing for them, but she turns the tables on them by singing a song that stirs up the Sicilians to attack the French. The key is in the phrase 'Your destiny is in your own hands' – 'dans vos mains', ominous words that she repeats five times. But the French soldiers, the worse for drink, miss her meaning.

Gradually, however, the intertwined dilemmas of the three principals come to monopolize the music, so that the act of massacre that occurs in the final moments of the opera seems both ill-prepared and wantonly cruel, since it destroys the happiness of Henri and Hélène, whose marriage Montfort has generously agreed to. He is another tyrant who, like Attila, turns out to be more magnanimous than his patriotic but vindictive enemies.

Overall, *Les vêpres* is less convincing, less sincere than its immediate successor, *Simon Boccanegra*; but heretical as this may sound, it seems to me to be musically richer, more brilliant and inventive, with the wealth of melodies that *Boccanegra* lacks. Its neglect in Britain is astonishing. The production by English National Opera in 1984 was the first London staging since its premiere there in 1859. Despite this the critical response was tepid. The rediscovery of Verdi still has some distance to go.

The late William Mann entitled an essay on *Simon Boccanegra* 'Verdi on Politics and Parenthood', and politics and parenthood are indeed the central and intertwined preoccupations of this opera.[26] If this were a Shakespeare play, the woman known in the opera as Amelia (who is really Simon's daughter Maria) would be called Perdita, the daughter who was lost and then found. It is through the reconciliation of father and daughter and their love for each other that Boccanegra achieves the political reconciliation of class-based factions that is his aim as ruler. The price of that reconciliation is his own life.

Like *Les vêpres*, *Boccanegra* takes it subject from Italian history, in this case fourteenth-century Genoa. But unlike its predecessor this is not a tale of struggle against foreign oppression. In that respect *Les vêpres* was, as Rodolfo Celletti has pointed out, 'his last opera with a patriotic *risorgimentale* theme',[27] though by no means his last operatic reflection on the theme of patriotism. Responding to the changing Italian political situation, Verdi's operas now take in new and often more complex political themes. The theme in *Boccanegra* is unity, internal harmony and an end to class conflict. Boccanegra, as Doge of Genoa, strives constantly for that harmony; especially in the council chamber scene, which Verdi added to the score when he came to revise it in 1881, he appears as the advocate and prophet of Italian unity. That theme had appeared before, in *La battaglia di Legnano*, the most openly and thoroughly patriotic of all his operas, and the scene in which the Lombard ambassadors plead for unity against Barbarossa is the obvious predecessor of the council chamber scene, although musically it is cruder.

In the Prologue to *Simon Boccanegra* we see how Paolo and Pietro, leaders of the popular party in Genoa, persuade a somewhat reluctant Simon to stand for election as Doge by suggesting that this is the only way in which he, a mere pirate ('il corsaro', as the crowd call him), could marry Maria, daughter of the aristocrat Jacopo Fiesco, who hates Simon for having seduced her. The episode takes place with great speed, but the impression is given that Paolo expects Simon to be a mere figurehead for the popular party over which Paolo wields the real power. This turns out to be a mistake, but it is one often made by over-devious political manipulators. The disappointment of this expectation may account in part for the viciousness with which Paolo later turns against Boccanegra. At the very moment when Simon discovers that his beloved Maria is dead, the crowd returns, hailing him as Doge. His one personal motive for seeking the office has been snatched away. So ends the Prologue.

The remainder of the action takes place twenty-five years later (twenty-five years was more or less the time between the historical Simon's accession as Doge and his death). The Prologue had been solely for male voices. Now the mood lightens: we are in a garden near the sea, and the young woman known as Amelia Grimaldi is reflecting on her state as an orphan and on the contrast between the modest home of her childhood and the austere grandeur of the Grimaldi palace. She is in love with the young nobleman Gabriele Adorno, who presently appears, but their love is shadowed for her by the fearful knowledge that Gabriele is plotting against the Doge; she also believes that Boccanegra is planning to marry her to his favourite, Paolo. The prospect of happiness is being undermined by political scheming on every side.

The political conflict in *Boccanegra* is a class conflict. Until Paolo turns against him, the Doge's fiercest enemies are the nobles Fiesco and Adorno. Paolo seeks to exploit this by trying to persuade first Fiesco and then Adorno to murder the Doge. Fiesco, outraged, rejects the idea as dishonourable. To Gabriele, Paolo suggests that Boccanegra intends to seduce Amelia, and the excitable young man – he is, after all, a tenor – prepares to murder the sleeping Doge. Amelia prevents him, and when it is revealed that Simon is her father, Gabriele's shame leads him to change sides. Finally his marriage to Amelia and Simon's nomination of him as his successor hold out the hope that the class strife that has bedevilled Boccanegra's period as Doge may at last come to an end. But not before Paolo, furious at having his expectation of marrying Amelia frustrated, has poisoned Simon. In the trio that follows Gabriele's attempt to kill the Doge, the latter asks himself whether he must hold out the hand of friendship to his enemy. He answers yes, for the sake of peace in the state. May my tomb be an altar to Italian friendship. At the point of death he refers to his own martyrdom. He knows what he has achieved, and what it has cost him.

The moment at which these themes are most clearly developed is in the council chamber scene that ends Act One of the revised version of the opera. This stupendous scene, one of the most exciting and powerful in all opera, would alone justify performances of this once neglected work. It is an essentially political scene, yet it draws together all the major figures in the story. It opens, rather like Act Three of *Otello*, with the curtain rising on a meeting that has started some time earlier. The Doge is transacting routine business, but then comes to the poet Petrarch's plea for peace between Venice and Genoa. This plea too has its basis in real history, and it was Verdi who suggested to Boito its incorporation in the scene. It is received with hostility by Paolo and the councillors. Then proceedings are dramatically interrupted by the noise of an angry crowd in the streets, which turns out to be chasing Gabriele with cries of 'Morte ai patrizi' ('Death to the nobles'), and later 'Morte al Doge!' Nevertheless, Simon orders the gates to be opened and the rival parties are admitted. There follows a superb confrontation between Gabriele and the Doge, in which Gabriele accuses Simon of being the man behind the abduction of Amelia that he has just frustrated. Amelia appears to give her account of events. No culprit is named, but both parties are convinced that blame lies with the other.

It is at this point that Simon intervenes with his eloquent plea for peace, not only between the parties in Genoa but, by implication, in Italy as a whole. This rises to its climax with the wonderful phrase

E vo gridando: pace!
E vo gridando: amor!

an adaptation of Petrarch's own words. All respond to this moving appeal in an ensemble over which Amelia's voice soars, making a personal plea for peace to Fiesco. This does produce at least a temporary calm, and the scene ends with the chilling and (melo?)dramatic confrontation between Simon and Paolo.

It is striking that Verdi in the 1880s should have returned to the theme of Italian unity that was naturally so great a preoccupation in the 1850s. Apart from wishing to improve what he recognized was the rickety structure of the opera, it seems likely that he felt, in the context of the uninspiring politics of the new Italy, that there was still something relevant to be said about the need for unity and patriotic spirit, and that the revision was Verdi's way of reminding his fellow Italians of the ideals that had inspired their long struggle in the earlier part of the century.

I have said nothing about the moving and utterly characteristic scene in which Simon and Amelia discover that they are father and daughter. Here Verdi explores further the theme of parenthood that was so dear to him. *Simon Boccanegra* is close to its predecessor *Les vêpres siciliennes* in its handling of this theme. For in both operas it is clear that the ruler needs his child and his child's love as an antidote to the burdens and loneliness of power. It is a theme in Shakespeare's *Henry IV* and *King Lear* (an operatic version of which Verdi constantly planned to write, but never did), and Verdi returns to it in *Don Carlos*. The exploration of the nature of government is a feature of these 'middle period' works, and Verdi provides us with a varied gallery of rulers, from the generous and far-sighted Boccanegra and the forgiving Gustavus to the racked but inflexible Philip II and the stony-hearted Amonasro.

Un ballo in maschera, which is based on the story of the assassination of King Gustavus III of Sweden, is a less political opera than its ostensible theme might suggest. Naturally the story fell foul of the Neapolitan censors even before it was staged. They were concerned not so much about the expression of liberal ideas, but about anything that implied disrespect for the institution of monarchy. Even in more liberal Rome, where the opera had its premiere in 1859, there were objections from the Vatican censor, and the whole story had to be transferred from Sweden to the rather improbable setting of colonial New England, with Gustavus becoming Riccardo, Earl of Warwick and Governor of Boston.

   Despite all this brouhaha, *Un ballo in maschera* is far less concerned with public issues than with private passions, and the way in which these feed into politics. The two long-standing conspirators have their grievances against the king: one has had property confiscated, the other a brother killed. They could well be representatives of the nobility whose privileges the historical Gustavus curtailed. But at no point do they elevate their opposition to the political level: they do not speak of justice or oppression, but simply of personal vengeance. When the decisive step is taken, and the king's closest counsellor and friend, Anckarstroem, joins them, it is similarly for personal reasons: he has discovered the king at a nocturnal assignation with his wife Amelia, and he too wants his revenge. Prior to Anckarstroem's involvement, Verdi treats the two conspirators as rather comic figures, muttering away at the bottom of the big ensembles, usually to the effect that the time is not yet ripe to strike. Anckarstroem is a more effective conspirator and assassin because his sense of betrayal is stronger, and his baritonal rage, powerfully voiced in the aria 'Eri tu', is much greater. He is also better placed to obtain the confidential information necessary to effect the murder, as we see from his conversation with Oscar at the ball.

Anckarstroem is a powerfully drawn and by no means unsympathetic figure. It emerges in the last scenes of the opera that the king has resolved to put temptation out of reach by sending Anckarstroem to Finland as ambassador, and with him Amelia. He will not attend the ball to get a last glimpse of Amelia. But warnings of a plan to kill him alter his plans. Courage and reputation demand that he attend and defy the threats. By these twists of the plot, and by giving Gustavus his only scene of isolated reflection just before the fatal ball, Verdi and Somma seek to dispel any thoughts we might have of comparing this playful and passionate ruler with the playboy duke of *Rigoletto*, and to counterbalance the sympathy that Anckarstroem inevitably gains from his agony of betrayal and misery.

So Gustavus remains at the tragic centre of this swift and compact drama. And it is through him that a significant political dimension is added to the opera. For what we are offered here, as in *Simon Boccanegra*, is a portrait of a basically good ruler; Gustavus's benevolent sway is flawed, perhaps by a degree of the wilful frivolity so tempting to any absolute ruler, but indisputably by an illicit love for the wife of his best friend and most trusted adviser.

As to the frivolity, what are we to make of his response in the first scene of the opera to the Chief Justice when he brings forward the case of Madame Arvidson (Ulrica), recommending that this supposed troublemaker be banished? On the one hand Gustavus can be seen as exercising both mercy and a rational scepticism appropriate to the Age of Enlightenment: let us find out for ourselves whether there be any harm in her. On the other it seems arbitrary and even insulting that, rather than accept his Chief Justice's opinion, he should turn directly to ask his court favourite, the page Oscar, for his opinion on the matter. This response has all the typical wilfulness of the absolute ruler, even if he is an enlightened one.

As for the king's proposal to visit the fortune-teller in disguise, we should note first that the responsible Anckarstroem advises against it, and second that the use of disguise is not simply a passing joke: disguise is necessary to rulers who wish to act in ways that are either morally outrageous – such as the Duke in *Rigoletto* – or socially unacceptable – such as Gustavus here or Macbeth in his more seriously motivated consultations with the witches. The implication is always that what these monarchs are doing is incompatible with their public dignity and reputation. Since the sceptical Gustavus is in any case indisposed to believe Arvidson's prophecies, and derides them when they are made (even if a trifle nervously, to judge from the opening of 'E scherzo od e follia'), it is clear that this visit is very much an act of self-indulgence on his part. It shows him in an attractive but ambivalent light. Is Anckarstroem right in thinking his behaviour irresponsible?

The figure of Oscar is a remarkable invention. But he plays no vital role in the plot. So why did Verdi attach such importance to him? He embodies the atmosphere of gaiety and brilliance that Verdi wants to suggest was characteristic of the Swedish court, and indeed of the king himself. Without Oscar the whole opera would be much more sombre. His contribution to its atmosphere, its *tinta*, is indispensable. But we may also see him as epitomizing the frivolous and careless side of the king, the side that causes him to run the risks that lead to his death.

Despite this frivolity, and despite the passion that overwhelms both him and Amelia in their confessional love duet in Act Two, Verdi's Gustavus is a ruler who is genuinely loved by his people, as is clear from the chorus in his praise which ends Act One. He sees that love as the secure basis of his power and rule:

> Del popolo mio
> L'amor mi guardi, e mi protegga Iddio.

(May the love of my people guard me, and God protect me.)

This is his response when Anckarstroem warns him that people are plotting against him. Anckarstroem has the list of names, but Gustavus refuses to look at it. This refusal may seem like foolishness and over-confidence, or like Boccanegra's clemency towards his enemies, or even suggest a death wish, a hankering after martyrdom as suggested in David Alden's production for English National Opera in 1989. But it is a refusal that Gustavus adheres to, right to the end, when the crowd is calling for death for the traitor Anckarstroem.

The king reasserts his authority, 'Signor qui sono', and pardons everyone, inspiring even Ribbing and Horn to exclaim along with everyone else, 'Core grande e generoso!' Thus magnanimity pays off, even if Gustavus pays for it with his life.

A remarkable number of the details of the opera are historically accurate. Gustavus did pardon those involved in the conspiracy to murder him, whose leaders were called Ribbing and Horn, and only Anckarstroem, the actual assassin, was executed. The conversation about the conspirators that Gustavus has with Anckarstroem in Act One is based on a deathbed conversation with his favourite Armfelt.

> Bello il poter non è, che de' soggetti
> Le lagrime non terge

(Power is not fine if it cannot wipe away the tears of its subjects)

So sings Gustavus in his very first utterance. That Verdi should have followed *Simon Boccanegra* with a second opera in which a merciful and magnanimous ruler pits the example of his own generosity of spirit against the ethics of vengeance and vendetta that have been traditionally dominant in his society can surely be no coincidence. Gustavus and Boccanegra (somewhat anachronistically in the case of the latter) are presented as harbingers of a much longed-for, more humane and civilized society, in which the barbarous codes of feudal factionalism are banished for ever. Writing these works in the later 1850s, Verdi surely hoped, and perhaps believed, that Victor Emmanuel of Piedmont might fill such a role for all Italy when the great moment came.

The most panoramic, the most inclusive of all Verdi's operas is *La forza del destino*, first performed in St Petersburg in November 1862. Piave's libretto was adapted from a play, *Don Alvaro o La fuerza del sino*, by the Spanish liberal writer and politician Angel Perez de Saavedra, Duke of Rivas, and it was the 'truly vast' character of this story that Verdi especially liked. Usually Verdi was preoccupied with sustaining narrative and dramatic tension by eliminating everything that held up the action or was irrelevant to the opera's central themes. But in this case he deliberately enlarged the already generous scope of Saavedra's play by adding material taken from another play about war, Schiller's *Wallenstein's Camp*. *La forza del destino* is a sprawling work, especially in its ill-shaped third act. But Verdi knowingly opted for spread rather than compression; the sense of a range of social types and situations, and an action spread across the map of Europe, is integral to the opera's character. George Martin has dubbed it 'Verdi's imitation of Shakespeare'; we might also be tempted to call it Verdi's *War and Peace*.[28] It includes his most profound and imaginative treatment of war, and his richest portrayal of organized religion.

The Force of Destiny is how the title is always translated. Despite the archaic ring of these words, they do convey the sense of fate that all three of the principal characters refer to more than once, and which is felt in a particularly oppressive way by the hero, Don Alvaro. This sense of fate emerges with special clarity in his superb recitative and aria at the opening of Act Three. 'Sara infelice eternamente . . . è scritto' ('I shall be eternally unhappy . . . it is decreed'). In the aria he refers to himself as 'Che senza nome ed esule. In odio del destino' ('a nameless exile, defying fate'). Alvaro incarnates with a special intensity the condition of the exile, which is a recurring preoccupation in Verdi's operas. Usually, the exile yearns to return to his or her homeland, but although Alvaro plans to return with Leonora to his native South America in Act One, once he has despaired of finding her, return comes to seem pointless. Now he wanders from land to land, homeless and hopeless. His music is throughout imbued with a sense of being accursed; having accidentally killed Leonora's father, when at the end of the opera he fatally wounds her brother Carlo, who then kills Leonora herself, it is small wonder that Alvaro should curse God for the horrors fate has visited upon him. The original 1862 ending, in which he hurls himself to his death shouting 'pera la razza umana' ('let the human race perish'), was surely true to the logic of the situation and to his responses. Joachim Herz used this ending in his production of the work for Welsh National Opera in 1982, in order, according to Peter Conrad, 'to make the work more philosophically acceptable to himself' – as if it had not in fact been composed by Verdi and Piave.[29] But its utter bleakness was not popular with audiences, and Verdi agonized a good deal over this 'infernale scioglimento' ('infernal denouement') before replacing it with the trio with which we are now familiar.

The idea of fate or doom – 'destino avverso', as Alvaro calls it – is characteristic of Spanish romantic pessimism; but it can be, and has been, argued that this idea, in the context of *La forza del destino*, is a mystification: there is no impersonal overarching force driving the characters to disaster, and everything is perfectly explicable in terms of human choices and actions and the social pressures and conventions which determine them. Leonora's brother Carlo, whose pursuit of vengeance provides the dynamic of most of the action, may see himself as the appointed instrument of fate; but this is plainly a classic piece of what Sartre called 'bad faith', an attempt to shuffle off responsibility for his own actions. It is his sense of what the honour of his family requires that drives him on: a traditional social code reminiscent of the Mafia, not some vague fate or destiny.

Similarly Leonora is doomed to unhappiness because she is caught between two conflicting attachments: to her family and to Alvaro. Both her father and her brother despise Alvaro, on class and racial grounds. She of course does not share their disdain, but neither does she want to put herself at odds with them. Hence her reluctance to elope with Alvaro. The accidental death of her father the marquis is the disaster that means that at a stroke she has lost Alvaro, whilst being saddled with grief for her father and dismay at her brother's determination to hunt down not only her lover but herself. Small wonder that she should seek to escape into the hoped-for tranquillity of the hermit's life.

But it is with Alvaro above all that we can see clearly that impersonal fate is not the driving force of the opera: Alvaro's unhappiness is not endemic or metaphysical, but due essentially to a single fact: the prejudice evoked by his racial background, and his consequent sense of being isolated in a hostile society. Not without reason, Alvaro tends to interpret any slight as an expression of this hostility, unintended if not intended. Thus in Act One it looks as though he interprets Leonora's reluctance to elope with him in this way, which may be unjust but is hardly surprising, since as soon as her father appears, he explicitly insults Alvaro by suggesting that his behaviour is just what one would expect from someone of his base origins. The marquis has already urged his daughter to forget about this foreigner who is unworthy of her, 'lo straniero di te indegno'.

If the Marquis of Calatrava is insulting, his son Carlo is a vicious racist. He never misses an opportunity to abuse Alvaro in racist terms, once he has discovered who he is. In the last act it is his racist insults, followed by a blow on the face, which finally provoke the peaceable

Alvaro into fighting a fatal duel with him. So, as Nicholas Payne has written about Alvaro, 'It is the laws of society that have condemned him: racial prejudice, conventions of honour, the circumstances of war.' No abstract or impersonal fate or destiny is to blame.[30]

I should add that the background to Alvaro's experiences and the explanation for his presence in Spain lie in Spanish dominion over South America (this is the middle of the eighteenth century). Alvaro is in Spain to obtain the release of his father, the Viceroy of Peru, who has married the last descendant of the Incas. It is through his mother that Alvaro claims royal descent, and he is naturally angry that he, of all people, should be treated as an inferior and an outcast by the Spanish. But it is equally 'natural' that the Calatravas, as aristocrats within an imperial culture, should despise and hate those they believe to be of inferior or tainted blood.

La forza del destino was not Verdi's first opera with a Spanish/South American background. Alzira, written for Naples in 1845, is based rather distantly on a play by Voltaire in which the basic conflict is once again between the indigenous Americans and their Spanish conquerors. The Spanish governor of Peru, Gusman or Gusmano, wishes to marry the the Inca princess Alzira. He loves her, but he also sees the political usefulness of the union, as does her father, the chief Ataliba, who thinks it could bring an end to the conflict with Spain, to whose power he has already submitted.

But Alzira is in love with another Inca chief, Zamoro, as he is with her. When Zamoro is taken in battle, Gusmano tells Alzira that unless she consents to marry him Zamoro will be killed. The situation is similar to that in Tosca, but less crudely sexual. Under this pressure, Alzira consents. When Zamoro hears the news he resolves to murder Gusmano, which he does in the midst of the festivities for the planned wedding. In his dying moments the Spaniard remembers his Christian faith, and forgives and blesses the Inca pair. But for most of the opera the Spanish behave with the customary arrogance of conquerors, and it is Zamoro who displays the virtues of the civilized and the Christian. Thus as the opera opens, a bloodthirsty group of Indians who have captured Gusmano's father, Alvaro, are preparing to put him to death; but Zamoro, their long-lost leader, suddenly appears and, not wishing the joy of the reunion to be stained with blood, lets Alvaro go free. Tell your people, who call us savages, how you owe your life to a savage, he sings. And when he tells his followers how he was tortured by Gusmano, he repeats the point, exclaiming, 'E i barbari siam noi' 'It's we who are supposed to be the barbarians'.

Zamoro seems in more than one respect a sketch for Alvaro in *La forza del destino*, not only in exemplifying a greater magnanimity than his Christian opponents, but also in the vein of melancholy that suffuses the *cavatina* 'Irne lungi ancor dovrei', in which, just before the final denouement, he contemplates a further spell of life as a fugitive, burdened with shame and separated from the woman he loves. Interestingly, like Alvaro's 'O tu che in seno', this song is preceded by a sad clarinet solo.

The unifying thread of *La forza del destino* is the vendetta or hunt pursued by Carlo not only against Alvaro but also, and even more horribly, against his own sister, Leonora, who has degraded her noble family by her intimacy with this 'base Indian'. His vendetta represents a terrible perversion of normal family feelings. This is one of the aspects of the opera which make it especially interesting. Usually, as we have seen, Verdi depicts family relations with great sympathy and depth of feeling. But Carlo can be seen as exemplifying the destructiveness of the family when it is treated as an idea or an institution to be upheld at whatever cost, rather than as a set of loving relationships.

Religion also receives unusual treatment in this opera. It is certainly the only one of Verdi's operas in which the spiritual beauty and comforts of religion are dwelt on more than its fierce and vengeful aspects. The latter are not wholly ignored. The monks, like priestly choruses in so many Verdi operas, clearly get a great deal of pleasure out of threatening evildoers with divine punishment. They sing their 'Maledizione' chorus at the end of Act Two with great relish. Then there is the comic figure of Fra Melitone, who belongs to the well-established tradition of satirical portraits of monks whose spirituality is doubtful, to say the least. In fact it is not clear which of the so-called Christian virtues Melitone actually possesses. His sermon to the soldiers is in the style of a crabby schoolmaster rebuking naughty children, only half-seriously; and he is plainly out of sympathy with the crowd of beggars – 'bricconi' ('rascals'), he calls them – whom he has to feed in Act Four.

But Melitone is overshadowed in every way by the austere but benign figure of the Padre Guardiano, who embodies a genuine spirituality, and it is he and the fervent Leonora who set the tone for the long second part of Act Two. Leonora's prayers at the beginning and end of this sequence are exceptionally beautiful. It is these radiant and passionate pleas, and the grave tones of Guardiano, that provide the dominant image of religion in the opera, and it is a positive and consolatory one.

The third major theme to receive unusual treatment is war. Verdi usually treats this theme by stressing, on the one hand, the heroism of those who are willing to die to liberate or defend their country, and, on the other hand, the grievous human costs of such heroism. In *La forza del destino* neither of these two aspects is wholly neglected. But Verdi looks at war from a new angle. War is presented from the point of view of its victims, the peasants whose land is plundered and laid waste, and the young men who are forcibly conscripted into the armies; but it is also examined, more conspicuously and more originally, from the point of view of hangers-on, the commercial baggage-train that simultaneously services the army and seeks to profit from it. In this rumbustious but disreputable pageant of appendages the principal figure is Preziosilla, who is politely described in the cast list as a 'young gipsy girl' – which no doubt she is. But she is also a cheerleader and entertainer for the troops, and in addition does a bit of informal recruiting along the way. 'E bella la guerra! Evviva la guerra!' is the chorus of her first song at the inn in Act Two. Then there is Trabucco, whose whining tenor is intended to make him sound like a caricature Jew, and who is in the business of offering low prices to soldiers who are selling what goods they have because they need cash. It is a squalid picture that Verdi paints, and the more we see of it the hollower becomes the gaiety that Preziosilla so insistently displays.

By the time we reach the Rataplan chorus with which she tries to raise morale at the end of Act Three, we have seen too much of this *bella guerra* to be so easily persuaded. Budden insists that she is merely 'a good-hearted girl . . . all too typical of that kindly world of common sense from which the principals are excluded'. This seems a bland, not to say evasive, characterization. Consider what has happened before she reappears to offer her final celebration of war. Alvaro has been wounded, so seriously that he is expected to die. A group of starving peasants has appeared begging for bread, and followed at once by a group of conscripts longing to return home. These laments are heartlessly interrupted by Preziosilla and the *vivandières*, offering them their 'consolations'; then comes Melitone's mock sermon, full of puns. Comparison of these scenes with Brecht's *Mother Courage* is derided by Budden as 'a post-Brechtian anachronism'. But the reference seems apt to me.[31]

As Budden himself has pointed out, Verdi had long been anxious to make use of the picture of military life presented in Schiller's play *Wallensteins Lager*, and at last, in Act Three of *La forza del destino*, he saw his opportunity. Schiller's play, the first and shortest part of the Wallenstein trilogy, is an extraordinary piece of work, in effect an extended conversation, with interruptions, about military life among a group of soldiers taking part in the Thirty Years War (which was also, as it happens, the setting for *Mother Courage*). It is realistic, anti-heroic, unsentimental. Undoubtedly it appealed to that side of Verdi that always recoiled from the cruelty and tragedy of war. He draws on Schiller for the text of Melitone's sermon, but also for the women who make themselves sexually available to the soldiery, and the peasants begging for bread.

> It's a merry life, it can't be gainsaid,
> To gallop over another man's head.

Lines like these were doubtless too strong meat for operatic audiences, but it would be odd if Verdi, having turned to this particular source, had not intended to convey something of the same resolutely unvarnished picture of war.

It is also relevant to recall that the opera was composed in the aftermath of the disillusioning war of 1859 between France and Austria, which Italian patriots had hoped would achieve the dream of a free and united Italy, but instead left Austria still in control of the Veneto and the Pope still ruling the Papal States. Verdi wrote to Clarina Maffei: 'What a result! What blood spilled for nothing! How our poor young men have been deluded. And Garibaldi, who has even made a sacrifice of his old and constant convictions in favour of a king, has still not achieved his wishes. It's enough to drive one mad!'[32]

We should note, even if it is not of great musical significance, that in the opera the war is placed in Italy, the enemy is once again Austria, and the battle in Act Three is that fought in 1744 at Velletri near Rome in which the Austrians were defeated by Neapolitan and Spanish forces. When Preziosilla is busy drumming up recruits in Act Two, a general cry goes up of 'Morte ai Tedeschi' ('death to the Germans'), and she refers to them as:

> Flagel d'Italia eterno
> E de figliuoli suoi
> (eternal scourge of Italy and of her children)

The patriotic note is worked in, despite its inappropriateness to the denizens of a Spanish inn.

With *Don Carlos* we come to what is surely Verdi's masterpiece among his treatments of political themes, for it is neither essentially a drama of personal relations where the characters are involved in politics or public life almost incidentally, as is the case in *Otello* and *Un ballo in maschera* to some extent; nor is it solely a drama of public issues in which individuals are wholly subsumed into their public roles and become exclusively symbols or representatives of political forces or groups, like Zaccaria in *Nabucco* or Procida in *Les vêpres siciliennes*. Here Verdi, thanks in part to Schiller, portrays a range of characters, all vividly individualized, all of whom are involved in a mesh of conflicts that are both personal and political. Of the six leading figures, only one, the Grand Inquisitor, is a purely public and political figure; only one character, the Princess Eboli, could plausibly be seen as a purely private person, caught up in political conflicts against her will. Philip II, the king of Spain, the queen, Don Carlos and the Marquis of Posa are the more complete and credible individual characters precisely because they are both political *and* private beings. Conflicts between personal feelings and loyalties and political hopes and responsibilities occur within each of them, and the drama becomes a far more complex affair than the simple clash between duty and feeling that had been a staple of musical drama since its inception.

It is rare for a single production of a work to compel a revision of traditional evaluations of it; yet that, I think, was the case with the production of *Don Carlos* first mounted at Covent Garden in 1958 by the great film and opera director Luchino Visconti. Until then *Don Carlos* had been either neglected or underrated. It was not seen at all in Vienna until 1933, and after its first run of performances at the Paris Opéra in 1867, for which it was written, in French, that house did not revive it again for nearly one hundred years. When Beecham performed it at Covent Garden in 1933 after decades of neglect, the Wagnerian Ernest Newman dismissed the music as mostly bad and followed up his criticisms with a generalized attack on Verdi as a poor dramatist and a worse psychologist.[33]

But the integrity and comprehensibility of the opera suffered even before the first performance from the need to make cuts, which even Verdi recognized, simply to reduce its length. These cuts impaired the political meaning of the work, and the tradition thus established of pushing its political meaning to one side has survived in performance up to the present day. The most damaging of these first cuts comes at the very opening of the opera – the opening, that is, always assuming that it is the five-act version that is being referred to, not the truncated version which entirely omits Act One. Originally the work opened with a sombre prelude making much use of the gloomy grace notes that are most familiar from the opening to Act Four and the soliloquy for King Philip for which it sets the scene. Then we hear a chorus of woodmen and their wives telling of their hardships. Winter in the forest of Fontainebleau compounds the miseries of wartime, and they want to know when the war with Spain will end. When Elisabeth de Valois appears, she responds with sympathy, promising that the war will soon be over. The climax of the chorus comes with these words:

> Avec la paix, o travailleurs,
> Nous reverrons des jours meilleurs.

(With peace, o labourers, we shall again see better days.)

There then follows the scene for Don Carlos with which the opera normally opens.

Quite apart from the odd abruptness of the revised beginning, the inclusion of this first scene has two merits. First, it immediately establishes the European political context within which the principal characters have to live and make their decisions. Their decisions are seldom purely personal: issues of war and peace, freedom and oppression, are bound up with them. Second, this scene explains the particular hard decision that Elisabeth takes later in the act when, after she has met and fallen in love with Don Carlos, the Spanish Infante, they learn that, after all, she is destined to marry not him, but his father, King Philip II. It is the renewed entreaties of the impoverished forest women that persuade her to agree to this proposal, even though she is thereby sacrificing her hope of happiness. As Count Lerma reminds her, 'Une guerre cruelle est finie à ce prix' ('this is the price for ending a cruel war'). It thus becomes clear that Elisabeth shares, to some extent, the political attitudes of Carlos's friend Rodrigo, the Marquis of Posa; so when in the final act she urges Carlos to continue Posa's struggle on behalf of Flanders and its freedom – another section of the work that has often been cut in performance – her words seem in no way gratuitous or out of character.

Don Carlos is an opera that it is hard to cut without making nonsense of the way its characters behave. That it has nevertheless been so frequently mutilated reflects not only a lack of faith in the work as a whole on the part of both managements and audiences but also, in view of what has been cut, a casual disregard of its political dimension, a disregard that has historically been all too typical of the operatic world. Yet that dimension is, I would suggest, essential to the work. Elisabeth's fateful decision to marry a man she does not love, and does not come to love, is inspired by political considerations; from that decision, comprehensible only in relation to the opening chorus, flows much of what follows: Carlos's reluctance to leave Spain and the court, Philip's unhappiness, his adultery with Eboli, and his mistrust of his son.

After the Fontainebleau act, the rest of the action takes place in Spain, but we are never allowed to forget that this is an opera about European rather than Spanish politics. Elisabeth never forgets the land she has left behind. When her lady-in-waiting, the Countess of Aremberg, is dismissed, Elisabeth's touching farewell suggests that she would be happy to return with her to France:

> Tu vas revoir la France,
> Ah! porte-lui mes adieux!

And she muses on her homeland, 'France, noble pays', in her last-act soliloquy. Her exile may be elevated, but it is no less sad for all that.

But the country – never seen in the opera – that looms largest over the action is of course the Low Countries, referred to in the text as Flanders. As in Goethe's *Egmont* and Beethoven's response to that play, so in Schiller's *Don Carlos* and Verdi's interpretation of it, the revolt of the Netherlands is taken as the symbol and starting point of the modern struggle for liberty, national, religious and personal. At only one point in the action, the grandiose spectacle of the coronation cum *auto-da-fé* in Act Three, do Flemish deputies actually appear, sponsored by Carlos, to plead their cause with the king. But by then we are well aware that the war in Flanders is the great political issue that places the king at odds with his son, and with his most trusted adviser, Posa, and to a lesser extent the queen as well. Flanders is the issue Posa urges Carlos to take up and make his own, and which leads to their famous duet of solidarity and dedication to liberty ('l'amour de la liberté'). It is also the issue over which Posa challenges the king himself in the interview that concludes Act Two. It is Carlos's involvement with the Flemish that leads to his imprisonment and to Posa's death at the hands of the Inquisition.

Of course, much of this is fiction rather than history. The historical Carlos shared some of the manifest instability of the operatic figure, and he was harshly treated by his father, dying in prison in 1588 at the age of twenty-three. But there is little reason to think that he was at all concerned with the issues of Flanders or religious freedom, even though legends to that effect grew up soon after his death. The figure of Posa, both in Schiller's play and the opera, has frequently been described as an anachronism, an idealist 'who would hardly have lasted a day at Philippe's court'.[34] No doubt this is true (indeed, Verdi himself recognized it, calling Posa 'an imaginary person who could never have existed in Philip's reign'),[35] but that is beside the point. Schiller and Verdi wanted to dramatize the issue of liberty, and chose to do so by making it the core of a confrontation between Philip II (upholder of the traditional authority of both Church and State) and Posa (the champion of liberty). The Spanish king would never have listened to the heretical spokesmen for the Flemish people, but he has to listen to a trusted counsellor in his own court; that much at least is plausible. And however inaccurate the details may be, the sense of a political situation dominated by one overriding issue of war or peace, authority or toleration, which invades the lives of all those involved, generating divisions in ruling groups and even within families, is powerfully conveyed. We need look back no further than the traumas the United States went through in the course of its war against Vietnam to find a contemporary parallel.

The dialogue between Philip and Posa that ends Act Two caused

Verdi difficulties in its composition, and Budden has suggested that this was really because being 'nothing less than a political argument about the value of freedom' it was 'hardly a natural subject for an opera'.[36] But it was at Verdi's suggestion that this scene was included in the scenario, as well as the comparable scene between Philip and the Grand Inquisitor in Act Four. To my knowledge, no one has ever suggested that the latter is anything but one of the most powerful scenes Verdi ever composed, and Budden suggests that this 'is because, beneath the cut and thrust of logic, it deals in feelings rather than intellectual ideas'.[37] The implied antithesis is not really very convincing. Both are essentially scenes of heated political argument. It is true that the later scene is a direct confrontation between the power of the State and the power of the Church, a confrontation which is also a personal struggle between the two men who embody those powers, and therefore it has a tension which does not belong to the earlier scene. But Posa's passion for peace and freedom comes through strongly and effectively in the earlier scene. There are few more astonishing and powerful moments in all opera than that of Posa's response to the king's claim that he is bringing the peace that prevails in Spain to Flanders. To this the marquis bursts in with

> Arrière
> Cette paix! La paix du cimetière!

(Away with such a peace! The peace of the graveyard!)

And on the word *cimetière*, or the Italian *sepolcri*, the orchestra explodes with a cataclysmic fury that has to be given time to subside before Posa can elaborate on what he means, and appeal to the king to replace terror and misery with liberty. The whole paragraph, which Verdi inserted when he came to revise the opera in the 1880s, is magnificently eloquent. Now in his seventies, once again Verdi pours out his compassion for the victims of war and repression, and reminds us of his lifelong devotion to liberty, for nations and for individuals. The production book of 1884 states explicitly that 'the two characters who stand face to face . . . represent two great principles in the history of mankind'. This certainly sounds like Verdi himself.[38]

In at least one respect *Don Carlos* is more daring than anything Verdi had done before: it embodies his most unqualified, frontal attack on the Catholic Church. Of course a play set at the time of the Inquisition was a gift, from that point of view. But once again we should note that it was at Verdi's request that the crucial encounter between the king and the Grand Inquisitor was included in the opera. Even as the conflict between nation and papacy was coming to a head in Italy, Verdi sought to dramatize the conflict of Church and State in the most vivid way. And as between the two, Verdi leaves us in no doubt that it is the Church that is the more powerful and the more ruthless. Philip wishes to shelter both his son and Posa from the Inquisition. The cleric is unrelenting, and even threatens the king himself with the Inquisition. At the end of this chilling interview Philip, defeated, comments, 'L'orgueil du Roi fléchit devant l'orgueil du prêtre.' ('The king's pride bends before that of the priest.') His phrase descends through two octaves to a low F.

It is an agent of the Inquisition who shoots Posa dead in Carlos's prison. Subsequently, it is the appearance of the Grand Inquisitor that overawes the angry crowd which gathers at the prison. In the *auto-da-fé* scene we have a classic Verdian confrontation within the overall ensemble between the churchmen and the rest. The scene opens with a cheerful crowd praising the king, but the mood changes as soon as the monks appear, dragging their victims to the stake and chanting grimly about the day of wrath. When the Flemish representatives appeal for mercy, their pleas are supported by Elisabeth, Carlos, Posa and the people, while the monks, as ever, support Philip in his refusal to listen. These suppliants are rebels, they remind him. The scene ends as the flames rise from the pyres where the 'heretics' are being burnt.

The opera was certainly perceived as being anti-Catholic. The Empress Eugénie, who attended the 1867 premiere, turned her back on the stage during the scene between the king and the Grand Inquisitor, reportedly at the moment when the king tells the cleric to be quiet: 'Tais-toi, prêtre.' Even as late as 1950 the opera was picketed in New York by protesters who objected to its anti-Catholicism. It is unlikely that the protesters were mistaken. Verdi had no love for the organized power of the Roman Church, as we have seen, and his hostility to the secular power of the papacy, which remained as the final obstacle to Italian unification in the late 1860s, was probably increased by the publication in 1864 of the notorious Syllabus of Errors, in which Pope Pius IX denounced all the basic liberal principles as among 'the principal errors of our times'. These included freedom of conscience, religious toleration, freedom of discussion, and the idea that the Papacy should reach an accommodation with 'progress, liberalism and recent civilization'. It is not hard to see in *Don Carlos* Verdi's response to the Syllabus, and a reaffirmation of his belief in the very ideas that Pio Nono had denounced as 'errors'. 'Of all Verdi's operas *Don Carlos* was the most finely tuned to the politics of its day,' George Martin has written.[39]

Martin has written interestingly about Posa, arguing that his behaviour shows him to be a more complex and ambivalent character than the model of liberal idealism he has usually been seen as. As far as Posa's actions are concerned, rather than Verdi's music, Martin has a good case. Posa is treated as a confidant by both the king and Carlos, and these two roles are irreconcilable. In persuading Carlos to surrender his sword to the king in the *auto-da-fé* scene he appears to side with the king. But for the most part he is actually working against Philip, through his support for the Flemish rebellion. In the end he saves Carlos through his death in the prison, but it was the pressure he put on Carlos to involve himself with the Flemish issue that landed Carlos in prison in the first place. The truth is that it would be impossible for Posa to take up the Flemish cause in the context of Philip's court without being devious and even manipulative.

But the music does, I think, show Posa to be noble and idealistic. To some commentators, notably Julian Budden, this also makes him boring and one-dimensional: 'musically rather uninteresting'. Even his death scene is 'bland and heroic . . . but somewhat monochrome'.[40] It is hard to be sure whether this is a purely musical judgement, or whether Budden, like some other commentators, is simply out of sympathy with the kind of liberal idealist that Verdi portrayed in Posa. I have always found the entire prison scene, and Posa's farewell to Carlos and life, apt and moving.

If there is a tendency to undervalue Posa as a musical character, there is a corresponding tendency to view the king with a good deal more indulgence than did Verdi himself. It is quite true that the king's soliloquy is magnificent, and that in his confrontation with the Inquisition, our sympathies are inevitably with him. He is given an exceptionally full realization, in a whole series of scenes, and his personal sadness places him in that gallery of burdened, unhappy rulers that includes Wotan and Boris Godunov as well Verdi's Francesco Foscari, Montfort and Boccanegra. But Verdi never allows us to forget that Philip II is also an inflexible ruler and a harsh husband. The scene with the Inquisitor is immediately followed by a meeting with Elisabeth in which the king accuses her of adultery with Carlos: the very sin of which he himself is guilty, as Eboli is shortly to confess to the queen. And in both the final scenes of the opera Philip appears in the company of the Grand Inquisitor, reminding us that when push comes to shove, Church and State unite against the challenge of rebellion and the threat of liberty. Verdi had visited Philip's famous palace, the Escorial, a few years before beginning work on *Don Carlos*. He did not like it. 'It is severe, terrible, like the fierce sovereign who built it.'[41] From Nabucco on Verdi had always looked for the complexity and colour in his tyrants and villains, but that did not blind him to the roles they played. Verdi was a realist, not a sentimentalist.

A further word should be said about Elisabeth, who is too easily seen as an apolitical victim, at sea in the world of male power politics. I have already noted that the drama begins with her politically motivated decision to accept the plan of marriage to Philip. Moreover, it is she who dominates the last act, which opens with her magnificent aria and continues with the last of her three duets with Carlos. This may easily be seen simply as her farewell to the man she loves and to her hopes of happiness, and no more. Such an interpretation is made more plausible when the *marziale* section of the duet is cut, heightening the pathos. But this is misleading. Elisabeth has taken a brave decision: to send Carlos off to Flanders to continue the work begun by Posa. She recognizes that this may well mean death for herself. So there is grief here, but there is also bravery, and commitment to a noble cause, and that is part of the meaning of both the aria and the duet.

It is true that Verdi himself cut the *marziale* section, in 1872, but he restored it in the more far-reaching revisions of the 1880s, so there is no reason to think that he regarded it as weak or superfluous. And as in *Simon Boccanegra* and *Un ballo in maschera*, the conclusion, if fully realized, though tragic, is not *only* tragic or negative. There is hope as well, and that is very much in the spirit of Verdi himself.

The reputation of *Don Carlos* has grown greatly in the past forty years. It is now much better appreciated than it used to be. But a full understanding of it will always elude those who, consciously or unconsciously, disregard the political dimension, which shapes the drama and the fate of the characters from beginning to end.

The musical splendours of *Aida*, apart from its opportunities for spectacle, will always ensure its popularity. But it is evident that Verdi was working here with a scenario a good deal less original and challenging than any he had tackled since *The Sicilian Vespers*. Verdi seems to have recognized this himself when he first read the synopsis: 'It is well done; it offers a splendid mise-en-scène, and there are two or three situations which, if not very new, are certainly very beautiful.'[42] The story is clear, coherent, but hardly original; apart from Amneris, perhaps, the characters are not especially complex or subtly drawn. Amonasro is fierce and passionate, but somewhat monotonous. Aida herself has spirit as well as pathos, but lacks individuality. Radames, although made sympathetic by his love for Aida and his compassion for her people, is limited and conventional – 'the eternal school captain', as Budden has called him.[43] They cannot interest or move us as deeply as the leading figures in *La forza del destino* or *Don Carlos*.

But perhaps their very lack of individuality, of complexity, is part of the meaning of the opera. For what we find portrayed here is the absolute triumph of a system over all those individuals and groups who oppose or deviate from it. And part of its ascendancy consists precisely in the absence of individuality among those it controls. Consider what happens in the later stages of the opera. Radames is trapped by Aida into revealing the Egyptians' battle plan to her father Amonasro, the Ethiopian king. Overcome with remorse, Radames surrenders himself to the priests. It turns out that his inadvertent betrayal is immaterial: the Ethiopians are defeated anyway. That makes no difference: he is condemned to be buried alive, and the protests of Amneris, who is, after all, the king's daughter, are as ineffectual as if she were trying to demolish his prison with her own furious fingers. The theocratic system of Egypt has crushed Ethiopia, destroyed the lives of Amonasro, Aida and Radames, and brushed aside the anger of a princess. It is a terrible, despairing conclusion, mitigated only by the mutual devotion of Radames and Aida.

Aida is often thought of as an Egyptian opera: naturally enough, since it is set in Egypt, was composed to an Egyptian commission, and had its premiere in Cairo in 1871. Everyone remembers the scenes in which the Egyptians are cheered off to the battlefront ('Ritorna vincitor') and return victorious, to be greeted with the equivalent of a New York ticker-tape victory parade. If these are thought to be the core of the opera, Aida can seem a rather bombastic and imperialistic work. And it has sometimes been interpreted in that way. Under Mussolini (a later conqueror of Ethiopia), one production presented a Blackshirt Radames triumphing over the barbarous Africans. Seen from outside the West, its first half at least may look and sound like a triumphalist work from the high noon of European imperialism.

But this is to miss the emotional and even the musical balance of the work, and also the significance of its title. Aida is the emotional centre of the opera, and with her her country, Ethiopia. Aida is the classic Verdian exile, her plight worsened by the humiliation of slavery, and her yearning for her country is as strong and important to her as her love for Radames. Her superb Act Three aria, 'O patria mia', might well be considered the very heart of the opera, especially as the feelings she expresses here explain why she succumbs to her father's pressure to act as the bait to trap Radames. So it comes as a surprise to find that this aria was a late addition to the score. Aida's attachment to her homeland affects even her patriotic Egyptian lover, who in their Act Three duet seems finally to accept that flight to Ethiopia offers the only chance of happiness for them both – as Amonasro certainly understands. But even in Radames's first aria, 'Celeste Aida', he shows that he understands her longing to return home. As for her first aria, in a sudden, dramatic shift of focus our attention is directed to her unhappiness, abruptly undercutting any tendency we might have to identify uncritically with the bellicose mood of the Egyptians. They have been glorying in the prospect of war, Amneris has exultantly urged Radames to return as a conqueror – 'Ritorna vincitor' – and everyone else takes up her words. The stage empties, and Aida repeats the same words, horrified to think she has been urging Radames on to victory over her father, her brothers, her country. Thus Verdi reminds us that victory for some is always defeat for others.

Verdi did not like or even admire the civilization of ancient Egypt: 'a land which once possessed a grandeur and a civilization which I could never bring myself to admire'.[44] Those who let themselves be carried away by the pomp and circumstance of the triumph scene in Act Two may overlook the ways in which it replicates the *auto-da-fé* scene in its predecessor, *Don Carlos*. At Radames's request, the Ethiopian prisoners are brought before the king, and Amonasro pleads for mercy. In the big ensemble that grows out of this plea, it is the high priest Ramfis and his fellows who demand that the prisoners be put to death, while the *popolo* urge the priests to be merciful.

Throughout *Aida* it is the Egyptian priests who incarnate the most unbendingly cruel and bloodthirsty aspects of their national culture. It is they who, in the first scene, lead the demands for Egypt to respond to the Ethiopian challenge with war – 'Guerra! Guerra!' When in the next scene the priests invest Radames with armour, Ramfis prays that his sword may be a thunderbolt bringing terror and death to the enemy. It is to the priests that Radames gives himself up when he believes that he has betrayed his country. It is the priests who try him, denounce him and decide on his punishment, inspiring Amneris to denounce them as ministers of death, whose thirst for blood is never sated: 'Ne di sangue son paghi giammai'.

Verdi's anti-clericalism was never more overt than in *Aida*, and there were topical reasons for this. He was composing the opera at the time of the Franco–Prussian War and the collapse of the Papal States. The latter might have been expected to excite Verdi's patriotism, but the episode was too sordid, and too much of a compromise with church power, to afford him much pleasure. And when in the following year the collapse of the Paris Commune was followed by the massacre of many thousands of the Communards, Verdi wrote to a friend in Rome, 'Your priests are certainly priests, but they aren't Christians. The Papal Court couldn't find a word of pity for those poor martyrs of Paris, and that is really scandalous.'[45]

It seems likely that Verdi intended a comparison between his operatic Egyptians and the Prussians, whose success in the Franco–Prussian war he regretted and whose growing power and ambition he (rightly) feared. When it came to devising words for the vindictive priests in the triumph scene, he told his librettist Ghislanzoni, 'You must . . . add eight more [lines] for the priests to the effect that "we have conquered with the help of divine providence. The enemy is delivered into our hands. God is henceforward on our side". (See King William's telegram.)'[46] The telegram he referred to was the one sent by the King after the Prussian victory at Sedan.

Verdi was no militarist, and although he was more than capable of investing the scenes of pageantry in *Aida* with all the requisite brilliance and grandeur, even in the first two acts he does not conceal the harshness of the Egyptian regime, while in the last two only the repressive and malevolent aspects of this priest-dominated system are apparent. Nor is the system based solely on repression. Part of the tragedy of Radames is that he is so much a part of that system that he does not know how to defy it or break away from it. Amonasro tries to drag him away at the end of Act Three, but all Radames can see is that he has betrayed his country and dishonoured himself. So he insists on turning himself in – to the priests. His silence when they make their formal charges against him is the silence of a man who feels the guilt of which he is accused. Amneris finally perceives the iniquity of the system more clearly than Radames, with his simplistic ideas of loyalty, ever could. The Egypt of *Aida* is indeed a closed society, even a monolithic one, but Budden is surely wrong to suggest that the opera conveys 'an implicit acceptance' of such a society.[47] Such a message would be contrary to everything that Verdi believed in. Ultimately, it is the ruthless cruelty of that society that stays in our minds, not its capacity to stage impressive victory parades. *Aida* is a fearsome tragedy, not a mindless celebration.

With *Aida* we have reached the end of Verdi's great line of political, or partially political dramas. *Otello* and *Falstaff* were to come, as well as the revisions of *Simon Boccanegra* and *Don Carlos*, which show that he neither changed nor abandoned his fundamental convictions in later years. Nor, of course, were his two final masterpieces without their connections with the earlier works. Indeed in *Otello* we hear the final refinement and even sublimation of many features of his earlier works, including the Risorgimentale ones. There is the last of the comradely duets, this one, of course, being shot through with strains of irony and horror. There is the huge ensemble at the end of Act Three, as grand as anything he had composed for Paris or Cairo, and entirely justified by its context, for what we are witnessing once again is the ruin of a public figure, whose fall is a cause for general dismay, not a mere domestic tragedy. And in Act One we hear Otello, the hero and lover, successful and happy for a moment as so few of Verdi's tenor heroes had been. But there are no topical references, such as we can find in

Don Carlos and even *Aida*, and the old patriotic note is not sounded. As George Martin has said:

> In earlier days he might have composed an *Otello* in which Desdemona sings of Venice *O patria mia*. Instead he concentrated with more power than he had ever brought to an opera before on the two great mysteries of existence, love and death.[48]

Falstaff too, despite being the only comedy since *Un giorno di regno* more than fifty years earlier, has links with earlier works. Verdi's talent for comedy was apparent in parts of *Un ballo in maschera* and *La forza del destino*, and espisodes of light-hearted brilliance are to be found even in darkly tragic works like *Rigoletto, La traviata* and even *Otello*. But we can also see in *Falstaff* a merry variation on the pattern of conflict between a scheming aristocrat and the supposedly gullible, available lower orders, especially the women, which is also the pattern of *Luisa Miller* and *Rigoletto*. Falstaff, the decaying aristocrat with his rag-tag retinue, is pitted against the prosperous bourgeoisie of Windsor, whom he foolishly supposes will be impressed by his status and title; as in *Figaro*, it is the lower orders who win the day. As in *Figaro*, too, it is the women who get the better of the men, including not only the predatory aristrocrat but also the jealous husband or husband-to-be. But the class dimension is only lightly sketched in; it is far less important than it was in Mozart's *buffo* operas. Verdi's Windsor is a magical, serene world. He has at last moved beyond all the struggles and tragedies, political and personal, that had dominated his life and art, and has found, through music as always, 'nothing . . . for tears . . . nothing but well and fair', working once more, and for the last time, with his beloved Shakespeare.

5

Wagner: from Revolution to Racism

It has sometimes been said that, apart from Jesus of Nazareth and Napoleon, no single individual has been more written about than Richard Wagner. This need not be taken too seriously; but that it can be said at all is indicative of the degree of fascination and perplexity that this composer has uniquely aroused. It is certainly the case that Wagner's politics, their significance in German history, and their relation to his operas have been more discussed, and with greater passion, than those of any other composer. With good reason: for the issues are complex, full of uncertainty and ambiguity, and are far from being finally sorted out. If, indeed, they ever can be.

Most notoriously, there is the unavoidable, embarrassing fact that Wagner and his works were adopted as cultural symbols by Hitler and the Third Reich. And while it is always the case that works of art, like other creations, can be appropriated and misused for purposes remote from, and even antithetical to, those of their creators, in this case the question has to be asked: was Wagner's work misused by the Nazis, or are there elements in it that made that appropriation appropriate? That question, which many Wagnerites would like to see put to rest, continues to be asked for two serious reasons: because Wagner's thinking and writing were at times, and especially in his last years, openly and virulently anti-Semitic and racist; and because there was a continuous cultural and political tradition that linked Wagner's Bayreuth of the 1870s with the ideas and politics of the Third Reich.

Both these last assertions are doubtless disputed in some quarters – as are virtually all assertions about Wagner – but unconvincingly, in my view. But the central issue, and the most hotly debated, is whether and to what extent his political views, and especially his racist ideas, found their way into his operas, or music-dramas, as he preferred the later of them to be called. This is a book about politics *in* opera, rather than about the politics or political uses *of* opera; so this chapter will concentrate on that central issue.

Wagner was a political being. Yet there are plenty of commentators who have sought to deny even this, or to play it down. Wagner was 'really' or 'ultimately' only concerned with art, his art, they claim, and got involved in politics only in order to advance his artistic aims and projects. 'Political convictions meant nothing to Wagner except in relation to the idea of musical drama, the measure of all things for him,' according to Carl Dahlhaus.[1] A more suspect commentator, Houston Stewart Chamberlain (Wagner's son-in-law and an early supporter of Hitler), said much the same: 'In reality, Wagner never at any time had any sort of sympathy with *politics* properly so called. Politics and diplomacy, to Wagner's mind, go only skin deep.'[2]

According to such commentators, even Wagner's involvement in the revolutionary upheavals of the years 1848–49, which led to his being exiled from Germany for the next eleven years, was apparently motivated only by artistic concerns: 'The revolutionary activities which led to his exile were only marginally political,' according to Peter Burbidge.[3] And despite these admitted revolutionary activities, 'politics as such hardly impinged at all on his inner life', according to Curt von Westernhagen.[4] Suggestions of this sort are abundant in the Wagnerian literature. Let us then look briefly at Wagner's political views and involvements.

For someone who was allegedly unconcerned with politics, Wagner seems to have got embroiled with them remarkably often in a life of seventy years. As a very young man (he was born in 1813, the same year as Verdi) he welcomed the Year of Revolutions, 1830. Of the uprising in Leipzig he later wrote, 'the historical world began for me from this day; and naturally I was wholeheartedly for the revolution'.

These events inspired him to compose a 'political overture', which was later lost. He was moved, too, by the plight of the Polish revolutionaries who sought refuge in Leipzig after their uprising was suppressed in 1831. Their cause inspired another overture, *Polonia*, which he completed in 1836.[5]

In those years Wagner was involved with the movement known as Young Germany, a typical liberal nationalist movement of that time, and a leading figure in that movement, Heinrich Laube, published Wagner's first musical manifesto in 1834 and offered him an opera libretto he had written on the subject of the Polish national hero Koskiusko. But even at this stage Wagner was committed to writing his own libretti. All Wagner's early operas, from *Das Liebesverbot* through *Rienzi* to *Der fliegende Holländer* and *Tannhäuser*, embody to some extent ideas he absorbed from his involvement with Laube and Young Germany: in particular, ideas about the sacredness of love regardless of convention and custom, and the open celebration of sensuality.

When revolution broke out all over Europe once more in 1848, Wagner was again among its enthusiastic supporters. He wrote a poem welcoming the uprising in Vienna in March 1848, and was associated in Saxony with Vaterslandverein, 'the leading republican grouping', and was a regular contributor to the *Volksblätter*, a republican weekly, soon proscribed, edited by his friend and fellow musician, August Röckel. It was through Röckel that Wagner met the anarchist revolutionary Bakunin.[6] When in the spring of 1849 Röckel fled to Prague to avoid arrest, Wagner took over responsibility for producing the paper. Then in May revolution broke out in Dresden. At least two political meetings were held in Wagner's garden, and he may have been responsible for ordering the making of hand grenades. He printed and distributed a leaflet urging the Saxon troops to side with the people against the invading Prussians, and at the height of the conflict he had the task of monitoring troop movements from the top of a church tower. As Derek Watson has written, 'Although he tried to underestimate his commitment to the uprising in later years, the very detail of the account of it given in *Mein Leben* shows that he was close to the ringleaders.'[7]

Röckel and Bakunin were among those subsequently arrested, and Wagner escaped arrest by sheer chance. Röckel was condemned to death; the sentence was later commuted to life imprisonment. There is little doubt that Wagner, if arrested, would have met the same fate. As it was, he had to spend the next eleven years in exile from Germany, until in 1860 he was the beneficiary of a limited amnesty.

In exile he was still under police surveillance for several years, and remained in contact with many of his fellow political exiles, including Georg Herwegh and the architect Gottfried Semper, and by correspondence with the imprisoned Röckel. Nevertheless, after the Dresden debacle he turned away from direct political involvement for the most part, and concentrated on the immense project of writing and composing *The Ring*. After he became familiar with the writings of Schopenhauer in 1854 his entire outlook on politics and life itself was changed.

He never lost sight, however, of his ideal of a music that would speak to and for the people, the *Volk*. He was never content to be a mere composer, a purveyor of entertainment for audiences he despised. He always saw his artistic projects as being also political: part of a programme for reviving the spirit of the German people and welding it together. He wrote to Constantin Franz in 1866:

> . . . my own artistic ideal stands or falls with the salvation of Germany; without Germany's greatness my art was only a dream: if this dream is to find fulfilment, Germany, too, must necessarily attain to her preordained greatness.

He repeated this view to King Ludwig of Bavaria a month later.[8] In his relations with the king, he caused annoyance by acting as an unofficial adviser to the king on policy matters, including how Bavaria should react to the 1866 war between Prussia and Austria. After Prussia's victory Wagner, who had previously despised Bismarck, decided that Germany's destiny, and his own, were now tied to the Prussian leader's. In 1870–71 he was an enthusiastic supporter of the war against France; he wrote a patriotic ode 'To the German Army before Paris', which he sent to Bismarck, and a tasteless farce about the plight of the besieged Parisians. He also composed his *Kaisermarsch*, dedicated to Kaiser Wilhelm I.

In his last years at Bayreuth Wagner became increasingly preoccupied with the supposed threat that the Jews posed to the health and survival of the German nation, and was caught up in the vogue for racist theorizing which was fast gaining ground in Europe and North America at that time. Indeed 'caught up' gives too passive an impression of Wagner's role in this process. One of those who attended the first performances of the complete *Ring* cycle at Bayreuth in 1876 was the French theorist of race Count Joseph-Arthur de Gobineau. This visit marked the beginning of a close association with Wagner in the last years of the composer's life. Gobineau was the author of *Essai sur l'inégalité des races humaines*. First published in the 1850s, it had not attracted much attention until, 'entirely thanks to Wagner' according to Derek Watson, this 'pioneering' work of racist theory was 'given a rebirth'.[9]

Gobineau's views were more pessimistic than Wagner's, but they shared a preoccupation with racial purity and the evils of so-called miscegenation. These obsessions were then interwoven with Wagner's long-standing and ever-growing hatred of the Jews, and in this form became a dominant theme in the writings of Wagner's last years, including his essays in the *Bayreuther Blätter*, the magazine first published in 1878 to propagate the gospel of Wagnerism – a creed which was by no means purely aesthetic in content. Eager to rescue Christianity from its embarrassingly Jewish origins, Wagner even put forward the fatuous idea that Jesus himself was not a Jew. In that magazine the ideas of Gobineau were also vigorously promoted, if anything even more strongly after the master's death in 1883 than before.

This highly condensed summary, which gives little indication of the extent to which Wagner was immersed in, or even obsessed with, political issues at various times of his life, ought nevertheless to be enough to dispel the tendentious notion that Wagner was in some way 'above' or remote from politics.

Admittedly, it is hard to pin down Wagner, politically. Although a nationalist, he was not a straightforward liberal nationalist in the style of Verdi or Smetana. His nationalism was entwined with racism. But there were also egalitarian and even socialist elements in his thinking. He envisaged Bayreuth as a theatre for a classless audience, to which there would be free admission. *The Ring* certainly contains radical and socialist ideas. We might conclude that in his politics Wagner was muddled or, more charitably, complex and ambiguous, but certainly not that he was unpolitical. It remains to consider how far his politics are reflected or embodied in his operas.

Of the works composed before 1848, when Wagner began work on the gigantic project of *The Ring*, only one, *Rienzi*, is directly and strongly political. The early and generally unperformed works, *Die Feen* and *Das Liebesverbot*, as well as the three principal works of the 1840s, *Der fliegende Holländer*, *Tannhäuser* and *Lohengrin*, focus on romantic themes, above all the hero's quest for salvation, which, though not without political implications and, especially in *Tannhäuser* and *Lohengrin*, a nationalist dimension, do not place politics or public issues at their centre.

But *Rienzi* is Wagner's first and most inflated attempt at a Parisian-style grand opera, and also his most single-mindedly public work. In later life Wagner tended to repudiate *Rienzi*, since it represented everything that his theory of music-drama was a reaction against. And perhaps in deference to his views, it is often omitted from surveys of his works. It is, nevertheless, an interesting and revealing work when related to his opus as a whole. It was the work with which he hoped to make his name as a composer, by having it put on at the Paris Opéra. This hope was not realized, and the disappointments and poverty of his early years in Paris (1839–42) lay at the root of his later chauvinist hostility to all things French. But *Rienzi* was staged with great success in Dresden in 1842, and soon became one of his most popular works.

Rienzi, the Last of the Tribunes was based primarily on Sir Edward Bulwer-Lytton's novel of the same name. Cola di Rienzo was the man who, with the support of the Papacy, led a successful popular uprising against aristocratic rule in Rome in 1347. As leader he took the title 'tribune', naming himself after those who were the representatives of the people, or plebs, in ancient Rome, and ruled the city for seven months until he lost the support of both pope and people, and was overthrown. Papal agents brought him back to Rome seven years later, but his hour had passed, and he was murdered soon afterwards. Wagner conflates this untidy historical sequence into a single episode depicting the rise and fall of this legendary revolutionary figure.

Rienzi first appears as the unmistakable man of destiny. A character-istic stage direction reads: 'The Nobles are speechless with astonish-ment at Rienzi's commanding presence and his obvious power over the people.' The opera has opened with a scene which anticipates *Rigoletto*, in which a band of aristocratic men are trying to abduct Rienzi's sister Irene from her house. Part of Rienzi's appeal is his promise to put an end to this upper-class licentiousness, as well as the feuding between the Orsini and Colonna families that is tearing the city apart, and to restore law and order to Rome.

We can detect at once the ambiguity of Rienzi's politics. He is at one and the same time the popular leader against the excesses of the aristocracy, and the strong leader who will put an end to disorder and restore the city's ancient glory. In fact he is not an egalitarian, and assures Adriano Colonna that he does not aim at 'the destruction of your class' but to turn you 'from robbers into true aristocrats'. His downfall, although it is plotted by his aristocratic enemies throughout the opera, takes place when his allies, the people and the Pope, desert him. This is presented as an act of betrayal. It is the people who have failed their leader, and with his final words he denounces them accordingly:

> Wretches; unworthy of this name!
> The last Roman curses you!
> May this town be accursed and destroyed!
> Disintegrate and wither, Rome!
> Your degenerate people wish it so!

This might remind us of Hitler's railings against the German people in defeat, and the ambiguity of Rienzi's politics surely carries a strong suggestion of fascism. Hitler's friend in his early years in Vienna, August Kubizcek, recalled that it was a performance of *Rienzi* that first turned Hitler's ambitions away from art towards politics. Hitler did not deny this, and as Führer he became the owner of the autograph of the opera, which is presumed to have been destroyed in the conflagration of 1945. The association with Hitler, however embarrassing, seems to me not at all fortuitous in view of the type of leader and the type of politics that the opera depicts.

Departing from the novel, Wagner chooses to portray Rienzi as unmarried, and even gives him words in which he describes Rome itself as his bride. Rienzi is in some ways a more political version of the lonely heroes of *Der fliegende Holländer* and *Lohengrin*, figures of integrity whose sense of mission forever precludes them from commitment to ordinary human relationships, and who are finally let down or betrayed by the unworthiness of others. Except for Parsifal, these figures are doomed to failure and, usually, a tragic death. John Deathridge has rightly pointed out that *Rienzi* reveals that Wagner's political pessimism antedates *The Ring* and the failure of the revolutions of 1848–49.[10] But for a Berlin performance in 1847 Wagner altered the final words quoted above into a prophecy of the hero's return:

> As long as the eternal city does not cease to exist,
> You shall see Rienzi return again.

The new words reflect the more positive political mood in Germany at that time and, perhaps half-consciously, strengthen the sense of identity between Rienzi and the composer himself. It was a revealing slip when Wagner told a correspondent in 1841 that Rienzi was twenty-eight when 'he carried out his great undertaking'. In fact it was Wagner who was twenty-eight when he wrote the letter; Rienzi was thirty-four in 1347.

Wagner is perhaps the greatest example in music of what Keats found in Wordsworth: the egotistical sublime. Not only are all his heroes to some extent projections of himself, and often self-pitying ones. It is clear that in some works the projection extends beyond that. Thus Wagner sees himself as both Sachs *and* Walther, Wotan *and* Siegfried, Gurnemanz *and* Parsifal. There is not the sense in Wagner, except to a limited extent in *Rheingold* and *Die Meistersinger*, of attempting to portray actual societies, past or present, as say Mussorgsky and Verdi attempt to do. His stage works are gigantic projections of his own obsessions, dreams and fantasies. He has all the musical, dramatic and communicative powers necessary to draw us into sharing these preoccupations; but it is this all-encompassing egotism that accounts for the claustrophobic atmosphere of so much of his work, so that while we may be possessed by it, we also escape from it with a (perhaps half-guilty) sense of relief.

If one wished to dwell on the non-political aspects of Wagner, it would be natural to focus on *The Flying Dutchman*. The shadow of Beethoven looms over this work. Daland, with his obsession with money and his desire to find a rich husband for his daughter, Senta, is plainly modelled on *Fidelio*'s Rocco; Erik plays the equivalent role to Jaquino, the neighbourly long-time suitor who tries vainly to deflect the woman from her obsession with the mysterious, glamorous stranger. The open fifths which open the overture derive from the opening of the Choral Symphony, the work of Beethoven that impressed Wagner above all others. But it is the contrast with *Fidelio* rather than the similarities that is most striking. The Dutchman is not a victim of political injustice needing to be rescued from imminent murder; he is metaphysically doomed to endless restlessness as a result of a blasphemous defiance of God and nature. We are in the world of myth and legend, not the everyday world of prisons and oppression and struggle. Florestan obviously deserves our sympathy; it is much less clear that Vanderdecken does.

Retrospectively, Wagner sought to emphasize the German, or Nordic, character of *The Flying Dutchman*, and to stress its origins in German legend and his own experience. This was in line with his later fervent nationalism.[11] In fact his first version was a scenario written in French in 1840, and represented yet another attempt to win performance and fame in the French capital. And his principal source was an ironic account of the legend provided by Heinrich Heine; but it would have been embarrassing to the mature Wagner to acknowledge a debt to this celebrated Jewish radical.[12]

The German nationalist note is sounded much less unambiguously in his next two operas, *Tannhäuser* and *Lohengrin*, both of which are given a medieval German setting. *Tannhäuser und der Sängerkrieg auf Wartburg* was, as this double title indicates, a conflation of two different stories: the legend of Tannhäuser and Venus and the entirely unconnected story of a song contest that took place at the Wartburg castle during the reign of Hermann, Landgrave of Thuringia (1190–1217). It was the latter strand that carried the stronger nationalist overtones. For, as Timothy McFarland has explained, in the nineteenth century it was 'certainly the most famous castle in Germany'. Its associations with Luther's epoch-making defiance of the Emperor Charles V led to its being the location for a major nationalist demonstration in 1817, the tercentenary of the Reformation. This made the castle into 'a potent ideological symbol of German nationalism' and, adds McFarland, 'When Wagner wrote Tannhäuser . . . these political and historical associations were paramount in the public mind.'[13] Hence the lavish salutations to the castle itself, from Elisabeth ('Dich, teure Halle'), from the court and from the Landgrave, have a political resonance beyond the appearance of courtly routine. More centrally, *Tannhäuser* is a complex and perhaps indecisive study of the dialectic of sensuality and freedom, profane and sacred love. The victory of religion over sexuality is much more apparent than real, and Wagner was scornful of interpreters who 'insist on reading into my *Tannhäuser* a specifically Christian and impotently pietistic drift'.[14] But there is also a German nationalist dimension to the opera, even if it is not of central importance, and even if Wagner was later to exaggerate the extent to which he had consciously produced a truly German work based on truly German sources.

Exactly the same is true, and more explicitly so, of Wagner's next work, *Lohengrin*. This 'romantic opera' is a slightly uneasy mixture of fairytale and, in its culmination, personal tragedy, yet set in a specific historical context. It opens with an actual Saxon king, Henry the Fowler (919–36), appealing to the people of Brabant (in present-day Belgium), as fellow Germans(!), to join with him in resisting a Hungarian invasion: 'Need I tell you of the affliction so often wrought upon German soil from the East?' This is the critical situation in which the nameless knight (Lohengrin) appears to vindicate the good name of Elsa (who is falsely accused by Telramund of murdering her brother Gottfried) but also to lead the Brabantine troops into battle in response to Henry's appeal. And when finally he has to abandon this project, he leaves with a prophecy that 'Germany shall never, even in remotest days, be vanquished by victorious Eastern hordes!' Thus the salvation of Germany provides a context and a subtext to the main themes of the opera which, it has to be said, are far more to do with faith and doubt, Christianity and paganism, and with the Wagnerian hero's familiar search for a woman who will place unquestioning trust in him and his quasi-metaphysical mission. In this case the trust must literally be unquestioning: Elsa has to promise not to ask him his name. Her failure to keep this promise leads to the collapse of their marriage and his mission. It is a grim tale, which incorporates in the figure of Ortrud, the pagan sorceress who successfully undermines Elsa's trust in Lohengrin, Wagner's first portrait in sound as well as words of real evil.

Yet the overall impression left by *Lohengrin* is one of romantic radiance. Thomas Mann used to say that the Prelude to the opera was the quintessence of romanticism – he should have said of *German* romanticism – and the ethereal colour and texture of that Prelude pervade much of the whole opera, not least the enchanting bridal chorus at the start of Act Three, as well as Lohengrin's own arias, Elsa's dream, and the wonderful melody that brings the great duet between Elsa and Ortrud in Act Two to its uneasy conclusion. *Lohengrin* is one of my favourites among Wagner's operas, but it is one of the least political of his works. It marks the end of Wagner's career as a composer of romantic, medieval grand opera. With his next project, *The Ring*, and his next completed work, *Das Rheingold*, the composer embarks on a radically different course.

Der Ring des Nibelungen

More than six years elapsed between the completion of *Lohengrin* in April 1848 and that of Wagner's next opera, *Das Rheingold*, in September 1854. Eighteen months later he had finished *Die Walküre*, the second part of *The Ring*, and by August 1857 he had composed the first two acts of *Siegfried*. Then Wagner turned aside to undertake *Tristan und Isolde* and other projects, so not until 1871 did he finish the score of *Siegfried*. *Götterdämmerung* was completed in 1874, some twenty-six years after the project first took shape. This extended process might indicate a sequence of rather loosely connected dramas. In fact the reverse is true. It was Wagner's firm grasp of the tetralogy as a single entity with a clearly perceived culmination that enabled him to bring this unprecedentedly vast project to completion despite almost every kind of difficulty and discouragement. But an epic of this length, devised and composed by a genius of Wagner's complexity, was bound to be a many-layered, variegated work, not without loose ends, puzzles and internal contradictions. The sixty-year-old man who composed *Götterdämmerung* was very different, as a person and a musician, from the thirty-five-year-old author of *Siegfrieds Tod*, the scenario on which the final part of the tetralogy was based. His world-view had also changed radically since the project first took shape in his mind. The intellectual key to this change, it is generally agreed, was his encounter with the thinking of Schopenhauer, to whose writings he was introduced, ironically, by his revolutionary friend Georg Herwegh. Schopenhauer's *The World as Will and Idea* probably clarified, articulated and solidified ideas that were already forming in his mind. There are certainly indications that Wagner was developing a more pessimistic world-view in the years after 1849 even before he had read Schopenhauer.

The project was originally a utopian one. It was to show an old world dominated by power, coercion and greed being superseded by a new order inspired by love, spontaneity and freedom. Despite their tragic end, Siegfried and Brünnhilde represent this new world, by contrast with the old order dominated by Wotan and the gods and corrupted by the struggle for possession of Alberich's ring and the power it brings with it. It might seem perverse to locate this idealistic narrative in the mythologized early stages of human (and German) history, but there are two plausible reasons for this. One is to give universality to the theme of the drama by removing it from the present, or any specific society. The other is that there is an echo here of Rousseau's perspective on human history and prehistory: in the beginning human beings had certain simple virtues that the development of 'civilization' has all but obliterated. It is those simple virtues, mainly incarnated in Siegfried himself, that we need to recover.

At the very least this perspective implies the possibility of change in human society and human behaviour. This is precisely what Schopenhauer denies. For him the human condition is a permanently wretched one, in which suffering has an unavoidable role. To rail against it is futile and pointless. Resignation is the only rational response. Having begun *The Ring* in a more affirmative frame of mind, Wagner now tried to incorporate what he learnt from Schopenhauer. It was probably not a coincidence that he was composing *Die Walküre* at the time. His reading of Schopenhauer probably enhanced the intense sympathy with which he treats Wotan's recognition of failure in his great Act Two monologue. But Dahlhaus is surely right to argue that the work as a whole cannot support a Schopenhauerian interpretation.[15] For it to do that, Wotan would have to have become the central figure, and the 'end' for which he longs would have to be the end of the world not, as is the case, the end of the rule of the gods. And however much we may feel that Wotan is the most sympathetic figure in *The Ring*, he is not for all that the most central.

It is not Wotan but Siegfried who dominates the two last and longest evenings of the tetralogy, and his supplanting of Wotan is what Wotan himself had foreseen and willed. The change of name of the final drama from *Siegfrieds Tod* to *Götterdämmerung* only underlines this point. It is the gods whose doom is final, while Siegfried's death is the tragedy that is still intended to open the way to a new order of things, however slender the hope of that may be after we have witnessed all the corruptions and betrayals of *Götterdämmerung*. But the many different versions of the end of the whole work, and the many redraftings of Brünnhilde's peroration, indicate how difficult it was not only to bring this huge project to a convincing conclusion, but also to balance the positive (utopian) and negative (Schopenhauerian) elements – both of which are present in the completed work. In 1880 Wagner's wife Cosima recorded in her diary that Wagner 'takes a look at the ending of *Twilight of the Gods* and says that he would never do anything as complicated as this ever again'.

Politics runs right through the cycle, as I hope to show. But there is a sense in which *Das Rheingold* is the most politically explicit and, from a radical point of view, perhaps the most exciting, of all Wagner's works. It is also the most allegorical. Human beings as such make no appearance. Its cast includes gods, giants, dwarfs and the three daughters of the river Rhine. Taken at face value, it tells in what is, for Wagner, an unusually speedy way, a vivid if sometimes frightening and shocking story. It is, in other words, a typical German fairy story. Comparable elements occur later, especially in *Siegfried*, with its dragon-slaying and its speaking bird. Sir Peter Hall, producer of *The Ring* at Bayreuth in 1983, was reported as saying that '*The Ring* is about gods and saints and dwarfs and spells – not politics.'[16] But it would be ridiculous to suppose that a composer of Wagner's immense ambitions, a composer who took himself as seriously as Wagner did, would offer his adult audiences nothing more than a child's story of the struggle between dwarfs, gods and giants for possession of a magic ring. As Bernard Shaw wrote, '*Das Rheingold* is either a profound allegory or a puerile fairytale . . .'[17]

Shaw is still, in my view, the best guide to the meaning of this allegory. His interpretation of *The Ring* is widely known, and also widely dismissed, as an attempt to 'impose' a view of it which is variously dubbed as 'Fabian' or 'Marxist': two very different descriptions, although some who have used them seem to regard them as more or less interchangeable. But Shaw's perception of a socialist element in the cycle is, even *a priori*, more than plausible. The drama was first conceived at a revolutionary moment in European history in which, as we have seen, Wagner himself was dramatically involved. Shaw suggests that the Russian anarchist Mikhail Bakunin, whom Wagner had met, provides the model for Siegfried. Wagner had also been much impressed by the ideas of the radical young Hegelian thinker Ludwig Feuerbach, and it was to Feuerbach that he dedicated his essay of 1849 'The Artwork of the Future'. Feuerbach was an important influence on the young Marx, who was an almost exact contemporary of Wagner, being born in 1812. But there is no evidence that Wagner was familiar with any of Marx's writings.

The crucial question is, however, whether Shaw's interpretation of *Das Rheingold* makes sense in terms of both the music and the words. I think it does. Many commentators have taken up Deryck Cooke's epitome of *The Ring* as a conflict of power versus love – and rightly, I think. But in the first part of the cycle at least the power that is contended for is a very specific power: economic power, the power over production which is given by possession of Alberich's ring. Later on, this specificity is lost sight of, but in *Das Rheingold* it is crucial to the whole work. Consider the first scene. The gold lies there at the bottom of the Rhine, watched over by the three Rhinemaidens. They know the potential power of the gold, but it does not interest them. They enjoy it 'in an entirely uncommercial way, for its bodily beauty and splendour'.[18] The dwarf Alberich comes, and tries to get hold of each of the Rhinemaidens in turn, but without success. When the sun shines down on the gleaming gold, Wellgunde tells him of its potential power, but Woglinde adds that he who would achieve this power 'must pronounce a curse on love', something the lecherous dwarf is hardly likely to do. But there they are wrong. Frustrated in his advances to the three watery women, Alberich is in just the mood to renounce love. He does so, seizes the gold and makes off with it. He has made the hard choice between power and love, and when we next see him in the dwarfs' realm of Nibelheim, he has forged the ring, and through the ring controls his fellow dwarfs, who now work to produce wealth for him.

Nibelheim, to which Wotan and Loge descend in order to steal the ring from Alberich, is an image in sound as well as theatrical terms of the industrial capitalism that was fast developing in western and central Europe in the 1830s and 1840s. The gods come to Nibelheim in the same spirit of envious curiosity as some contemporary tourists visited an industrial city like Manchester.

> Of Nibelheim's dusky land
> we've heard a most marvellous tale.

Like any industrial city of that time, it is a place where money can be made, but not enjoyed. As Wotan points out:

> In joyless Nibelheim
> with gold there's nothing to buy!

But Alberich has his answer to that:

> . . . with my wealth
> from the darkness I'll rise,
> rise and be master of all things;
> the whole wide world
> I'll buy for myself with the treasure![19]

Even the gods on their 'glorious heights', an established leisured class who despise 'those who work below', will yield to his power. Women, whom he could not persuade to love him, will be available to him through the power of money: a prediction that comes true, as Wotan reveals in *Die Walküre*. And the key to all this is the productive power concentrated in the ring itself. So, when Alberich has been captured, he is reluctantly willing to surrender all the wealth the Nibelungs have produced, provided that he can retain the ring, through which that wealth can be re-produced and replaced. Similarly Wotan tries to cheat the giants by handing over all the treasure taken from Alberich, while keeping the ring for himself.

The price of economic power is the renunciation of love. But not only that. Alberich's curse on the ring is also a prophecy, as curses always are. Possession of the ring and its wealth will not bring happiness, and those who aspire to possess it shall also ruin their lives with envy and anxiety:

Its wealth shall yield
pleasure to none . . .

Care shall consume
the man who commands it,
and mortal envy
consume those who don't –
striving vainly
to win that prize.
But he who obtains it
shall find no joy! . . .

Who owns the ring
to the ring is a slave . . .

Alberich's warning is reinforced by Erda's, and once Wotan has surrendered the ring to the giants, they fall to quarrelling over it, until Fafner murders his brother to music of horrifying brutality. But while Alberich knows how to *use* the ring, Fafner is content with mere possession of it. Metamorphosed into a dragon, he simply sits on his treasure until he is conquered and killed by Siegfried. Alberich understands the difference between productive power and mere wealth. So does Wotan. Fafner does not.

The gods nevertheless succeed in outwitting Alberich. Like the old ruling class that they may be intended to represent, they may not be as rich as the new industrialists, but long experience has made them cunning. They exploit the boastfulness and vanity of Alberich, the self-made dwarf, the nouveau riche who cannot resist the fatal invitation to show off his newly acquired power. He falls into the trap that Loge has set for him.

Das Rheingold, like all Wagner's operas, is carefully named. The gold itself is at the centre of the drama, nowhere more disturbingly so than in the scene where Freia is bought with it, and it is piled up beside her until she is invisible to the besotted Fasolt. Shaw puts his finger on the meaning of this sordid scene:

Not unless there is gold enough to utterly hide her from them – not until the heap has grown so that they can see nothing but gold – until money has come between them and every human feeling, will they part with her.[20]

If Wotan, Alberich and the giants are all corrupted by greed to the point where they are prepared to commit crimes like theft and murder, the Nibelungs, including Alberich's brother Mime, are enslaved by the power of capital, and the Rhinemaidens are robbed to create it – much as the eighteenth-century rural poor were robbed of common lands by enclosure. Mime explains to the visiting gods how the Nibelungs used to work for themselves, but now:

> for him alone
> we sweat and we slave
> . . . so by day and night
> we serve the greed of our lord.

It may have been sentimental of Wagner, through Mime, to suggest that pre-industrial work was 'carefree' and creative. But many radical as well as conservative opponents of the new industrial capitalism believed that to have been the case. William Cobbett believed that 'when *master* and *man* were the terms, every one was in his place, and all were free. Now, in fact, it is an affair of *masters* and *slaves* . . .'[21]

In response to Mime, Loge promises that 'we can set free / the suffering Nibelung folk'. But for this to happen the original crime must be undone, and the gold returned to the Rhinemaidens, which does not happen until the very end of the whole cycle. The whole of the third scene of *Das Rheingold*, including, of course, the prelude and the postlude with their insistent hammerings, are the most vivid evocation of the dark, harsh world of early industrial capitalism in nineteenth-century music. Many years later, in 1877, Wagner visited the London docks, and found there an embodiment of Nibelheim: 'This is Alberich's dream come true – Nibelheim, world dominion, activity, work, everywhere the oppressive feeling of steam and fog.'[22]

In their great struggle for power and wealth, the chief protagonists, Alberich and Wotan – Licht-Alberich, as he calls himself later on – not only damage themselves and their fellows, they also violate nature. *Das Rheingold* opens with one of the most daringly original strokes in all music: 136 bars of E flat arpeggios, gradually accumulating in richness of texture, but unchanging in harmony. It is a gesture that at once establishes the immense scale and the weighty significance of what is to follow. It can be taken as representing the beginning of the world, but also the purely harmonious, euphonious character of the natural world before it was subject to human interference. Alberich's seizure of the gold is an act of theft but also an assault on nature. The productive power of the ring can be obtained only by exploiting nature rather than simply enjoying it, as the Rhinemaidens do. As soon as he has torn the gold from its rock, a symbolic darkness descends on the Rhine; the waters remain dark (as the Rhinemaidens complain later, in *Götterdämmerung*) until the gold is finally returned to them.

This is not the first violation of nature, however. That was the work of Alberich's rival, Wotan. He tore a branch from the World Ash-tree from which to fashion a spear that is the symbol of his authority and law. As a result, as the Norns explain in *Götterdämmerung*, the tree slowly died, and the spring that bubbled beside it dried up. Like Alberich, Wotan pays a price for his vandalism: he loses the sight of an eye. But nature suffers too.

Rousseau located the fatal 'wrong turning' taken by humanity far back in prehistory, and associated it with the invention of private property, the principle of possession, and a breaking of the links between 'man' and nature; just so, Wagner places the original crimes against both nature and humanity deep in the mythological past. It is a perspective that is both pessimistic and utopian: pessimistic because wrongs so deeply and so long embedded in human history cannot easily be put right; utopian because there is also the distant hope that the original harmony can be restored. Humanity is corrupt not by nature, but against nature.

The grandeur of the final pages of *Das Rheingold* – the passage known, when rendered orchestrally, as 'The Entry of the Gods into Valhalla' – is profoundly deceptive. As Loge, their cynical servant, comments:

> They are hastening on to their end,
> though they think they are great in their grandeur.

In effect he is addressing the audience, as narrator or chorus, and so setting a certain distance between us and what is happening on stage and in the orchestra. But even Wotan admits that Valhalla is built on a foundation of greed and deceit, and is less a symbol of power than a refuge from the evils that are to come. Wotan contracted with the giants to have it built in return for handing over to them Freia, the goddess of love. He only escapes from this outrageous deal by stealing the gold and the ring from Alberich and persuading the giants to accept these instead. The music tells us how shaky the basis of Valhalla is when, in the marvellous transition from Scene One to Scene Two, we hear the motif of the ring gradually transmuted in the motif of Valhalla. In the pompous conclusion to the opera words and music set up an ambiguous dialectic. For the final words are those of the robbed and lamenting Rhinemaidens:

> Goodness and truth
> dwell but in the waters:
> False and base
> all those who dwell up above.

The C flat minor chords that fall on the two key words (*falsch*) (false) and *feig* (base) partially undermine the D flat major of the concluding bars.

Das Rheingold has the largest and most varied cast of the four parts of *The Ring*. The focus is less on individuals than on the gods, the dwarfs, giants and Rhinemaidens as conflicting social groups, all engaged in struggle for possession of the gold or ring. It is about power, and power prevails over its opposite value, love. Those who represent love (Freia and Fasolt) or even domesticity (Fricka) or innocent pleasure (the Rhinemaidens) lose out to the male seekers after power. It is a kind of anti-love story, picturesque and vivid, but portraying a harsh public world of greed and ruthlessness. The consolation is that we know that this heartless social order is doomed. No society that sacrifices human values to the pursuit of wealth and power can survive indefinitely. Its internal conflicts, what Hobbes called 'the war of all against all', will ultimately destroy it. But it is not until the next part of the cycle that the alternative values really assert themselves with any effectiveness.

Die Walküre has always been the most popular part of *The Ring*, and Act One in particular is often given concert performances, and even recorded, on its own. This popularity, easily understood in musical terms because of the profusion of melodic and lyrical invention in Act One, is nevertheless ironic. Act One of *Die Walküre* is the one act in the entire cycle whose cast consists solely of human beings: it is a classic triangle of bullying husband, unhappy wife and handsome young lover. In this act we can almost forget about Wotan's plans and the direction of the whole cycle in our absorption in this simple, basic human drama. But what this suggests is that many music-lovers are not entirely at ease with Wagner's mythology and grand design, and would secretly prefer him to have written 'normal' operas about 'real' people, uncomplicated by epic themes and heavily significant symbols. Wotan's farewell to Brünnhilde in Act Three can move us in the same simple way: a father bids a final fond farewell to his favourite child.

All this is a part of Wagner's grand design. If we are fortunate enough to see or hear *Die Walküre* soon after *Rheingold*, we shall be struck, as Wagner surely intended, by the contrast between the hard political conflicts of the one and the tender human emotions evoked by its immediate sequel. But there are complications, even in Act One of *Die Walküre*, which no attentive listener and watcher can ignore for long. There are many backward musical references, especially to the Valhalla motif, which make it clear that Wotan is lurking somewhere in the background to this story. Indeed Wagner at one time planned to have Wotan appear to plant the sword in the tree but, with his usual sound artistic judgement, abandoned the idea. And what about that sword? The drama at this point hardly requires it, so, despite its obvious sexual symbolism, the musical climax that Wagner builds around its withdrawal from the tree makes it plain that more than human forces are at work in Hunding's forest home.

But above all there is the issue of incest. That Siegmund and Sieglinde are brother and sister can hardly be missed, since Wagner makes this discovery a climactic point of their scene together; it is with the rapturous cry of 'Braut und Schwester' ('Bride and sister') that Siegmund prepares to make love to her as, in Wagner's tactful stage direction, 'the curtain falls quickly'. (There is nothing, incidentally, in those directions about the lovers rushing out into the forest at the end of the act, as some bowdlerized accounts of this scene would have it.) As Shaw observed, the act ends at the point where 'the conventions of our society demand the precipitate fall of the curtain'.[23]

The idea of brother and sister becoming lovers was not Wagner's invention. It was there in the Volsung Saga. But the prominence given to it in *Die Walküre* is very much Wagner's responsibility. He is trying not to embarrass, but to challenge us. He saw nothing wrong in incest, as we know from his comments on the Oedipus story: 'Did Oedipus offend against human nature when he married his mother? Certainly not. Otherwise nature would have shown its offence by not permitting any children to be born to the marriage; but nature, if no other power, was quite content.' That was in *Opera and Drama*, written in 1850.[24] His endorsement of both adultery and incestuous love is in line with the celebration of sensuality that he learnt from Young Germany; the Walsung twins are part of the challenge to the old world of laws, rules and conventions. When Fricka, guardian of conventional morality and monogamous marriage, expresses her outrage in Act Two, Wotan retorts:

> Unholy
> call I the vows
> that bind unloving hearts.

Wagner's view, partially inspired by his own experience, was that a loveless marriage is no marriage at all; although he had the usual male vested interest in sexual freedom, it is fair to point out that he was appalled by the treatment of women as property by their husbands; that, of course, is the position of Sieglinde in relation to Hunding. Wagner attached great social significance to uninhibited sexual love, and Siegfried's role as a rebel and outsider is partly established by his being the offspring of an incestuous union (perhaps, too, by his involvement in another, for Brünnhilde is his aunt).

Thus the impression that Act One of *Walküre* is a semi-detached section of the cycle is to some extent illusory. But not wholly so. Although Acts Two and Three place the Siegmund/Sieglinde relationship firmly in the context of the cycle as a whole, in terms of the plot *Die Walküre* remains the most dispensable part of the tetralogy. For Siegmund's revolt represents Wotan's false start: an attempt by the god to recover the ring by proxy, which is doomed because, as Fricka quickly perceives, it is fraudulent. Siegmund is not the free being who is needed to inaugurate the new order. He is Wotan's tool. It is for that reason that he has to die. He is the innocent victim of Wotan's misconceived plotting or, as Deryck Cooke said, 'surely . . . the most contemptibly betrayed of all Wagner's heroes'.[25]

Nevertheless, Siegmund's death, and even more his readiness to defy death for the sake of his love for Sieglinde, mark a turning point in the cycle as a whole. It is Siegmund's refusal to go with Brünnhilde to Valhalla leaving Sieglinde behind that opens Brünnhilde's eyes to the reality of love, and leads her in her turn to defy Wotan. For her defiance of her father, she is of course punished, but by the paradox which is at the heart of the cycle, he needs that defiance if the curse of the ring is finally to be undone.

Wotan, meanwhile, has accepted that he and his fellow gods are doomed, and this acceptance is expressed in the great monologue, addressed to Brünnhilde as if she were part of himself, which lies at the heart of Act Two. Some commentators adopt a defensive or apologetic tone in relation to this scene. This seems to me unnecessary. It takes us not only into the heart of Wotan himself, but also to the heart of what is tragic in the cycle as a whole. From here until the death of Siegmund at the end of the act we apprehend the terrible costs that are exacted in terms of human suffering by this social order committed to convention, force and greed; we share the despair of the god or ruler who longs to see free beings walk the earth, but knows that they cannot be produced by manipulation or decree, and who therefore turns away with disgust when he discovers only echoes of himself in what his power can achieve:

> With loathing
> I can find but myself
> in all my hand has created!

In this sharp antithesis between freedom and power, freedom and law, which Wotan so eloquently articulates, there is more than a hint of the anarchist world-view which Wagner may have absorbed from his contacts with Bakunin.

Die Walküre is the most tragic of the four parts of *The Ring*, and what makes it tragic is not only the wretched fate of Siegmund and Sieglinde, but the fact that Wotan finds himself compelled to inflict that fate, and also to punish his beloved daughter Brünnhilde, against his own deeper desires and impulses. The agonies of rulers who punish and execute their own subjects with a heavy heart are, or should be, less touching than the fate of their victims. But Wotan is a more complex figure than that. He is a divided man (god) who belongs to the old order but knows and accepts that it is finished, who is so tied into it that he cannot nourish the forces he wishes to see arise and displace it.

> . . . observe him closely! he resembles *us* to a tee; he is the sum total of present-day intelligence, whereas Siegfried is the man of the future whom we desire and long for but who cannot be made by us, since he must create himself on the basis of *our own annihilation*. In such a guise, Wotan – you must admit – is of extreme interest to us . . . [26]

Indeed he is, and nowhere more so than in Act Two of *Walküre*. But still, he belongs to the present and the past. It is Siegfried who is the man of the future, and it is to him and his eponymous opera that we must now turn.

The problem with *Siegfried* is, in a word, Siegfried. There can be no doubt, no mistake about it: Siegfried is intended to be the tragic yet ultimately redemptive hero of the whole cycle. He is Wagner's 'man of the future'. Yet even devoted Wagnerians have been dismayed by the actual character of this putative hero. Is Siegfried really the Wagnerian ideal man?

Everything in the cycle that comes before him is intended to point forward to Siegfried and the tragic action through which the world is cleansed of the old corruption and a new start is made possible. Siegfried with Brünnhilde – and the partnership of man and woman is essential to the project – represents the new, free and more human society that can, and perhaps will, come into being after the collapse of the flawed and tainted world order presided over by Wotan. As Wagner explained, in one of those all-important letters to Röckel:

> . . . my Nibelung poem . . . had taken shape at a time when, relying upon my conceptions, I had constructed a Hellenistically optimistic world for myself which I held to be entirely realizable if only people wished it to exist. . . . I recall now having singled out the character of my Siegfried with this particular aim in mind.

In another letter he wrote, 'in Siegfried I have tried to depict what I understand to be the most perfect human being.'[27] So much, then, for Wagner's intentions in relation to Siegfried. How are they realized?

We first see Siegfried in relation and contrast to Mime, Alberich's brother, who though no longer confined to Nibelheim is still tied to manual labour at his forge in the forest. Mime falsely claims to be Siegfried's father, but he is in effect his foster parent, having brought him up after Sieglinde died in giving birth to him. Mime's long-term plan is to get Siegfried to kill Fafner the dragon. He will then poison Siegfried and obtain the ring. Mime is as much obsessed with the ring and its power as are Alberich and Wotan. But he still belongs to the world of joyless, repetitive toil, and it is of his wearisome work that he complains in the first words of the drama, while we have been reminded in the orchestral prelude that we are not far from the dark land of Nibelheim (Wagner originally planned to reintroduce the Nibelung dwarfs into the drama at this point).

Siegfried, by contrast, makes his appearance as in every way a free being. He is free from the bondage of labour, but also free from the greed for power and property that obsesses the dwarf brothers. When he picks up the ring and Tarnhelm from Fafner's hoard, it is

> because the woodbird said I should.
> I know not their use

Mime is oppressed with care, obsessed with scheming. Siegfried is carefree, lighthearted and fearless. His first entry makes an obvious contrast with that of Siegmund at the opening of *Walküre*. Siegmund is the fearful, hunted man; Siegfried has been hunting, and brings home a bear. Mime is petrified with fear.

It is an aspect of Siegfried's uncorrupted nature that he enjoys a unique rapport with nature, symbolized by his ability to understand the language of birds. And whilst to Mime the forest is a place of terror, for Siegfried it is the terrain of pleasurable adventure. This rapport signifies the renewal of that harmony between humanity and the natural world that was disrupted by the theft of the Rhinegold and Wotan's wounding of the World Ash-tree which, he reveals in his conversation with Mime, is now dead.

We could also say that Siegfried's openly expressed loathing and revulsion for Mime is a natural, instinctive reaction against the dwarf's barely concealed malevolence and evil. But I think we are bound to feel uneasy about the tirades of abuse and insult that the young hero heaps upon the old dwarf, who is, after all, his foster father. And if we are tempted to excuse Siegfried's rudeness to Mime, what are we to make of his response to the Wanderer in Act Three? Siegfried is not to know that he is dealing with his own grandfather, but when Wotan suggests that he should honour the aged, Siegfried explicitly invokes Mime as his justification for not doing so. Siegfried has to overcome Wotan's resistance, but his impatience and contempt for the old man who tries to bar his way is, to say the least, not particularly endearing.

But there is a further and still more disturbing dimension to Siegfried's treatment of Mime, and that is its thinly disguised racism. When Mime tries to claim that he is Siegfried's father, the young man rejects this idea on the grounds that the two of them obviously belong to different orders of beings. I have seen my face in a stream, says Siegfried, and I resemble you

> no more than a toad
> resembles a fish.
> No fish had a toad for a father!

If we add to this the degree to which Mime's way of singing conforms to Wagner's notorious description of the supposed Jewish manner of speech in his essay 'Jewishness in Music' ('Das Judentum in der Musik') – if it is the case that both dwarfs are intended as anti-Semitic caricatures – then it begins to look as if Siegfried's intuitive reaction against Mime is meant to represent the natural disgust that those of superior race are supposed to feel towards inferior beings. This is one of several points in Wagner's musical works where there must be at least a suspicion that his adherence to racist theories and his persistent anti-Semitism play a significant role. And blood purity does play a role in the scheme of The Ring. When Siegfried and Gunther swear their oath of blood-brotherhood (Blutbruderschaft) in Act One of Götterdämmerung, Hagen does not join in, explaining:

> My blood would spoil all your drink;
> my blood's not pure
> and noble like yours;

Hagen is, of course, Alberich's son. Moreover, Siegmund's final words of exaltation in Act One of Walküre seem to suggest that incest, far from being objectionable, has the virtue of confining procreation to those of the same 'blood'.

To return to Siegfried himself. It is in fulfilment of his destiny as harbinger if not creator of the new human order that he sweeps aside all the elements of the old order, dragons, dwarfs and gods, in the course of his advance towards Brünnhilde and the ring of fire that surrounds her. To enter that ring, it is necessary that he should be fearless. But must he also be witless? In *Siegfried* his courage enables him to overcome every obstacle that stands between him and Brünnhilde; in *Götterdämmerung* this same heedless onward drive leads him straight into the traps Hagen lays for him. To whom does he listen, apart from the Woodbird? He pays no attention to what Wotan has to tell him. Brünnhilde, too, has much to say, but Siegfried again finds it hard to listen. He tells her:

> You sing of the past,
> but how can I listen,
> while I have you beside me,
> see and feel only you?

It may be said that it is natural for him to be overwhelmed by his first encounter with a woman, but his inattentive ardour reminds me too much of Lieutenant B.F. Pinkerton trying to hustle the far more sensitive Butterfly into their wedding bed. And when the final trap is closing on him, and the Rhinemaidens appear to warn him and beg him for the return of the ring, he is deaf to what they have to say. Or rather, he interprets their warning, and their explanation of the curse on the ring, as a threat to be defied, and as typical women's reaction to his resistance to their advances. This is hardly a very intelligent response. In fact it is a piece of misplaced chauvinist patronage.

How conscious, how aware, is Siegfried of what he is doing, of what happens to him? The obverse of his energy and impetuosity is that he seems not to understand his own life, so that at its very end he seems to have learned distressingly little from all he has lived through in so short a time. It is clear that this question arose even before the music of the last two dramas was written, for Wagner tries to deal with it in his correspondence with Röckel:

> . . . my hero should not leave behind the impression of a totally unconscious individual: on the contrary, in Siegfried I have tried to depict what I understand to be the most perfect human being, whose highest consciousness expressed itself in the fact that all consciousness manifests itself solely in the most immediate vitality and action . . . [28]

The convoluted syntax of the last clauses is the giveaway: this really is no answer at all. And Wagner surely makes matters worse by immediately citing the scene with the Rhinemaidens as demonstrating that 'Siegfried is infinitely wise, for he knows the highest truth, that death is better than a life of fear . . .' It is not clear that this *is* the choice before Siegfried at that moment; his incomprehension of what they are telling him means that it is left to Brünnhilde to perform the necessary act of restitution by returning the ring to the Rhinemaidens.

These are some of the reasons why Siegfried as 'the most perfect human being' and 'the man of the future' has appeared to many commentators grotesquely inadequate. Ernest Newman, that most devoted of Wagnerians, dubbed him 'an overgrown boy-scout', while Carl Dahlhaus described him as 'an insensitive, foolish bully to start with and later . . . a would-be deceiver who is himself deceived'.[29] Robert Gutman refers to him as 'the hooligan Siegfried', and Theodor Adorno characterized him as 'a bully-boy, incorrigible in his naivety, imperialistic in his bearing'.[30] No doubt it was these very characteristics that excited admiration for Siegfried among the Nazis: Siegfried as the arrogant, aggressive and above all mindless Nordic hero.

Wagner, however, is emphatic that the end of the old order is to be brought about by Siegfried *and* Brünnhilde:

> Not even Siegfried alone (man alone) is the complete 'human being': he is merely the half, only with *Brünnhilde* does he become the redeemer; . . . a suffering, self-immolating woman finally becomes the true, conscious redeemer: for it is love which is really 'the eternal feminine' itself.[31]

Remembering what Wagner also said about women being treated as property, it is clear that in *The Ring* at least women are being accorded a more positive role than in the earlier operas. It is Brünnhilde who, after Siegfried's murder, understands what has to be done and carries out the act of reparation needed to wipe out the original crime. The gold is returned to the Rhine, and as Valhalla burns in the sky, reconciliation and hope are suggested by the return of the theme originally heard in connection with Sieglinde's expression of thanks to Brünnhilde. Wagner referred to it as 'the glorification of Brünnhilde'. The Valkyrie certainly makes a more positive hero than Siegfried.

Even her furious determination to avenge herself on Siegfried when she discovers that he has apparently deserted her for Gutrune is at least a positive act, whereas Siegfried's susceptibility to Hagen's amnesiac drug shows how his very innocence exposes him to manipulation by his enemies.

Yet both Siegfried and Brünnhilde are so readily drawn into Hagen's dark world of treachery, rape and murder that their credibility as the representatives of a new and better social order is inevitably called into question. They too are corrupted by the accursed ring. For them it is symbol of love: its power is of no interest to Siegfried. Nevertheless, it is through the ring that Brünnhilde becomes aware of her betrayal, and both of them refuse requests to return it to the Rhinemaidens.

In the final act of *Götterdämmerung* Wagner expends all his musical and dramatic gifts on re-creating the tragic stature of Siegfried and Brünnhilde. Siegfried is able to remind us of his vitality, innocence and charm in his final narration, whilst his dying greeting to Brünnhilde recalls their happiness together; his funeral march, if grandiose, synthesizes at least ten motifs from the entire cycle. Brünnhilde, in her peroration, attains dignity, compassion and wisdom. But is it enough? It was she who betrayed Siegfried to Hagen. Her 'Liebestod' can hardly be as unambiguous as Isolde's rapturous paean of devotion.

Wagner had great difficulty in finding the right conclusion to the whole cycle, and Brünnhilde's final words in particular were drafted and re-drafted. The uncertainties and puzzles have not been entirely eliminated from the ending as we have it. Wagner originally envisaged the gods being saved by the return of the gold to the Rhine. Siegfried and Brünnhilde would ascend to Valhalla as their triumphant rescuers. He rightly sensed that this was too glib, too much in the style of conventional grand opera – a style to which, as Shaw argued, he had already made too many concessions in some parts of *Götterdämmerung*, especially Act Two – quite apart from being politically conservative rather than radical. Instead he opted for the fiery destruction of Valhalla, a vision that reflected his rather apocalyptic mood in the years after 1849. He told Theodore Uhlig in 1850:

> I no longer believe in any other revolution save that which begins with the burning down of Paris. . . . Does that alarm you? . . . just as we

need a water-cure to heal our bodies, so we need a fire-cure in order to remedy (i.e. destroy) the cause of our illness – a cause that is all around us.

Ten months earlier he had told Uhlig, 'There can only be a single moment in the revolution, a token of affirmation in the process of destruction. Destruction alone is what is now needed . . .'[32] These words are remarkably close to Bakunin's celebrated dictum, 'The urge to destruction is a creative urge.'

So the end of the cycle reflects Wagner's post-1849 obsession with a 'fire-cure' to cleanse the world. But the question that Röckel raised remains unanswered: 'why, since the Rhinegold is returned to the Rhine, [do] the gods nevertheless perish?'[33] Again and again we hear that the return of the gold will rescue the gods from their doom. But in the end it does not, and the title of the final part of the cycle indicates that Wagner was determined that the gods must perish to make way for the new order. And since they represent the old order of states, force and laws, that is logical enough. But this perspective contradicts the original design, in which Wotan was to survive, a monarch presiding over a republic in the manner envisaged by Wagner for Saxony in 1848. And since Siegfried and Brünnhilde are dead too, the question of who is to establish the new society in a world burnt and washed clean of the old corruption remains unanswered, as it was in Wagner's own post-1849 political speculations.

The moments of hope and reconciliation with which the cycle ends sound even more fragile when we consider what has preceded them. *Götterdämmerung* is by far the darkest part of the whole cycle. Once the exultant duet between Brünnhilde and Siegfried is over, and the hero has set out on his fateful journey to the Rhine, he enters the gloomy, treacherous world of the Gibichungs: the glory fades from the music at the end of Siegfried's Rhine journey, and sinister motifs replace it. From here on an aura of evil hangs over the work, and nowhere more heavily than in Act Two which, from its opening nocturnal dialogue between Alberich and Hagen to its concluding trio of murderous plotting, is not relieved by a single ray of moral light or even normal human sensitivities.

This act is the one where we can most clearly *hear* what it is in Wagner that anticipates the barbarism of the Third Reich. Hagen's vassals have sometimes been portrayed on stage as stormtroopers. It is easy to see why. Not only do they come on stage spoiling for a fight. Their noisy unanimity has a shouted brutality about it which sounds to me to be as close to an expression of fascism in musical terms as has ever been achieved. Equally horrible is the music to which Siegfried and Gunther take their oath of blood-brotherhood in the first act, and the brutal music with which the act ends, when the disguised Siegfried tears the ring from Brünnhilde's finger and forces her into the cave – 'with every appearance of impending rape', as Robert Donington put it.[34]

To say that Wagner endorses this barbarous culture would be absurd. These are clearly the forces of evil at work. But this musical evocation of evil and brutality is so strong, so vivid, and these forces so completely engulf Siegfried and Brünnhilde at this stage in the drama, that we can only wonder who or what could stand against them. Thus the utopianism of the original design, though not wholly lost, is threatened and undercut both by the inadequacy of Siegfried (as a prototype of the man of the future and as a counterweight to Wotan) and by the disturbing power of Wagner's creation, in the final part of the great cycle, of a world of pervasive violence, hatred and duplicity.

Nothing will be said here of *Tristan und Isolde*, except to observe that this is surely, in its intended character, the most deliberately anti-political of all great operas. It is therefore made much of by those many commentators who wish to stress Wagner's distaste for politics, his supposed absorption in the timeless and mythical. But it is the *only* work of his maturity, and the only one of his last seven music-dramas, in which politics has this entirely negative signification. In *Die Meistersinger* and *Parsifal*, as in *The Ring*, it is an entirely different story.

Die Meistersinger von Nürnberg

Note the title. It is not 'The Adventures of Walther von Stolzing'. It is not 'The Humiliation of Sixtus Beckmesser'. It is not even 'The Shoemaker Poet'. No one individual is the focus of this drama. Here the community contains the individuals, and at the end of the opera even Walther, the aristocratic outsider, is reconciled to membership of the town's most prestigious artistic elite, the Mastersingers. There are many similarities with *Parsifal*. Walther, like Parsifal, is the young outsider whose courage and independence rescue a community in decline. And in both operas the outsider effects that rescue with the support and assistance of a rather isolated older and wiser member of that community. Hans Sachs is a more active, energetic Gurnemanz, able to recognize an unorthodox talent when all his more hidebound colleagues can see is the unorthodoxy. One theme of *Die Meistersinger* is the one later to be orchestrated by Richard Strauss in *Ein Helden-leben*: that of the genius versus the critics, creative originality in conflict with the petty rule-obsessed carping of the professional critics, those favourite butts of the supposedly misunderstood artist. Wagner sees himself as both Walther, the innovative outsider, and Sachs, the perceptive patriot who rises above the rules and rescues German music from incipient stagnation. Beckmesser is, famously, a caricature of the Viennese critic Eduard Hanslick, who had initially hailed Wagner's genius but later turned against him and championed the music of Brahms, which Wagner despised. In an early draft, Beckmesser was actually called Hanslich; Hanslick himself was invited to a reading of the libretto by Wagner in 1862, but he recognized himself as the target of Wagner's cruel comedy and walked out.

Die Meistersinger is a bourgeois comedy, not merely in the sense that it is about a bourgeois community, but also because it celebrates the triumphant survival of that community and its successful incorporation of Walther, the aristocratic outsider. In the sensible, workaday world of Nuremberg, Walther the knight cuts an exaggerated, anachronistic figure. He woos Eva in the first scene in elaborately courtly language, whilst her maid, Magdalene, makes typically down-to-earth responses. His hand flies to his sword when he hears the Nightwatchman's horn in Act Two, and his reaction to the obstacles put in the way of his marriage with Eva is to suggest a romantic elopement, which Sachs sees at once would be a disaster. No one else wears a sword in Nuremberg. As Adorno noted, there is more than a hint of Don Quixote's absurdity about the untamed young Walther.[35] It is almost as if Wagner were mocking the chivalric and militaristic conventions that play so large a part in his own dramas of the 1840s, *Tannhäuser* and *Lohengrin*. And perhaps he was, since he first conceived of *Die Meistersinger* in the mid 1840s as a kind of comic pendant to *Tannhäuser*.

In its realism and historical specificity, *Die Meistersinger* is unique in Wagner's output. If we try hard, we can locate *Tannhäuser*, *Lohengrin* and even *Tristan* and *Parsifal* in more or less specific times and places, but apart from the German references in *Tannhäuser* and *Lohengrin*, particularity of time and place is not important to any of these works, to say nothing of *The Ring*. But *Die Meistersinger* is a tale of sixteenth-century Nuremberg, and the libretto is peppered with detailed historical references, such as Eva's comparison of Walther to Dürer's picture of David vanquishing Goliath, or the use of the historical Hans Sachs's ode in praise of Luther in the last scene of the work. Not only that, but considerable attention is paid to the mundane details of daily life in the town. Hans Sachs really does make shoes; his apprentice David works long hours for delayed rewards. Magdalene, too, has her hands full keeping an eye on Eva and coping with her various whims and requests.

Wagner started with the idea of a community, and it is that community whose themes dominate the overture, which he composed before the opera itself. Later the individuals at the centre of the drama came to assume more importance in his scenario, especially Sachs, whose themes do not feature at all in the overture. But the work begins and ends with that community, and it begins and ends in the C major of the Mastersingers' themes. When the overture or prelude comes to its exultant conclusion, it is the massed voices of the community, still in C major, that we hear first from the stage. That is also the key of Walther's prize song, which may perhaps be taken to symbolize his ultimate incorporation into the singers' guild. *Die Meistersinger*, like *Parsifal*, is a fable of the triumph of the community over the individual. But the relationship is a dialectical one: community and individual need each other. Nuremberg needs Walther as much as Walther needs Nuremberg. In the same way Wagner was convinced that Germany needed him, even as he saw himself as quintessentially German.

For no work of Wagner's is more self-consciously and explicitly German, both in its music and its words. *Die Meistersinger* is one of the supreme artistic achievements and expressions of German nationalism; it is not surprising, even if it is embarrassing, to find that the most extreme of German nationalists, the Nazis, gave it a place of honour in their own narrow and racist version of 'true' German culture. Wilhelm Furtwängler conducted a special performance in March 1933 to mark the founding of the Third Reich; even before that, in 1924, performances at Bayreuth had been greeted by Nazis with the singing of the national anthem and shouts of 'heil'.[36]

It is entirely understandable that some lovers of *Die Meistersinger* and devotees of Wagner should react to this by claiming that the opera really has little or nothing to do with German nationalism. Thus Deryck Cooke wrote, apropos of *Meistersinger*, that 'if we knew as little of his life and opinions as we know of Bach's – which is nothing – we should never guess from his art that his personal political viewpoint was that of an extreme right-wing German nationalist'. But the more we know about this opera and its context, the more clearly does its nationalist meaning stand revealed. Most discussion of this has focused on Sachs's final peroration, in which he warns of the danger of the German people and empire falling under false French domination (Barry Millington has explained why *walsch* can only mean 'French' in this context), unless the national spirit is kept alive through holy German art ('die heil'ge deutsche Kunst'). Millington points out, quite fairly, that 'The passage is not a call to arms but an affirmation that even foreign domination cannot obliterate the German spirit so long as it resides in the art of the old masters and they are respected.' Even so, Wagner had been inclined to cut out this passage, but was persuaded by Cosima to retain it, perhaps against his better judgement. With its anti-French references and its lauding of an art that is 'German and true', it is difficult in the light of subsequent history not to find this passage unattractive if not sinister. To suggest, as did Cooke, that its context is 'purely historical', that is, purely sixteenth-century, is not plausible, any more than it would be to say that *Nabucco* was purely about the situation of the Jews in Old Testament Babylon.[37] *Die Meistersinger* is an opera of the 1860s and Sachs's warning belonged to the 1860s as much as to the 1560s. It would be absurd to think that Wagner intended no contemporary relevance.

But even without this passage, the opera as a whole is a work of German nationalism. The community Wagner depicts is a specific one, Reformation Nuremberg, and it is worth asking why he chose it. The city had become a symbol of German independence and German history. As a city, it had survived 'intact from the idealized heroic age of Albrecht Dürer and Martin Luther'. The real sixteenth-century Nuremberg was an international banking and trading centre, more like the Venice of Shakespeare's *Merchant of Venice* than the 'self-contained, rather inward-looking community of skilled craftsmen' depicted by Wagner.[38] Wagner uses the names of real Mastersingers, but assigns to them generally more modest occupations than they had in real life. As Newman observed, 'These people were probably not artisans, in the sense in which Wagner employs that term, but well-to-do business men . . .'[39] But it was the more picturesque, quasi-medieval image of Nuremberg that dominated nineteenth-century mythology, and it was this that Wagner chose to elaborate and endorse in *Die Meistersinger*. In his letters to King Ludwig written while he was at work on the opera, Wagner waxed lyrical about Nuremberg and its significance:

> Nuremberg, the old true seat of German art, German uniqueness and splendour, the powerful old free city, well-preserved like precious jewel. . . . Do you know what this strange old town of Nuremberg now means to me? It is the abode of the 'art-work of the future', the Archimedes point at which we shall move the world – the inert mass of the stagnating German spirit![40]

Nostalgia for the lost community, for *Gemeinschaft*, has played an important part in modern German politics, not least in the right-wing reaction against the democracy of the Weimar Republic, and this too helps to explain the popularity of this work with the Nazis. The passages in which Nuremberg itself is invoked, above all perhaps in Sachs's monologue at the opening of Act Three, must always have evoked a particularly strong response in German nationalist hearers. Sachs apostrophizes his beloved Nuremberg, lying in the heart of Germany ('in Deutschlands Mitten / mein liebes Nürnberg!'), and his words correspond to Wagner's own and to what Wagner told his publisher Schott he had intended to portray: 'I am counting on having depicted *the* real nerve-centre of German life and on having displayed its originality'.[41]

It is in relation to this distinctively German ideal community that it may be plausible to suspect that Beckmesser is another of Wagner's disguised anti-Semitic caricatures. It may not be without relevance that Wagner at one time supposed that Hanslick was Jewish (perhaps on the assumption that any enemy of his *must* be Jewish). Apart from that, however, as Barry Millington has pointed out, aspects of his character, his behaviour as described in the stage directions, and even his manner of singing – as well as certain sources for the text – correspond all too closely to Wagner's characterization of 'the Jew' in 'Das Judentum in der Musik'.[42] One of Wagner's shrewdest critics and admirers, Thomas Mann, apparently suspected anti-Semitic caricature here.

Suggestions of this kind are apt to be greeted not with rational curiosity or scepticism, but with angry hostility. This is understandable, since they hardly enhance the attractiveness of this deeply loved work. But even its most fervent admirers generally admit that the treatment of the town clerk is cruel to the point of sadism. Like Malvolio in *Twelfth Night*, he hardly deserves the crushing humiliation that is inflicted on him, in this case by a rather shabby deception on the part of the 'noble' Sachs, who is, to say the least, economical with the truth in relation to the prize song. That the town clerk is made the town's laughing stock can leave a nasty taste behind. As Dahlhaus said, *Die Meistersinger* is 'the brainchild of an untrustworthy sense of humour'.[43] The humour of the work is nearly all at Beckmesser's expense, and it is decidedly heavy-handed: the scene of his attempted serenade of Eva, and that of his visit to Sachs's workshop, are both over-extended. What delights us in *Die Meistersinger* as in other great and humane comedies is not so much its humour as its good humour.

The deliberate Germanness of the opera extends beyond its words and its chosen setting to the music itself. After the adventurous chromaticism of *Tristan*, Wagner here makes a very self-conscious return to diatonicism, to a sometimes academic counterpoint, and to an attempt to evoke the national past by pastiche of some of its musical forms and styles. It is all rather calculated. After *Tristan* there could be no return, at least for Wagner, to a 'natural' diatonicism. As John Deathridge has written, 'The style of *Tristan* is the latent precondition for the style of *Meistersinger*.' Consequently, 'The diatonicism of *Die Meistersinger* is somehow dreamlike, not quite real in the 1860s.'[44] Nietzsche spotted this archaizing tendency when he wrote about the prelude in *Beyond Good and Evil*. It corresponds exactly to the mythologized version of Nuremberg itself that Wagner presents to us.

In the end *Die Meistersinger* is a much less serious attempt to get to grips with history itself than some other nearly contemporary operas, those of Mussorgsky, for example. It should rather be seen as Wagner's most explicit attempt to revive or re-create a specifically German art and so, in his view, meet a specifically German need of the moment: to restore the national spirit by reminding the nation of its glorious traditions and inheritance, social as well as musical. *Die Meistersinger*, which is often viewed as timeless, like a Shakespearian comedy, is in fact very much a work of the 1860s, the moment of German unification and national assertion in central Europe. That topicality helps to explain its immediate success, and its continuing special popularity in Germany itself.

Parsifal

At irregular but frequent intervals an article appears in which a musical commentator tells us that, contrary to most opinions, *Parsifal* is really a straightforward, unambiguous work, whose difficulties are more apparent than real. This claim is near to being self-contradictory since, if it were true, there would hardly be the need to write yet another interpretative article to prove it. How many articles are there about the 'real meaning' of *Rigoletto*?

It seems better to start by recognizing that *Parsifal* is a complex and difficult work, ambiguous enough for serious students to interpret it in widely differing ways. It has a good claim to be regarded as the most ambivalent and enigmatic opera ever composed. Lucy Beckett's Cambridge Opera Handbook treated the opera as a Christian work. To Robert Craft, however, the opera's Christianity is a 'sham'. 'Wagnerism is the true religion of *Parsifal*', he suggests. Robert Gutman goes further, arguing, '*Parsifal* is not only un-Christian, it is anti-Christian.' Instead Wagner 'set forth a religion of racism under the cover of Christian legend'. Another commentator asserts that 'no stretch, or rather contraction, of the interpretative imagination will yield a primarily political *Parsifal*'.[45]

As always, much depends on what is meant by 'politics', and it is of course true that, except in *Rienzi*, Wagner is seldom concerned with politics as we encounter it in, say, *Guillaume Tell*, or *Don Carlos* or

Khovanschina. It is the larger themes and grander perspectives that preoccupy him, and they are not readily separated from his concern with religion and the spiritual, or the psychic health of the individual and the community. If it is claimed that *Parsifal* is 'about' redemption or regeneration, or self-knowledge and self-abnegation, it does not follow from this that politics is thereby excluded from the drama. So whilst it might be perverse to claim that *Parsifal* is *primarily* political in its preoccupations, it would be equally perverse or blinkered to suppose that politics has no part in this, Wagner's final work, which he always intended as a kind of summation of his ideas and his message to the world. In particular we need to consider the relation of *Parsifal* to the views Wagner formed in the years of its composition, which found expression in the series of essays published between 1878 and 1881.

Parsifal begins not with Parsifal himself, but with the condition of the community he is destined to rescue: the community of the knights of the Grail at Montsalvat. We are rapidly made aware of the crisis and decay that have overtaken this institution. Its leader, Amfortas, in an attempt to recover the sacred spear that has been stolen from the community by the magician Klingsor, succumbed to the enticements of the woman Kundry. As a result he suffered a wound (in the side) which troubles him continuously and makes him long for death, whilst his sexual guilt makes him reluctant to perform his duty of unveiling the Grail (a ritual on which the knights depend for spiritual nourishment, much as the gods in *Das Rheingold* depend upon Freia's golden apples and fall into decline when deprived of them). Like Oedipus, Amfortas is a guilty ruler whose guilt poisons the community he rules over.

Much of this we learn from Gurnemanz, whose long if selective and sometimes cryptic narrative of past events forms the core of the opera's long first scene. But much, too, is revealed by the behaviour of the other members of Montsalvat. Gurnemanz may represent the true values of that community, but he is often at odds with the others. He has to defend Kundry against the aggressive taunts of the young squires, and when one of them calls her a 'savage beast', she enquires ironically, 'Are not the beasts holy here?' They are all indignant when Parsifal shoots a swan, but their demand for punishment seems at odds with the principles of charity and non-violence they are supposed to uphold. Even more vindictive is their treatment of Amfortas in the opera's final scene, when they bellow at him over Titurel's coffin to uncover the Grail for the last time ('zum letzten Mal!'). You must, you must, they shout menacingly, and the confrontation is only defused by the dramatic appearance of Parsifal bearing the spear he has recovered from Klingsor.

Parsifal re-enacts Amfortas's failed mission. He visits Klingsor's magic castle, and is erotically tempted first by the Flower Maidens, who quarrel over him as the Ladies in *The Magic Flute* quarrel over Tamino, and then by Kundry, transformed into a beautiful young seductress. The moment when she kisses him is the moment of revelation for Parsifal. He immediately understands how Amfortas acquired his wound, and how it is to be healed. He resists Kundry's further blandishments, recovers the holy spear, and returns with it to Montsalvat. Parsifal becomes the saviour and new leader of the all-but-collapsed community of the Grail.

There are echoes of both Siegfried and Walther von Stolzing in this. Like Walther, but in a far more exalted vein, Parsifal comes to rescue a community that has sunk into decay. Like Siegfried he is innocent and fearless, until he encounters a woman. But while *The Ring* was based wholly on pagan mythology, *Parsifal* makes extensive use of Christian references and rituals. The Grail, which was a stone in some early versions of the legend, is a cup that contains the blood of the Saviour or Redeemer, while the spear that wounded Amfortas in the side is the spear with which Christ's side was wounded as he hung on the cross. The first act ends with an enactment of the Mass or Eucharist, with bread and wine being distributed among the knights. In Act Three, which takes place on Good Friday, Kundry washes and anoints Parsifal's feet and head in the manner of Mary Magdalene, and Gurnemanz hails him as king. Wagner's use of Christian symbols and rituals is explicit and self-conscious. But far from establishing the Christian character of the work, it seems daring to the point of blasphemy. Christianity admits of only one God and one Redeemer; yet here is Wagner making Parsifal the object of the same gestures of worship as Christ himself. What are we meant to understand by this identification of Parsifal with Christ?

Nietzsche was disgusted by *Parsifal*. He saw it as a surrender to Christianity, 'an apostasy and reversion to sickly Christian and obscurantist ideals'. He jeered: 'Richard Wagner . . . suddenly sank down, helpless and broken, before the Christian cross.'[46] But Nietzsche, for all his brilliant perceptions of this work, as of Wagner's work as a whole, had misunderstood what Wagner was about.

Wagner had never been an orthodox Christian, and he did not become one at the end of his life. He explained his position in a letter of 1880 to his disciple Hans von Wolzogen:

> . . . although we are merciless in abandoning the Church and the priesthood, and, indeed, the whole historical phenomenon of Christianity, our friends must always know that we do so for the sake of that same Christ whom . . . we wish to preserve in His total purity, so that – like all the other sublime products of man's artistic and scientific spirit – we can take Him with us into those terrible times which may very well follow the necessary destruction of all that at present exists.[47]

A diary note from the following year is even more explicit: 'If Christ is for us in the end even still merely a most noble poetic fiction, then it is at the same time more realizable than any other poetic ideal – in the daily communion with wine and bread.'[48] Wagner was like many other nineteenth-century non-believers: they were not cheerful pagans or agnostics. They were disturbed or even tormented by their inability to believe, and were always anxious to find new forms in which what they valued in Christianity or religion could somehow be retained or renewed. Matthew Arnold was a classic instance. So was George Eliot, who was among other things a translator of Feuerbach, and so was Wagner. Not surprisingly Wagner saw art, especially his art, of course, as the ideal vessel in which the valuable essence of religion could be preserved when discredited old dogmas and myths had been discarded. This was the message of the essay of 1880 'Religion and Art':

> One could say that at the point where religion becomes artificial it is for art to preserve the essence of religion by grasping the symbolic value of its mythic symbols, which the former would have us believe in their literal sense, so that the deep, hidden truth in them might be revealed by their ideal representation.[49]

Cosima shared this view, and it was this lofty view of the quasi-religious role of art that gave her and the Master's disciples their sense of mission about Bayreuth. 'Believe me, my friend, our art is a religion,' she wrote to Hermann Levi, the first conductor of *Parsifal*. 'It has been made possible for art to rescue what is most holy to us from all dogmatism and rigid formalism.'[50]

The bearing of all this on *Parsifal* is obvious. It is not so much a Christian as a consciously post-Christian work, committed to rescuing and transmitting the 'deep, hidden truths' contained in Christian theology and symbolism from the wreckage of organized religion itself. Hence the near-blasphemous identification of Parsifal with Christ is a deliberate attempt to reuse certain stories and ceremonies connected with Christ, so demonstrating that their validity transcends that of the dying dogmas of Christianity itself. It is noticeable that Christ is nowhere directly referred to in *Parsifal*. There are many references to the Redeemer (*Erlöser*) and the Saviour (*Heiland*), but this figure is never explicitly identified as Jesus of Nazareth.

Christians may well find the 'spirit' of Christianity in this work, but it seems clear that Wagner's intentions were rather different. Wagner is less interested in the idea of a single act of redemption performed once and for all by Christ, far more in the idea that people and communities can be repeatedly redeemed or rescued by acts of self-denial and dedication. The Schopenhauerian idea of renunciation of the will is as important here as any specifically Christian element. While Amfortas was unable to control his sexual urge, Klingsor tried to control his by self-castration, which was regarded by the early Christian Church as a mortal sin. There are to be no short-cuts to self-control. Kundry's mocking question to Klingsor, 'Are you chaste?', enrages him because he knows that despite self-mutilation he has failed to exorcize sexual desire. It is Parsifal's decision to resist Kundry that saves both Amfortas and, paradoxically, Kundry herself.

But Amfortas's sin is not simply his failure to remain chaste; it is his sexual contact with a racial inferior. His blood is thus corrupted, and he can no longer act as the leader of a male community committed to preserve the pure and sacred blood contained in the Grail. This is the burden of his agonized lament in Scene Two of Act One. He constantly contrasts his own guilty blood with the holy blood in the Grail cup. One of Nietzsche's comments on *Parsifal* was 'too much blood'. Not much blood is actually shed, apart from that of the swan, and that of the knights of Klingsor whom Parsifal wounds offstage. But the imagery of blood pervades the work. 'Blut' must be one of the commonest nouns in the text. Blood has, of course, its significance as a Christian image, and Wagner makes use of that. But we can hardly overlook the fact that for Wagner it also had a racial significance. On the same day that he put down the reflection on Christ quoted above, Wagner also wrote this in his notebook:

> In the mingling of races the blood of the nobler males is ruined by the baser feminine element: the masculine element suffers, character founders, whilst the women gain as much as to take the men's place.[51]

This, surely, is Amfortas's case. The leader of the Grail knights has mixed his blood with that of a 'baser feminine element'. That is the source of the corruption that obsesses him.

Incredible as it may seem to us, or to orthodox Christians, Wagner in his last years mixed up racist and Christian ideas in a farrago of notions about the redemption and regeneration of the human race: racial mingling, or miscegenation as it came to be tendentiously labelled, had led to the decline of humanity as a whole; the superior races had coupled and intermarried with the inferior, and had been dragged down as a consequence. Wagner combined this general notion with his long-standing anti-Semitism, according to which Jews inevitably corrupted those who had intercourse with them: 'even interbreeding does not harm him . . . if a Jew or Jewess intermarry with the most extraneous races, a Jew will always be born'.[52]

Wagner's friend of these years, Gobineau, shared this view and drew from it the pessimistic lesson of the inevitable decline of civilization. This was the point at which Wagner diverged from the theorist of racial inequality:

> Wagner's more optimistic view was that redemption was possible through the agency of Christ. . . . The Saviour's blood was pure – the highest possible development of the human species. The Redeemer's blood perhaps flowed, suggests Wagner, in a supreme endeavour of redoubled power to save humanity from final decay. By partaking of that blood, as symbolized in the sacrament of the Eucharist, even the lowest races might be raised to the most godly purity.[53]

This is what Westernhagen described as turning Gobineau's ideas 'in a spiritual direction'![54]

In the light of this thinking, which found its ultimate expression in Wagner's essay of 1881 'Heroism and Christianity', it would be almost perverse to deny that this unsavoury blend of racism and religion finds a reflection in *Parsifal*. Perverse, because commentators do not have any difficulty in recognizing how some of Wagner's other ideas and preoccupations find their way into his music-dramas. Thus it is natural and right that we should associate Gurnemanz's rebuke to Parsifal for shooting the harmless swan, as well as his Good Friday observations on the renewal of harmony between humanity and nature, with Wagner's strong commitment to vegetarianism, his opposition to vivisection, and his belief that a carnivorous diet lay at the root of human degeneration. But if commentators can easily accept that Wagner's regard for animals finds its way into *Parsifal*, why do they resist the suggestion that his racism is there as well? It is resisted simply because it is an embarrassment to Wagner's admirers; but the similarities between the opera and Wagner's writings and opinions in the period of its creation are so striking that it comes close to dishonesty to disregard or discount them. We have already noticed that ideas of blood purity played a role in *The Ring*. How much more likely that they should feature in *Parsifal*, product of the years in which race and racial purity became an obsession in the Wagner household. From this point of view *Parsifal* becomes a fable about racial degeneration and regeneration. Parsifal's refusal of Kundry is an affirmation of racial purity, which then enables him to rescue the beleaguered Grail community from its decline. That community becomes a metaphor for the Aryan race, or the Germans, threatened with decline and extinction by interbreeding, but saved by a reassertion of the principle of racial exclusivity.

Once *Parsifal* is placed in the context of the ideological concerns of Wagner's later years, it is not so difficult to understand the particular fascination this work had for Adolf Hitler. Winifred Wagner recalled Hitler visiting Wagner's grave in 1923 and coming away saying, 'Out of *Parsifal* I make a religion', whilst Hermann Rauschning recorded the Führer as deriding the apparent Christianity of the work, and asserting, 'it is not the Christian Schopenhauerist religion of compassion that is acclaimed, but pure, noble blood . . . the king is suffering from the ailment of corrupted blood'.[55] Hitler was wrong to discount the Schopenhauerist element in *Parsifal*, and the centrality accorded to the principle of compassion. But he was not wrong to find in the work elements that accorded with his own racist imaginings. The idea often put forward by well-meaning but over-partisan apologists for Wagner, that there is a great gulf between his racist ideology and that of the Nazis, simply does not stand up to the evidence, although it does not follow that Wagner would have approved of the actual policies of the Nazis, or their barbarous style of politics, let alone the mass murder of the Jews. It is not only that the ideological tradition identified with Bayreuth and sustained by Wagner's family and followers in the half-century after his death helped to create the ideological climate in which Nazism could triumph in Germany. It is also the case that this tradition was not, in essence, a distortion of Wagner's intentions or a misrepresentation of many of his views, particularly in his final years. Wagner's elaborated and paranoid racism provides the concealed thematic substructure of his final opera, *Parsifal*.

It may be questioned what relation all this has to the music of *Parsifal* which, it is often suggested, is 'all that matters'. But it is curious that Wagnerians should seek to discount Wagner's words and ideas. Opera, or music-drama for that matter, is never 'pure' music in any case; and in Wagner's case there is obviously meant to be a consistency between words and music, a synthesis of the two, since the composer is the author of both. The musical notes are *not* 'all that matters'. It is through music primarily that the work's meaning is conveyed, but not exclusively; normally it is in conjunction with the words and the action to be seen on the stage.

As to the music of *Parsifal*, three observations may be made. The first is that music can never be as politically specific as words can be. As Martin van Amerongen has well put it: 'there is no specifically Fascist kind of music, just as there is no anti-Fascist chord of a diminished seventh . . .'[56]

Nevertheless – and this is my second observation – we may find aspects of the music do correspond to what has been inferred from other sources, including the verbal text, to be the meaning of the work. The unison chorus of the Grail knights, which opens the Grail ceremony in Act One, apart from being some of the less distinguished music in the score, might strike us as having a crude, aggressive character which, whatever Wagner may have intended, places the community of Montsalvat in an unattractive light. We might think that the comparatively feeble, conventional character of the work's final chorus also exposes the limitations of Wagner's attempt to exploit the ethos of Christianity while not actually believing in its basic doctrine. And many listeners have commented on the ultimately cloying, claustrophobic atmosphere of the work, which might be the musical expression or consequence of the cult of an exclusive community which the work extols.

But there is a third possible response, which is simply to see a disjunction between the extraordinary originality, psychological profundity and occasional sublimity of the music, and the tawdriness of the ideas in and behind the verbal text. This is the approach taken by one noted conductor of the work, Pierre Boulez, who could not be accused of any sympathy with Wagner's politics: Wagner the musician was always able to transcend Wagner the muddle-headed, second-rate ideologue of reactionary German politics.[57] This was essentially the view too of Claude Debussy, who had some fun at the expense of the ideas and characters of the opera, declaring Klingsor to be 'the only moral character in the drama', but yielded to no one in his admiration for the music: '*Parsifal* is one of the loveliest monuments of sound ever raised to the serene glory of music.'[58]

This could be the only way to enjoy *Parsifal* in an entirely unqualified, unambiguous fashion; but of course it depends upon *not* responding to the work as a whole, upon constructing a kind of selective attention, which contradicts the very nature and experience of opera. It is better to recognize the inherent ambiguities and complexities of *Parsifal*, as of so much of Wagner's work, and accept that our responses can only be equally complex and ambivalent.

Wagner's politics have usually been an embarrassment to his musical admirers. Right-wing admirers, such as Curt von Westernhagen, who in the 1930s put forward an essentially Nazi interpretation of the composer, naturally seek to play down his early socialist and revolutionary ideas, and his involvement in the Dresden revolution of 1849. Liberal and left-wing devotees are upset by his anti-Semitism and racism. Especially since 1945 there has been an understandable desire to rescue Wagner from his associations with Hitler and Nazism, and this has led to a good many commentators trying to play down his anti-Semitism and racism, and to stress the supposed gap between

Wagner's views and 'the unspeakable credo of Hitler'. These efforts are not, in my judgement, very convincing. As I have indicated, the association of Wagner's name and work with Hitler and Nazism is far from fortuitous.

A more sensible and sophisticated approach is taken by writers such as Deryck Cooke and Bryan Magee. These commentators offer no defence or plea in mitigation of Wagner's racism, chauvinism and anti-Semitism. They argue simply that, odious as his views on these matters were, they have no impact on or relevance to his work as a composer. His music-dramas are happily free from the taint of his obnoxious racist obsessions. Anyone who recognizes Wagner's musical and dramatic genius, and who responds to the power and beauty of his work, must wish that this were so. But it is inherently unlikely that a composer with Wagner's large ambitions for his own work would systematically exclude some of his most passionately held beliefs from his major creations. And throughout this chapter I have tried to suggest the ways in which Wagner's political views and experiences did in fact find their way into his operas. To look at his works from this angle is, of course, partial and selective. But this dimension of his work has been so neglected, or even wholly denied, that something must be done to redress the balance.

6

Russia, Czechoslovakia and a Footnote on England

(NATIONALISM II)

German nationalism was not typical of nineteenth-century European nationalisms. It was never as strongly interwoven with political liberalism as elsewhere. Germany was not, like Greece or Italy, an occupied country. There was therefore a tendency to compensate for this by inventing imaginary external threats against which the nation could be rallied, and so unified. France was the most popular of these fancied threats, and it was by making war on France in 1870 that Germany was finally united. Many aspects of the unique German variant of nationalism are reflected in the life and work of Wagner.

One might expect Russian nationalism to have had a similar character. Russia was, after all, the centre of a vast empire, against which nations like the Poles and Finns had to struggle for independence. But the parallel with Germany (or Britain) breaks down because of the alliance in tsarist Russia between nationalism and political radicalism. To discover an authentically Russian musical idiom was to identify yourself with, and give a voice to, the long-suffering, oppressed but still great and good Russian people. The heyday of Russian opera – the period between 1870 and 1900 – coincided roughly with the period of populism, when intellectuals looking for a hope of radical change placed their faith in 'the people'.

As with nationhood itself, a national musical idiom was something that had to be both created and discovered. It meant, usually, the conscious incorporation into 'serious' music of forms, rhythms, melodic shapes, harmonies and scales that already existed in the folk or popular music of the country itself. Sometimes, as in the case of Chopin, it involved the use of national dance styles and rhythms, such as the polonaise and the mazurka. In other countries, such as Hungary and England, composers such as Kodály and Bartók, Holst and Vaughan Williams involved themselves in the collecting of folk songs.

But there could be no more profound demonstration of the deep personal significance of nationalism than the fact that, for so many different composers, the discovery or invention of a national idiom was also the discovery of their own personal musical voice. They cease to be anonymous imitators and acquire a distinctive, recognizable idiom of their own. There is no clearer example of this than Mikhail Ivanovich Glinka, the composer whom virtually every succeeding Russian composer venerated as the founder and father of 'true' Russian music. Glinka, like several other Russian composers, was an amateur and part-time composer – in effect, to begin with a dilettante, happy to supply drawing-room performers with piano variations on popular operatic arias of the day and agreeable divertimento-style chamber music like the Trio Pathétique (written in Italy in 1832), a work not without colour or character, but not very individual either. Paradoxically, it was this visit to Italy that convinced Glinka that, as he later put it, 'I could not sincerely be an Italian.' And so homesickness, 'a longing for my own country led me gradually to the idea of writing in a Russian manner'.[1] When he returned home he began work on his first opera, A Life for the Tsar; at the same time he composed his Symphony on Two Russian Themes. But as far as the opera was concerned

> The main thing is the choice of subject. In any case, I want everything to be national: above all, the subject – and the music likewise – so much so that my dear compatriots will feel they are at home, and so that abroad I shall not be considered a braggart or a crow who seeks to deck himself in borrowed plumes.[2]

'Borrowed plumes' would have been an imitation of the Italian or German styles. But to compose truly Russian or national music, that was to do something authentic and original. And so, in 1836, it was.

Ivan Susanin or A Life for the Tsar (the more obsequious title by which the opera is usually known in Britain was adopted for the opera only at the last moment),[3] tells the story of a peasant who, during the Polish invasion of Russia in 1613, helped to save his country by deliberately leading the Polish army into an ambush, knowing that he was bound to lose his own life in the process. This story, whatever its veracity, was popular in the patriotic period after the Napoleonic invasion of 1812, and Glinka's teacher, the Italian Cattarino Cavos, who settled in Russia in 1798, had composed an opera on this theme in 1815.

Bernard Shaw once described Shakespeare's *Henry V* as 'a national anthem in five acts'. Glinka's first opera is a national anthem in four acts. The composer had some trouble in finding a suitable librettist, but eventually found one in the person of Baron Georgy Rosen, secretary to the tsarevich. As so often, the final libretto reflected the composer's ideas as much as, if not more than, the librettist's, but there was evidently no dissent between them on the note of patriotism that was to be sounded from beginning to end of the work. In the first act Sobinin returns from the war ready to marry his betrothed, Antonida, Susanin's daughter. But Susanin refuses to permit the wedding until the war is over. Like Tell in Act One of his opera, this grizzled patriot finds it impossible to contemplate or participate in wedding festivities at a time of national crisis. In the original version Susanin refuses to allow the wedding until a new tsar has been elected. but Sobinin has the news that this has happened: the first of the Romanovs, Michael, has been chosen, and this leads Susanin to join in the general rejoicing. The text of my USSR-made recording, how-ever, makes no mention of any of this. It is not for the tsar but for Russia that Susanin makes his great sacrifice.

Act Two is the Polish act, much as Act Three is in the revised *Boris Godunov*, although Mussorgsky's treatment is far more substantial, both dramatically and musically. Glinka's act is essentially a dance sequence, attractive but lightweight, and relaxes dramatic tension too far. The Poles are represented purely collectively, and are consistently caricatured as both cruel and frivolous. They will be defeated because they do not take their enemy seriously. When the Polish soldiers appear in Acts Three and Four they bring their mazurka rhythms with them, and while this may seem inappropriately jolly, it does remind us of the arrogant frivolity of these invaders, who do not understand what they are up against. For, as the people sing in Act One, no doubt with Napoleon in mind as much as any earlier invader:

> Whoever has made war on Russia
> Has always wrought his own destruction there.

The Polish aristocrats are particularly contemptuous when they learn that the Russian uprising against their rule is being led by a mere peasant, Minin. So the opera has a dimension of class as well as national conflict. The enemy are effete upper-class foreigners, pitted against a brave and patriotic peasantry. No wonder that this opera, with a suitably doctored text, was nearly as popular in Soviet Russia as it was under tsarism, when it opened every new season in both Moscow and St Petersburg. The West has always seen Poland as a victim nation, crushed between its two powerful neighbours, Russia and Prussia–Germany. So it is of some significance that two of the major political–historical Russian operas of the nineteenth century hark back to the early seventeenth century, when it was Russia that was threatened by a vigorously expansionist Poland.

Act Three provides the dramatic turning point of the work. The Russians are celebrating Minin's military successes and preparing for the delayed wedding when the Poles suddenly burst in, demanding to know where Minin is, and to be shown the way to Moscow. (In the original version, they are seeking to capture the young tsar.) Susanin manages to send a messenger to warn Minin, while agreeing to guide the Poles on their way. After the Poles have left with Susanin, Antonida's women friends arrive, singing their lovely bridal chorus in 5/4 time, only to discover the disaster that has befallen the family. The act ends with a chorus of anger and defiance.

In the final act a scene in which Vanya rouses the people to try and rescue his father is followed by Susanin's final act of self-sacrifice. Awake and alone among the sleeping Poles, he prays for strength, and recalls his family with love, before the Poles awake to discover that they have been led into a trap. They kill Susanin before they themselves are attacked. The Epilogue is a final scene of rejoicing and praise for Susanin in Red Square. Once again all references to the tsar were removed from the version performed in the USSR.

Given its theme of devotion to the first of the Romanovs, the success of Glinka's opera with the Russian court and ruling class was unsurprising. It became a patriotic duty to attend a performance of it. But the crucial factor was, of course, Glinka's music. There had been operas on patriotic themes before this, but none of them had achieved a lasting success. Glinka's music is fresh, lively, full of melodic invention and superbly colourful orchestration. The opera is also well and clearly constructed, unlike its more original successor *Ruslan and Lyudmila* which, for all the greater sophistication and originality of its music, is so confused and incoherent as to deter all but the most determined when it comes to staging it. Musically *Ivan Susanin* is more uneven and inconsistent, in that sections of real inspiration and of recognizably Russian character are mixed up with more conventional passages in which Glinka is content to follow the conventions of Italian opera.

Nevertheless, *A Life for the Tsar* is an astonishing achievement, not only in inventing a Russian idiom for Russian opera, but also in itself, as a drama of patriotism that contains much beautiful music and becomes deeply moving when it focuses on the splendid figure of Susanin himself. His soliloquy in the final act has justly become a classic of the Russian bass repertory. Some years before Glinka had even conceived the idea of writing an opera, his old school friend, Nicolai Melgunov, had formulated a clear view of what a really Russian opera would be:

> The person who can write a Russian opera is one who, having saturated himself sufficiently in our own folk melodies, will transmute them within himself, and then in their spirit will write his own music, which will be national not because it will remind us of melodies we already know, but because it will conform to our musical demands and feeling.[4]

This can be taken as a classic analysis of how a national musical idiom is developed. We can say that Glinka, like Smetana, Bartók and Vaughan Williams after him, wrote his own folk tunes, rather than simply borrowing ones that already existed. Melgunov was enthusiastic about the opera when it appeared, and another critic, Yanuary Neverov, noted shrewdly that the mere stringing together of existing tunes could never produce either dramatic impetus or artistic unity, and that Glinka's achievement was something far more impressive and subtle.[5]

It was not through this one opera alone that Glinka opened up paths for later Russian composers to explore. The blend of magic, fantasy and exoticism in *Ruslan and Lyudmila* provided a model for Borodin, for Tchaikovsky in his ballets, and above all for Rimsky-Korsakov in his later operas. Tchaikovsky identified a single short orchestral work, *Kamarinskaya*, which Glinka himself described as a 'national scherzo', as the acorn from which the distinctively Russian symphony grew, with its preference for variation over orthodox Austro-German symphonic development. Glinka's short orchestral works, including the Waltz-Fantasie and the two so-called Spanish Overtures, are so brilliant and melodically attractive that their absence from Western orchestral programmes is incomprehensible, even if it is conceded that staging his operas, and especially *Ruslan and Lyudmila*, poses large problems.

Mussorgsky: Opera and History

It might be thought that Glinka's achievement in inventing Russian opera more or less overnight would have ensured the demise of Italian imitations and a decline in the trade in imported operas. This was not so, and it was not until the 1860s that radical and nationalist composers such as Alexander Dargomyzhsky and Modest Mussorgsky began to explore the paths Glinka had opened up more than twenty years before. Their ideal, their principle, was that of radical artists throughout history: truth to nature; and it was Dargomyzhsky, in his extraordinary opera *The Stone Guest* (left unfinished at his death in 1869), who provided the model that Mussorgsky tried in some respects to follow.

The British composer Constant Lambert once remarked that he was probably the most inappropriately named of all composers, with the possible exception of Modest Mussorgsky. A good joke, but unfair to them both. Mussorgsky was not vain or arrogant, but he was artistically ambitious. He wished to put the Russian people and their history onto the operatic stage, and that is what he achieves to a remarkable extent in his two grandest projects, *Boris Godunov* and *Khovanschina*.

BORIS GODUNOV

Like, it sometimes seems, three-quarters of Russian operas from *Ruslan and Lyudmila* onwards, *Boris Godunov* is based on a text by Pushkin; it follows that text very closely at many points, although inevitably in a compressed and selective form: Pushkin's play has twenty-four separate scenes and a large cast. For the purposes of opera, compression was clearly necessary, and this the composer skilfully achieved. The first version of the opera had seven scenes, the revised version nine. In the latter, the two Polish scenes that make up Act Three were added, as was the final scene in Kromy forest, while the scene in front of St Basil's Cathedral was omitted. The additional scenes were derived from Pushkin's play, although the sinister figure of the Polish Jesuit Rangoni is Mussorgsky's own invention.

Pushkin had set out to write a play of Shakespearian richness, and there are certainly echoes of Shakespeare in the finished play. But Pushkin was also concerned to write something true to history, at least as he knew it, and this posed a problem: as John Bayley has put it, 'History gives the impression of not being interested in drama.'[6] Consequently, in both play and opera there is no contact or confrontation between the two opposed protagonists of the drama, Tsar Boris and his challenger and supplanter, the false Dmitri (here depicted as the monk Grigory who masquerades as the 'disappeared' tsarevich). The entirely fictional confrontation between those rival queens Elizabeth of England and Mary Queen of Scots that Schiller invented for his play, and is central to Donizetti's opera *Maria Stuarda*, is exactly the kind of colourful embroidery of historical truth that Pushkin and, even more emphatically, Mussorgsky were determined to eschew.

It would be wrong, however, to imagine that the composer was overmuch concerned with literal historical truth. For example, he, not Pushkin, invented the scene in which the monk Pimen's narrative of the miracle at the tomb of the dead tsarevich precipitates Boris's final collapse. Whether or not the historical Boris was haunted by guilt over the tsarevich's death is uncertain, although it seems likely that it was not murder but an accident. In any event he made great efforts to clear the matter up, appointing one of his sworn enemies, the Boyar Shuisky, to conduct the enquiry into the tsarevich's death.

Despite Mussorgsky's inventions, an audience with a knowledge of

Russian history would not have seen *Boris Godunov* as historical fiction or romance. Much in it corresponds closely to actual developments during Boris's reign as tsar from 1598 to 1605. Boris did have the reputation of being a loving father to his children, he did seek to groom his son Fyodor as heir to his throne, and the scene with the map is a reminder that Fyodor during his brief reign as tsar did commission a map of Russia. Boris was anxious that his election as tsar should be as near unanimous as possible, and the ostentatious grandeur of his coronation was designed to legitimize his succession to the throne. It is also true that the false Dmitri fixed up a marriage with the daughter of a Polish nobleman, Marina Mniczek, and that the deal involved his becoming a Catholic and committing himself to Catholicizing Russia. Dmitri's reign, alongside Marina, lasted less than a year before he was replaced by the Boyar Shuisky, whose reign was also short. This period, known as 'the time of troubles', began to come to an end with the accession of the first Romanov tsar in 1613 – the moment that provides the context for Glinka's *A Life for the Tsar*. It seems clear that the century between the reign of Ivan the Terrible, who died in 1584, and the accession of Peter the Great in 1689 was seen as the formative period in the evolution of modern Russia, so the placing of both Mussorgsky's historical operas as well as *A Life for the Tsar* in this period is not accidental.

How central is Boris Godunov to *Boris Godunov*? The answer depends in part upon which version of the opera is studied, or performed. In the original version, performed in Britain in 1989 by Opera North, the guilt-ridden tsar appears in four of the seven scenes, and dominates the last three, the whole opera ending with his death. Histrionic basses of the old school naturally tend to favour this version. Nevertheless, two major scenes in the first version, that of Pimen and Grigory in the monastery, and that at the inn near the Lithuanian frontier, introduce characters who, apart from Grigory, have no important part to play in the story of Boris himself. But it is clear from the attention that is paid to them, and especially to Pimen and Varlaam, the dissolute monk, that Mussorgsky had something more in mind than the drama of the tsar as an individual figure: that is, an attempt to place Boris in the context of Russian society, a society whose various aspects are represented by the chorus and the range of subsidiary characters, which is extensive even in the first and shorter version of the opera.

The contrasting figures of Pimen (the devoted chronicler of the nation's history, grieving over his country's fate) and Varlaam (the illiterate, drunken vagrant whose version of that same history is a gloating ballad about Ivan the Terrible's slaughter of the Tartars at Kazan in 1552) represent the true spirit of the Russian Church and its corruption. They probably owe something to the contrast between the austere Padre Guardiano and the grumpy, secular-spirited Fra Melitone in Verdi's *La forza del destino*, which had had its premiere in St Petersburg in 1862. But Pimen is a more powerfully affecting figure than Verdi's abbot because he represents the best in national as well as religious feeling: the Church as guardian of the nation's history and morality.

The other emblematic figure who grieves over his country's plight is, of course, the Simpleton. This is a role for a character tenor, and since, like Trabucco in *La forza del destino*, he is baited by a crowd, he too may be a Verdian inspiration. The holy fool, or *gurodivy*, was a familiar figure in Russian tradition. Children in their ignorance might torment him, but adults would leave him superstitiously alone. Like an outcast court jester, he had a licence to say what he wanted to, and it was accepted that he might speak unspeakable truths, if only in the form of oracular riddles. Hence the Simpleton is the only person who dares accuse Boris to his face of murdering the tsarevich.

It was not the composer's own idea, when he turned to revise the opera, to end it with the Kromy forest scene, but once the idea had been suggested to him by Vladimir Nikolsky, he embraced it with enthusiasm: 'Mussorgsky was in raptures and in a few days he reconstructed and fitted this final scene.'[7] This scene, and its placing at the end of the opera, is one of Mussorgsky's inspirations. It locates Boris firmly in the wider historical context of the 'time of troubles'. And it does more than that. It leaves us to reflect, not on the death of the 'tyrant' Boris, but on the plight of the Russian people, as hopeless as it was when the opera, and Boris's reign, began.

The scene is sometimes referred to as one of 'anarchy'; but that description tells us more about the commentator than the scene itself. What is initially represented is one of those moments, not so rare in history, when the people rise up against those whose normal everyday role is to exploit them, oppress them, command them; the oppressed give vent to their long-suppressed hatred and resentment. Mussorgsky's version of this is anarchic to the extent that his crowd is without leaders, but also without plans or perspective. It only wants to revenge itself on the Boyar Krushchov, whom it has captured. This project is interrupted first by the arrival of Varlaam and Missail, announcing the arrival of the new tsar, then by the Polish Catholic monks, and finally by the appearance of the Pretender Dmitri himself. The crowd, together with Varlaam and Missail, is ready to string up the Latin-intoning monks, not realizing that they are the harbingers of the new Polish-backed ruler. It is a further blow when Dmitri immediately releases the captive Boyar: the cries of 'slava' with which the crowd follows him on his progress towards Moscow remind us that at the beginning of the opera it was cheering his predecessor in exactly the same way. Nothing has changed. The new ruler has not put down the mighty from their seat, nor has he exalted the humble and meek. The stage is set for the reappearance of the Simpleton or Innocent, singing his heartbreaking lament for the Russian people, behind which we can hear the tramping tread of the weary and the heavy-laden through all the centuries. Does any opera end with a deeper sense of compassion and utter desolation?

In all the public or outdoor scenes of the opera, the chorus represents the Russian people. Where appropriate, as in the coronation scene, this chorus can produce great blocks of sound and speak with one voice. But it does not have only one voice. It has an internal life of its own. It divides into groups who argue among themselves and discuss the significance of the events they witness and take part in. Mussorgsky exploits this dual character in the first two scenes. In the first scene the first voice we hear is that of the police officer, bullying the crowd into pleading with Boris to accept election as tsar. But the people are plainly fed up with playing this role, and when they are told to go to the Kremlin and await further orders, they shuffle off with cynical resignation. Against this background the choral splendours of the coronation scene which follows take on an ambiguous character. Is this the same rent-a-crowd? Is it singing because it has been told, 'Your business is rejoicing'? Mussorgsky may have taken the Epilogue to *A Life for the Tsar* as the model for this scene, but in this context the rejoicing cannot be the unequivocal celebration it was at the conclusion of Glinka's epic. It is in the doubtful relationship between the new tsar and his people that the seeds of Boris's tragedy lie. So when, much later, the people plead with Boris in front of St Basil's Cathedral for alms and bread to relieve their hunger, and Boris makes no reply, we know that he has been defeated by the misery of the people he rules over, who are ready to look elsewhere, anywhere, for a chance of rescue from starvation. Hence their welcome for the Pretender in the final scene.

It is in this grandly conceived and depicted social and historical context that Mussorsky, following Pushkin, places the complex figure of Boris. He is sometimes compared to the guilt-ridden Macbeth, but a more apt comparison is with another Shakespearian ruler, Henry IV, who, like Boris in this version, came to the throne only by way of murder, and could neither forget it, nor win for himself the legitimacy he knew he needed. Both monarchs hoped that their sons could achieve that legitimacy, but Boris's tragedy engulfs his entire family; and his son and daughter, even though their fate is not specified, appear in the opera as doomed innocents in a world of terror and ruthlessness.

Although in the opera Boris's guilt is taken for granted, it is wrong for him to be portrayed as a psychopathic, bloodstained monster. Not only is he haunted by his crime, not only is his personal disintegration movingly portrayed, but he is manifestly distressed by the misfortunes of the country he rules over, a task made no easier by the malevolence and untrustworthiness of those through whom he must govern, as represented by the repulsive Shuisky. But most moving of all is Boris's love for his two children: Xenia, saddened already by the loss of her betrothed, and Fyodor, whom his father tries to prepare for power. Whenever Boris thinks of Xenia, we hear a phrase in the orchestra, or shared between orchestra and voices, that seems the quintessence of parental tenderness. It is part of the opera's complexity that the murderer–tyrant should also be the focus of the only sincere human relationships in the work.

The only other possible focus in this opera is the relationship between Dmitri and the Princess Marina, but commentators who see the Polish episodes as introducing 'a romantic element' into the opera have misunderstood what is happening in these scenes.[8] It is possible that Dmitri is genuinely attracted to Marina, although he can hardly be unaware of the *Realpolitik* advantages of the alliance. As for Marina, her interest in Dmitri is in a man who, she hopes, will bring her power and fame:

> Princess Mniczek longs for glory,
> Princess Mniczek thirsts for power!
> I shall sit as your Tsarina
> on the throne of Russia.

This is also the design of the Jesuit Rangoni, and although Marina finds him loathsome, like Philip in *Don Carlos* she cannot ultimately resist the power of the Church. So while Dmitri and Marina pledge themselves to each other, he hovers gloatingly over them like some bird of prey. Mussorgsky in effect turns the tables on those who complained of the absence of love interest in the opera by showing how even love can become an arm and agent of politics and ambition.

The introduction of Rangoni provides another model of religious corruption – the subordination of religion to political scheming and blackmail – to set against the integrity of Pimen. Of course, the composer uses these scenes, as did Glinka, to contrast the frivolous, high-living Poles and their arrogant expansionism with the plight of the Russian people whose fate, as we see in the Kromy scene, is a matter of complete indifference to them as it is to the ambitious Dmitri. Thus the Polish scenes, contrary to what is sometimes suggested, are well integrated into the work as a whole, and reinforce all the major political, national and religious themes of the opera, as well as giving more substance to the Pretender, who in the earlier version disappears altogether after the scene of his escape to Lithuania.

The extended version of the opera involves no significant extension of Boris's role, so it does alter the balance of the work as a whole. But Boris's tragedy, which is the tragedy of his country, lies at the centre of the opera which, despite its episodic construction, has a clear narrative pattern. To that extent *Boris Godunov*, with all its vast scope and complexity, does conform to conventional expectations of opera as a narrative and individual-focused form. It is in these respects that Mussorgsky's other major historical–political project, *Khovanschina*, is so extraordinarily radical and challenging.

KHOVANSCHINA

The title could perhaps be translated as 'The Khovansky Affair', but the Khovanskys are hardly more central to the opera than any of its other major characters. Once again Mussorgsky chooses his material from seventeenth-century history, and if the opera does have a single individual as its focus, it is someone who appears at most only once in the work, and sings not a note: the young tsar, Peter the Great. Its title and subtitle ought really to be *Peter the Great*, or *The End of Feudal Muscovy*. For its theme is the demise of the various groups and forces that, representing the old feudal and anarchic Russia, stood in the way of Peter's establishment of a 'modern' centralized autocracy.

Three major groups are represented here: the feudal nobility (the old boyar class, here represented by the Khovanskys, father and son); the tsar's private army, the brutal and lawless Streltsy musketeers, first set up by Ivan the Terrible, who have acquired an independent power of their own; and the champions of the old, unmodernized forms of the Orthodox Church, the Old Believers (led by Dosifei). All three of these groups meet their doom in the three final scenes of the opera. Even the Westernized modernizer, Prince Galitsin, does not escape the purge, although his fate, exile, is less final. Only Shaklovity, who puts his patriotism and ruthlessness at the service of the new tsar, escapes the nemesis of the old order. Peter himself does not need to appear, because Mussorgsky and his librettist Stasov were interested not primarily in him or even in what he represented, but in the impact of the drastic upheaval upon the old Russia. They measured his achievement by what he had swept away.

Mussorgsky and Stasov were clear and explicit about their purposes, about the kind of work they intended to produce. *Khovanschina* was to be 'a national musical drama', and so it was subtitled. 'It is', in Isaiah Berlin's words, 'an attempt to re-create a moment in the history of the Russian people, in which the personages are embodiments of historical movements, for each of which the composer attempted to find its own unique type of musical expression.'[9] Stasov described Ivan Khovansky as representing 'ancient, fanatical, deep, dark, unfathomable Russia', while Galitsin is 'the representative of Europe which some, even in the party of the Princess Sophia, had begun to understand and value'. And 'in the centre of the plot I wanted to put the majestic figure of Dosifei, the head of the Old Believers, a strong energetic man . . . a deep spirit . . .'

Such a project is in obvious danger of becoming schematic to the extent that the representative individuals become mere caricatures or puppets, lacking that third dimension that would bring them to musical and dramatic life. But that is not a fault in *Khovanschina*. Mussorgsky was much more of a musical dramatist than Glinka or Borodin or even Tchaikovsky. He was not tempted by a generalized lyricism, and the major figures in the opera are mostly as vividly characterized as their counterparts in *Boris Godunov*.

A related feature of the opera, which has certainly stood in the way of its success, is its lack (unlike *Boris*) of a central focus on the fate of one or two individuals. This lack, which many experience as a difficulty, is in fact one of its most radical and significant aspects. Mussorgky and Stasov set before us this range of representative figures, some more sympathetic than others, but none of them especially attractive, and steadfastly refuse to allow us to fasten upon one or other of them as the focus for our interest and sympathy. To a degree that is naturally rare in music drama – given music's unique capacity to communicate at the emotional level – we are compelled, by the episodic structure of the drama, to distance ourselves from the characters on stage, to watch and listen with sympathy without abandoning objectivity. With the partial exception of Janáček's *From the House of the Dead*, I can think of no other opera that not only aims at this kind of balance between detachment and sympathy, but also actually achieves it. It constitutes a challenge to modern Western individualistic expectations, and should extend our awareness of what opera (and drama) can encompass.

Mussorgsky and Stasov were concerned with historical truth. But historical truth was not for them the same thing as fidelity to particular facts. They took great liberties with facts and dates, conflating events for the sake of a more coherent and concentrated narrative.

Ostensibly the opera is set in 1682 when, following the death of the young Fyodor III, authority was formally divided between the half-brothers Peter and Ivan, with Ivan's sister Sophia as Regent. But it also takes in some of the events of 1689, when a plot involving Galitsin and Shaklovity failed to establish Sophia as absolute ruler and push Peter aside; Galitsin was exiled, while Shaklovity was executed. The

Streltsy were tortured with great cruelty and executed; in the opera, however, they are forgiven by a magnanimous tsar. Likewise, the historical Ivan Khovansky was formally executed along with his son, whereas in the opera he is dramatically murdered. The opera refers to many mass suicides by Old Believers (though the movement in fact continued until well into the eighteenth century) but the historical Dosifei was actually opposed to such actions. These deviations from strict historical accuracy only underline the fact that Mussorgsky and Stasov were interested in the meaning of these developments rather than in creating a literal chronicle of them; they were theatrically minded enough to invent scenes like the murder of Ivan Khovansky rather than adhere to the historical truth.

Given the originality of *Khovanschina*, and the success with which Mussorgsky's dramatic genius overcomes some of its difficulties, the question remains: why are we not speaking of a masterpiece comparable to its great predecessor? *Khovanschina* contains some splendid and effective scenes, among them that of the murder of the older Khovansky, and also the scene of political argument between Galitsin, Khovansky and Dosifei, a scene which, like the scenes between Philip and Posa and Philip and the Grand Inquisitor in *Don Carlos*, really ought to dispose of the still prevalent belief that opera cannot encompass intellectual or political argument and debate. The elder Khovansky is a magnificent character, and other leading figures, Galitsin, Shaklovity, Dosifei and Andrei Khovansky, are all adequately delineated. Marfa, the Old Believer who has been spurned by Andrei but is still passionate about him, is given some eloquent music (eloquently sung by Irina Arkhipova on the Bolshoi recording). The ethos of pre-modern Russia is vividly created in the music: the hooligan behaviour of the Streltsy, the obsessive, death-oriented fanaticism of the Old Believers (the fundamentalists of their day). It is a brilliant moment when Galitsin, having summoned Marfa to prophesy his future, is so terrified by what she foretells that he orders his servant to have her drowned straightaway. The façade of sophistication and scepticism suddenly collapses, revealing the old superstition and cruelty that lurk only just beneath the surface.

Not the least of the score's beauties is the familiar Prelude depicting dawn over Moscow but also, as David Lloyd-Jones has suggested, depicting the dawn of modernity represented by Tsar Peter.[10] The theme recurs briefly when Marfa relates how she has been rescued by Peter's guards to the unanimous astonishment and alarm of Golitsin, Khovansky and Dosifei (another thrilling moment); in producing for the first time a complete version of the opera, Rimsky-Korsakov used the theme to bring the unfinished scene to an end. This procedure was criticized by Calvocoressi, but I think Rimsky-Korsakov's instincts were sound.[11] This is the first moment in the work when Peter's power is asserted, and as such it marks the beginning of the end for the assembled representatives of the old order.

But what does all this add up to? It is the sheer incoherence and lack of forward impetus that make *Khovanschina* so unsatisfying, despite its deep originality and its musical splendours. The amount of attention devoted to Andrei Khovansky and his involvement with the German girl Emma, and with Marfa, is excessive given the marginality of this subplot to the opera's central theme. His immolation along with the Old Believers in the final scene is not credible, and is presumably introduced to bring a dramatic touch to what would otherwise be an oratorio-like conclusion. By contrast, the important figure of Golitsin has only one scene, and the reasons for his exile are never made clear. *Khovanschina* is even more episodic than *Boris Godunov*, and the three final scenes of the denouement are short and inadequately prepared for by the three earlier scenes, which are often static or tangential to the central theme. So, the opera is an artistic experiment of quite exceptional interest and ambition, which certainly does not deserve its general neglect. But it is structurally too flawed and musically too uneven to achieve the classic stature of *Boris Godunov*.

It ought to be added, however, that it is difficult to be sure what *Khovanschina* consists of, let alone see or even hear a complete performance. The English libretto for a BBC broadcast in 1982 omitted scenes and characters (Susanna, the German pastor) without any indication of the fact. The plot summary in *Kobbé* is similarly incomplete, and the Bolshoi recording conducted by Boris Khaikin, while including some scenes not present in the BBC libretto, omits others that were. When every allowance has been made for the chaotic state in which the composer left his opera, and for the different editions prepared by Rimsky-Korsakov and Shostakovich, it seems to be treated in an even more cavalier fashion than *Boris Godunov* has been.

A late product of the Russian nationalist school was Borodin's *Prince Igor*, which was left unfinished by its composer when he died in 1887. Like its predecessors by Glinka and Mussorgsky, this is an epic opera through which Borodin, who wrote his own libretto, sought to recover the Russian past and revive the national sense of identity. Although there is some individuation of characters, the opera is not, essentially, about individuals. It is about Russia and its historical destiny, and the forces that threaten that destiny from within and without, the latter being represented here by the savage but splendid Polovtsians. But the patriotic mood, here as elsewhere, is not conspicuously triumphalist. As represented above all by Yaroslavna, that mood is one of brave, patient, often grieving endurance. Russia's great destiny has yet to be fulfilled.

As in Italy, the spirit of Russian nationalism touched even composers, such as Tchaikovsky, who were not explicitly committed to the nationalist cause. Tchaikovsky took themes from Russian history for several of his operas, including *The Oprichnik* and *Mazeppa*. Rimsky-Korsakov, too, although his most characteristic operas belong to the style of magic and fairytale established by *Ruslan and Lyudmila*, produced as his first opera *The Maid of Pskov*, an historical drama set in the time of Ivan the Terrible. His later operas combine fantasy with political satire; one of them, *The Golden Cockerel*, ran into trouble with the tsarist censors on that account, and also because of the composer's known political liberalism.

Finally, by way of an epilogue to the nineteenth-century nationalist tradition, mention must be made of an opera composed in the early 1940s which nevertheless clearly belongs in the same category, Prokofiev's *War and Peace*. This adaptation of Tolstoy's vast novel is, by common consent, remarkably successful. Prokofiev divides his opera into two parts, corresponding roughly to the periods and themes of peace and war. The first part ends dramatically with the news that Napoleon has crossed the frontier into Russia, and the second concentrates on the defence of Russia against the French, in which the leading role is assigned to Marshal Kutuzov. In deference to Soviet ideology the tsar makes no appearance and, as in the adapted *A Life for the Tsar*, loyalty to the tsar is replaced by simple patriotism.

Prokofiev and his future second wife Mira Mendelson began work on the libretto in April 1941, and he had completed eleven scenes in piano score by the summer of the following year. It seems that the Nazi invasion of Russia in June 1941 provided a further stimulus; the composer later wrote that it became clear to him 'that the emphasis would have to be placed on the events closest to 1812'.[12] The work was never performed complete in his lifetime, even in concert perform- ance, and he continued to revise it up to his death on 7 March 1953, the same day as that of Stalin himself.

The word 'Stalinist' is widely and loosely used, and almost always as a term of abuse; so I may be misunderstood if I describe *War and Peace* as a Stalinist opera. But there is an innocuous sense in which it undoubtedly is. Soviet audiences at least could hardly help equating the French invasion of 1812 with the German invasion of 1941, or seeing in Marshal Kutuzov an historically disguised, and of course idealized, portrait of Marshal Stalin, the farseeing patriotic leader who saves his country at a time of terrible danger. The portrait is a flattering one, and its relation to reality is questionable, since Stalin's war leadership was probably not the triumph of the military genius that official Soviet propaganda proclaimed it to be. But that is really beside the point. For Russians the 1941–45 war was a war of national survival, and Stalin played the same symbolic leadership role in that struggle as Churchill did for the British.

It might be expected that the very topicality and propagandistic value with which Prokofiev's project was so dramatically endowed would have led to the composition of a crude, shallow and ephemeral piece of wartime propaganda. But *War and Peace* is a clear proof that art and propaganda *can* mix, and do not necessarily contradict each other. Prokofiev shared the national sense of crisis, and perhaps discovered in himself unsuspected depths of attachment to his native country, to which he had returned in 1933 after fifteen years of self-imposed exile. Whatever the reasons, the strength of feeling in the patriotic choruses of the opera, as well as in its more intimate scenes, is unmistakable, especially if the performance begins with the powerful choral epigraph announcing the danger to Russia – as happened in the splendid performances staged by English National Opera in the 1970s and early 1980s. As their producer Colin Graham said, this opening chorus is the sound of 'a whole nation speaking out against the oppressor'.[13]

Not many people nowadays would anticipate a sympathetic por- trayal of Stalin with a warm glow of excitement. It is testimony to

Prokofiev's achievement, but also to Stalin's image among the Russian people during 'the Great Patriotic War', that we find that Kutuzov, the grizzled unpolished soldier who has risen from obscurity to the top of the army, is an impressive and, in his patriotic soliloquy in Scene Ten, a very moving figure.

Prokofiev's *War and Peace* has more to it than Soviet patriotism and flattery of Stalin, of course. The composer was first tempted to tackle Tolstoy's novel by the episode in which Natasha meets once more the wounded Prince Andrei, which struck him as 'the perfect operatic scene'. And Andrei's death, with its fleeting recollections of the delicate waltz from Scene Two, when his relationship with Natasha began, is indeed one of the most touching things in the score. My point is only that the patriotic and propagandist elements do not, on the whole, detract from the opera, but on the contrary, form a major element in its overall success.

Czech Opera

BEDRICH SMETANA

In the first lines of Smetana's first opera, *The Brandenburgers in Bohemia*, a Czech knight sings passionately about the damage these foreign occupiers are doing to 'our land and our language'. Smetana, a passionate Czech nationalist, had had to learn that language, with considerable difficulty, when he was in middle life. Like all Czechs of the educated classes, he was brought up speaking and reading German, the official language of the Austro-Hungarian Empire of which the Czech lands were then a part.[14] Smetana had to learn what patriotism involved. Nationalism had to be invented in Czechoslovakia, and he was at the centre of that process as a matter of his own volition. Language has always been a political issue, especially in empires. German had been imposed upon the Czech lands as recently as 1784, as part of the allegedly modernizing reforms of the Emperor Joseph II. Czech had survived, however, as a popular language, and from the 1820s onwards there was a deliberate nationalist campaign to keep it alive. A leading figure in this campaign was Josef Jungmann, who produced a five-volume Czech–German dictionary in the 1830s, and was also director of the school in Prague that Smetana briefly attended in 1839–40.

A German visitor to Bohemia in 1833 concluded that the Austrian policy of Germanization was based on the arrogant assumption that the Czechs were a branch of 'the great German family'. But, he added, 'The Bohemians are not Germans, in their language, in their feelings, in their habits, in their prejudices, nor, above all, in their institutions.'[15] The preservation and revival of the language was paralleled by an attempt to sustain or create an independent musical tradition. Patriotic songs and choruses were composed, and folk songs were collected and published. What came to be thought of as one of the most characteristic of Czech dances, the polka, was an invention of the 1830s. Some of Smetana's earliest compositions were polkas and other dances written for the piano.

As a composer he developed slowly, but he was an obviously musical child, and he was only six years old when he gave a public performance of a piano arrangement of the overture to *La muette de Portici*, a work he was often to conduct in the 1860s and early 1870s. It was the revolutionary year 1848 that seems to have awoken his political and nationalist feelings. He was active on the barricades in Prague, and was inspired to compose: marches for military band, a unison 'Song of Freedom' using a Czech text, and a Grand Overture in D major. But not until the 1860s, when there was some liberalization of Austrian rule and it became clear that the new Provisional Theatre in Prague – it was provisional pending the building of the planned National Theatre – would be available for opera and operetta as well as drama, did Smetana come into his own as a composer and conductor. The first opera to be performed at the Provisional Theatre when it opened in 1862 was *Les deux journées*, a suitably revolutionary and egalitarian choice. At the same time a competition 'to encourage the composition of Czech national opera' was announced by Count Jan von Harrach, a member of the Old Czech Party. Two prizes were given, one for an opera 'based on the history of the Czech people', the other to be 'of gay content and taken from the national life of the people in Bohemia, Moravia or Silesia'.

Smetana returned to Bohemia after six years working in Sweden, and set to work on *The Brandenburgers in Bohemia*. His second opera, *The Bartered Bride*, although seemingly tailor-made for the opera of 'national life' prize, was not in fact composed for the competition. *The Brandenburgers* was eventually and somewhat grudgingly awarded the prize for the best historical opera.

By the time Smetana had begun to compose his first opera he was nearly forty, and clear not only about his musical and political purposes, but also about his style and methods. A few years earlier he had been stung by the remark of a Viennese conductor that for all their instrumental talent the Czechs seemed incapable of producing music of real quality. He vowed then and there to dedicate himself to the creation of a national music. But he did not envisage a music that either incorporated or echoed folk songs. His view was that 'imitating the melodic curves and rhythms of our folksongs will not create a national style let alone any dramatic truth – at the most only a pale imitation of the songs themselves'.[16] All this may seem surprising to those who hear in *The Bartered Bride* the quintessential music of the Bohemian countryside, but we should note that Smetana was often accused of being too German and even too Wagnerian in his music to produce the authentically national music the Czechs were searching for.

None of this affects the fact of Smetana's personal commitment to the creation of a distinctively Czech musical tradition, or his standing as a composer, or, as a matter of history, his success in composing a number of works, such as *Ma Vlast*, that have assumed a special position in the musical and political life of the Czech peoples.

As for *The Brandenburgers in Bohemia*, this story of the German occupation of Bohemia in the late thirteenth century has never lost its political relevance. The opera is set in the year 1279. The German troops are behaving with all the arrogance and lawlessness of occupying armies through the ages; nevertheless they enjoy a degree of collaboration from the dominant German merchant class in Bohemia. It is left to the lower orders, 'the people', to mobilize a patriotic resistance. The opera has a class as well as a national dimension.

The first half of the opera maintains considerable dramatic excitement and coherence through a variety of scenes. In Scene One Oldrich, a knight, urges the necessity of armed resistance against the handwringing reluctance of Volfram Olbramovic, the Lord Mayor of Prague. Only when news comes of the looting of Prague and the abduction of the queen and the crown prince is Volfram convinced of the need for resistance. In Scene Two we see his daughter Ludise rejecting the approaches of one of the German merchants, Tausendmark; the scene ends when he returns with German soldiers to abduct her and her two sisters.

Scene Three, set in Prague, begins as a scene of revolutionary celebration by the poor, reminding us of Lenin's dictum that revolutions are the festivals of the oppressed. Their leader is Jira, a runaway serf, who emerges as by far the most positive male figure in the opera. He and the chorus assert the age-old popular principles of social equality and fair shares for all:

> As long as the lords have enough
> There is enough for us too!

The celebration culminates in lively dances; then Ludise rushes in appealing for help, hotly pursued by Tausendmark and the soldiers. What happens next is crucial not only to the plot, but in revealing the social radicalism of the opera. Volfram and the other notables appear, and when Tausendmark claims that he was rescuing Ludise and her sisters from 'the rabble', the notables automatically believe him, against the protestations of Jira and the people. Tausendmark makes it plain that he can hardly bear to speak to someone as inferior as Jira. 'I don't speak with the rabble,' he announces. To which the whole chorus retorts angrily: 'We aren't rabble! We're the people!' It calls on him three times to withdraw his insult: 'Odvolej!' Nevertheless, Jira is arrested, and Act One ends in dramatic confrontation. From this class bias, this willingness to believe the respectable rich rather than the disreputable poor, spring all the subsequent misfortunes of Ludise and her sisters.

Act Two opens with a sombre scene of country people preparing to evacuate their village; the scene is dominated by a choral prayer which, inevitably perhaps, sounds rather too oratorio-like. This is followed by a court scene in which Volfram presides over an inquiry into what happened to his daughters. Once again Tausendmark's word is believed against Jira's, who denounces the partiality of the court and is sentenced to death. 'Execute him on time', are Volfram's parting words. This too is an impressive and musically well-integrated scene.

But from this point on the opera loses its way. The scene shifts again to the three women, now incarcerated in their country home, and the rest of the work is focused on the convoluted happenings surrounding the efforts to rescue them. We are left ignorant of the fate of Jira or the popular response to his sentence until he reappears in the last ten minutes of the opera. Tension sags badly, and the collective focus of the work, affirmed so strongly in the first act and a half, is lost. The rescue of the three sisters is simply not an adequate symbol or substitute for the complex of class and national conflicts that have so powerfully dominated the first half of the opera.

The Brandenburgers in Bohemia was finished in April 1863, but had to wait for its premiere until January 1866. It made a huge impact: 'No work of such calibre had ever been written previously by a Czech composer.'[17] The troubled history of independent Czechoslovakia, which suffered invasion by the Germans in 1938, and by the Russians thirty years later, in 1968, has given *The Brandenburgers* a constant political relevance. It was understandably popular after the defeat of the Nazis in 1945, and between then and 1968 received 146 performances at the National Theatre in Prague. Performances that autumn, after the Warsaw Pact invasion, naturally enough became occasions for clear if discreet demonstrations against the invasion. The work then disappeared from the repertory for the next sixteen years, until a new production was staged in 1984.[18]

Despite its structural weaknesses, *The Brandenburgers in Bohemia* is an impressive work, which does not deserve its nearly total neglect outside Czechoslovakia. The scene of popular revolutionary tumult and celebration is especially effective, and the combination of the patriotic theme with that of social revolution reminds us that nationalist movements are seldom purely nationalist: political independence is often seen as the precondition and prelude to social and economic reform or revolution. How far this theme was introduced by the librettist Karel Sabina rather than Smetana is not clear, but Sabina was a leading figure in the Czech nationalist movement in the 1860s. He was also the librettist of Smetana's next opera, *The Bartered Bride*, premiered only five months after *The Brandenburgers*. (A more accurate English title would be *The Sold Bride*: the conventional translation is a picturesque euphemism.) Given the double collaboration between Smetana and Sabina, I think we are justified in attaching some significance to the social character of *The Bartered Bride*.

Smetana was justifiably annoyed that some critics made belittling comparisons of his *opéra comique* with those of Offenbach; he pointed out that his model was in fact *The Marriage of Figaro*. And both are, indeed, comedies of marriage and misunderstanding, of conflicting plans and plots. But one obvious difference is that Smetana's opera includes no aristocrats, whether to interfere or to act as benign patrons of the villagers. Smetana and Sabina portray a more or less autonomous community which is also strikingly egalitarian. It would be wrong to suggest that they idealize it. In fact, despite the tendency of many productions to prettify the piece or else play it broadly for laughs, it is actually a rather realistic work which does not evade the sordid and mercenary side of village life. For example, marriage in the village is treated as a contractual arrangement made by parents on behalf of their children, in which considerations of money and property are usually paramount.

But the work nevertheless rests on a democratic act of faith that was quite unusual in opera in the mid nineteenth century. It was assumed that the collective life of an ordinary village, and the happiness and unhappiness of its inhabitants, provided more than enough material for a full-length opera that would both touch and entertain. That this was a risky assumption is perhaps indicated by the fact that *The Bartered Bride* took a few years to establish itself. Brian Large writes: 'The Prague audience . . . coming as they did from society or middle-class circles, found the plot too naive, even too rustic.'[19] Smetana revised the opera several times (adding, among other things, the dances that have helped to ensure its lasting popularity) before it reached its final form in 1870, after which its popularity came to overshadow all the other, more serious operas that the composer valued more highly.

John Tyrrell has written that *The Bartered Bride* is 'one of Smetana's least overtly patriotic operas'.[20] This is true. But integral to Smetana's project of creating a national music, as part of a national culture and consciousness, was the idea that there should be operas in which the everyday life and distinctive customs of the people should be portrayed. Subject matter was always important to cultural nationalism. Nationalists wanted to show that it was not necessary for composers to draw on the international stockpile of myths and plots. The use of specifically national myths, legends, history and literature would generate something fresher and more authentic, they believed, and

would be likely to reach a wider audience and touch it more profoundly. All the nationalist opera composers wanted to reach an
audience beyond the traditional court and upper-class coteries. And
opera was not marginal to the nationalist struggle in the Czech lands.
According to John Tyrrell 'opera became the chief vehicle of Czech
cultural nationalism'.[21]

Dvořák was one of those who in 1872 put their names to a manifesto
in support of Smetana, which declared that 'with *The Bartered Bride* he
blazed a trail for Czech light opera, indeed we may say is the creator of
that genre'. Smetana had his enemies, but even in his lifetime he was
widely recognized as the man who had, in the words of the manifesto,
laid 'the foundations of our future dramatic national music'.[22]

The grandest of Smetana's explicitly nationalist projects was *Libuse*,
which was intended to mark the coronation of the Emperor Franz
Josef as king of Bohemia, but the event never took place. Consequently, although *Libuse* was composed between 1868 and 1872, it
was not performed until the opening of the National Theatre in 1881,
by which time the composer was totally deaf. Smetana wanted *Libuse*
'to be used only for festivals which affect the whole Czech nation'.
And he was equally clear that it was not a conventional opera 'but a
festive tableau'. As Large has written, it 'has the grandeur of an ode. It
is not opera in the traditional sense but a magnificent pageant, a hymn
to the nation, cast in six tableaux.'[23] Thus it stands rather uneasily
somewhere between the oratorio and music–drama. Parts of it are too
static to be easily staged, but in other scenes the music is strongly
dramatic – in the scene, rather too reminiscent of Wotan and Brünnhilde, between Lutobor and his daughter Krasava, for example – or
clearly suggestive of a stage picture, as in the scene at Premysl's farm,
with its offstage music for the harvesters and Premysl's farewell to his
farmworkers when he answers Libuse's invitation to join her as her
prince-consort.

Libuse ends with the famous series of prophecies in which this
legendary queen of Bohemia looks ahead to her nation's difficult but
heroic future, conjuring up a series of episodes; the work concludes
with everyone affirming:

> The Czech people shall never perish,
> They all hell's horrors will ever resist! Slava! Slava!

Libuse is a splendid figure, grand yet emotional, emblematic of course, but never dehumanized. But just as vital to this ode to the nation is the evocation of 'Bohemia's woods and fields' in the scenes at Premysl's farm. The lime trees he touchingly salutes are presented as symbols of the nation's 'virtue and strength'. Quite as much as the references to heroism and history, these scenes take us to the heart of nationalism as an attachment to a particular place as a home, a father- or mother-land. Nationalism, then, in *Libuse*, is seen in its simplest, least troublesome form.

Smetana's great musical successor, Antonin Dvořák, also attached great importance to his operas, and likewise saw them as valuable contributions to the developing national culture. Shortly before his death in 1904 he told an interviewer, 'I wish to devote all my powers to the creation of opera. Not from a desire for personal glory, but because I consider it to be the best form for the nation.'[24] But with the exception of *Rusalka*, Dvořák's operas did not achieve the success of his orchestral and instrumental music or even, initially, that of his choral works. Nor were they markedly political or explicitly national-ist in the style of Smetana's grander efforts, though of course the distinctive character and success of his symphonies and instrumental music owe much to his use of Czech and Slavonic elements, such as the dances – dumka, furiant and polka. It is arguable, I think, that it was this Czechness that saved Dvořák from being merely another imitator of Brahms and, to a lesser extent, Wagner. Like other Czech composers, including Janáček, Dvořák was sympathetic to Pan-Slavism, the idea of an alliance of Slav peoples against the domi-nating German powers, Germany and Austria. Hence his two sets of Slavonic Dances, and especially the second set, opus 72, which includes Ukrainian dumkas, a Polish mazurka, a Slovakian odzmek, and a Serbian kolo.

Leoš Janáček

Unlike Greece, Italy and Germany, the countries of central and eastern Europe incorporated into the tsarist and Austro-Hungarian empires had to wait until 1917–18 for their independence. So nationalism continued to have an important influence on the music of Finland, Hungary, Poland and Czechoslovakia well into the twentieth century. Of these countries only Czechoslovakia had established a really strong operatic tradition. Its outstanding inheritor was Leoš Janáček.

Born in 1854, Janáček was a passionate nationalist and, like the earlier Czech composers we have discussed, wanted to serve the national cause through his music. Except for Italy in the first half of the nineteenth century, nowhere in Europe were music and the national cause more closely identified than in Bohemia. But Janáček was not from Bohemia. He was born and lived most of his life in the Slovakian area of Moravia, and his attachment was to Moravia. This undoubtedly disadvantaged him when he tried to establish himself in Prague, which he dearly wished to achieve; and while his first really successful opera, *Jenufa*, had its premiere in Brno in 1904, it was not until 1916 that it reached the National Theatre in Prague, and then only in a version reorchestrated to make it more acceptable to conventional musical tastes.

Like other musical nationalists, Janáček spent some of his early life collecting folk songs. A number of his earliest works, including his second opera *The Beginning of a Romance* and the better-known *Lachian Dances*, incorporate Moravian folk tunes directly into larger structures. But by the time Janáček came to his third opera he had adopted the more sophisticated approach that we have already come across with Smetana, Glinka and others.

Like *The Bartered Bride*, *Jenufa* is a story of village life but, as has been observed, it is a story quite close in character to some of the Italian and French *verismo* narratives of the same period. The bare bones of the story, with its jealousy-inspired face-slashing and the murder of a newborn child by a step-grandmother then driven nearly mad by what she has done, are melodramatic; it is not hard to imagine the mad scene that an Italian composer would have provided for the Kostelnicka in the final act. The melodrama led some critics to express hostility and scepticism towards the play on which the opera is based, Gabriela Preissova's *Her Step-Daughter*. But the author had learnt about both incidents while she was living in Moravia, and the play and the opera go to some lengths to create a truthful picture of Moravian village life. The programme for the first performance claimed: 'it is the first opera which consistently wants to be Moravian'.[25] The change of title, however, indicates a shift of emphasis. In the play the Kostelnicka was the central figure. Janáček, who fashioned his own libretto, shifts the emphasis to the younger woman, Jenufa, and her heroic readiness to understand and forgive her foster mother becomes the moral and emotional culmination of the opera. Jenufa and the Kostelnicka are the first in a series of profoundly sympathetic portrayals of women in tragic situations, which are among the most striking features of Janáček's operas.

With the partial exception of *The Excursions of Mr Brouček*, however, it is not in the operas of his maturity that Janáček expresses his nationalism. More significant in this respect are the Piano Sonata of 1905, which is a musical commemoration of the death of a man who was shot dead during a demonstration demanding the creation of a Czech university in Brno; or the *Sinfonietta*, composed in 1925–26, which he dedicated to the Czechoslovak armed forces and called originally *Military Sinfonietta*; or the *Glagolithic Mass*, which uses an old Slavonic language in preference to the usual Latin.

Be that as it may, *The Excursions of Mr Brouček* is dedicated to Czechoslovakia's first president, Tomáš Masaryk. There are two excursions, or dreams. The first takes Mr Brouček to the moon, where he finds a company of aesthetes who are shocked by his philistine lack of imagination and sensitivity. The second takes him back to the fifteenth century and an encounter with the Hussites, and here too he disgraces himself by failing to share in the patriotic will to resist the Emperor Sigismund. He is determined not to be conscripted into the Hussite army: 'What would I gain thereby?' he asks, typically. He shocks the patriots by telling them, 'I do not care at all about military glory.' 'Sigismund, Schmigisbund . . . He hasn't done me any harm.' After the Hussite victory, Brouček is discovered hiding. He tries to lie his way out of the situation, but is denounced for his cowardice. Back in the real world of late-nineteenth-century Prague this pocket Falstaff is inclined to boast of his role: 'I mightily helped to liberate Prague!' But he adds, 'please don't tell it to anybody!'

Overall, Janáček endorsed Svatopluk Cech's satire at the expense of the small-minded, philistine, cowardly and unpatriotic bourgeois of the Czechoslovakia of his day. Brouček is a landlord, always complaining about his tenants and always worrying about his property and property in general. 'I wanted people to be disgusted by him, to want to destroy him and stifle him at first sight – but, in the first place, mainly in themselves. So that we may be reborn in the heavenly purity of our national martyrs.'[26]

But the format of *Brouček* does not permit of the directness of a national epic like *The Brandenburgers in Bohemia*. It is unavoidably more ambivalent, and if Brouček is satirized, so too are the lunar luminaries and the exceedingly earnest Hussites. Even when Cech himself appears at the opening of the fifteenth-century excursion to lament the decline of patriotism, his lament is immediately followed by Brouček's remark, 'We must make a note of this interesting short-cut.' Brouček's lack of vision is being guyed, but at the same time the grandiose oration of the poet is deflated. And the excursion to the moon includes a lunar parody of the words of the new Czech national anthem. Whether or not Janáček intended or realized it, the opera reflects a changing world. As Jan Smaczny has written, 'the day of the impassioned and dignified national statement was fast disappearing . . .' Janáček the artist grasped this even if Janáček the patriot had no intention of subverting his own political cause.[27] Brouček may be a contemptible fellow, but he is at least a distant relative of that classic Czech anti-hero Schweik, and of Brecht's war survivor, the ironically named Mother Courage. Our century naturally tends to regard Brouček's antipathy to 'military glory' with a more than sneaking sympathy.

Nevertheless, Janáček seems to have felt more at home with the material of the patriotic excursion: for whereas the composition of Part One, dealing with the lunar excursions, was protracted (the composer called on the services of no fewer than five different librettists), the second excursion was written in eight months in 1917. Its composition was prompted by the prospect of national independence at last. 'A new era is at hand. It is just around the corner. What about holding up to it the clean mirror of the battle of Vitkov Hill?' Janáček suggested to his librettist F.S. Prochazka.[28] And there is no mistaking the fervour in the choral episodes particularly, where Janáček uses the famous Hussite hymn, 'Hear ye, warriors of God', which Smetana had also used in *Libuse*.

An English Epilogue: *Hugh the Drover*

The rather self-conscious treatment of nationalism in *The Excursions of Mr Brouček* has a kind of parallel in an English opera composed at almost exactly the same time, Vaughan Williams's *Hugh the Drover*, which will provide the ambivalent epilogue to this chapter and our considerations on nationalism and music.

Hugh the Drover belongs to Vaughan Williams's early period as a composer, although he was around forty at the time of its composition (like Janáček, he was a late musical developer). It also belongs among his works most influenced by folk music, incorporating a number of genuine folk tunes, but also including a large amount of original music that is meant to sound like folk songs and dances. The musical character of the work required a village setting, but it also required that it be set in the past, since the kind of rural community life that involved folk-dancing, not to mention prize-fighting, putting people in the stocks and celebrating May Day, had certainly disappeared from the England of 1910. So the story was set in the Cotswolds in the period of the Napoleonic Wars.

Mary, the daughter of the constable, is to be married to John the Butcher, a boorish macho chauvinist. Unhappy at the prospect, she is swept off her feet by the romantic figure of the nomadic Hugh. But their plans to elope are frustrated by Hugh's arrest. The outsider is suspected of being a French spy. In the end he is rehabilitated by the recruiting sergeant, who recognizes him as a patriotic friend who saved his life on one wintry occasion. 'I tell you, His Majesty has no better friend in England than Hugh the Drover.' Amidst cries of 'God save the King', John the Butcher is pressganged into the army and taken off to fight 'old Boney', while the happy pair ride off into the wider world.

Vaughan Williams himself had in mind 'something on the lines of' *The Bartered Bride*, as he explained to his librettist Harold Child, a staff writer on *The Times*. *Hugh the Drover* was to be a distinctively English work in the same mould:

> I have an idea of an opera written to *real* English words, with a certain amount of *real* English music and also a real English subject, might just hit the right nail on the head.[29]

There is indeed a musical similarity between Marenka's famous Act Three aria and Aunt Jane's 'Life must be full of care', also a half-sad reflection on married life and love. But, alas, Vaughan Williams's librettist was not up to providing what was needed, and the composer, at least at this stage of his career, had insufficient sense of what was needed dramatically to make the project work. The resulting 'ballad opera', with its fair, its dancing, its prize fight, stocks and recruiting party, is relentlessly picturesque and closer to the mythical 'merry England' of the picturebooks than to the earthy realism of Smetana and Janáček. Hubert Foss summed up the opera's main defects admirably:

> There is something of charades about *Hugh the Drover*. The nationalism is fervid but self-conscious. . . . Hugh . . . is so picturesque, with his boxing match, his stocks, his escape, and his love triumphant, as to be unconvincing . . . for once . . . Vaughan Williams accepted this charming compromise between literature and life as the real thing . . .[30]

Much of the music is attractive, and the love music is almost Puccinian in its passion: in the vein of the slow movement of *A London Symphony*, or the brief passage in the *Serenade to Music* that was written especially for Eva Turner, the great British Turandot of those years. *Hugh the Drover* is certainly worth the occasional English revival, but the truth is that it did not 'hit the right nail on the head', as the composer had hoped, and the interesting question is: why not?

Even a better libretto could not have saved the opera, I think, because the whole project was ultimately an under-motivated exercise in antiquarianism. What could be the function, the *raison de'être*, of English nationalist opera in the early twentieth century? This was not a country struggling for political independence, or needing to establish its separate identity – except in one relevant respect, that of music. Vaughan Williams was concerned, like nationalist composers elsewhere in Europe, to bring his country's music out from under the baleful shadow of Mendelssohn and Brahms and create an authentic national music based on folk or popular idioms. One problem in England was that, as a result of early industrialization and the even earlier abolition of an independent peasantry, those idioms were in a far less live and vigorous state than in, say, Hungary or Moravia. Vaughan Williams, Holst, Cecil Sharp and others collected folk songs and dances from almost the last people to remember them. Far from being the soil in which a rooted popular art could grow, it was a dying culture to which these enthusiasts tried to give last-minute respiration.

But if there was a musical rationale behind the English folk-song school of composers, the political dynamic was wholly absent, or at least quite different in ethical character from the liberal nationalist cultural projects of Italy or the Czech lands. If *Hugh the Drover* had any political meaning in the context of pre-1914 England, it could only be as a light-hearted piece of recruiting propaganda, in which the spectre of Bonaparte, a popular bogeyman in the early nineteenth century, as Thomas Hardy testified, was conjured up to remind the (southern) English of the still-present danger of invasion from the Continent.

But this version of nationalism, even if it is charitably seen as purely defensive, does not require the vision and dedication of the classic struggle for independence, nor does it have anything of the revolutionary social content of *Boris Godunov* or *The Brandenburgers in Bohemia*. It might suggest a comparison with *War and Peace*, another opera of national defence, but the urgency and absolute seriousness of Prokofiev's epic only underline the lightweight and unconvincing character of the nationalist sentiment in *Hugh the Drover*. The opera, for all its charm and lyricism, is too self-conscious, too evidently faked to carry conviction, and I think demonstrates that national or nationalist opera cannot be created at will, regardless of its political and cultural context. *Hugh the Drover* was, as Peter Pirie acutely observed, 'a peculiar and perilous undertaking at so late a date'.[31] The successes of English opera in the twentieth century, which came mainly after the end of World War Two, were, as we shall see in Chapter Nine, achieved in response to more genuine challenges.

7

Women in Opera

As far as its composition is concerned, opera has always been an overwhelmingly male affair. Until Judith Weir made her mark in recent years, it was hard to think of more than one or two women composers of operas: Ethel Smythe and, more recently, Thea Musgrave being the exceptions that come to mind. It may be that, as in so many other areas, women's achievements lie waiting to be recovered from the patronizing or unthinking neglect of generations of men. We are only just beginning to pay due attention to such sadly overshadowed figures as Clara Wieck-Schumann and Fanny Mendelssohn, some of whose songs were published as being her brother's work. But opera, unlike domestic music, is not often composed without some prospect of performance; until quite recently, therefore, it would have been only a very assured woman indeed who, whatever her musical talents, would have turned to composition in this form. There may not, in this case, be a great deal to be recovered.

Be that as it may, opera as we know it has been written and composed by men, and the question has to be asked: how has this male near-monopoly affected the portrayal of women in opera? Have they been as regularly mispresented, stereotyped and caricatured as in other cultural modes?

We ought first to note that classical music as a whole and opera in particular are fields that have so far been comparatively neglected by modern feminist criticism, which has cast such a revealing light on so many other fields of culture. The portrayal of women in opera is a subject in itself – too large for adequate treatment here – and requires debate as well as study. My purpose is to do no more than offer a few – I hope – provocative thoughts and observations which might perhaps help to stimulate further and fuller investigation.

One of the first feminist studies was Catherine Clément's *Opera, or the Undoing of Women*. This was first published in France in 1979, but it was not until 1988 that it appeared in an English translation.[1] As its title succinctly indicates, Clément argues that women get a poor deal in opera: essentially they figure as victims and sufferers, very often to the point of death:

> Opera concerns women. No, there is no feminist version; no, there is no liberation. Quite the contrary: they suffer, they cry, they die. . . . Not one of them escapes with her life, or very few of them do.[2]

She offers a list of women who die on the operatic stage:

> Nine by knife, two of them suicides; three by fire; two who jump; two consumptives; three who drown; three poisoned; two of fright; and a few unclassifiable . . . that is just the first sorting.[3]

There can be no doubt that women as victims do feature strongly in tragic opera. From the Verdi canon Clément cites Gilda, Violetta, Aida and Desdemona. She could have added a good many more. Both Abigaille (*Nabucco*) and Leonora (*Il trovatore*) poison themselves. The other Leonora (*La forza del destino*) is stabbed to death by her own brother, whilst Luisa Miller is poisoned by her frenzied lover.

But at least most of Verdi's women die of definite, ascertainable causes: disease, or various versions of violence. In the more phantas-magorical world of Wagner women expire, often for no very clear reason, when their role in the drama is done (Kundry), or when the hero upon whom they depend as their *raison d'être* leaves the scene (Elisabeth, Elsa and perhaps Isolde), or when a redemptory sacrifice is required (Senta, Brünnhilde). That the woman's fate hinges upon that of the heroic man is clear in the cases of Senta and Elsa, less clear in those of Elisabeth and Kundry.

Puccini's obsession with woman as victim was so great that he introduced the theme into one of his few operas with a happy ending, that is, significantly, an intended rather than achieved happy ending: *Turandot*. The slave-girl Liu is hardly necessary to the plot, although she introduces a note of tenderness that the icy princess lacks, and her death is even more gratuitous. Her hopeless devotion to Calaf culminates in her stabbing herself rather than reveal his name under torture. A stage direction tells us that, 'She casts her lost eyes about, looks at the Prince with supreme sweetness, goes staggering over to him and falls at his feet, dead.' To describe this as quintessential male fantasizing is almost superfluous. Examples could be multiplied, and Clément multiplies them. There can be no doubt that this is a fruitful line of enquiry.

Clément's approach is open to three major criticisms, however. The first is that she hardly pauses to acknowledge that what she is writing about is tragic opera, and that the convention of tragedy, in opera as in drama and other forms, involves suffering and usually culminates in death. It is not only women who die at the end of operas. Tannhäuser dies after Elisabeth; it is Tristan's death that Isolde laments and celebrates, as Brünnhilde provides Siegfried with his funeral oration before immolating herself. Manrico dies as well as Leonora, Radames alongside Aida, Rodolfo poisons himself as well as Luisa. Conversely, Ernani dies but not Elvira, Gustavus but not Amelia, Boccanegra is poisoned but his daughter survives him. Women may feature more as innocent victims than do men, but men do not escape nemesis either.

Even if we allow her concentration on tragic opera, it is surely important to attend to how and why women suffer and die, and not simply to the bald facts of suffering and death. Norma is a tragic figure, but not one of less stature than male tragic figures such as Alvaro (*La forza del destino*) or Otello – far from it. While it is true and significant that many of them are destroyed by male power, male arrogance or male violence, it certainly does not follow that we are encouraged to withhold our sympathy or admiration from them. No one says of Desdemona or Cio-Cio-San that 'she got what was coming to her' or words to that effect, as quite frequently happens when cases of rape or even wife murder come before British courts and British judges. Women suffer at the hands of men, in opera as they do in real life, but the balance of sympathy is weighted more towards women in opera than it usually is in the real world.

This is not to impute hitherto undetected feminist leanings to composers such as Bellini or Puccini. It is to do with the structure of tragedy and with the particular musical opportunities, for pathos and brilliance, available through the female voice, especially the soprano voice. A feminist of an earlier generation, Brigid Brophy, developed this point in her study *Mozart the Dramatist*:

> . . . it is the female voice, and par excellence the soprano, which exerts the most vivid pressure on our imagination . . . opera is a creation not exclusively for but round the soprano. *Prima donna* is a term without a masculine.

She argues that the primacy of women's voices in opera reflects the emergence of women onto the historical stage in the late eighteenth century. Opera 'not merely drew attention to women but pointed up the injustice of assuming that nature had made them in every respect inferior to men'.[4] If this is a reference to women's ability to sing, the point is a weak one. The ability of some women to sing beautifully might merely enhance the male conception of them as bewitching but brainless. On the other hand the appearance on the operatic stage of characters such as Susanna, Leonore/Fidelio, Norma and Violetta could not but compel a revision of traditional male perceptions of women and their abilities and virtues, if they were taken at all seriously. The prominence of women in opera was far greater than their presence in the public life of the nineteenth century; given that they do not feature in opera merely as victims and stereotypes of femininity, that prominence was likely to have some emancipatory effect, as Brophy suggests.

The most serious weakness of Clément's book, however, is its general failure to consider the roles given to women in non-tragic opera. The Mozart/Da Ponte operas are very scantily considered, except for an unavoidable few paragraphs on Don Giovanni/Juan, and the overt misogyny of *The Magic Flute* is taken more or less completely at face value. There is no mention at all of *Fidelio*, which seems too blatant a way of evading opera that does not fit with her overall thesis. The resourcefulness and intelligence of the women at the centre of many comedies, including several of Rossini's, *L'elisir d'amore, Falstaff* (which she discusses, but not in this respect) and *The Bartered Bride*, is ignored. Much comedy is a mode of revenge, sometimes light-hearted, sometimes quite savage, against the revered and established aspects of society. *Opera buffa* had this subversive background from the start, and it is not surprising to find that, in opera as in drama, a reversal of the normal power relations between men and women, as between masters and servants, provides a stock theme or situation. Of course such stories are themselves a form of fantasy which may in turn nourish complacent myths: women as 'the power behind the throne', and so on. But they may also be an expression, however flippant, of deep-seated resentments or repressed aspirations. Comedies like *Figaro* and *Falstaff* and *Don Pasquale*, for all their male authorship, can be seen in this light. Self-deluding men meet their match. Men can laugh at this, too, secure in the knowledge of their real power and privilege; but women may well respond more fervently, and identify themselves more deeply with these fables of fortunes reversed and vain fools outwitted.

But let us take the argument back onto Clément's chosen terrain, and consider a number of tragic or semi-tragic operas, and the way in which women appear in these works. I have chosen to look briefly at five generally very familiar works: *La traviata, Carmen, Eugene Onegin, Katya Kabanova* and *Lulu*.

La traviata, which is often seen today as one of the most sentimental of operas, when it was first performed was Verdi's most modern and most shocking work. At its British premiere in 1856 no translation of the libretto was available, no doubt in view of what *The Times* referred to vaguely as its 'foul and hideous horrors'; when a year later what became the Obscene Publications Act was introduced into Parliament, Dumas's *La Dame aux camélias* was flourished as exhibit number one for the prosecution.[5] The opera's title is never translated which, for the romanticizers, is just as well. Meaning literally 'the fallen one' or 'the lost one', the term was a familiar euphemism for a prostitute. There can be little doubt that Verdi knew what he was doing when he chose to turn Dumas's very recent play into an opera, and in fact he wanted it done in contemporary costumes and settings – something that the Venice management would not allow.

At first glance, the opera, far from being shocking, seems a morality tale to suit bourgeois tastes. A successful courtesan (Violetta) tries to attain respectability by giving up her disreputable if colourful life in

Paris and settling down in the country with her lover, Alfredo Germont. But his family, represented by his father, is outraged. The family's respectability and the reputation of Alfredo's sister are being damaged by the liaison. Violetta gives up the attempt to escape from her past and, eaten up by consumption, abandoned by her friends and harassed by her creditors, she dies in an atmosphere of penitence and piety. Alfredo is left free to marry a 'good woman'. It might almost be thought to be a happy ending.

But of course it is not. The whole point of the opera that Verdi composed is that it is a tragedy in which Violetta Valéry is the heroine as well as the victim. She is the victim of a relentless obsession with respectability that is quite ready to see her happiness destroyed, if that is what is needed. But she decides voluntarily to give up her relationship with Alfredo for his sake and for his family's; the public insults she subsequently endures from him do not cause her to break her undertaking. She is the only one of the three principals with a clear-sighted perception of her own position in society, and of how her actions may affect others. There is a useful comparison to be made with both the Massenet and the Puccini versions of the story of another famous courtesan whose worldly success eventually precipitates her tragic fall: Manon Lescaut. Neither version attempts to endow Manon with any special moral qualities. But Violetta is indisputably at the moral heart of La traviata.

We can see and hear that the readiness with which she accedes to Germont's demand that she leave Alfredo reflects not a pallid submissiveness, but her sense of guilt and fatalism – already voiced in the soliloquy–aria with which she ends the first act – her sense that a lasting, loving relationship is not for her, is merely a dream. So when Germont appears and makes his terrible demand, she exclaims, 'Il previdi . . . v'attesi' ('I foresaw it, I knew it'). Perhaps she ought not to feel guilty and insecure; but that she does is entirely credible, given the kind of society she inhabits. Yet Verdi's portrayal of the Germonts, and especially of Germont père, is by no means unsympathetic, and in the end Germont is prepared to accept Violetta as a daughter, even as earlier Violetta had begged him to. But it is her generosity and courage that we are invited to admire above all. 'God may forgive me, but man never will,' she exclaims bitterly, and there is no doubt that it is the harshness of conventional morality that is being indicted.

Some commentators, notably Julian Budden, resist the suggestion that Verdi had any personal reasons for treating the Marguerite Gautier/Violetta Valéry story so sympathetically.[6] But *La traviata* was written at a time when Verdi was living with Giuseppina Strepponi in Busseto and the liaison was attracting censorious gossip from the locals. It was this that provoked Verdi's letter of January 1852 to Antonio Barezzi, in which he asserted 'my nature rebels against conformity'. The letter also contains a notable passage about Giuseppina:

> In my house there lives a lady, free and independent, who, like myself, prefers a solitary life. . . . Neither I nor she is obliged to account for our actions. . . . In my house she is entitled to as much respect as myself, more even.

This is so close, in its tone of dignified reproach, to Violetta's reproof to Germont when he bursts into her house ('Donna son io, signore, ed in mia casa') that it seems most unlikely that Verdi was not struck by certain similarities between the play/opera and the situation of Giuseppina. It is an intimate opera, a modern opera of domestic life, and I think David Kimbell is right to see it as 'the most explicit of his offerings to Giuseppina Strepponi. It is their private opera, an artistic sublimation of their relationship.'[7]

Whatever may be the truth about this, there is, I think, no dispute that in *La traviata* Verdi offers a double challenge to conformity. He presents the conventional and hypocritical male morality, which condemns a prostitute or even a so-called 'loose woman' to a lifetime of shame and exclusion, as harsh and unjust; and he goes further and presents one of these social and moral inferiors as actually superior in wisdom, sensitivity and consideration to the men who surround her. If we can get away from the habit of treating *La traviata* as a romantic costume drama, we can still find the radical treatment of convention and morality in this opera challenging today. Violetta is a victim of male society and its rules, but it is that society that stands condemned, not her.

Carmen, some people might be tempted to say, is another matter. Bizet's opera of that name, which has one of the best libretti ever written, is in some ways far more modern than *La traviata*. It is a much less familiar kind of story, and it is strikingly free of the explicit morality of Verdi's work. A standard view of Carmen is that she is the archetypal *femme fatale*, the heartless hussy who breaks men's hearts without compunction, but breaks one too many and gets her come-uppance, albeit a rather extreme and nasty one, at the hands of Don José. Carmen, on this account, is not much more than a spirited whore.

The concept of the *femme fatale* is such a conventional one that it is surprising to find it so automatically employed by many otherwise sophisticated commentators. A woman – it could equally be a man, but the phrase *homme fatal* has, of course, not entered the language in the same way – attracts stronger feelings than she can reciprocate. She ends, or tries to end, a relationship when she tires of it. The man refuses to accept this, becomes obsessive, and obsessively jealous, and eventually kills the woman. In what way is the woman responsible for this pattern of behaviour, or for her own death? Yet, subtly or not so subtly, the idea of the *femme fatale* contrives to suggest that she is.

Certainly Don José's view of what happens to him is that the woman is responsible. And it is just possible that that view of Carmen could be derived from Prosper Mérimée's original story, in which it is José who tells the story of their relationship. But the viewpoint of the opera is different. The opera abolishes José's privileged position as narrator. Carmen now appears far more as an independent character, and not merely as the object of José's obsessive love. She is directly before us, and both the libretto and the music give her a much fuller and more balanced characterization than she received in the original story.

In the story José accuses Carmen of being an inveterate liar: 'I don't know if that girl has ever spoken a word of truth in her life. But when she spoke, I believed her, I couldn't help it.' By and large the opera shows Carmen behaving in a different way. She never conceals her view of love and lovers, which is that both are essentially transient. This is the message of her famous songs, the habanera and the seguidilla. The habanera is simultaneously an enticement and a warn-ing to Don José. He responds to the enticement, but predictably ignores the warning. When at the end she tells him, 'Carmen jamais n'a menti' ('Carmen has never yet lied'), she speaks the truth. She has concealed nothing. She is infinitely more clear-sighted than he.

Episode after episode makes it plain that he has neither the tempera-
ment nor the background to join Carmen wholeheartedly in her
lawless life as a gypsy and a smuggler. His conventional background is
embodied in Micaela, the demure but courageous girl whom the
librettists Meilhac and Halévy brilliantly invented as a foil to Carmen.
He makes no use of the file Carmen sends him when he is in prison,
and when the bugles summon him back to barracks he is ready to go,
giving up the opportunity to spend the night with her. Only the
accident of the fracas with his superior officer, Zuniga, forces him to
become an outlaw. But it is too late. He has already aroused Carmen's
contempt by his failure to break with the army for her sake. The
relationship is doomed.

He cannot accept this. He cannot accept that she is a free being, who
enters into relationships freely and withdraws from them with equal
independence. 'Libre elle est née et libre elle mourra' ('Free she was
born and free she will die') she tells him in the final scene, and that is
indeed how she dies at his hands, refusing to yield to his bullying
threats. Fatalistic she may be, according to the conventional lore of
gypsies, but her fatalism produces courage, not passivity.

Carmen is thus a victim of male violence in the most direct way. She
pays the ultimate price for her outright refusal to submit to the will of a
male, who clearly could not endure this affront to his expectations of
how a woman, loved by a man, ought to behave.

But is there anything in the opera, in words or music, to suggest
that Don José is justified in his actions, or that he alone deserves our
sympathy? I think not. It could be argued that José is in some ways the
more tragic figure, precisely because he is so hopelessly divided, so
little in control of his emotions and of his terrible propensity to
violence. It may be a little hard to call him 'a maternally dominated
psychopath',[8] but this verdict is a useful counterbalance to the traditional (male) view which sees him as a decent, innocent soldier lured to
his downfall by a woman without either serious feelings or moral
scruples. Carmen seems to me one of the operas we understand much
better in the wake of modern feminism. We appreciate better Carmen's qualities, her extraordinary independence and control over her
own life; and we understand better why she dies: such independence is
more than many men can tolerate. 'She acts like a man, that is all.'
Precisely, and that is what men find so hard to accept.

Eugene Onegin is an opera whose title is misleading in at least two ways. It is not really about a single individual so much as about a group of friends who act as a microcosm of a whole society. And if there *is* one individual who is its emotional core, it is not Onegin, but Tatyana. That was always Tchaikovsky's intention, and that is what he achieved. If nevertheless Onegin deserves his top billing, that is because he is the heedless, destructive catalyst of all the opera's significant developments.

Tchaikovsky recognized from the start that Pushkin's great narrative poem would be the basis for a rather unconventional kind of opera.

> I do not want kings and queens, popular uprisings, battles, marches, in a word anything that belongs to grand opera. I am looking for an intimate but powerful drama on the conflict of circumstances which I have seen or experienced, and which can move me inwardly.[9]

That was what he found in Pushkin's *Onegin*, and although his own work involved a significant shift in balance and mood away from Pushkin's original, Tchaikovsky achieved something absolutely authentic and convincing in its own right. He did not call the resulting work an opera, but 'lyric scenes', and as in Mussorgsky's *Boris Godunov* of a few years earlier, these scenes are only some episodes in a narrative, while others are not staged at all.

Tchaikovsky composed Tatyana's letter scene first of all, since this was the scene that most captivated him, and it remains the emotional heart of the work as a whole. There is no sense that the composer is patronizing the seventeen-year-old girl who impetuously pours out her heart to the older and more sophisticated Onegin. On the contrary, Tchaikovsky identifies with her wholeheartedly, and treats her rejection by Onegin in the following scene as a demonstration of his coldness and patronizing insensitivity. Only at the end of the opera does Onegin realize his mistake, and experience the same feelings towards her as she has always felt towards him: as Tchaikovsky shows by giving him her themes from the letter scene. 'Ah happiness was once so near us!' they sing together. But it is too late. Tatyana has made her commitment to the elderly (45-year-old) Prince Gremin, and has no intention of breaking it. Besides, who knows how serious Onegin is? Tatyana suggests that though he was not interested in her when she was a naïve country girl, now that she's rich and married to someone important, he is attracted by the idea of seducing her.

> For what a conquest it would seem
> If I should yield to your persuasion!

Of course Onegin denies this, and no doubt with sincerity. But he may not really understand his own feelings, whereas Tatyana, the grown woman, is clear-sighted in a way that Onegin, the unsettled, dissatisfied wanderer, is not.

Catherine Clément, who writes particularly well about this opera, dubs it 'Eugen Onegin, or how girls repeat their mothers' history'. For, as she points out, the opera opens with Madame Larina and the nurse making jam and listening to the Larin girls singing a melancholy duet. The mother recalls how she had been in love with a guardsman, but had been compelled to marry a husband of her father's choice whom she did not love. Unhappy at first, she grew resigned to her lot; she and the Nurse draw the moral of the story:

> God sends us habit from above
> In place of happiness and love.
> The proverb's true.

By the end of the opera the pattern has been repeated in the life of Tatyana. She is married to Gremin, and 'the time to make preserves has come'.[10] It is a tragedy of a kind, but one quite without melodrama, with an ending as uncertain and unsatisfactory as life itself. If it touches and disturbs us more deeply than many apparently more harrowing tales, it is precisely this realism and lack of exaggeration that achieve the effect.

Like *La traviata*, like *Carmen* – so different from the latter in so many ways, even though Tchaikovsky was an early enthusiast for Bizet's misunderstood masterpiece – this is an opera which is truthful about what happens to women, but which neither gloats nor glories in their misfortunes. On the contrary. Tchaikovsky, like Verdi, makes the woman the focus of sympathy and of moral dignity. Even the young Tatyana's writing of the letter, which anyone (including the mature Tatyana) might be tempted to regard as a piece of adolescent foolishness that the more sensible Onegin is right to rebuff, even if he does so in an unacceptably snooty fashion, is not so treated by Tchaikovsky, who clearly respects Tatyana's courage and unconventionality. *Eugene Onegin* requires no special, critical glossing by producers or performers to bring out its feminist significances. It was written only a few years after *Carmen*, and both operas reflect, even if only intuitively, a changing and growing awareness of women, women's positions in society, and women's grievances.

Janáček's *Katya Kabanova* is another opera based on a Russian classic, in this case Ostrovsky's famous play *The Storm*; again like Tchaikovsky with *Onegin*, the composer shifted the balance and emphasis of the literary original to focus more sharply on the woman at the centre of the story. This is clearly indicated by the change of title. Ostrovsky's play is a work of social criticism, directed against the backwardness, intolerance and vindictiveness of Russian small-town society in the middle of the nineteenth century. Katya is a victim of this narrow, repressive environment, but the play does not focus on her with the single-mindedness of the opera, for which Janáček devised his own libretto. Ironically, the one moment in the opera when we do get a glimpse of the superstitious ignorance of the town – in their reactions to the storm at the opening of Act Three – is one of its least effective, precisely because it goes against the overall grain of Janáček's adaptation, and belongs to the play rather than to the opera.

There is a sense, then, in which Janáček depoliticizes the play (which clearly belongs to the oppositional literature of tsarist Russia) for his own purposes. But those purposes can themselves be seen as political, in so far as it is the representative nature of Katya's situation and her tragedy that he so powerfully succeeds in conveying. Katya, to be sure, is yet another operatic victim of male bullying and callousness – although her chief enemy and humiliator is her mother-in-law – and of social morals that operate one set of standards for men, another for women. But, as with Violetta, it is with the woman that the composer identifies and persuades his audience to identify; as Cynthia Marsh has written, 'her tragedy is so vividly portrayed that she appears to represent the condition of women in general'.[11]

But too much can be, and has been, made of the elimination of social comment. If it were true that 'Janáček treated the social background almost with contempt',[12] then Katya's own agonies and dissatisfactions would become almost unintelligible. It is not merely that she is trapped in an unhappy marriage to a man still under the heavy domination of a tyrannical mother. That repressive, claustrophobic home environment is an expression and microcosm of the provincial society within which all the characters have to survive; it was suggested by the composer's friend, Max Brod, that the husband Tichon's mother, Kabanicha, is a domestic embodiment of the tsarist principle of absolute, unquestionable authority: 'She stands symbolically for tsarist Russia, with its morality of blind obedience to arbitrary command.'[13] But what gives this tragedy its special, acute poignancy is that Katya is not an explicit, self-aware rebel against this intolerant society. She suffers from its cruel, cramping restraints, and longs for freedom, the freedom of the birds, as she tells Varvara in Scene Two. But she has internalized the values of marital fidelity and stability, so that her love for another man, Boris, fills her with guilt and anxiety – to the extent that she begs Tichon to stay with her, not go away, and it is she who suggests that she swear an oath not even to think of another man while he is away. If Boris had taken her away as she begged him to, perhaps her life could have had a new start. But she is left to endure the censure of her husband, her mother-in-law and her town:

> The people will stare at me
> when I go through the streets,
> mocking and laughing at me.

And, since she herself, at one level, accepts the justness of that censure, she finds herself in a hopeless position. 'What more can I live for now?' Even Varvara and Kudryash, who enjoy a guilt-free relationship and believe that Katya has done nothing to reproach herself for, nevertheless feel compelled to leave the town as the tragedy approaches its crisis. How much more dreadful is the situation of the conscience-stricken Katya.

Emotionally she is at odds with her society. Why is she unhappy? What has gone wrong? She wants to belong, to be happy within society, not to revolt against it, not to flee from it. In a sense therefore she is a far more deeply representative woman than those who can cheerfully challenge received roles and values. Millions upon millions of women throughout history must have wondered, as she does, why the roles they have been allotted in society – as wife and mother – do not bring them the unlimited happiness that myth so tenaciously attaches to them. Many, like Tatyana, choose the path of stoical adjustment. But Katya's position is infinitely less comfortable than Tatyana's, and her perception of her situation more confused. Her suicide is the ultimate response to tensions within herself and within her life that she cannot resolve. It is a psychological drama, therefore, but not on that account one without a social dimension, a dimension that modern feminism has made it easier for us to recognize.

In this opera and in the earlier *Jenufa*, Janáček displays an exceptional empathy with his women characters. One might think that the grotesque Kabanicha contradicts this, and certainly Janáček goes further than Ostrovsky in stressing her cold cruelty (she is given the opera's final chilling words to sing, whereas the play ends with Tichon's expressions of dismay). But if we are tempted to think that Janáček lacks sympathy with older women, his treatment of the Kostelnicka in *Jenufa* refutes this. Jenufa's understanding and forgiveness of her foster mother's terrible crime of infanticide is so generous and heroic, and is invested by Janáček with such radiant music, that it is clear that we are being invited to consider her actions in the same compassionate light. We shall find the composer lavishing a similar compassion on the condemned murderers of *From the House of the Dead*.

What stands out equally clearly is the relative feebleness of the male characters in both operas. Steva, to whom Jenufa is engaged and by whom she is pregnant, is vain and silly, and accepts no responsibility for her pregnancy or for the child when it is born. Laca, his glowering half-brother, is full of resentment at his subordinate role, and slashes Jenufa's face in a fit of jealous passion. Eventually he and Jenufa are drawn together by their sufferings: Laca is a character who matures in the course of the opera. But he displays nothing like the moral stamina and courage of Jenufa. It is she who hauls him out of the pit of violent resentments into which he has sunk.

In *Katya Kabanova* none of the men possesses even Laca's capacity for self-redemption. Tichon is unable or unwilling to protect his wife against his mother's insults and humiliations. Her lover, Boris, for all his protestations of love, is equally subservient to his uncle, Dikoy, who orders him to go away when Katya publicly confesses her adultery. The thought of going with him occurs to her, but not, it seems, to him. The affair is over; he abandons her to her fate.

Jenufa is a victim of male violence as directly, though not as fatally, as Carmen. Katya is compelled, by the prospect of endless social ostracism as well as by her own sense of guilt, to take her own life. Her equally culpable lover feels no comparable shame or compulsion. *Katya* conforms to a pattern in which women figure as victims, destroyed by pressures that do not bear on men in the same drastic way. Yet Janáček so structures these stories and portrays the characters that it is the women who elicit not only our sympathy, but our understanding and our admiration.

With the possible exception of *Carmen*, a work of almost classical objectivity, each of these operas is so constructed as to make the woman at the centre of the story the moral as well as the emotional focus of the work. The same cannot exactly be said of Alban Berg's *Lulu*, which is closer to *Carmen* in this respect. Lulu, who certainly has feelings of her own, and, like Carmen, knows herself far better than do the men who pursue her, is the emotional focus of the opera: the object of the loves and lusts of many men and one woman. And the opera is certainly, in moral terms, a challenging and disturbing work. But Lulu herself disclaims all acquaintance with beliefs, ideas, morality. In response to a series of questions about her beliefs from the painter who becomes her second husband, she answers seven times, 'Ich weiss es nicht,' like Parsifal responding to Gurnemanz's enquiries. Like Parsifal when he first appears, Lulu is a wholly innocent creature, a child of nature who belongs nowhere and to no one. (*Erdgeist* – 'Earth Spirit' – is the title of one of the two Wedekind plays from which Berg made the libretto of his second opera.) But unlike Parsifal she remains that way until the very end: sadder, certainly, and perhaps wiser, but not essentially changed. Like Carmen, she has her own integrity: she remains true to herself. In her 'Lied', which is sung to Dr Schön, the one man she really loves, she reminds him that she has never pretended to be anything other than what she is. Lulu's essence can be seen as pure sensuality or even sexuality. But that is not to say that she is available, or wants to be available, to any man or woman who desires her. When the blackmailing Marquis tries to sell her to a Cairo brothel as an alternative to handing her over to the police, she rejects this indignantly as another kind of imprisonment. Reduced to prostitution in the final scene, she is finally compelled to sell the one thing that she really values in herself.

The men who desire her, and to whom she responds (within limits), do not understand her and do not really try. This is expressed by the fact that they all endow her with names of their own choosing: Nelly, Eva, Mignon. Only the rather mysterious old man, Schigolch, who is not her father although he is sometimes thought to be that, calls her Lulu. The others are patently trying to turn her into the realization of their fantasies. When these efforts predictably collapse, Lulu is seen as to blame. Two of her husbands – the doctor who dies of shock when he comes home to find her making love to the painter, and the painter who commits suicide when Dr Schön fills him in on Lulu's past – die more or less before her eyes. Lulu responds with shocking callousness. The truth is that she feels no involvement with either man, and no responsibility for their deaths. She hardly belongs to the everyday human world. Like Tristan and Isolde, like Helen in Tippett's version of *King Priam*, she knows nothing of normal moral obligations.

The character of Lulu has inevitably attracted the stock label, *femme fatale*, often from commentators from whom more subtlety might be expected. Professor George Steiner, for example, has written: 'She is the *femme fatale*, the *belle dame sans merci*, the man-eating, man-devouring vamp.' It is true that love or desire for Lulu leads several men and one woman to their deaths. To that extent the label is apt. And of course it could be argued that this stereotypical version of woman is reproduced in the work of Wedekind and Berg. In fact I think they achieve something much more truthful. In what sense is Lulu 'a woman as tiger, as man-eater, as destroyer'?[14] In what sense does she deliberately, or even unwittingly, encompass the deaths of her lovers, admirers and husbands – with the sole, ironic exception of Dr Schön, whom she shoots? No more than Tippett's Helen does she encourage their advances, or mislead them with false promises of unending happiness or permanent liaisons. In another idiom, she might sing:

> Men cluster to me
> Like moths about the flame.

But that does not make the flame responsible for the hapless obsession of the moths. Like Carmen, Lulu goes her own way, follows the logic of her own existence.

That is too much for the men to endure. In the end her lovers are also her destroyers. *Lulu*, as Pierre Boulez has said, 'is definitely a "morality play", a sort of *Rake's Progress* . . .'[15] Berg constructed it so, with his usual careful elaboration. The rise and fall of Lulu divide the opera exactly into two halves. Her rise culminates in Scene One of Act Two, when she is married to the capitalist, Dr Schön. Her shooting of him leads to her imprisonment, and the second half of the opera charts her decline. In between comes the *ostinato* interlude, composed to accompany a film depicting the climactic events of her arrest, trial and imprisonment, and itself constructed as a musical palindrome. It was Berg's own idea that the singers who play Lulu's three husbands, the doctor, the painter and Dr Schön, should also in the opera's final scene play her three clients as a prostitute in London. These doublings are proposed not for the sake of economy, but to make the specific point that the men who love her also abuse and destroy her. Schön reappears as Jack the Ripper. Lulu is drawn to him as she is not to her other customers, and he murders her and her faithful friend and admirer the Countess Geschwitz in the final moments of the opera.

But Berg's 'morality play' is quite different from the Stravinsky/Auden version of the classic eighteenth-century story, *The Rake's Progress*. Stravinsky and Auden match the use of traditional musical forms, such as *cavatina/cabaletta* arias, with an equally traditional invocation of old-fashioned morality. This is what happens to the dissolute and unprincipled man, and not even the true love of Anne Truelove can rescue him from madness and death. It is all very neat. Lulu, however, is punished not so much for what she does as for what she is, and we are invited to reflect on the hypocrisy of the men who apparently worship her, but end by reducing her to prostitution and death.

When Berg first read Wedekind's plays, a quarter of a century before he turned them into an opera, it was Wedekind's celebration of sensuality that enthused him most:

> At last we have realized that sensuality is not a weakness . . . but an immense strength – the centre of all our being and thought. Only

through an understanding of the sensual can one arrive at a true idea of the human psyche.[16]

Lulu is the incarnation of that sensuality; but it is more than simple sensuality that she represents. Otherwise why should prostitution be so obnoxious to her? Her availability to men is rationed by her determination to preserve her independence and to be true to her own feelings. Sensuality must, ideally, be guided by love. Hence she is unlikely to make a successful prostitute. As the perceptive Schigolch says, in the final scene, 'She can't make a living from loving, since her life is love.' ('Die kann von der Liebe nicht leben, weil ihr Leben die Liebe ist.')

Berg did not despise prostitutes. He told his fiancée, Helene, that he found 'a prostitute's position no more or less offensive than associating with people whom you and many others consider quite unobjectionable'.[17] This comment was not gratuitously shocking. It arose because his lesbian sister, Smaragda, had a relationship with a prostitute. Smaragda tried to commit suicide on one occasion. *Lulu*, like *Wozzeck*, has its autobiographical elements: Berg makes Alwa a composer, not a writer. Berg extends the sexual radicalism of the opera from its celebration of sensuality to its open and deeply sympathetic portrayal of the lesbian Countess Geschwitz. Geschwitz is regarded as a freak by Lulu and most of the men in the opera. But this attitude is clearly not shared by Berg (or Wedekind), even though Berg confessed, 'I find her harder to set to music than all the rest of Lulu's "satellites" put together.'[18] Geschwitz's devotion to Lulu is consistent and self-sacrificing. She is a figure of some nobility. Berg endows her with a halo of string sonorities, and it is she who sings the brief but intensely beautiful and poignant *Liebestod* which brings the opera to an end and provides Lulu with her epitaph.

Lulu is often referred to as sordid and squalid – as also is *Wozzeck*. In terms of its story and events it is not entirely clear why it should have attracted such adjectives when very similar stories like that of Manon Lescaut, or equally unpleasant tales like that of *Rigoletto*, now normally escape such descriptions. But the Manon story, in either version, and *Rigoletto*, are costume dramas, partially populated by aristocrats and persons of title. They therefore possess distance and glamour. Although Wedekind's plays are nearly a century old, both they and Berg's operas belong inescapably to the modern, urban world. Whatever period a production might be set in, the essential drama and characters are all too close to the world with which we are familiar: the world of capitalist newspaper proprietors, stock market crashes, and murderers who specialize in killing prostitutes. It is not surprising that *Lulu* is found to be 'utterly unpleasant'. It is almost impossible to turn it into escapist entertainment.

Nevertheless, Berg's supreme achievement is to invest this story and its characters with humanity and even dignity. The final scene, in which Lulu brings her clients up to the attic where she is living with Geschwitz, Alwa and Schigolch, and in which first Alwa and then Lulu herself and Geschwitz are murdered by the Negro and Jack the Ripper, is certainly, in its narrative content, sordid and horrific. And Berg's music expresses the horror of the final murders. Yet taken as a whole, this scene is powerful, almost grandly moving, full of compassion for the situation of Lulu and her friends. As in the final act of *Rigoletto*, with its botched contract murder and sexually available woman, squalor is raised to the level of tragedy. Berg's understanding of what prostitution is, and why it occurs, is here embodied in music that makes everything credible and terrible. There is no hint of cartoon or satire, such as we might find in Weill or Stravinsky. This scene in particular is one of the great achievements of Western opera.

With the partial exception of Tatyana, all of these operatic heroines end badly. Two of them are directly victims of male violence. Another is driven to suicide. They certainly belong to Catherine Clément's gallery of women as victims. My point is a simple one. In at least four of these operas – *Carmen* is a more ambiguous case – the balance of empathy and admiration is with the woman, who is not only a target of male misunderstanding, abuse and cruelty, but also to one degree or another a courageous or even heroic figure. Of course many operas – perhaps any opera – can be given a feminist slant or interpretation. None of the works briefly discussed here needs special attention of that kind. The sympathy and understanding for women that they display are manifest. Against the odds, given the near monopoly of its creation by men, opera speaks more eloquently for women, for their qualities and achievements, and against their humiliations and sufferings, than we might expect.

8

Interlude –
Opera without Politics:
Puccini and Strauss

Only two opera composers of the early twentieth century produced
works that have become staples of the standard repertory: Puccini and
Richard Strauss. Neither composer is associated, through their music,
with politics. Yet whereas Strauss carefully avoided subjects that had
more than a vestigial political dimension – with the strange exception
of *Friedenstag*, a work of the 1930s which I have not heard, and which
still (in 1992) awaits its British stage premiere – Puccini presents
something of a paradox. The plots of two of his three most popular
operas, *Tosca* and *Madama Butterfly*, possess an inescapable political
element. Why did this determinedly non-political composer choose
such subjects? It is something of a puzzle, on which the standard
commentaries in English cast no light. *Tosca* provides a model of how
an essentially political story can be emptied of political content in a
way that leaves us puzzling about meaning and motivation. *Madama
Butterfly* is a more complex case, not least because of the revisions
Puccini made after its unsuccessful premiere.

Tosca

The story of Tosca is melodramatic, but not improbably so. The
central situation, in which a man of power uses his hold over a

woman's lover to get her to surrender herself to him, is both familiar and credible. Even the juxtaposition of the lover's torture to the bullying of the woman can be seen as dramatically acceptable, however horrible. The final twist, in which the lover's mock execution turns out to be real, adds more cruelty to the tale, but can again be accepted as a black conclusion to a dreadful story. Mock executions are by no means a theatrical device: Dostoevsky was one famous victim of this cruel ordeal.

Tosca had its first performance in Rome on 14 January 1900 and was based on events that took place in the same city almost exactly one hundred years earlier, on 17 June 1800. The invasion of Italy by French armies led by Napoleon Bonaparte in 1796 led to the expulsion of the old dynastic rulers, including the Pope, and the setting up of radical republics in northern Italy as well as in Rome and Naples. By 1800 these republics had collapsed, both for lack of public support and under the pressure of military counterattack by the anti-French European powers. With the vital assistance of a British fleet under Nelson, the old order was back in power, and taking a terrible revenge on those who had dared to challenge and displace it – as it always does. In the opera, Scarpia, the police chief, is the agent of this systematic vengeance. Angelotti, formerly a consul of the Roman republic, is one of those being hunted down. He is loosely based on one of the actual consuls, Liborio Angelucci. Cavaradossi, a radical sympathizer who hides him, is tortured to reveal his hiding place. He refuses to speak, and it is not he but the singer Tosca who, out of love for him, reveals where Angelotti is concealed.

The establishment of the radical republics marked the beginning of the national struggle which culminated in the achievement of Italian independence and unity in the 1860s. Verdi heard Illica read the libretto in 1894 at the Paris home of the French playwright Victorien Sardou, author of *La Tosca*, and was apparently much impressed, 'especially by a long farewell to art and life which Illica had written for Cavaradossi to sing shortly before his execution'.[1] It is not difficult to imagine what Verdi would have made of this subject. It must have appealed strongly to his patriotism, his idealism and his deep understanding of political conflict.

But there is hardly any of this in Puccini's version, from which the political element is excluded so far as the story permits. In the libretto only a single line tells us what Angelotti is, or was, and why he is on the run. Cavaradossi recognizes him and exclaims, 'Il Console della spenta republica romana', and Angelotti explains that he has escaped from the Castel Sant'Angelo. Similarly we learn little of Scarpia's role beyond a single rapid speech of Cavaradossi's, where he is characterized as

> That dirty bigot who beneath the cloak of religion
> gratifies his squalid lusts and passions.
> He can bend
> to his evil ambition
> churchman as well as hangman!

When Scarpia is given the opportunity to reveal himself to us, in his soliloquy at the opening of Act Two, he says nothing about his official role or about the sources of his power. He simply gloats over the coming deaths of Angelotti and Cavaradossi, and revels in his own appetite for the violent conquest of women – for rape, in other words. Scarpia owes his power and opportunities to a turn of the political wheel. He is hunting down not criminals, but political opponents. It is implausible that he suggests no political motive, or at least justification, for his cruelty. Yet he is not even given words in which to denounce his enemies as subversives, heretics and so forth. A single brief reference to the painter as 'un volterrian', a disciple of Voltaire, is all we have by way of explaining his suspicion of the painter in Act One.

Tosca, we can accept, is a non-political person. This, in effect, is what she confesses in 'Vissi d'arte'. Cavaradossi recognizes this, when he explains to Angelotti that he cannot tell her what is going on, since she believes that nothing should be concealed from the priest to whom she makes confession. She is the non-political person who is utterly bewildered by the events in which she becomes embroiled, and whose instinctive reaction is always to put the safety and well-being of her lover first. This is consistent and credible.

But the depoliticization of Cavaradossi as well as of Scarpia is not. When Cavaradossi meets and recognizes Angelotti in the church, he immediately agrees to conceal him. Under torture he stubbornly refuses to reveal Angelotti's whereabouts. These actions can only be explained in terms of his political commitment. Yet this is barely hinted at. There is a moment when he briefly expresses his scorn for Scarpia, and another when, after the torture has stopped, news comes of Napoleon's victory at Marengo and the painter is allowed a moment of rejoicing. But his joy is in hysterical vein, and after four short lines turns into a denunciation of Scarpia. It also distracts attention from Tosca's betrayal of Angelotti, for which Cavaradossi would surely have rebuked her. This news, which would have meant so much to a man who had just endured torture for the same political cause, is treated by Puccini as no more than another item in the feud with Scarpia, and a further twist with which to screw up the theatrical excitement – nothing more. The final absurdity comes when Cavaradossi learns from Tosca of the death of Scarpia. This must be, for him, both a political and a personal triumph. But all it inspires is the maudlin and lacklustre 'O dolci mani', which is both inappropriate and inadequate.

In Act Three the heroic farewell to life and art that Verdi so admired disappears entirely, being replaced by 'E lucevan le stelle', a recollection of an erotic encounter which collapses into self-pity: 'Svani per sempre il bel sogno d'amore' ('The lovely dream of love has vanished for ever'). For a man facing death for his political convictions, this is grotesquely inappropriate.

It can reasonably be said in Puccini's defence that he knew his own abilities and limitations, knew that the heroic Verdian note was beyond him, and was, indeed, not suited to the kind of work he wanted to write. That is no doubt correct; but he can only create his type of drama, a drama of intense, exclusive personal relationships, out of *Tosca* by making Cavaradossi's courage appear bizarre and almost unintelligible. Even Giuseppe Giacosa, co-librettist with Illica, was upset by what Puccini did with Cavaradossi: 'it seems' he wrote to Puccini's publisher and impresario, Ricordi, 'that for you and Puccini, Mario Cavaradossi should be nothing but a *signor tenore*'.[2] This will not worry those who do not look for coherence or plausibility in the opera house; but it is a good example of what happens when a determinedly non-political composer takes up an intrinsically political subject. Keeping politics out of politics is not a recipe for intelligibility.

There remains the question of torture, and Puccini's use of it as the core of the drama in Act Two. This is, of course, not the only opera by

Puccini in which torture figures; the torture and death of Liu in *Turandot* are, in one way, even more objectionable because they are so superfluous to both the plot and character development. But there is a gratuitous nastiness in *Tosca* too. The threat of death would surely have been enough to extract the necessary information and submission from Tosca, instead of which the composer and his librettists generate the maximum of crude tension and horror by having Cavaradossi tortured just offstage, his cries of pain audible to us as well as to Tosca.

Puccini's evident fascination with cruelty and suffering can be seen as a rather distasteful psychological phenomenon. But in the light of twentieth-century experience in particular, to take pleasure in cruelty and suffering can hardly be regarded merely as an individual foible. Sadistic cruelty has been given a licence by many modern political regimes, and fascism, specifically, provided it with a justification. Puccini anticipates the sophisticated, obsessive cruelty and pleasure in cruelty that were conspicuous features of fascism. And this, it can be argued, is what makes *Tosca* a more modern and prophetic work than it could ever have been in the hands of Verdi.

Bernard Williams, in one of the few interesting comments on *Tosca* (and Puccini) that I have come across, suggests that it is 'the one really twentieth-century subject among Puccini's works. . . . It really asks to be set in this century, above all in Mussolini's Italy, with Scarpia as a Fascist boss. Many things in the opera fit such a time and such a regime. . . .'[3] This idea was presumably the inspiration behind Jonathan Miller's production for Florence and the English National Opera in 1986–87. The action was shifted to Rome in the spring of 1944, when, after the collapse of Mussolini's regime, the Nazis had occupied the city and were busy hunting down, interrogating and torturing members of the Italian resistance.

In the ENO programme Gaia Servadio recounted the extraordinary story of how the young film director Luchino Visconti, then a member of the resistance, was arrested and taken to the headquarters of the Italian Special Squad, where he was questioned and beaten up by its head, Pietro Koch. Simultaneously the actress Maria Denis, who was in love with Visconti, was brought to the same place. Koch became infatuated with her, and she finally persuaded Koch not to hand over Visconti to the Gestapo: *Tosca* with a happy ending. Koch was later captured and executed.[4] This and other material in the programme did much to support Williams's argument. The updating of the opera in this production was highly effective, and gave *Tosca* a seriousness it needs if its sheer nastiness is not to seem gratuitous – as perhaps in the the final analysis it always must.

Madama Butterfly

Puccini's next opera also has a political dimension, which is necessary to an understanding of the story and its principal characters; yet once again the composer, this time in the process of revising the work after its unsuccessful first performance at La Scala in February 1904, tinkered with it in such a way as to confuse its inherent logic. Once again the focus of the opera's politics is the *signor tenore*, the America naval lieutenant Pinkerton.

However Puccini may have reacted to David Belasco's play *Madame Butterfly*, you have to be almost wilfully non-political not to recognize in this story a parable and epitome of the impact of Western imperialism upon the non-Western world. Pinkerton can perhaps be seen simply as an unusually (or more than usually) insensitive and callous man; but even at that level it is hard not to reflect on the circumstances that make it possible for him to treat Butterfly so cruelly. He is in a position to leave her behind, believing he will return, when in fact he intends to go back to the United States and marry 'una vera sposa americana'. But Cio-Cio-San has no such freedom. She must remain in Nagasaki, isolated from her family and culture because she has committed herself wholly to her American husband and his culture, and regards herself as an American. In Act Two she refers to America as 'my country', 'mio paese', and welcomes Sharpless, the US Consul, 'in casa americana', into an American house.

The tragedy is hers, not his, not simply because she is one of an itinerant sailor's many brief liaisons, but because he takes advantage of her innocence and of the attractive power of the American way of life, which she sees as superior to that of her native Japan. To write, as Mosco Carner did, that the cause of her tragedy is simply 'the incompatibility of East and West' is to resort to one of those evasive euphemisms with which people habitually camouflage an awkward political truth.[5] It is not the equality of the two cultures that determines the form of the tragedy, but precisely their inequality, and the ability of the globally powerful Americans to use and discard people (and especially women) from less powerful, and less cynical, societies.

Pinkerton is not a weak or well-meaning man who allows himself to be drawn deeper than he intended into an unfortunate dilemma. His first dialogue with Sharpless makes it excruciatingly clear that he knows exactly what he is doing. Cio-Cio-San is like a butterfly that he must chase even if her wings are damaged in the process. This, he tells his worried companion, is the philosophy of 'lo yankee vagabondo'. He will marry her, but the Japanese wedding contract is not to be taken seriously. He proposes a toast to the day when he gets married in earnest to a 'real American wife'. And at that very moment we hear the touching, ecstatic music of Butterfly and her companions as they climb the hill to the house, until Butterfly's voice soars above them:

> Io sono la fanciulla
> Piu lieta del Giappone,
> Anzi del mondo.

(I am the happiest girl in Japan, in fact in the world.)

The calculated deception makes this song poignant, but it also underlines the fact that it is Pinkerton who controls the situation, and creates the tragedy. The marriage they go through means everything to her, nothing to him. In the extended duet which ends Act One there is again a poignant contrast between Butterfly's tremulous, exalted rapture and pleas to Pinkerton to 'love me a little, like a child', and his crude male eagerness to get her into bed: 'Vieni, vieni'. What is for him the gratification of a passing sexual whim ('grillo') or infatuation is for her the turning point of her young life.

The final expression of Pinkerton's imperialist presumption, partially masked as compassion, comes when the lieutenant and his American wife return to Nagasaki to take away the son born to Butterfly after his departure – for the child's own good, naturally. Only membership of a society that assumes its own superiority can give people the confidence to take a young child away from its mother. This proposal removes Butterfly's last reason for going on living.

But Pinkerton's treatment of Butterfly is only the most outrageous aspect of his contemptuous attitude towards Japan and the Japanese.

When the house servants are introduced to him, he cannot be bothered to attend to their proper names, and announces that he will call them 'muso primo, secondo, e muso terzo' – 'face', or even 'mug', one, two and three. He is insulting about Japanese food, referring to 'candied flies and spiders', impatient of traditional courtesies, and entirely disrespectful towards Butterfly's relations. Much of Pinkerton's arrogance was cut when Puccini revised the opera extensively for its Paris premiere in 1906, and even before then Puccini had tried to soften the harsh impression created by Pinkerton by adding the remorseful aria 'Addio, fiorito asil' when he reappears to claim the child. In the Paris version Kate Pinkerton's conversation with Butterfly was transferred to Sharpless, and the scene in which the Consul tries to give Butterfly the money Pinkerton has left for her was cut altogether. Whatever the reasons for these changes – and they were urged on Puccini by Albert Carré, the director of the Opéra-Comique – they softened the harshness of the original and made it more acceptable to American audiences, though not much more so to Japanese ones. But in the end no amount of remorse and sensitivity on the part of Pinkerton and his *sposa americana* can redeem his character or diminish the horrible tragedy of what has occurred. They only blur the basic outlines of the characters and the plot.

Mosco Carner, one of the great experts on Puccini, found it simply impossible to accept the political meaning of *Butterfly*. He observed that 'Communism has in fact seized on *Butterfly* as propaganda against colonial imperialism', and referred scornfully to 'the supposed Marxist moral of the plot', as if this was all so much crude distortion of what the opera actually is.[6] And when Joachim Herz returned to much of the original version for his 1978 production for Welsh National Opera, it was denounced as a 'despicable forgery' by Rodney Milnes (in the *Observer* of 30 September 1984), as if an East German producer could only be expected to falsify a work for political reasons.

It is certainly a puzzle that so resolutely non-political a composer as Puccini should have chosen such an inherently political story. We need not doubt that his real interest is in Butterfly herself, and it is she who dominates the long second act of the opera – and dominates not simply by being its focus, but by virtue of the dignity and determination with which she rejects every invitation to abandon her hope or to give way to self-pity and despair. She is a victim, but not a pathetic one. Her behaviour and her resolution are heroic. As Tom Sutcliffe has written: 'There's no evidence that he [Puccini] was a premature feminist, or opponent of colonialism. Yet is not *Madama Butterfly* one of the most telling indictments of American imperialism and the casual exploitation of women?'[7] We need not ascribe this indictment to any intention of the composer; but the work stands independent of its author's intentions, and if we ignore or soften its political meanings, we diminish it. Like much of Puccini's work, it hovers on the edges of sentimentality and melodrama. It can be dragged back from the brink by acknowledging its wider, and still highly topical, implications.

Of the rest of Puccini's work, there is not much to be said in this context. However, we might note that in his last, uncompleted opera, *Turandot*, Puccini finds an appropriate context for his preoccupation with cruelty in that the whole story is about the barbarous exercise of absolute power. Particularly in the magnificently dynamic and well-structured Act One, Puccini evokes with great vividness and grandeur a society in which the whole people cower under the shadow of an arbitrary depotism. Carner suggested a comparison, in the crowd scenes, with *Boris Godunov*, and this is apt, even though in Puccini's opera the people recede into the background as the Calaf–Turandot relationship comes to the fore. John Louis DiGaetani has developed this theme in an interesting way, pointing out that these crowds, like the crowd in Shakespeare's *Julius Caesar*, are easily swayed and clearly need leadership and direction. By the end of the opera there is the prospect that this leadership will be provided by Calaf. Perhaps, suggests DiGaetani, 'Puccini had the same hopes for Mussolini'; there is evidence that the composer viewed Mussolini and his regime with some sympathy.[8]

I will say something of *Il tabarro* in a later context. Otherwise the political elements in Puccini's operas appear either incidental or accidental in relation to the composer's real concerns. For all the popularity of a handful of his works, the range of his sympathies, of the moods and characters he can evoke, is narrow, and his general evasion of politics is an aspect of that narrowness. He knew his own strengths and made the most of them. Those who draw attention to his limitations (like Joseph Kerman in his classic study, *Opera and Drama*) attract an immense amount of hostility. These limitations exist nevertheless, and however much we may enjoy his music, it is absurd to deny their existence.

Richard Strauss

In the summer of 1898 Richard Strauss began work on a tone poem that he at first referred to as his *Eroica*, and which soon acquired its familiar title, *Ein Heldenleben* ('A Hero's Life'). The comparison with Beethoven's symphony was Strauss's own idea: 'true, it has no funeral march, but it *is* in E flat major and has lots of horns, which are of course well versed in heroism . . .' [9] Strauss was then thirty-four; Beethoven had been thirty-three when he composed his Third Symphony nearly a century before. The comparison, or contrast, is in every way revealing. The hero of Beethoven's work was to have been Napoleon, and even without that specific focus it remains an objective, outward-looking work, embodying the epoch-making political and military conflicts of the immediately post-revolutionary era.

Strauss's response to the *Eroica* is an overtly autobiographical work. Not that Strauss saw himself as a hero in any real sense, as he confessed to Romain Rolland in 1900:

> I am not a hero; I haven't got the necessary strength; I am not cut out for battle; I prefer to withdraw, to be quiet, to have peace. I haven't enough genius. I lack the strength of health, and will-power. [10]

So there is more than a touch of self-mockery about this tone poem. A work that casts your critics as the hero's enemies, and makes a battle with them its centrepiece, cannot be taken too seriously, and is not so intended. The self-consciousness and irony of *Ein Heldenleben* are part of what makes it acceptable to modern taste.

But this lightheartedness only underlines the contrast with Beethoven. Strauss, having started out with the idea of an heroic piece using Beethoven's heroic key of E flat (it is also the key of the so-called 'Emperor' concerto), finds that he cannot come anywhere near emulating his model. So instead of a great public work, we have an autobiographical piece (complete with a portrait of his wife), one purpose of which seems to be to mock the very idea of heroism.

The contrast between these two related works, set at the beginning and end of the nineteenth century, tells us much about what had happened to music in that time, but also helps to explain why opera, in the hands of its last great conventional practitioners, ran into a cul-de-sac and needed, for its resuscitation, to move off in entirely different directions. That neither Puccini nor Strauss could strike the heroic note might be held to reflect only the very different social and political climate of their times, with the period of liberal revolutionary struggles now far in the past. But much more disturbing is their lack of interest in political themes of any kind and, in Strauss's case particularly, the almost complete exclusion of the public dimension from his operas. *Salome* and *Electra* may be compared with their near contemporary *Tosca* in one respect, in that they too are dramas set in a political context of which little or nothing is made. Strauss's operas are studies in extremes of individual psychology; and although it is possible to see Herod as a ruler whose fears and anxieties spring more from the insecurities of his political position than from personal neurosis, there is no evidence that either Oscar Wilde or Strauss was much interested in that aspect of the drama, or even in the political and religious tensions that focus on the figure and fate of Jokanaan (John the Baptist).

After these two condensed and powerful works, Strauss notoriously veered into prolixity and pastiche with *Der Rosenkavalier*; thereafter it sometimes seems as if the flight from reality – certainly, the flight into privacy – becomes more pronounced with each succeeding work. *Ariadne auf Naxos* is a brilliant and touching exploration of theatricality, invention and illusion, in which layers of artifice are piled upon each other. *Die Frau ohne Schatten*, though inflated, is cumulatively very moving in its celebration of humanness and human regeneration. *Intermezzo* is a modern domestic comedy, and so on. There is a degree of variety and a degree of social interest. A valuable study could be made of the Viennas of *Der Rosenkavalier* and *Arabella*, and the way in which these two operas, set roughly a hundred years apart, provide vignettes of the changing social character of that city.

Arabella had its premiere in Dresden in July 1933, some five months after Hitler became Reichskanzler. Strauss was by then nearing seventy, and it was not to be expected that a composer as little interested in the political world as he was would go into exile or adopt a position of opposition to the Nazi regime. In fact he allowed himself to be incorporated into the façade of cultural distinction that the Nazis were anxious to maintain. Ever pliable, he replaced Toscanini as conductor of *Die Meistersinger* at Bayreuth in 1933, when the Italian refused to perform in a Nazi-controlled state. Strauss accepted the position of president of the Reichsmusikkammer set up by Goebbels, and he composed the hymn for the opening of the Berlin Olympic Games in 1936. He put his name to the letter denouncing Thomas Mann for his 'unpatriotic' attitude towards Wagner, which convinced Mann that it was not safe for him to stay in Nazi Germany. In private Strauss despised the Nazis, but he nevertheless let himself be used by them. As John Cox observed apropos of Strauss, 'The propaganda value of great artists is easily overlooked by artists and even by the public, but never by rulers.'[11] Strauss protested to Hitler, 'I have never been active politically nor even expressed myself in politics.'[12] But it was precisely this indifference to large public issues that made it possible for the Nazis to exploit Strauss's prestige as the greatest German composer of his time.

This is a book about politics *in* opera, rather than the politics of opera composers. But Nazi Germany was the context of the last five operas that Strauss composed, and it seems to me that the sheer vapidity of some of these works – *Daphne*, for example – reflects not only the composer's lifelong indifference to politics, not only the garrulity of a composer who was running out of musical ideas, but also a preciousness and triviality that were forced upon him if he was to produce works that could be performed without difficulty in the repressive context of the Third Reich. This was the tragic impasse into which Strauss, the non-political opera composer, was driven at last.

To this general conclusion there is one startling, even puzzling exception: *Friedenstag* ('Peace Day'). The day in question is 24 October 1648, the date of the end of the Thirty Years War (although in the opera's final form all references to particular times and places have been removed). *Friedenstag* is an opera in praise of peace and reconciliation, which condemns the miseries of war and also the mentality of the military man who knows and understands nothing but war. William Mann described the music as 'exceptionally tough in tone of voice', and Michael Kennedy has called it Strauss's 'most austere' opera.[13] It is, by their accounts, an impressive work, and an exceptional one in the composer's output. Although its librettist is named as Joseph Gregor, the idea and much of the outline were provided by Stefan Zweig, who had worked as Strauss's librettist on his previous opera, but as a Jew was now prohibited from collaborating with the composer.

That *Friedenstag* is a political opera there can be no doubt. Nor can there be much doubt about the significance of its composition in the mid-1930s. What is most astonishing, and perhaps needs special explanation, is that the opera was performed quite widely in Germany and Austria in the year before war broke out, achieving a total of 98 performances before it disappeared from the repertory. Perhaps *Friedenstag* ran against Strauss's normal inclinations. Nevertheless, he wrote it and got it performed; that suggests that Strauss may always have been capable of grander things than he usually achieved in the opera house, and that the path he chose to follow from *Der Rosenkavalier* onwards was not the only one open to him. Together with the two early operas and *Die Frau ohne Schatten*, *Friedenstag* gives us more than a glimpse of the other, more serious Strauss: a composer who would probably have found composition harder work, but who might have left us a smaller but more substantial body of works for the opera house.

Giordano's *Andrea Chénier*

Andrea Chénier could well be described as the political opera Puccini never wrote, although it should be said at once that Umberto Giordano had neither the inspiration nor the craftsmanship of his older contemporary. *Chénier* is cruder and far less well structured than Puccini's mature operas. There is a good deal of vulgarity, not to say melodrama, about it, and it has been roundly abused by some critics. To Rodney Milnes it is 'a dreadful opera', with 'its two hours jam-packed with empty rhetoric'. Milnes summed it up in Hobbes's famous phrase as 'nasty, brutish and short'.[14] But *Tosca* is far nastier, if musically not so brutish, and brevity is a virtue of both works.

Andrea Chénier certainly conforms to standard expectations of what Italian opera is like, and belongs clearly to its time and place, Italy in 1896. It has plenty of rather obvious theatrical effects, and picturesque details are inserted often without much regard for their relevance or dramatic function. The final duet, with hero and heroine going together to their deaths at the guillotine and shouting, fortissimo, 'viva la morte!', is more than I personally can stomach. Its final message – that the French Revolution ended by devouring its own children in a bloodbath preceded by mob trials – is unsubtle, unoriginal, and highly congenial to traditional operatic audiences.

Chénier is not a sincere work in the Verdian manner. As with Puccini, the aura of theatrical contrivance hangs heavily over it. Nevertheless, taken as a whole, this comparatively short opera gives us a detailed and perceptive picture of the evolution of the great French Revolution, in which politics is accepted as integral to the story, and not treated as incidental or accidental. The opera's portrait of the poet Chénier is quite close to reality, and three of his arias are based on Chénier's actual poems. Each of the first three acts provides a sketch of the Revolution at a different stage in its development, with three major characters standing in different relations to each other as a direct consequence of these political changes.

Act One is set in the château of the Comtesse de Coigny in the early months of 1789; it is altogether overshadowed by the impending revolution. The curtain rises on a busy scene of servants preparing a party. One of them, Gerard, reflects angrily on the luxury and frivolity of the life of his employer and her class, and with particular bitterness on the plight of his aged father, still humping furniture around for them after sixty years. Gerard embodies the social resentment that supplies one of the main dynamics of the Revolution.

But there are other dynamics, and these too are brought into play in this brief act, in which the highly artificial diversions of the aristocracy, complete with shepherdesses, are repeatedly disrupted by political incursions. First, the Abbé brings disturbing political news from Paris. Then the poet Chénier, invited to recite, delivers an aria that turns from meditation on the beauty of the earth to an impassioned denunciation of the suffering and injustice that mar that beauty. The company is naturally embarrassed. Chénier represents the middle-class idealism that was also channelled into the Revolution. Finally, a gavotte begins, but it is gradually drowned out by a fierce chorus of starving beggars, who are introduced into the house by Gerard with the announcement 'Sua grandezza, la Miseria' ('His highness,

Poverty'). Gerard is dismissed on the spot – 'reading has ruined him', says the Countess – and the opera's librettist, Luigi Illica, tells us in one of his innumerable detailed footnotes that Gerard has been reading Rousseau and the Encyclopaedists.[15] The dance begins again, ending the act on an appropriate note of irony and insecurity.

It is in Act Two that we see most of the positive side of the French Revolution, even though it takes place as late as June 1794, just before the fall of Robespierre, when the Terror was at its height. The act opens in festive vein, with Bersi, once Maddalena de Coigny's servant, revelling, or pretending to revel, in the delights of the revolutionary life. Then, at the moment when Chénier is ready to abandon his dream of meeting a woman he can really love ('Addio bel sogno'), we hear the approaching procession of revolutionary leaders, among whom an outwardly modest Robespierre is the dominant figure and the idol of the crowd.

It is clear from Illica's commentary, and from the cynical comments he puts into the mouths of Chénier and his fellow-moderate, Roucher, that he adopts the conventionally distrustful view of 'the mob' and its fickle capacity for hero-worship: 'la eterna cortigiana' ('the eternal courtesan') Chénier calls it. But the music, I think, tells a different story. The bystanders' disdainful comments are set against the enthusiastic cries of the crowd and, sweeping all before it, a magnificent string theme; at the same time Gerard, who is now among the revolutionary leaders, sings of his anguished passion for the elusive Maddalena. It has been suggested that the string theme is simply an expression of his love and has no political significance. But it ends with a clear echo of the Marseillaise. This is a great moment of exultation, in which Giordano and Illica skilfully and movingly bring together public enthusiasm and private doubts and passions.

Later, as dusk falls, we hear a patrol, a pastiche of the kind used in operas of the revolutionary period such as *Les deux journées*; Mathieu, the sans-culotte, hums the Carmagnole. The opera and its libretto are full of details of this kind, which help to create the atmosphere of the French Revolution, though sometimes in a rather cavalier manner, as with the Merveilleuses and Incroyables of Act Two, who belong historically to the period of the Directory, established the year after the execution of Robespierre. Nevertheless, those who treat the opera simply as a vehicle for an heroic, or stentorian, tenor, do its detail and craftsmanship an injustice.

In Act Three, we see the Revolution in difficulties. Mathieu has little success in persuading the people to contribute money to support the war in defence of the new republic. It needs the greater eloquence and standing of Gerard to elicit a response: an old woman, Madelon, proudly volunteers her grandson of fifteen to fight. This could be seen as a rather horrifying episode, but in fact it is moving, if terrible: the old lady is a dignified, even noble, figure.

In this act Maddalena and Gerard finally confront one another as Chénier's fate hangs in the balance, in a scene that may recall Act Two of *Tosca*, since Gerard, like Scarpia, demands a woman's sexual surrender as the price for saving her lover. But Gerard is a more complex and sympathetic figure than Scarpia. He reflects on his own corruption, on the conflict within him between political idealism and sensuality, in his aria 'Nemico della patria?'. In the end he is won over by Maddalena and, having earlier indicted Chénier, he now makes a last doomed attempt to rescue the poet from the hostility of the Public Prosecutor and the revolutionary tribunal. By the end of this act the drama is effectively over. Chénier has been condemned to death, and it only remains for Maddalena to effect the ruse by which she joins him in prison and on the scaffold (a conclusion to the story for which real history offers no warrant).

In Italy in the 1890s opera was no longer a vehicle for popular political aspirations. It was far more unambiguously a commercial entertainment. Giordano was a young composer who needed a success, and could hardly be expected to resist the temptations to rhetoric and melodrama that the subject and libretto offered him. Nevertheless, the opera presents a complex and balanced picture of the French Revolution and its impact on the three principal characters. For the most part it avoids simplifying it into the orthodox reactionary pattern, in which we see nothing but terror and tumbrils, mobs and murder. *Andrea Chénier* deserves a better press than it has lately received.

As it happens, if we are looking for an example of an opera in which politics is used merely to add a frisson of topicality to a conventional drama of revenge and pursuit, we need look no further than Giordano's next opera, *Fedora*, premiered in 1898. Like *Tosca*, this was based on a melodrama by Sardou, into which Sardou inserted a topical note by suggesting that the supposed murderer of Fedora's fiancé is a Nihilist who is also implicated in the assassination of Tsar Alexander II in 1881. Political assassination was a highly topical theme in the 1890s, but this contemporary reference is entirely otiose, and nothing substantial is made of it. Unlike *Chénier, Fedora* is an opera that exploits politics for superficial dramatic effect, but no more than that.

It was clear that works like *Turandot, Daphne* and even *Capriccio* had taken late Romantic opera so far from contemporary reality and contemporary concerns that some kind of revival was needed. New directions, new styles, new forms would have to be explored and invented if opera was to be rescued from exoticism and triviality, and become once again a vital cultural format, addressing contemporary concerns with the urgency that could be found in the contemporaneous plays of Chekhov, Ibsen, Shaw and Granville Barker. Some people still believe that the history of opera ended with *Der Rosenkavalier* and *Turandot,* often cited as the last two operas to enter indisputably into the core repertory. But this is an increasingly outdated view. There *was* a renewal of opera after Romanticism ran out of steam, and this renewal forms the subject of my final chapter.

9

Democratic Opera: Victims as Heroes

The impact of democratic ideas on music, and particularly opera, began with Mozart, and was enormously enlarged by the French Revolution. In *The Marriage of Figaro* the servants are as human and as capable as their employers and social 'superiors'. They have ceased to be merely comic. This readiness to recognize the dignity and decency of 'ordinary' people, to treat the lives of the 'lower orders' seriously, is apparent in works of the revolutionary period like *Les deux journées* and *Fidelio*, and later in the operas of radical nationalism like *Boris Godunov* and *The Bartered Bride*, both works of the 1860s. The same is true of Verdi's more class-conscious operas, such as *Luisa Miller* and *Rigoletto*.

Nevertheless, the tendency for opera to choose its subjects from remote times and civilizations, and its characters from the upper classes – to sustain a kind of snobbish romanticism – persisted. It was shocking when Verdi chose to make an opera out of a contemporary subject, as in *La traviata*, and challenging when Smetana in the 1860s and even Janáček in 1904 chose to make operas out of everyday village life. Tchaikovsky expressed his impatience with the orthodox exoticism when he chose to make an opera out of Pushkin's *Eugene Onegin*, and declared how pleasant it would be 'to avoid all the routine Pharaohs, Ethiopian princesses, poisoned cups and all the rest of these tales about automata'.[1]

This reference to *Aida* did less than justice to that opera's real substance, of course. But Tchaikovsky's opera, although set in a society not much less exotic to us than ancient Egypt, retains its sense of everyday reality, beginning with the jam-making in the first scene. Along with the attachment to exotic subjects went, most often, the employment of exotic language. Even a modern drama like *La traviata* was couched in the extraordinarily stilted and ornate conventional language of Italian opera. As Julian Budden has pointed out, 'So long as horses remained "steeds", church bells "sacred bronzes", and women instead of being married were "conducted to the pronubial altar", everyday reality was kept at a distance.'[2] And so the need arose, as it regularly does, for a break with convention, and a refreshment of both the language and the subject matter of opera. These were the aims of the *verismo* movement, which was so important in French and Italian opera in the 1880s and 1890s, and which had its parallels elsewhere: in *Jenufa*, for example, the first Czech opera with a prose libretto.

Verismo is a complex phenomenon, and an ambiguous concept. It is usually associated with subjects taken from 'low life', but also with melodrama, violence and emotional extremism. Thus, among Puccini's works, *verismo* is more often mentioned in connection with *Tosca*, on account of its strong and violent drama, than with *La Bohème* (despite its setting in artistic poverty), which is almost conflict-free. Because of *verismo*'s focus on situations of high drama, the brief one-act format suited it well. The famous prototype was Mascagni's *Cavalleria rusticana*, which won one of the prizes for a one-act opera offered by the music publisher Edoardo Sonzogno in 1889. Its first performance in Rome in 1890 created a sensation and made its composer famous overnight, although none of his subsequent operas enjoyed a comparable success. *Verismo* was a literary movement before it was an operatic one, and its leading figure was the Sicilian author of *Cavalleria rusticana*, Giovanni Verga. His aim was to observe and represent the lives of the poor and deprived as they actually were, without either passion or judgement. Verga was influenced by the ideas of the great French naturalistic and socialist writer Emile Zola, who was enthusiastically received when he visited Italy in the 1890s as, in Budden's words, 'the father of Italy's new operatic tradition'.[3]

Verismo, at least in its literary form, had a political as well as an artistic inspiration and purpose, and was related in its spirit to the emerging socialist movements in Europe. Ibsen and his Fabian champion and follower, Shaw, made the same kind of impact as Zola with their unflinching dramatizations of major social issues and conflicts. There is an interesting parallel with what Wordsworth and Coleridge, under the influence of the French Revolution and its ideals, proclaimed as their purpose in the famous Preface to the *Lyrical Ballads* of 1800. They rejected 'the gaudiness and inane phraseology of modern writers'. Instead their plan was:

> to choose incidents and situations from common life, and to relate or describe them, throughout, as far as was possible in a selection of language really used by men. . . . Humble and rustic life was generally chosen, because, in that condition, the essential passions of the heart find a better soil in which they can attain their maturity . . .

This could almost be a manifesto not only for *verismo*, but for the other efforts that were made in the early part of the twentieth century, and especially, perhaps, in the 1920s, to bring opera back into touch with contemporary reality, not only in terms of subject matter but also in terns of musical language. Janáček's concern with speech melodies, for example, is an attempt to de-formalize opera, and to create a musical convention of natural, everyday communication.

Some versions of *verismo*

Cavalleria rusticana, like *The Bartered Bride* and the slightly later *Jenufa*, takes place entirely within a self-contained village community. The fact that it is a tragedy is significant in itself; while it had always been conceded that rustics and servants could provide the material for comedy, tragedy required dignity, which was often taken to be synonymous with social standing; according to some conceptions, tragedy was by definition about the fall and destruction of the great. Only in a democratic age was it conceivable that the poor and the utterly insignificant could be deemed worthy or capable of tragedy.

Presumably quite deliberately, Mascagni's tragedy observes the unities of time and place prescribed for tragedy by Aristotle, and has its climactic murder take place offstage, to be reported, Greek-style, by a 'messenger'. Thus it invites comparison with classical tragedies such as those of King Oedipus and Princess Electra, even though no grand personages appear.

For most operatic audiences, impoverished Sicilian villages, which have not disappeared in the century since Mascagni and Verga, are now as picturesque as Smetana's Bohemia or that other Bohemia of Puccini's would-be artists. Today it is a producer's responsibility to try to re-create the shock of reality that audiences used to having the curtain rise on scenes of ancient Egypt or medieval Germany would have felt when first confronted with these dramas of the contemporary poor. The radicalism of *verismo* in some of its aspects is now largely forgotten. But it needs to be recovered if the full significance of this artistic movement is to be appreciated.

The radical social dimension of *verismo* is represented by Charpentier's *Louise*, which so impressed Janáček when he saw it in Prague in 1903, and by Puccini's *Il tabarro*. *Louise*, which was first performed in 1900, takes a more serious view of poverty and work in Paris than *La Bohème*, which had had its premiere four years before. Indeed it can be read as, in a sense, a commentary on *La Bohème*, since here too the artists, or would-be artists, of Montmartre figure, but now in constant juxtaposition with the ordinary workers of Paris, who disapprove of them. This is why Louise's proletarian parents obstruct her love affair with Julien. He is an artist, disreputable by definition, and the young couple are preparing to live together without marrying. The offence is against working-class respectability.

Yet the scales are carefully balanced. Paris, the city which is a 'fête éternelle du plaisir' in the eyes of Louise and Julien, is hardly as innocent as that suggests. The 5 a.m. street scene which opens Act Two introduces us to Le Noctambule, a sinister figure notorious for seducing gullible girls. Seduction is exactly what Louise's parents fear for their daughter. Both parents, but especially the father, of whom Louise is genuinely fond, give passionate expression to classic proletarian or socialist sentiments in the first and final acts, which both take place in their modest apartment and frame the more Bohemian action of the central acts. 'Les pauvres gens peuvent-ils être heureux?' ('Can the poor be happy?') asks the father in the final act. We are 'Tristes serfs

d'une besogne qui ne cesse jamais' ('the wretched slaves of an unending necessity'). 'It is Zola set to music,' one French writer exclaimed; it
is interesting that Charpentier, who wrote his own text, called the
opera 'un roman' (a novel).

Louise embodies many of the radical concerns of its time – and of
ours: not only the class issue, but also the question of personal
freedom, and especially the need for women to free themselves from
domination by both parents and their male partners. Although Louise
is finally driven out of the house by her angry father, there can be no
doubt that she would have left anyway. But whether she would or
could have returned to Julien, or would have found herself alone in the
great city, is not so clear.

Louise, like *La Bohème*, is in some ways a hymn to Paris, a tribute to
that city's European predominance in the period of the Third Republic
(1871–1940). This must account for some of its great popularity in
France, but its self-consciously proletarian orientation clearly did it no
harm either. It is sometimes classified as a work of French *verismo*, but
this verdict must refer to its choice of subject matter. It is in no way
melodramatic or violent, and its often sombre but melodious musical
idiom is closer to Massenet than to Puccini or Mascagni.

Il tabarro also is set in Paris among the Parisian poor. But this is not
the picturesque and probably temporary poverty of the young Bohemians: it is the permanent poverty of the urban working class. The
barge-loaders of *Il tabarro* may dream, like La Frugola, of a cottage in
the country, but it is only a dream. They know that their condition is
unchanging. The best they can hope for is to settle down back in the
Paris suburb of Belleville where they were born, and this is the dream
of Luigi and Giorgetta. So, like *Louise*, this opera celebrates the
modest joys of the common people's Paris. But even these are scarcely
available to the lovers, on account of the nomadic life that barge work
imposes. The mood and atmosphere of *Il tabarro* are sombre, and are
sustained without monotony through most of the opera's fifty-minute
span. The use, from figure 57 in the score, of an *ostinato* to sustain
tension and unify the later part of the score is particularly effective.
Puccini cannot resist, though, introducing more than a short opera's
fair share of picturesque touches: an organ grinder, a song-vendor
(who sings the story of Mimi complete with a quotation from *La*

Bohème), fog-horns, church bells, bugle calls, and a distant pair of lovers (Puccini also rather over-exploits distant voices).

Il tabarro represents an impressive extension of Puccini's range; but the American sleeve-writer who described this opera as the composer's 'one foray into what was then contemporary socialistic theater' rather overstates the case, as does Mosco Carner, from another angle, when he accuses Puccini of putting 'words into Luigi's mouth which read like those of a fanatical Marxist'.[4] It is true, and worth noting, that the monologue Carner refers to was not in the original play, but was added by Adami and Puccini. But Luigi's bitter complaints about his lot are simply those of any angry worker, not the 'fanatical Marxist' of Carner's heated imagination. He sings:

> Hai ben ragione: meglio non pensare,
> piegare il capo ed incurrar la schiena

(You're right: it's better not to think, just bow your head and bend your back)

And the truth is that here he sounds much like any other lachrymose tenor of Puccini. As in *Tosca*, the actual drama is one of love, jealousy and terrible revenge. Giorgetta's elderly husband Michele murders Luigi, her young lover, and hides the body under his cloak, which he opens up as Giorgetta comes towards him at the end of the opera. Yet the *Grand Guignol* ending is not essential to the work, which can stand anyway as an effective evocation both of Paris by night and of the cramped lives and frustrated feelings of the urban poor.

The one-act opera, as we noted, was typical of *verismo*. Even Delius tried his hand at it with *Margot la Rouge*, yet another opera set in Paris, and entered by the composer, without success, for another of Sonzogno's competitions in 1902.

Even briefer, yet similar in focus to these operas of Mascagni and Puccini, is a work that in musical style could hardly be more different, less Latinate: Vaughan Williams's *Riders to the Sea*. This is a setting, with remarkably few cuts, of J.M. Synge's play about a woman living on an island off the west coast of Ireland who loses her husband and all her sons to the sea. The play was inspired by, and based on, Synge's experience of spending several successive summers from 1898 onwards on the Aran Islands. He went there at the suggestion of W.B.

Yeats, whom he met in Paris in 1896, at a time when he was reading socialist writers. As Yeats recalled it, 'I said, "Give up Paris. . . . Go to the Aran Islands. Live there as if you were one of the people themselves; express a life that has never found expression." '[5]

In the last phrase we have the clue to what links *Riders to the Sea* to *verismo* and the other operas in this chapter. It is the idea of giving a voice to those who had never been heard, of making the inarticulate articulate through the eloquence of music, that is the democratic impulse behind all these works.

It has been said that 'it is the sea itself that is the chief protagonist' of the opera; moreover, here the sea is not, as in the earlier *Sea Symphony*, an exhilarating space for 'pleasant exploration' but a hard and relentless antagonist, a destroyer of lives.[6] We hear this sea in the orchestra from the very beginning of the opera, and although we never see it, its presence is there in sound throughout the work. The struggle of human beings with hostile elements was also the theme of the later *Sinfonia Antartica*, which grew out of the music Vaughan Williams composed for the film *Scott of the Antarctic*. The opera contains many anticipations of that later work, and also of the equally bleak Sixth Symphony, and especially its desolate epilogue. But there is a significant difference. Scott was an archetypal English gentleman–hero, and his expedition was an act of voluntary heroism. Maurya and her children struggle against the sea because they have to make their living as fisherfolk. It is sheer necessity that compels them to develop the virtues of courage, endurance and persistence, much as in the case of the leech-gatherer whom Wordsworth honoured in his great poem 'Resolution and Independence'. It is a mistake to say, as Raymond Williams did of the play, that 'the people are simply victims'.[7] They are not passive, and they are not broken by their sufferings.

In Vaughan Williams's opera this unbroken spirit is underlined by the entire structure of the work. Most of the opera is sung in recitative or arioso, with melodic commentary in the orchestral accompaniment; but as it moves towards its close and Maurya comes to dominate, the vocal line becomes more melodic and the austere textures are replaced by more tranquil and chorded passages. When finally she sings, 'They are all gone now . . . ', it is as if the whole work had been moving towards this deeply felt resolution. Her final words were adapted by Synge from a phrase in a letter from one of his Aran friends: 'What more can we want than that? No man at all can be living for ever, and we must be satisfied.' They are expressive not only of resignation, but also of a serenity of spirit that signifies not defeat but a human triumph. 'Ripeness is all.' Maurya is the victim as hero, and as darkness closes in on her and her family, there is no easy consolation or comfort, but there is a hard-won peace at last.

Wozzeck and Its Impact

At the heart of this chapter must stand Alban Berg's Wozzeck, the most influential opera of the twentieth century, and perhaps also its greatest. Its importance derives not only from the modernity of its musical idiom – it was the first full-length atonal opera – but also from the perfect integration of text and music. The subject matter was as radical as the musical style. Berg had found a play ideally suited to his musical genius; this is not to say that he encountered no problems in turning Büchner's play into an opera, but rather that he solved them triumphantly.

In theme and style, then, Wozzeck became the quintessential modern opera, and there is a pleasing coincidence in the fact that Berg was immediately seized with the idea of turning the play into an opera when he saw its first performance in Vienna on 5 May 1914, in the very last months of the old world that was to vanish in the cataclysm of World War One. Berg himself was soon conscripted, and it was not until 1918 that he was able to settle down in earnest to composing the opera. Thus Wozzeck can be seen as one of the many great works of art to have emerged from the European convulsions of 1914–18. And Berg put a good deal of his wartime experience into it, including the wordless chorus of sleeping soldiers in Act Two, Scene Five.[8]

But there is also the apparent paradox that for this (at the time) most modern of operas Berg should have chosen the text of a play which was written in 1836. How could such a work provide a modern basis for a modern opera?

The answer lies in the compelling synthesis of political and aesthetic radicalism achieved by its 22-year-old author, Georg Büchner. Büchner was born in 1813, the same year as Wagner, and, like Wagner to a lesser extent, he was caught up in the radical German politics of the early 1830s. Politically, Büchner is a link between the Jacobinism of Robespierre and the proletarian socialism articulated in the 1840s and after by Karl Marx. In Giessen in 1833 he helped to set up a Society for the Rights of Man, and his play *Danton's Death* witnesses his familiarity with the politics of the French Revolution. But unlike most revolutionaries of the 1790s, Büchner saw the conflict between rich and poor as 'the only revolutionary element in the world; hunger alone can become the goddess of freedom'. He also wrote that for the masses 'there are only two levers: material poverty and religious fanaticism'. Wozzeck (or Woyzeck, as he is named by Büchner), whose head is full of muddled reminiscences of the more apocalyptic scriptures, and who submits to the humiliations of being one of the doctor's 'cases' in order to earn a little extra money, exemplifies both.

Büchner was, in effect, a materialist who believed that morality grew out of prosperity: 'It is easy to be an honest man if one is able to eat soup, vegetables and meat every day.' That is what Wozzeck replies to the captain when in the first scene that pompous figure rebukes the barber for his lack of morality. Büchner may have been familiar with the writing of Thomas Paine, who makes a brief appearance in *Danton's Death*. In *The Rights of Man* Paine pithily pointed out the roots of crime in poverty:

> Why is it that scarcely any are executed but the poor? The fact is a proof . . . of a wretchedness in their condition. Bred up without morals, and cast upon the world without a prospect, they are the exposed sacrifices of vice and legal barbarity.

As a brief comment on the fates of both Wozzeck and Marie, the woman he lives with, this could hardly be bettered.

Büchner's political radicalism partially determined his aesthetic. He was scornful of idealization in art, and of conventional ideas of beauty and ugliness:

> We must not ask whether it is beautiful or ugly, the feeling that the work of art has life stands above these two qualities and is the sole criterion of art.

The idealists

> ought to try immersing themselves for once in the life of the most insignificant person. . . . These are the most prosaic people under the

sun; but the vein of sensitivity is alike in nearly all men, all that varies is the thickness of the crust through which it must break.

Beneath the fumbling articulacy of Wozzeck and Marie's maudlin sentimentality lies the 'vein of sensitivity' that Büchner wished to bring to our attention, and which finds its eloquent expression in Berg's music.[9]

Given Büchner's reputation as a radical and the chaotic condition in which he left the manuscript of *Woyzeck* – even its title was misread – it is not so surprising that the play was not published in any form until 1875, and did not reach the stage until 1913 (in Munich). Accidents apart, these delays testify to the extraordinary modernity of Büchner's play. It had to wait more than seventy years to gain proper appreciation.

Büchner came into his own after 1918, when he was recognized as belonging to the tradition of radical German art that the Left celebrated as reappearing in the culture of the Weimar Republic. As Peter Gay has written: 'at least in Weimar days, Büchner clearly belonged to democrats, socialists and Communists'.[10] Inevitably, therefore, the premiere of Berg's opera in Berlin in 1925 was an occasion for political controversy. The opera was an immediate success, but it was denounced by the nationalist Right as a work of *Kulturbolshewismus*; and after the Nazis came to power in 1933 Berg found it virtually impossible to get his work performed in Germany (although he made some rather abject attempts to prove his 'Aryan' credentials).

How far did Berg share Büchner's political attitudes, and how far does the opera embody the spirit of the play? Berg was not a politically committed composer in the manner of Verdi or Janáček. But he was always a person of liberal or progressive views, and like many of his contemporaries he was radicalized by his war experiences, to the extent that by 1919 he was describing himself as a 'fierce anti-militarist'; he even contemplated using an anti-war play by Paul Raynal as the basis for his second opera.[11] The miseries and humiliations of military life led him to identify with Wozzeck to some degree, as he told his wife Helene: 'There is a bit of myself in his character'.[12] Berg told Webern that 'the fate of this poor man, exploited and tormented by *all the world* . . . touches me closely'.[13] But he was also clear that the opera was about more than one man and his individual problems, and his hope was that in seeing and hearing the opera 'there is no one in the audience who pays any attention to the various fugues, inventions, suites, sonata movements, variations and passacaglias – no one who heeds anything but the social problems of this opera – which by far transcend the personal destiny of Wozzeck'.[14]

Thus, as Mark deVoto has written, 'for Büchner and Berg alike, Wozzeck's daily existence is that of Everyman under arms, at the mercy of the world gone mad'.[15] Musical structures were to serve the drama, and Berg makes the phrase 'Wir arme leute' ('We poor folk'), often used by Wozzeck and Marie, a leitmotif of the whole work: 'perhaps the most important motive of the opera', according to Douglas Jarman.[16] It is the tormentors and exploiters of Wozzeck and Marie, especially the captain and the doctor, who are heartless and mechanical in their behaviour, and Berg uses appropriate musical devices to convey this.

Although the very project of the play, inspired by the case of the actual Johann Christian Woyzeck, who was executed in 1824 for the murder of his mistress, testifies to Büchner's compassion and commitment, there is a certain clinical detachment about the play which reflects the author's scientific and medical education. Given Berg's highly expressive, or even expressionist, musical idiom, this 'objectivity' is not reflected in the opera, and Berg underlines his personal involvement with the drama by inserting a substantial orchestral interlude in D minor (the only overtly tonal music in the opera) after the scene of Wozzeck's suicide. In a lecture on the opera, he described this as 'the composer's confession, breaking through the framework of the dramatic plot, and likewise even as an appeal to the audience, which is here meant to represent humanity itself'. Some commentators, such as Joseph Kerman, regard this interpellation as a miscalculation.[17] But to my mind it enhances the marvellous humanity of this opera, whilst any danger of sentimentality is dispelled by the chilling final scene which, as Berg pointed out, brings the opera full circle, in that the final notes could easily lead back into the opening bars, and so recommence the cycle of misery which repeats itself from generation to generation. Like the ending of *Boris Godunov*, which it resembles, the ending of *Wozzeck* is bleak and honest, but not heartless. The pessimism of the conclusion is not cosmic. What we have seen is not the miseries of the human condition as such, but the remediable miseries of injustice, callousness and oppression. *Wozzeck* is therefore a political opera, challenging us to change the world rather than resign ourselves to its supposedly ineluctable wretchedness.

As is well known, Berg escaped from the potential problems of formlessness and absence of direction that atonality presented by composing the opera in extraordinarily tight and elaborate patterns of formal musical organization. These endow it with structure, clarity and economy, as well as providing a musical counterpart to the deterministic elements in Büchner's drama. But as we have seen, Berg was anxious that the music should be shaped 'in such a way that it is always conscious of its duty to serve the drama', and in this he was outstandingly successful. Despite its musical intricacy, and its consequent fascination for musical analysts, no one would think of *Wozzeck* as an academic work. It belongs to the theatre, and succeeds as theatre. 'For all its formidable complexity, *Wozzeck* has the directness and clarity of all great dramas.'[18]

Wozzeck rapidly made an impact, and in the decade between its premiere and Berg's death had received 166 performances in opera houses all over central Europe and beyond, including a production in Leningrad which Berg himself travelled to see. It was the right work on the right theme at the right moment, and its example and its success were of great importance to the subsequent history of opera. The young Shostakovich was among those who saw the opera in Leningrad, and it probably encouraged him when he turned to compose *Lady Macbeth of Mtsensk*, which has even been called 'the Russian *Wozzeck*'. Shostakovich's opera has more affinities with *verismo* than does Berg's. Both operas feature jealousy, lust and murder, but Berg's treatment is restrained by comparison with Shostakovich's, which is at times lurid and excessive. Shostakovich denied that he had been influenced by Berg's opera; but it is likely that the success of *Wozzeck* must have encouraged the Soviet composer to think that an opera on an ostensibly 'sordid' subject could be an artistic and popular success.

Another composer who saw *Wozzeck* and was deeply impressed was Janáček. He was indignant that anti-German protests compelled the Prague National Theatre to withdraw the opera in 1927, after only three performances. 'Injustice – what an injustice! They wrong *Wozzeck*. They have wronged Berg terribly. He is a dramatist of astonishing importance, of deep truth.'[19] In the next year Janáček turned to the composition of his last and perhaps greatest opera, *From the House of the Dead*, and it seems likely that Berg's chorus of sleeping soldiers suggested to Janáček his treatment of sleeping prisoners in the last act. And, as with Shostakovich, Berg's success with an apparently unpromising subject may have encouraged Janáček to venture even further beyond the conventional bounds of opera than he had done in its unorthodox immediate predecessors, *The Cunning Little Vixen* and *The Makropoulos Case*. But the opera that most directly continues and extends the tradition represented by Berg's two masterpieces is Bernd Alois Zimmermann's *Die Soldaten*. This opera, which was first performed in Cologne in 1965, is linked to Berg's masterpieces by a mesh of interwoven threads, without being in any way a pallid or parrot-like imitation of them.

Die Soldaten

Zimmermann's opera has a libretto that necessarily condenses, but is otherwise taken more or less word for word from, the play of the same name by Jakob Michael Reinhold Lenz, written in 1775. It tells of the downfall of a middle-class woman, Marie Wesener, who deserts her faithful but unglamorous lover, Stolzius, for a series of short-lived affairs with upper-class officers. None of them sees her as much more than a whore. Finally she is raped and reduced to beggary; Stolzius has his despairing revenge by murdering one of the officers, Desportes, and killing himself at the same time. The resemblances between Stolzius and Wozzeck, between Marie Wesener and both Marie and Lulu, and between Desportes and the Drum-Major in *Wozzeck* are strong and not accidental. For Lenz had a formative influence on Büchner, and was the subject of the latter's remarkable *novella*. Büchner's Marie was consciously modelled on Lenz's, although there are significant differences. What is more, it is common for students of German literature to trace an uneven line of non-naturalistic yet socially conscious drama from Lenz to Büchner, and at the end of the nineteenth century to Wedekind, and from Wedekind to Brecht. In turning to one of the originators of that tradition, Zimmermann was consciously following in the steps of Alban Berg.

The method of pushing forward the narrative through a series of short, sometimes disconnected, scenes is common to both Lenz and Büchner, and implies a highly flexible and non-naturalistic style of staging. There are thirty-five scenes grouped into five acts in Lenz's play. Zimmermann condenses these to fifteen scenes in four acts, which might appear to be a huge feat of compression, except that many of Lenz's scenes are extremely short, often only a few sentences long and involving only a single character. Some characters disappear in the operatic version, notably Marie's mother. But some of her lines are transferred to Marie's sister Charlotte, and many scenes are simply amalgamated.

Zimmermann was interested in musical collage as a method of depicting different events, or reactions to events, occurring simultaneously. Of course, the operatic ensemble has always been used for this purpose, and Zimmermann makes very effective ensembles out of the scenes of the officers' social life. But he goes further by running several different scenes concurrently, or by producing a multilayered musical texture. Thus the second scene of Act Two in both play and opera is interleaved with the second scene of the play's third act. While Marie and Desportes make love, Marie's grandmother sings a lament, and Stolzius's mother tells her son not to be bothered with that slut ('*ein Lude*'). The first scene of Act Four uses film, in the manner of *Lulu*, to depict Marie's murder; in the final scene, in which Wesener fails to recognize his own daughter when she begs him for money in the street, in the background we hear simultaneously a chaplain intoning the Lord's Prayer in Latin and a jazz band playing; finally everything else is drowned out by a tramping march as the soldiers move on.

Die Soldaten is an opera without heroes. It is about victims. And it calls on our sympathy not for the innocent victims of the crimes or stupidity of others, but for victims who help to accomplish their own destruction, who lack the resources, either material or spiritual, to resist the temptations that drag them down to personal degradation and dreadful crimes. The crimes of Stolzius and Wozzeck are acts not of wickedness but of desperation, committed by men who see their only hope of happiness or personal security being torn away, and can see no other way out of their abyss. Marie may be silly and easily deluded by fantasies of social success. But in a different, more privileged social context these weaknesses would do her no serious harm. Indeed, the urge to climb up the social ladder is often praised as healthy ambition. And how, we might ask, could a woman get on in eighteenth-century society except by exploiting her sexuality and attaching herself to a man of superior social rank?

Lenz was certainly conscious of this. He set out to reach 'the whole nation . . . in which the commoners are as important to me as the nobility'. And he wanted to 'represent the social classes as they really are, not as they appear to persons of the more elevated sphere'. His aim in *Die Soldaten* was 'to stem the decay of morals that is creeping down from the illustrious ranks of society to the lower classes, who have not the means of defence against it available to their betters'. Stolzius rages at Desportes, as they are both dying: 'If you can't live without ruining women, why must you turn to those who can't resist, who believe every word you say?'[20] And his most agonized protest could be taken as the theme of the entire opera: 'And must those who suffer wrong tremble, and only those who are guilty of wrong be cheerful?' In the play this is Stolzius's solitary complaint, but Zimmermann significantly makes it a concerted utterance at the end of Act Four, Scene One.

Zimmermann's musical texture is quite different from Berg's. It is recognizably post-1945 and post-Webern, by turns dense and fragmentary. The Act Three interlude (romanza), which makes conspicuous use of guitar, harp, celeste and solo strings, might remind us of Boulez, for example. This is a work uncompromising in its modernity, yet truly operatic. Zimmermann is considerate to his singers, and makes skilful use of Lenz's text to provide them with fine vocal opportunities. Thus Act One ends with an eloquent extended *arioso* for Marie, Act Two with Stolzius meditating on vengeance, and Act Three with a beautiful trio for women's voices. Above all, the total structure is clear, coherent and fast-moving: the drama moves inexorably to its logical, predictable conclusion. Its success owes much to Lenz's brilliant and powerful play. But Zimmermann matches it with vivid, dramatic and deeply felt music. At the time of writing (1992), *Die Soldaten* still awaits its first British production (Opera North had to abandon a planned production for lack of funds). This is something of a scandal. If there is now a substantial audience for *Wozzeck*, or Aribert Reimann's *Lear*, there is an audience for *Die Soldaten*, which is acknowledged as a modern classic in the German-speaking world.

Two Prison Operas

Prison scenes are common enough in nineteenth-century opera, but operas set entirely in prison are rare. *Fidelio* provides the first and greatest example. The twentieth century has added two more: *From the House of the Dead*, and Luigi Dallapiccola's *Il prigioniero*. As befits a darker and necessarily less sanguine age, neither work, unlike Beethoven's, holds out the prospect of release or liberation. Imprisonment without any certain prospect of release, such as has been endured by several million people in this century, is one of the most appalling ordeals that human beings have imposed upon each other. To make this the material of opera is a formidable challenge: it can seem almost blasphemous to convert horror and tragedy into a form of entertainment, a good night out. Yet this has always been the test and trial of great art: that it can absorb and illuminate even the worst that life has to offer; that it can find its beauty in truth, rather than seeking for beauty in itself. This was certainly Janáček's approach: 'I penetrate because there is truth in my work; truth to its very limit. Truth does not exclude beauty, on the contrary. . . . Life, I want life itself.'[21] For Janáček as for Berg, Wilfred Owen's famous sentence is apposite: 'The poetry is in the pity.'

Of these two prison operas Janáček's is in many respects the more audacious and challenging, both morally and aesthetically. Dallapiccola treats of a single prisoner, anonymous and symbolic, a victim of the Inquisition, to whom our sympathy is readily given. Janáček, taking as the basis for his opera Dostoevsky's account of his four years in a tsarist labour camp in *Notes from the House of the Dead*, presents to us a group of prisoners of whom only one is a political prisoner. The rest are, as we would say, common criminals, and mostly of a particularly brutal character: they are in prison for murder. We know what they have done and why they are there, because they tell us, more or less, in a series of narratives which make up much of the substance of the opera. Janáček, who devised his own libretto, does not evade the unappetizing truth about these men, and he is determined that we shall not evade it either. And yet, through his always generous and compassionate music, he asks us to feel for and with these men. The motto he set at the head of the score was itself taken from Dostoevsky: 'In every creature a spark of the divine.' The types of people whom tabloid newspapers habitually label 'monsters' or 'animals', that is as inhuman or subhuman, Janáček here presents to us, without disguising anything, as human beings who are not irredeemable or beyond sympathy:

> Why do I go into the dark frozen cells of the prisoners with the author of *Crime and Punishment*? Into the minds of the prisoners, and there I find the spark of God. It does not wipe away their guilt, but equally you can't quell the divine spark.[22]

Janáček goes on to instance the moment of Filka Morozov's death in the final act, when Shishkov curses him, but the Old Prisoner observes simply: 'He too had a mother.' In all this Janáček was only following the Russian novelist, who wrote: 'I am the first to testify that among those who suffered so terribly in that most primitive and oppressive environment, I sometimes encountered evidence of the most refined moral development.'[23] If we were tempted to think Janáček too generous in his treatment of these criminals, we could hardly make the same charge against Dostoevsky, who had lived for several years among them.

Fidelio is a 'rescue' opera, in which attention is held by Leonore's plan to save her husband. But the truth about prison life for most prisoners is that nothing happens and nothing changes, and Janáček faced the problem of holding attention for a group of men who at the end of the opera are, with one exception, in the same situation as they were at the beginning. It is true that the opera opens with the arrival of the one political prisoner, Goryanchikov, and ends with his release. When he has the temerity to remind the governor that he is a political prisoner, the governor is so enraged that he has him beaten, and Act One ends with his return from this dreadful punishment. Brief episodes of tenderness between Goryanchikov and the Tartar boy, Alyeya – the only real friendship among the prisoners – open and close Acts Two and Three. But these are framing devices. *From the House of the Dead* is not about Goryanchikov in particular. Indeed it is not about any two or three prisoners in particular. Janáček responds to his problem in the most radical way. He abandons narrative structure for the opera as a whole, and at the same time he jettisons the traditional focus on a small number of individuals. In place of these he offers us a collective portrait of the prisoners and their life, a mosaic of episodes and discrete narratives by individual prisoners, some connected, some standing on their own. So the opera contains narratives, but is not contained by one. And it ends where it began. Goryanchikov and the wounded eagle (ironically called 'the tsar of the forests') are free, but the other prisoners must return to work under the watchful eyes of their guards. (The weakly affirmative ending tacked on by some of the composer's more timorous pupils has now been generally and rightly abandoned.) The dream and theme of freedom (*svoboda*) is present in Janáček's opera, as it must be in any prison opera, and focuses on the figure of the eagle who goes free to a great chorus of acclaim from the prisoners; but it is just this dangerous outburst that prompts the guards to step in and drive the prisoners back to work. The bleak truthfulness of this work is matched by Janáček's compassionate lyricism to give an unforgettably moving picture of one of the central cruelties of modern societies and their politics; and it has the additional significance of abandoning the encompassing narrative of individuals characteristic of most opera in favour of a collective focus, which brings this particular opera close to some of the plays of Brecht.

If Janáček was impressed by *Wozzeck*, Dallapiccola's one-act opera owes several debts to Berg. Arnold Whittall has described Dallapiccola as 'the obvious continuer of Bergian eclecticism',[24] and *Il prigioniero*, with its echoes of Puccini – the very opening chords may recall those of *Tosca* – and even Verdi, illustrates that. The Italian composer found his own way to serialism, and adopted it 'because it allows me to express what I feel I must express'.[25] *Il prigioniero*, like Berg's two operas, demonstrates that the abandonment of tonality as a general rule need not produce either ungrateful vocal lines or any lack of emotional or dramatic eloquence. On the other hand Dallapiccola, like Berg, seems to have felt the need to use traditional forms to structure his work, so that the third scene of the opera, for example, is constructed on three *ricecares*.

As a boy during World War One, Luigi Dallapiccola was deported with his family from his native Istria by the Austrians and interned for nearly two years in Graz. Twenty years later in 1938 the introduction of anti-Semitic laws in fascist Italy inspired him to begin work on his *Canti di Prigionia*. 'Only through music could I vent my indignation,' he wrote later.[26] These three choral pieces led in due course to the opera *Il prigioniero*, which he composed between 1944 and 1948.

Initially it had great success, and received 186 performances in concert or stage form in the first twelve years after its radio premiere in 1949. But since then it has fallen into undeserved neglect, and even a rare concert performance at the 1986 Proms in London went unnoticed in the pages of *Opera* magazine.

The opera is a direct and manifestly deeply felt response to the experience of fascism; but, as with other operatic treatments of topical themes, Dallapiccola chose to place it in the context of a different age and place. The opera is based on a story by Villiers de l'Isle-Adam, 'La Torture par l'espérance', and is set (like *Don Carlos*) in the context of the sixteenth-century revolt of the Netherlands and the fierce repression of the Inquisition. In the Prologue the prisoner's mother recounts her recurring dream of Philip II, the king who rules not over men but over a graveyard – 'Non su gli uomini impera, ma sopra una cimitero' – a phrase that may remind us of Posa's outburst against Philip in Verdi's opera; in the remainder of the opera the priests embody the same spirit of remorseless power and cruelty as they do for Verdi.

The nameless prisoner is held in the Inquisition's prison at Saragossa. He is a partisan of the revolt, who rejoices when his jailor tells him of the success of the Sea Beggars against the Spanish. The Inquisition is a metaphor for the psychological tormentors who have become a speciality of modern tyrannies. The prisoner has been tortured physically, and this is discreetly but chillingly recalled; but now it is his spirit that is being broken by his jailor, who calls him his brother – 'fratello', sung repeatedly to an insinuating three-note phrase – and constantly urges him to keep his hope alive ('Spera, fratello, spera ardamente'), knowing that these hopes will prove illusory. Eventually the prisoner is released from his cell and wanders out into a garden rich with the scent of cedars under a starry sky. For a moment he thinks he is free, but then from the shadow of the cedars emerges the Grand Inquisitor, who embraces the prisoner with the same greeting: 'fratello'. He realizes that hope itself has been used as a form of torture – 'l'ultima tortura' – and the opera ends with his question: 'la libertà?'

It is not a comfortable ending, but neither is it as pessimistic as some commentators have suggested. The revolt of the Netherlands was, after all, successful, just as Italian fascism was also defeated in the end. Individuals may be crushed by oppression, but oppression does not always triumph. Because Dallapiccola's opera focuses on a single individual, it cannot avoid tragedy: anything else would be glib and unconvincing. But he followed up the opera by writing his *Canti di liberazione*. The opera should be seen in its chosen historical context, and also in the context of the composer's life and work. In itself, however, it is a reflection on the ordeal of imprisonment and the horror of total power: more single-mindedly sombre than Janáček's richer, more humanely detailed canvas, but powerful, sincere and true to the darkest experiences of its time. It is one of the great political operas.

Kurt Weill and 'Accessible' Opera

It remains to consider four composers who, in different ways and to differing degrees, have sustained the tradition of what I have termed 'democratic opera': opera about the conditions and troubles of 'ordinary' people, about the collective life of local or national communities, operas in which our sympathies are enlisted on behalf of the victims of persecution, oppression, injustice, or simply neglect and incomprehension. Of the four, Weill and Gershwin stand close to the tradition of the American musical. The other two, Benjamin Britten and Michael Tippett, have been the leading figures in the renascence of British opera since 1945.

Of these four composers, Kurt Weill, the brilliant young collaborator with Bertolt Brecht and Georg Kaiser, who fled from Nazi Germany to America and then devoted himself to the Broadway musical, is in many ways the least known and the most puzzling. It is doubtful that any innocent listener hearing, say, his early *Recordare* alongside a score like *Lady in the Dark* would ever suppose that they were by the same composer. Is there any thread of consistency in Weill's music and musical life?

We should notice, first, that once Weill began to compose for the theatre, with *Der Protagonist* (1926), he composed virtually nothing other than vocal music for the rest of his life, and the great bulk of it was for the theatre. After his brilliant apprenticeship to Busoni, he became as single-mindedly a theatre composer as Verdi, Wagner and Puccini had been. Second, in both his German and American incarnations, Weill was always concerned with the accessibility of music, and with reaching as wide an audience as possible. This was for political as well as musical reasons. Schoenberg and Webern both despised Weill and his music. As early as 1928 Schoenberg wrote, with reference to Weill, 'it is evident that art which treats deeper ideas cannot address itself to the many'.[27] The composer of *The Magic Flute* would have found that hard to accept, and so did Kurt Weill.

It was this concern with accessibility that, once he had settled in America, led him to set his sights not on the conventional opera houses but on Broadway. 'If there will ever be anything like an American opera, it is bound to come out of Broadway.'[28] It is a misconception to suppose that Weill's 'American' music was entirely unpolitical, or that he left his politics behind when he parted with Brecht and Europe. He came to America as a man and composer of the Left, and was immediately involved with the left-wing Group Theater of New York, for which he wrote the music for the anti-militarist satire *Johnny Johnson*. His second score, *Knickerbocker Holiday*, was another political satire. His most ambitious American project was *Street Scene*, a picture of daily life among the urban working class which he composed as a 'Broadway opera'; his final completed work was a musical adaptation of Alan Paton's famous novel of apartheid, *Cry the Beloved Country*, under the less specific title *Lost in the Stars*. This is not the record of an apolitical composer, and Weill should be recognized as one of those composers, like Gershwin, Richard Rogers, Leonard Bernstein and Stephen Sondheim, who made serious efforts to widen and deepen the scope of the musical, in terms not only of subject matter, but also of musical style. How far Weill succeeded is still a matter of musical debate.

The partnership of Weill and Brecht, which lasted on and off for six years from 1927 to 1933, was one of the great creative collaborations of the twentieth century. That it happened at all was something of a miracle. Brecht had a political suspicion of music as always potentially sentimental and irrational. He always wanted music to serve the words he wrote. Not surprisingly, Weill found it increasingly hard to accept the subordinate role this gave him, and so the two grew apart. Nevertheless the partnership with Brecht seems to have come at just the right moment for him, and stimulated him to produce several of his most brilliant scores, in which words and music combine to powerful effect.

The first fruit of the partnership was the *Mahagonny Songspiel*, a stage montage of songs strung on a slender thread, which made an immediate impact when first performed in 1927. This was an offshoot of the larger project for a full-length Mahagonny opera, which was already being planned. *Mahagonny Songspiel* was intentionally modern and popular in format and sentiments; it was music theatre rather than opera, and it pointed the way in which the Brecht–Weill collaboration was to develop.

Their next production turned out to be their most lastingly popular, *Der Dreigroschenoper*, or *The Threepenny Opera*. Written for the re-opening of a Berlin theatre, it was put together rapidly, in four months in the summer of 1928; the show's most famous song, the 'Morität' ('Mack the Knife'), was added at the last moment. Rehearsals were fraught and beset by accidents, and a disaster was confidently expected. Instead the show was an overnight success. Within a year of its premiere it had notched up over 4,200 performances all over Europe.

There seems to be a consensus among most writers on Brecht and Weill that *Der Dreigroschenoper* is an ambivalent, equivocal work, whose 'political significance' has often been 'overrated'.[29] It is certainly less severe and didactic than some that were soon to follow, such as *Der Jasager*. But much of this commentary seems to reflect the common assumption that entertainment and politics are inherently at odds. Brecht, however, was always clear that even didactic theatre had to be enjoyable. Otherwise who would learn from it? Who indeed would come to it? Nor does it seem to me a particularly equivocal work. True, there is some romanticization of crime and the underworld, but this is not inconsistent with the work's central theme: that the ethics of capitalism are mirrored in the ethics of organized crime and beggary, and that morality is simply a luxury which the poor cannot afford.

It is a fiercely materialist work, in the sense that it constantly draws our attention to the way in which material circumstances determine or at least condition human behaviour and attitudes. 'Money rules the world', observes Mrs Peachum, while her husband, who runs a begging syndicate, claims that we would all like to be virtuous, 'but conditions here won't have it so'. Finally the basic materialist principle is spelt out in the concerted finale to Act Two – 'Erst kommt das Fressen, dann kommt die Moral' ('Food is the first thing. Morals follow on') – a statement about morality which is also a statement *of* morality.

That *The Threepenny Opera* continues to be excluded from Kobbé's *Complete Opera Guide* is ironic in view of its title, but doubly so since the title and the format of the work were explicitly intended both to challenge and to relate to established operatic tradition. For *The Threepenny Opera* had a model in the classical tradition, and that was *The Magic Flute*. 'Mozart is the operatic composer *par excellence*', Weill had written in 1926. 'His writing is always filled with the passionate breath of the theater . . . but it also always exhibits that straight-forwardness of expression that constitutes the most essential charac-teristic of operatic music.' *The Threepenny Opera* contains a number of quotations from Mozart's *Singspiel*, particularly in the finales to Act One and to the entire opera. But in other ways the collaborators sought to mock some of the conventions of traditional opera. 'Pirate Jenny' is, in shape and content, a burlesque of Senta's ballad in *The Flying Dutchman*. Lucy plans her revenge on Jenny in a spoof colora-tura aria, and the absurd happy end, in which Macheath is rescued from hanging by a royal pardon, is explicitly justified as operatically necessary:

> Since this is opera, not life, you'll see
> Justice give way before humanity.

Weill claimed that *The Threepenny Opera* represented 'a new type of music theatre', which had reached an audience 'much wider than the normal concert- and opera-going audiences'.[30] Both claims, and especially the latter, were broadly true, and the work's success must have been hugely encouraging to a composer seeking to widen the audience for serious contemporary music. But popular success was a more ambivalent achievement than Weill perhaps realized. There have always been those who enjoy his pungent, witty yet memorably tuneful music, but prefer to ignore Brecht's equally pungent, not to say shocking lyrics, to say nothing of the message of the work as a whole. The pursuit of commercial success has always invited pro-ducers and performers to prettify and tone down *The Threepenny*

Opera. This became a recurring problem for Weill in his American years. At what point does accessibility involve throwing out the baby of musical and political substance along with the disposable bathwater?

To some extent the full-scale Mahagonny opera, which was completed early in the year following *The Threepenny Opera* (1929), ran into the same kind of problems. Anxious to avoid hostile, Nazi-inspired demonstrations, Weill was willing to disguise some of the more provocative political overtones of the opera, in vain, as it turned out. But despite these equivocations, intrinsic to *The Rise and Fall of the City of Mahagonny* is that it is an attack on capitalism and its values, on a society where money rules and everything, including women and sex, can be bought and sold. Mahagonny is a mythical city given over wholly to chiefly male pleasures: eating, drinking, fighting and sex. The one unforgivable sin is not to be able to pay for your pleasures, and this is the crime of Jimmy Mahoney, who stands everyone drinks but cannot foot the bill. He is put on trial and found guilty of various lesser crimes, such as being an accessory to murder; but it is his lack of money that earns him the death sentence. So Jimmy goes to the electric chair, and the chorus tells us implacably that there is nothing to be done about it. This finale is 'characterized by a blasting, aggressive hostility' which, says Ronald Sanders, 'is bound to leave an audience in a state of agitation'.[31]

Mahagonny is thus not simply a parable about the destructiveness of the unbridled pursuit of pleasure; it is also an assault on a society where money rules and poverty is the worst of crimes. At a time when the theorists of so-called libertarian capitalism argue that nearly every object of human desire should be made available on the market – prostitution, fatally addictive drugs, what you will – the nightmare city of Brecht and Weill is close to being the utopia of the wilder enthusiasts for unlimited capitalism.

For *Mahagonny*'s chilling story, Weill provides music of a fierceness and austerity quite different from the comparatively relaxed, cheerfully cynical mood established in *The Threepenny Opera*. Its unrelenting character is, ironically, partly established by the fact that *Mahagonny*, unlike the earlier work, is through-composed. In this respect it represented a move away from the principles that underpinned its predecessor, and not surprisingly Brecht was by no means happy about this development. He was too positive a dramatist to be able to accept the inevitably subordinate role of librettist. Yet the fact is that the effectiveness of *Mahagonny* in hammering home its message depends upon its musical continuity, on the far more careful integration of the songs into the musical texture of the whole, and on the cumulative power of such movements as the finales to the first and last acts. (The Act One finale begins with a chorale for male voices that is another of Weill's tributes to Mozart, since it clearly recalls the music for the Two Armed Men in *Die Zauberflöte*.) *Mahagonny* is, as Douglas Jarman has written, 'ferocious both dramatically and musically'.[32] Of course, it contains tender and beautiful music, such as the 'Benares Song' (which is, however, rather awkwardly inserted between Jimmy's trial and his execution), but its overall impact is bleak and harsh to the point where it is entirely understandable that it should have provoked audience hostility. But precisely that is the measure of its success. Neither Weill nor Brecht intended to bring us aught for our comfort. Some opera, like some drama, has to be disturbing above all. *Mahagonny* is a prime example of this genre.

The final product of the Brecht–Weill partnership was another through-composed work, the ballet-opera or ballet-chanté *The Seven Deadly Sins*, which was created after both men had left Germany in the early weeks of 1933 following the Nazis' rise to power. This work too is a sharp satire on the values of capitalist society, and once more it is placed in an imaginary American context, reflecting Brecht's continuing fascination with the sordid yet glamorous heartland of world capitalism, which neither he nor Weill had yet seen for himself. The sins of the title are the traditional ones, but Brecht, as one would expect, gives a bitter twist to conventional morality by making it plain that each of these is regarded as a sin only in so far as it obstructs Anna's career and world success. Thus, she should not be proud: not, that is, too proud to strip if that helps her to make her name. She should not be angry: not, that is, angry at injustice, since that anger only antagonizes people. She should not be gluttonous, since men do not fancy fat girls: 'There's no market for hippos in Philadelphia.' And so on. A quartet of male voices representing her family at home in Louisiana, with, grotesquely, a bass voice for her mother, offer her this advice at each stage of her geographical and social progress through American society; they, of course, are interested primarily in the material benefits they expect from Anna's self-control and worldly success. It is a brilliant scenario, which Weill realizes in equally effective musical terms, but it is not a particularly visual or theatrical piece. Not a lot is lost in concert performance – or so it seems to me.

I have done little more than cast a brief and highly selective glance over Weill's record as a composer of works for the musical theatre with a political dimension. Gradually, however, works that have long been neglected, such as *Street Scene*, *Lost in the Stars* and *Die Silbersee*, are receiving overdue performances and recordings. Within a relatively few years it ought to be possible to reach some kind of general perspective on both his musical achievement and his political commitments, and on the connections between them.

George Gershwin and the American Musical

Less than a year before the Berlin premiere of *Die Dreigroschenoper*, the first performance took place of the work that is generally considered to have marked the turning point in the evolution of the American musical: Jerome Kern's *Show Boat*, first seen at the National Theater, Washington on 15 November 1927. 'The history of the American musical theatre', says Miles Kreuger, 'quite simply, is divided into two eras: everything before *Show Boat*, and everything after *Show Boat*.'[33] What *Show Boat* demonstrated was that the musical did not have to restrict itself to the Ruritanian fantasies of Lehár and Sigmund Romberg, but could deal with substantial, even controversial, subject matter which yet lent itself successfully to exhilarating musical treatment.

The choice of Edna Ferber's popular family saga was Kern's own. The project was an ambitious one: to trace the fortunes of a group of hard-working entertainers over nearly half a century of United States history. This involved incorporating a variety of styles and rhythms by way of illustrating the passage of time. This aspect of the work is not entirely successful, since it is spanned into a series of disconnected scenes all crammed into the second of the show's two acts. The first and longer act focuses on a single moment in the story of the Mississippi show boat of the title, and it is life on and around the great symbolic American river that lies at the heart of this often moving score.

From the start of the overture we know that this is going to be no ordinary musical. Instead of offering the usual medley of hit tunes, it opens on a fierce chord of A minor and derives most of its material from the collective black lament 'Mis'ry's comin' aroun'', although 'Why do I love you?' gives it an upbeat conclusion. But this overture is essentially a piece of sombre scene-setting, which is followed by an equally striking opening scene. A gang of black stevedores sing:

> Niggers all work on de Mississippi
> Niggers all work while de white folks play

It is understandable that in many productions the word 'nigger' is replaced by something that is not insulting. But Kern and Hammerstein meant no insult, as is clear from what follows. On the contrary, they intended to shock by treating race relations in the Deep South without sentimentality, and by placing them at the centre of the story. Later the stevedores' chorus forms the trio section of 'Ol' man river', an immortal song whose burden is the same swaying lament over the endless cycle of work and brief escapes from work that Luigi articulates for the Parisian stevedores in *Il tabarro*.

The emotional heart of Act One comes when a jealous would-be lover tips off the state authorities that Julie La Verne, the company's leading lady, is a mulatto married to a white, and the two of them are forced to leave the troupe. The musical context is set by 'Mis'ry's comin' aroun' '. This was the first piece to be cut after the show's first performance had run for over four hours: a mistake, for it is some of the best music in this rich score, and one of the strengths of the score is the way in which the strict antithesis of songs and spoken dialogue is constantly broken down by the use of fragments and reminiscences in the orchestral or choral background; Scene Four, shorn of this introductory number, must lose a great deal of its meaning and impact.

Show Boat is a hybrid and uneven work. Some of it, especially the perhaps deliberately glib love songs – 'Only make believe', 'You are love' – harks back to the frothy world of operetta. Not all of the songs are integrated into the drama, and the disappearance of Julie from the story, except when she reappears briefly to sing the excellent but irrelevant 'Bill' in Act Two, robs it of much of its power. But the long first act is a magnificent achievement, and the basis of that success lies in the way it is rooted in the life, work and music of the blacks. 'Ol' man river', 'Mis'ry's comin' aroun'', and 'Can't help lovin' dat man' are the songs most central to the music of the act, and they are all black songs, for solo voices and chorus. The music itself challenges the racism that drives Julie and Steve off the show boat.

The new seriousness of music theatre in the later 1920s is a striking phenomenon. The 1920s have often been seen as a period of frivolity. In fact its creative artists worked in the shadow of the Great War, and were acutely conscious of being in a new and far less stable environment. This consciouness was reinforced by the global recession of the inter-war years, and not even the musical was immune to the realities of depression, unemployment and the hopelessness and insecurity they produced. In Germany Brecht and Weill, Ernst Krenek and others produced the music theatre of the depression. In the United States its leading composer was George Gershwin. To say this is controversial. Gershwin has been described as 'a man who was famous for being apolitical'.[34] Perhaps, in a sophisticated and specific way, this is true. But Gershwin had ambitions for his music: he wanted it to speak for and to his time. Above all he wanted to create an authentically American opera. His aims with *Porgy and Bess* were similar to those that Smetana had for his operas, and Vaughan Williams for *Hugh the Drover*: to produce something distinctively national, genuinely popular, and rooted in common experience. These were essentially political ambitions in the broad sense. And even if we acquit George of any concern with specific political issues, the same cannot be said of his brother Ira, who was his regular librettist. Ira always had radical sympathies, and this had the inevitable consequence that in the years of anti-Communist persecution after World War Two he came briefly under suspicion.

The genesis of *Porgy and Bess* was exactly contemporary with that of *Show Boat*. Gershwin read Edwin DuBose Heyward's novel *Porgy* in 1926, and wrote to Heyward immediately about the possibility of turning it into an opera. At that time, however, it was being converted into a successful play, and so the idea had to be dropped. Not until 1934 was the project taken up again. Meanwhile the Gershwin brothers had produced a series of political musicals which, in their particular way, reflected the mood and conditions of the times just as vividly as the novels of John Steinbeck and Christopher Isherwood, or the poetry of W.H. Auden and Stephen Spender. These were *Strike up the Band* (1927), *Of Thee I Sing* (1931) and *Let 'Em Eat Cake* (1933).

Strike Up the Band was an anti-war satire, with profiteers and swindlers as its particular target. *Of Thee I Sing* was even more ambitious. The songs were fully integrated into the plot, and the music was not confined to the songs. Ira in an interview described it as 'our first wholly integrated musical'. *Let 'Em Eat Cake* was too radical and political for the Broadway audiences of 1933, and was not a success. All three musicals can be considered as in some ways preparatory to the greatest of Gershwin's achievements in the theatre: *Porgy and Bess*.

'The production will be a serious attempt to put into operatic form a purely American theme. If I am successful, it will resemble a combination of the drama and romance of *Carmen* and the beauty of *Meistersinger*, if you can imagine that.'[35] Gershwin, in other words, had great ambitions for his opera. To invite comparison with two of the supreme masterpieces of opera was perhaps unwise, although as a melodist Gershwin can certainly compare with Bizet, and *Porgy and Bess* has some obvious affinities with *Carmen*. But while any of the set numbers in Gershwin's opera, ensembles as well as songs, are magnificent, his handling of what goes between, of recitative and conversation, often lacks the restraint and economy of the masterworks of opera. His writing is often over-scored and sometimes vapid. *Porgy and Bess* is not a flawless masterpiece. But there are few such in the entire history of opera, and Gershwin's only opera is undeniably magnificent and moving.

Some African-Americans have found this opera, the work of a New York Jewish composer, unconvincing and inauthentic. But in its own musical terms, and allowing for Gershwin's background in Broadway music, he succeeds in creating what Wilfred Mellers has called 'a folk-opera about a dispossessed people'. Its tragic yet intensely vibrant central pair are, of course, victims: of ignorance, exploitation and the other evils that spring from the structure of racial oppression. But they are victims who are in no sense isolated, but belong to a culture and community which are as much what the opera is about as it is about any particular individuals. Indeed, most of Act One, although it introduces us to Porgy, Bess and the other major characters, who are swiftly and skilfully characterized, is devoted to communal occasions: the crap game and the violence in which it ends, and the second scene of general mourning over the body of the murdered Robbins.

Religion is central to the life of this community, although not all its members take it as seriously as Serena. When she tries to dissuade her husband Robbins from the crap game, he tells her:

> Lissen what I say
> I works all the week; Sunday got to pray,
> But Saturday night a man's got the right to play.

Although religion is clearly a strength and a source of comfort to the community in times of distress – the soul of a soulless world, in Marx's phrase – it does not go unchallenged. Crown and Sportin' Life, the two men who between them corrupt and ruin Bess and so destroy her relationship with Porgy, are both heartless cynics; Crown is the worst kind of male bully, revelling in drunkenness, violence and his power over women, and unpardonably insulting to the crippled Porgy. But both are critics of the credulity and superstition that go along with religious belief in Catfish Row. Sportin' Life scoffs at those who foolishly believe that the storm is the prelude to the Day of Judgement, while Crown is the only man who dares to go out in the storm to try and rescue Clara and Jake. And then Sportin' Life's 'It ain't necessarily so' is so witty and exhilarating:

> De t'ings dat yo' li'ble
> To read in de Bible,
> It ain't necessarily so.

that it can hardly be received as the unambiguous voice of the Devil. Sportin' Life is the devil who tempts Bess/Eve with drugs. But he is a devil with at least two exceptionally good tunes: 'There's a boat dat's leavin' soon for New York' is another dazzling temptation.

This is a superstitious community, and conventional in terms of sexual morality. When Crown abandons Bess in Act One, they all shut their doors on her – the opera is full of biblical references as well as invocations – and it is left to Porgy to give her shelter. As he says, 'Between the Gawd fearin' ladies and the Gawd damnin' men that gal

ain't got a chance.' But it is a real community with a real culture and
vitality of its own. The only people who do not sing in the opera are
the white representatives of law 'n' order, who venture into Catfish
Row from time to time in largely futile attempts to track down crimes.
Music belongs to the black community, not to white authority.

A word should be said in defence of Bess, who is rather too easily
written off as 'a woman of easy virtue', as the CBS recording synopsis
has it. It is true that she knows her own attractiveness to men and is
prepared to exploit it: 'Some man always willin' to take care of Bess'.
But she also knows her own weakness, and makes genuine efforts to
escape from the culture of drugs and easy sex represented by Crown
and Sportin' Life. A less male-patronizing view would see her as a
rather isolated woman with few resources and cruelly exposed to
relentless pressure from two men who know exactly how to exploit
her weaknesses. She is as much a victim in her particular way as is
Porgy himself.

The politics of the American musical is a subject in itself, and it lies
beyond the scope of this book and this author. Unlike opera, which
has usually enjoyed some kind of patronage, first private, now mainly
public, which releases its creators from the obligation to achieve
immediate commercial success, the musical has always been a commercial form, and has been heavily conditioned by the settled tastes
and expectations of its audiences. Stephen Sondheim, who has taken
more risks with the musical than any other prominent composer, has
aptly adapted Lillian Hellman as follows: 'most people like to go to the
theatre to see pleasant people deal with pleasant problems, which is
what most musicals provide'. This can, of course, be done with wit,
style and exuberance, as in *My Fair Lady*. But when these pressures
and expectations are taken into account, what is extraordinary about
the American musical since *Show Boat* is how far its scope has been
extended by many of its leading exponents to take in themes and
characters a world away from the student princes and vagabond kings
of earlier years, and to deal with situations that are anything but
pleasant. The Broadway musical has often reflected the sentiments
and attitudes of East Coast liberalism. It is impressive to find Rogers
and Hammerstein placing race relations and the problems of 'mixed'
marriages at the heart of a hugely popular work like *South Pacific*,

and it is striking how many other musicals besides *South Pacific* have played variations on the theme of *Madama Butterfly*: difficulties in relations between America and the peoples of east Asia. It is a theme that has been treated with greatly differing degres of sentimentality and/or seriousness in *The King and I*, *Flower Drum Song*, and most recently *M. Butterfly* and *Miss Saigon*. But the most intelligent and sophisticated treatment is surely that of Sondheim in *Pacific Overtures*, to which I will turn in a moment.

Among many conscious efforts to write a 'serious' musical *West Side Story* deserves special mention, not only because of its daring and its success, but also because it is an explicit attempt to bring pity and dignity to the lives and hopes of the poor and the unlucky. The basic idea – that of translating the Romeo and Juliet story from the ruling families of Renaissance Verona to the ethnic slums of Manhattan – is not mere updating, but the democratization of a familiar legend. The original idea, of setting it as a conflict between Jewish and Catholic communities, was rightly discarded in favour of a clash between ethnic communities, a treatment that is as strongly topical as ever more than three decades later. In his diary Leonard Bernstein succinctly outlined his stylistic aims:

> Chief problem: to tread the fine line between opera and Broadway, between realism and poetry, ballet and 'just dancing', abstract and representational. Avoid being 'messagy'. The line is there, but it's very fine, and sometimes takes a lot of peering around to discern it.[36]

On the whole Bernstein and his collaborators, who included the young Sondheim as a lyricist, succeeded in treading that fine line. The dance sequences have real musical power. 'America' is an exhilaratingly witty song (the best in the show?), which explains brilliantly the reasons for immigration. Some of the love music is more commonplace – 'Tonight' is easy to remember without being truly memorable – and 'Gee, Officer Krupke' comes too late in the tragedy to be appropriate. What is appropriate is that no real way out of the tragedy is suggested: 'Somewhere' is a dream of how things might and could be better, but it is an expression of desperation as much as of hope. 'Somehow, some day, somewhere!' – the lack of specificity gives the game away. Bernstein commented after the first night, 'Not even a whisper about a happy ending was heard. A rare thing on Broadway.'

He was anxious not to fall into the 'operatic trap', as he put it. But like all the most substantial musicals, *West Side Story* questions the distinction between musical and opera – especially the *Singspiel* opera.

Stephen Sondheim soon graduated from providing lyrics for others to providing music for his own lyrics, and in the past twenty years he has had no rival as an innovator and experimenter in this field. If anything, he has grown more adventurous with the years, so that his recent musicals include one about the post-Impressionist painter Georges Seurat (*Sunday in the Park with George*), a brilliant synthesis of a number of familiar fairytales (*Into the Woods*), and, most recently, a collective study of some of those who have tried to kill, and sometimes succeeded in killing, American Presidents (*Assassins*).

Not surprisingly, not all of Sondheim's shows have had much appeal for the big audiences that flock to the latest Andrew Lloyd Webber spectacular, and probably none of his musicals has been less commercially successful than his most political to date, *Pacific Overtures*. Its theme is similar to that of *Madama Butterfly*, but it is treated in a wholly and significantly different way. Sondheim takes as his subject the historic intrusion into Japan of the American Commodore Perry in 1853, and the impact on Japanese life and culture of the country's subsequent exposure to Western capitalist customs and principles. But whereas the conventional way to handle such a theme would be to explore it in terms of a single narrative and a small number of individuals – three or four at most – Sondheim and his collaborators focus on the historical process itself, and individuals are firmly subordinated to that overall grand perspective. We do see what this devastating change meant to individuals, in terms of individual lives, but none of them is allowed to monopolize our attention in the conventional way. The presence of a reciter/narrator is a further distancing effect which militates against the emotional identification with particular individuals that is so fundamental to so much modern drama and opera. Moreover, Sondheim composed for this show music that seems to me utterly appropriate in its simplicity and restraint, but which is therefore worlds away from Broadway's traditional idioms, including the pretty orientalisms that a more conventional composer would naturally turn to when dealing with a theme of this kind.

Pacific Overtures is not a solemn show. It is full of wit, subtlety and colour, beginning with its brilliantly apt and ironical title. But it fails to meet so many conventional expectations that it has baffled some of its audiences and some of its reviewers as well. But if Sondheim succeeds in his mission to expand the scope of the musical and to bring to it some of the intelligence and sophistication that have never been thought out of place in the straight theatre, and if a political climate can be established in which the West can look more critically at the history of its relations with the rest of the world, then *Pacific Overtures* will come to be appreciated for the imaginative sensitivity with which it evokes the confusion, the bewilderment and corruption that are caused when one culture ignorantly invades another.

Benjamin Britten and Michael Tippett

Benjamin Britten and Michael Tippett both developed musically and politically in the context of the left-wing culture of Britain in the 1930s. Britten, born in 1913, was musically precocious, but Tippett, born in 1905, was a late developer, and he has allowed only a handful of his works of the 1930s to survive. Britten initiated the modern presence of British opera with *Peter Grimes* in 1945, and devoted much of his musical energy thereafter to the composition of opera (he composed five further full-length operas in the next nine years). Tippett's first opera did not appear until 1955, since when he has composed a further four over a period of thirty-five years.

Britten's precocious brilliance led to an intermittent collaboration with W.H. Auden, which produced some notable work, including the orchestral song cycle *Our Hunting Fathers* and the composer's first full-length stage work, *Paul Bunyan*. For both of them involvement with the Left was essentially confined to the 1930s. Although Britten remained a pacifist, in so far as politics enters his operas it is in the quintessentially liberal form of the conflict between society and the isolated or persecuted individual.

The pattern of Tippett's life is a very different one. Although he has won honours and great affection in his later years, he remains a less conventional figure than Britten became. Like Britten a pacifist, his beliefs have had a much more pervasive and profound effect on his work. He has always followed politics closely and has attempted to embody political ideas and current developments in his music, particularly in his operas. Though Tippett is less naturally gifted and virtuosically accomplished than Britten, his work generally escapes the facility and even smoothness that sometimes vitiate the impact of Britten's music. But Britten's opening up of prospects for British opera made Tippett's work possible, and it is to Britten that we must turn first.

Of Britten's operas I shall consider only two, *Peter Grimes* and *Billy Budd*. *Owen Wingrave*, an opera written originally for television, is a work centrally concerned with pacifism and its challenge to military and patriotic traditions, and so ought also to be considered, but, regrettably, I have neither seen nor even heard it.

Peter Grimes, whose premiere just after the end of the war in Europe in 1945 made such an impact on account of its astonishing musical and dramatic assurance, is, nevertheless, an extraordinarily ambivalent and even dubious work. Based loosely on parts of *The Borough*, George Crabbe's poem about Britten's home town of Aldeburgh and some of its inhabitants, it tells the story of a lonely fisherman who employs a series of workhouse boys as apprentices, who die under suspicious circumstances. Two people in the Borough try to help him: a retired sea captain, Balstrode, and the schoolteacher, Ellen Orford, whom Grimes has the opportunity to marry. But Grimes is too impetuous and self-willed to take their advice. Another apprentice falls to his death. The Borough turns into a lynch mob, determined to get Grimes. Half-crazed, Grimes takes Balstrode's last piece of advice: to drown himself with his boat. Life in the Borough returns to normal.

In Crabbe's poem Grimes is brutal and inarticulate, at the last a figure like Macbeth, haunted by the deaths for which he is at least partially responsible. But he is transformed by Britten and his librettist, Montagu Slater, into a tragic visionary, persecuted from the start by a spiteful community, which is determined to believe the worst of him. He is an almost Christ-like figure. His first utterances in the courtroom inquest into one of these apprentices' deaths are surrounded with a musical halo by the strings, as Christ's words are in Bach's *St Matthew Passion*; when some in the community express opposition to the plan to provide him with another apprentice bought from the workhouse, Ellen Orford offers the biblical retort: 'Let her among you without fault cast the first stone'. Her decision to go with the carter to fetch the boy is presented as a brave and generous act. Bob Boles, the Methodist fisherman, protests:

> Is this a Christian country? Are pauper children so enslaved that their bodies go for cash?

But he is portrayed as a hypocritical prig, inveighing against the drink and sexual pleasure he really craves for.

We have got no further than the Prologue and the opening scene of Act One, but already the slant that the music (far more than the libretto) puts upon the story is perplexing, not to say tendentious. Lawyer Swallow's advice to Grimes not to take another apprentice, but to work with a fisherman 'big enough to stand up for himself', sounds like good sense. Grimes's disregard of it, and the willingness of Mrs Orford to cooperate in the purchase of a 'workhouse brat', are at best foolish, at worst callous. Bob Boles is surely right in his protest. The music would persuade us otherwise, but in relation to the actual story this is special pleading.

The entire opera is slanted in this way: to present Grimes as a tragic figure, self-destructive but misunderstood and cruelly persecuted, whilst the community that hunts him down and drives him to his death is individually vindictive and collectively a hysterical mob. Crabbe's original account is far less one-sided. For example, one of the few phrases from the poem that finds its way into the libretto, 'Grimes is at his exercise', is, in Crabbe's version, an expression of calm, almost complaisant indifference towards Grimes's bullying of the apprentices. In Britten's hands it becomes the refrain of a chorus in which the Borough whips itself up into a frenzy of hostility towards Grimes. Crabbe's Grimes is haunted by the three dead apprentices. Britten and Slater reduce the number to two, and in his final soliloquy Grimes is more obsessed with his own persecution than with the dead boys. Mrs Sedley is ridiculed in the same manner as Bob Boles. She is portrayed as a silly and spiteful amateur sleuth, the Borough's malevolent Miss Marple, poking her nose into matters that are no concern of hers. But she is right: another apprentice *has* died, under doubtful circumstances. And if it is no concern of hers, or the Borough's, then whose concern is it? Desmond Shawe-Taylor raised these questions in his review of the 1945 premiere: 'What neither composer nor librettist seems to realise is that, after all, the sympathetic schoolmarm was wrong (and therefore, in effect, an accessory in the second boy's death), whereas Mrs Sedley was dead right.'[37]

The one apprentice whom we see, we don't hear. It is a silent role. Did Britten fear that if given a voice, this unhappy homeless child would tilt the balance of sympathy away from Grimes? It certainly seems a curious, even a disturbing, decision. Grimes is not a murderer but, to adapt Lady Bracknell, while losing one apprentice may be considered a misfortune, to lose two looks like carelessness. Grimes is a violent bully, as Ellen Orford knows – 'Well, it's begun', she sings, when she discovers the apprentice's bruises – and he is certainly guilty of neglecting the safety of the boys he employs, if nothing worse.

It can be argued that in making Grimes a grand, tragic figure Britten and his collaborators were seeking to broaden the range of our sympathies, as Janáček or Berg did with men or women guilty of violence and murder. It is another example of tragedy democratized. This is true, to an extent. As portrayed in the opera, Grimes shows brutality and sensitivity coexisting in the same person, and the opera shows how terrible is the fate of someone ostracized by the only small community to which he feels he belongs. But the treatment of Grimes by Britten and Slater is sentimental and loaded compared to the balance between objectivity (or honesty) and compassion that is achieved by Berg and Büchner, or Janáček and Dostoevsky. Grimes's cruelty and egoism are glossed over in a way that is wholly foreign to Janáček's agonized exploration of the lower depths.

Britten said, in retrospect, that as pacifists during World War Two, he and Peter Pears felt estranged from the country they returned to, and so identified quite strongly with Grimes the outsider.[38] One can add that their position as homosexuals in a generally intolerant 'straight' society would also have prompted such an identification.[39] But these consideration merely exacerbate the problem with *Peter Grimes*. The position of the person who is at odds with society for reasons of conscience or sexual orientation readily evokes sympathy; that of a brutal and violent man who refuses to heed even the best motivated advice, much less so. Yet even in such cases sympathy might be created, provided every hint of whitewashing or tendentiousness was avoided. But that is not the case with *Grimes*. So, for all its musical splendours, *Grimes* remains a deeply flawed work. A romanticized individual is pitted against a travestied community. The result is not, in my experience, to enhance our sympathy for the lonely misunderstood outsider, but to call in question the validity of this stock liberal antithesis, in which the individual can be so easily represented as the victim of an uncomprehending collective, notwithstanding that he is at least partially responsible for the deaths of other individuals even more vulnerable and unfortunate than himself.

Billy Budd is, I believe, a greater and more powerful opera than *Peter Grimes*, which is not free from a rather self-conscious picturesqueness, epitomized in the awkwardly cued 'round' in the pub: 'For peace sake, someone start a song.' *Billy Budd* has in abundance the intensity and single-mindedness that the earlier opera does not always display.

The action of the opera is entirely confined to events on board the *Indomitable*, a 'floating monarchy' whose king is Captain Vere, and the ship functions, as it so often does in literature, as a microcosm of the human world, and of the society on shore that it exists to defend. The class structure of the onshore society, whose lineaments are often obscured by ideological myths and complexities of detail, is expressed on board ship with rigidity and harshness. There are the officers, who are of course gentlemen, and there are the 'men': in essence the same dangerous, unenfranchised 'rabble' that exists on shore, but here tamed by the relentless brutality of so-called naval discipline and by their isolation and confinement within the ship. Between these two classes stand the non-commissioned officers, whose task it is to carry out the acts of brutality with which it would be impolitic for the respectable officers to soil their hands, and reputations. The system depends upon coercion; but those whose position rests on that coercion, and who bear the ultimate responsibility for it, are not seen to be involved in it. Their hands appear to be clean, and the veneer of civilized benevolence is sustained.

All of this is manifest in *Billy Budd*. The beatings, the unscrupulous pressganging of civilians into service are unsparingly depicted in the opera's opening scenes. The immediate agent of this cruelty is Claggart, the master-at-arms. It is therefore he who attracts the hatred of the crew, whilst the man who must bear the ultimate responsibility for all that happens within his miniature monarchy, Captain Vere, 'Starry Vere' as he is known, is revered by them (they sing a chorus in his praise at the end of what was originally Act One of the opera). Not until Billy is hanged for striking and accidentally killing the hated Claggart do the men give any hint of revolt against the officers. And even then that revolt is portrayed in a wordless chorus of murmurings and groanings, as if the men would be too inarticulate, too bestial in fact, to formulate any coherent complaints against their superiors. True, this episode follows the account given of it by Melville in the original story, but the librettists (E.M. Forster and Eric Crozier) did not have to follow their source. This episode suggests a very conventional view of 'the mob' as, in the old phrase, a 'many-headed monster'.

This view is the more incongruous since the whole story is set in the immediate aftermath of the celebrated mutinies at Spithead and the Nore in 1797. The officers are acutely nervous, and take fright even when the entirely innocent Billy is heard singing a farewell to the ship he has been snatched from: 'Farewell, old *Rights of Man*'. They are constantly on the lookout for the influence of 'French', or revolutionary, ideas. Yet despite the precise timing of the opera's events, at no point is there any hint that the crew of the *Indomitable* have been affected, let alone inspired, by the recent stirring revolts in the navy. When the pressed novice returns from his flogging, his comrades, far from expressing any indignation, merely sing a generalized lament about being 'lost for ever on the endless sea'. This seems like an evasion. Perhaps, given the concept of Billy's innocence, it would be pointless to expect that he should protest at his own impressing. Nevertheless, the resignation with which he accepts everything that happens to him, including the injustice of his execution, may strike some of us as less saintly than pathetic. Meekness is not easily distinguished from acquiescence in oppression and injustice.

The animal-like response of the sailors to Budd's execution, described in the libretto as a '*capricious* revulsion of feeling' (my italics), is another evasion. Still, we are close to the end of the opera, and to suggest that the climactic event of the execution might set off a series of further developments would be untidy, even if realistic.

Yet the historical context of the story is vital to an understanding of everything that happens. It is because Britain is at war with revolutionary France, and – perhaps even more importantly – because the establishment is at war with the influence of revolutionary ideas within Britain itself, and even within the navy, that Vere feels that

Budd's action cannot be treated with leniency. He must suffer the full, final punishment, not because he is guilty as an individual, but because the counter-revolutionary war requires it. So Vere offers no defence, no plea of mitigation on Billy's behalf, although Billy twice appeals to him to do so, and even the officers are dismayed by his implacable silence. Justice to an individual matters less than the maintenance of order and moral discipline. Vere knows that he has the prime responsibility for the death of an innocent man, and this knowledge haunts him for ever after, as one would expect. But there is no indication that he reconsiders his action. He had to act, not as a man but as a naval officer and as part of a system committed to war and the defence of the existing social order. He did what the role required of him. And this, apart from the political situation that dictates the tragic outcome, is the second significantly political dimension of this powerful work. For, as Tom Sutcliffe pointed out, 'Britten was always showing people caught in a system that perverts their natural goodness and stops them being themselves.'[40]

Even so, Britten once again seems to fudge the hard issues by endowing Vere, like Grimes, with a tragic quality which may lead, and may be intended to lead, us to sympathize with him rather than with the victim of his ruthless if not misconceived notion of duty. Vere, in the version of the story by Britten and his librettists, is the centre of interest rather than Billy himself; but is he really deserving of so much sympathy? He is a cultivated man who reads the classics. He does not share the crude chauvinism of his subordinate officers, and he is not deceived by Claggart's scheming and lies. None the less, he fails to save Billy. E.M. Forster wrote that his first task as a librettist was 'to rescue Vere from Melville' and to place Billy, not Vere, at the heart of the story. 'How odiously Vere comes out in the trial scene!' he remarked.[41] In the opera this odiousness is mitigated perhaps, but not fundamentally altered. At the moment of testing, he fails, and given his intelligence and apparent decency, the failure is the more abject. As the central figure in the drama he is marvellously well drawn, and can command our interest throughout. But the person who allows his role or occupation to determine his or her actions against his own con-science and moral knowledge is not in the end admirable. He is dangerous because he is a pliable tool of institutions committed to brutality and evil.

At the end, in Vere's tranquil recollection of these far-off events, we are given to understand that he feels himself to have been saved, redeemed even, by Billy's goodness and forgiveness. 'I could have saved him, I could have saved him,' he sings, and 'O what have I done?' But the immediate next-bar response to that is that 'he has saved me and blessed me'; he goes on to sing the words of Billy's final soliloquy: 'I've sighted a sail in the storm, the far-shining sail, and I'm contented.' The work's fundamental musical conflict, stated in the opening bars, between B minor and B flat major, with B minor being (significantly) the key in which Spithead and the Nore are recalled in the conversation between Vere and his fellow officers, is finally resolved in favour of a peaceful and comforting B flat major.

Am I alone in finding this glib, unconvincing and, indeed, repellent? Vere knows that he could have saved Billy's life, knows that Billy was essentially innocent, and yet can find comfort, absolution even, in the magnanimity of his victim. Billy's very lack of anger or resentment ought surely to haunt him the more profoundly. And it is extraordinary that Forster, whose most famous pronouncement was probably his declaration, on the eve of World War Two, 'if I had to choose between betraying my country and betraying my friend, I hope I should have the guts to betray my country', should have apparently endorsed a libretto whose message appears to be the exact opposite.[42] Vere betrays Billy for what would be called patriotic reasons. Such actions can, of course, be justified. But that such betrayals should be rewarded with spiritual peace and forgiveness is hardly credible, and certainly not creditable.

The end of *Billy Budd* is not an isolated moment of weakness in Britten's work. The same tendency, to compensate for the musical treatment of harsh themes with a comfortable, conciliatory conclusion, is evinced to some degree by the final movement of the *Sinfonia da Requiem*, which falls rather too consolingly on the ear after the fierceness and anguish of what has preceded it; and even more so by the conclusion of the *War Requiem*. After the terror of the final 'Libera me' has dissolved into the wonderful austerity and restraint of the setting of Owen's 'Strange Meeting', the consolatory 'In paradisum' ensemble, which is built up over the words 'let us sleep now', seems facile and banal. Britten has evoked the horrors of war so vividly, and with such compassion, that a conclusion that eschews the tragic dimension, as this does, is simply inadequate. It is as if Britten, like Janáček's pupils but unlike Janáček himself, had not finally the capacity to confront the black finality of such destruction of human lives and hopes. Perhaps this is why he never realized his project of an opera based on *King Lear*.

Even though Britten was still in his thirties when *Billy Budd* was composed, his treatment of the crew's response to Billy's death, of the theme of mutiny, and of Vere's dilemmas as a figure of authority all indicate how far he had travelled from the radical politics of his youth. In later works, it is hard to detect any concern with large social or political issues, apart from the pacifism which inspired the *War Requiem* and *Owen Wingrave*. The one exception might be *Gloriana*, which followed two years after *Budd* in 1953.

Gloriana provides a moving, complex portrait of an ageing ruler who has to subordinate her personal feelings to her public duty, like Vere; her relationship with her subjects at different social and political levels is vividly depicted. But Essex's rebellion, and his ambitions and those of his sister, Lady Rich, are poorly handled. His defiance seems to be motivated by little more than personal pique: the political substance of it is missing, as is Essex himself after the end of Act Two. The portrait of Queen Elizabeth belongs to the same gallery as those of Boris, Philip II, Mozart's Tito and other operatic studies of rulers isolated by their power and divided between their personal affections and their political obligations. But the opera as a whole, with its many setpiece dances and songs, has too much of the character of an historical romance-cum-pageant to bear serious comparison with the great political masterpieces of Verdi and Mussorgsky.

The contrast between Britten and Michael Tippett could hardly be greater. Tippett has been a lifelong experimenter, in both form and style. Britten's operas conform to established naturalistic conventions, for the most part. But of Tippett's five operas only one is at all plausibly regarded as a realist work. The others are all replete with symbolic figures and references, and are never given any precise time of location other than 'the present'. And yet, paradoxically, they are always contemporary and topical. All Britten's operas are set somewhere in the past, which does not, of course, necessarily deprive them of topicality. Yet after *Billy Budd* the sense of grappling with modern

issues is not generally strong. With Tippett there is never any doubt
that he is striving to address the problems of today. He elects to do this
by using myths from the past, as in *King Priam* and to some extent in
The Midsummer Marriage, or by inventing his own, or by blending the
two. His libretti, which he writes himself, are full of borrowings,
echoes, allusions and quotations. They are quintessentially modernist,
in the style of T.S. Eliot's *The Waste Land*, a work whose influence the
composer has readily acknowledged, and from which he adapted the
figures of King Fisher and (Madame) Sosostris in *The Midsummer
Marriage*. These texts have been much criticized, and they are not free
from awkwardness and even the occasional absurdity. Tippett sometimes, as in *The Ice Break*, one of his shortest operas, tries to pack too
much into a brief span: the text, and the audience's attention, are
overloaded. But the texts are integral to the operas, and are unique and
characteristic. There is never any sense of routine, or conventional
literariness, about them.

Perhaps none of his operas is entirely successful. *The Ice Break* is
overloaded; *New Year*, at first hearing and seeing, seems incoherent in
its combination of public rituals with private dilemmas; the last act of
King Priam is too long and lacking in tension, whilst the last act of *The
Knot Garden* hardly begins to resolve the tensions and problems so
eloquently set out in the first two acts. The disappearance of the central
couple, Mark and Jennifer, for half of *The Midsummer Marriage* is
awkward. But Tippett has always refused to play safe. He may not
always realize his aims completely, but the aims are serious and
exciting. Tippett's grand projects, even when only partially successful, stir us more deeply and address our central concerns more
powerfully than do the well-crafted, self-contained works of less
ambitious composers. His achievement is a great one. He has proved
that opera, a form that sometimes seems to belong to the past even as
its creators locate their stories in the past, can speak about, as well as
to, the late-twentieth-century world.

Both Britten and Tippett were pacifists, but though Britten's pacifism was the inspiration for certain major works, it would be hard to
guess that the composer of *Billy Budd* was a pacifist. Tippett's pacifism
is more of a comprehensive philosophy, and affects his work more
pervasively. It is the basis of his lifelong preoccupation with the causes
and consequences of violence at every level and of conflict and

aggression of every kind. It is not only war that concerns him, but the individual psychology of which, as he sees it, war is the most extreme manifestation. These preoccupations found expression in one of his first works to achieve popular success, the oratorio *A Child of Our Time*. The episode that provided the starting point for this work was the attempted assassination of a Nazi diplomat in Paris in 1938 by a young Polish Jew, Herschel Grynspan, which the Nazis then used as the pretext for a concerted attack on Jews and Jewish property, the so-called Kristallnacht. Tippett of course felt deep sympathy for Grynspan and for the persecuted Jews, but he was convinced that the resort to violent resistance was futile because it only bred further violence. The oratorio was thus the first of Tippett's pacifist works. But Tippett felt strongly that an oratorio or an opera could not simply be the expression of an individual point of view: it had to be the embodiment of collective experience. Hence he uses Negro spirituals in *A Child of Our Time* to play the role played by the chorales in the Bach Passions:

> I felt I had to express collective feelings and that could only be done by collective tunes such as the Negro spirituals, for these tunes contain a deposit of generations of common experience.[43]

Their use has been criticized, and it is true that it involves some awkward stylistic gear changes. But Tippett's settings of the spirituals are inspired, and they play exactly the role that the composer envisaged for them: of tying the oratorio to a common and familiar experience of oppression, wonderfully expressed in simple music.

One of the strengths of all Tippett's operas is the way in which he connects individuals and their behaviour with general social and political issues. Personal dilemmas always have a wider significance; public issues are always dealt with in terms of their impact on individuals. So, in *The Midsummer Marriage*, a pastoral and lyrical work, set like Shakespeare's comedy in a forest on midsummer's eve, the figure of King Fisher, the businessman whose response to every opposition or obstacle is to resort to power or force, represents all that Tippett, the pacifist and socialist, finds most destructive and negative in the everyday world of money and power. He is deaf and blind to the magic of the forest, to all the mysterious forces of the natural and spiritual worlds which represent everything that makes for life, insight and sympathy. King Fisher stands for spiritual death-in-life, the dehumanization that is the root and precondition of aggression in personal and political relations.

The opera as a whole is a hymn to the wholeness, the unity of body and mind, sensuality and spirituality with which Tippett has always been preoccupied. It owes a lot to *The Magic Flute*: too much, perhaps, for while the comparison between Mark and Jennifer and Tamino and Pamina presents no problems, the addition of a secondary pair, Bella the secretary and Jack the mechanic, is something of an embarrassment. Not only are they socially 'inferior', but clearly they cannot undergo the mysterious transforming experiences vouchsafed to Mark and Jennifer. Although they rise to the occasion to the extent of defying King Fisher's sacrilegious orders, they represent a modest, prosaic level of imagination and aspiration in the same manner as Papageno and Papagena. They aim at nothing more ambitious than getting married and having children. This patronizing portrayal of 'ordinariness' forms a jarring element in the extraordinarily sustained lyricism and exaltation of the opera as a whole.

There are many for whom *The Midsummer Marriage* remains Tippett's only approachable and lovable opera, and it is not hard to see why this should be so. Tippett's early tonal lyrical idiom, which is also the idiom of the Concerto for Double String Orchestra and the Corelli Fantasia, is close enough to the familiar English pastoral idiom most commonly associated with Vaughan Williams not to present too many problems for the conservative listener. None of his four subsequent operas owes much to that idiom. But Tippett is a composer of deep, lifelong preoccupations, and for that reason it is especially important to see his work as a whole. His first opera was an unrepeatable exercise in radiant lyricism. In his next he turned to face directly the question of war and its roots, appropriately enough since, like Britten's *War Requiem*, *King Priam* was commissioned for the opening of the new cathedral at Coventry, a city which had been devastated by German bombing in 1940. For this opera and this subject the composer, by then well into his fifties, fashioned a new and more suitably abrasive musical language. He perceived that 'the music had to be spare, taut, heroic and unsentimental'. It required, he knew, a departure 'from the lyrical style of most of my music in the past', and its replacement by 'a hard, tough, declamatory style, that would reflect inevitability'.[44]

The harshness and austerity of the music came as a surprise, yet in some ways *King Priam* is the most conventional of Tippett's operas. David Matthews has written, 'All Tippett's operas are modern myths,' but most of these myths are the composer's own invention, or at least embellished borrowings. *Priam* is the only opera for which the composer made use of a familiar public myth, and it is also the one with the plainest and most direct narrative structure. Its central conflict, that between personal, private feeling and what are understood to be public necessities and duties, is also a staple theme of much opera since the inception of the form. The particular originality of *King Priam* lies in Tippett's success in dramatizing a set of variations on this theme, all within the Trojan royal family.

The composer described the opera, perhaps provocatively, as 'essentially an "opera of the family" '. But this should not be taken to mean a drama of purely private relationships. On the contrary, the quarrels and tensions within the family all arise out of the political crisis in which it is engulfed. The three leading women represent responses to this crisis so different that there is no real communication between them. Hecuba, the queen, puts public and political duty before everything, and even suppresses maternal feelings to this end. In the opening scene of the opera Priam and Hecuba learn from a wise old man that their newborn son will cause 'as by an inexorable fate, his father's death'. Hecuba does not hesitate. A threat to Priam is a threat to Troy. She orders that the child be killed. Priam is more troubled. In a fine soliloquy, he meditates on the conflict between being 'a father and a king', and on the injustice of determining the fate of a helpless child. Yet he finally agrees that the child should be killed.

The attempt to resist fate is doomed to fail. Paris survives, to elope with Helen, wife of Menelaus, and so provoke the Trojan War. Paris and Helen seem almost wholly absorbed in their passion for each other, oblivious of the vast political and human consequences of their self-indulgence. Andromache, wife of Hector, reproaches Helen for this. But Hecuba in turn rebukes Andromache for her naïveté:

> Daughter, you are a fool.
> No war is fought for a woman.
> If, because of Helen,
> the Greeks landed from their thousand ships,
> It is Troy they want, not Helen.

If Helen represents a withdrawal from politics and society into pure sensuality, her sister-in-law Andromache represents another version of withdrawal: into domesticity and the traditional woman's roles of wife and mother. She is the Fricka of this opera. Hecuba exposes her narrowness, too. When Andromache asserts 'My place is here in my home,' the queen retorts, 'And what will be your home if Troy is taken?' Neither version of withdrawal offers any escape from the political conflict Helen has helped to precipitate. Both Paris and Hector are killed in the war.

But as the catastrophe of the war unfolds in Act Three – and it is a structural weakness that so much of the drama's development is packed into the final and longest act – Priam is overwhelmed by a sense of the futility of the war and the sequence of revenge killings, to which no end can be foreseen. He withdraws from the world of fighting and action and prepares himself for the death he now accepts as inevitable. At this moment of withdrawal it is not Hecuba his wife, nor Andromache, but Helen alone of the three women whom Priam agrees to see. She is the only person with whom the king feels any affinity as he approaches death. It is an inspired stroke. Helen's sensuality suddenly appears as a positive, if unconscious alternative to the wearying macho aggressiveness of Hector and Achilles.

King Priam is a strong, unflinching work which eschews the consolatory conclusion of the *War Requiem*. Priam attains a kind of pacifist enlightenment, but too late to halt the killing. No gods or peacemakers appear to point the way ahead. Only Hermes, the messenger of death, urges us to 'feel the pity and the terror as Priam dies' and calls on 'divine music' to 'Melt our hearts / Renew our love'. Tippett never abandons hope, but he knows how hard it is to sustain that hope in the face of the history of this century. In his Third Symphony he faces this challenge directly by quoting the opening bars of the finale of Beethoven's Ninth Symphony, then replacing Schiller's Ode with a set of verses of his own devising. This is typically audacious, but Tippett makes it compelling precisely by *not* attempting to imitate, let alone emulate, Beethoven's heaven-storming rhetoric or his grand musical structure.

Tippett is a master of musical quotation. In his third opera, *The Knot Garden*, it is the 'divine music' of Schubert that so effectively melts our hearts when a moment of peace is arrived at in Act Two as

Flora sings a verse of 'Die liebe Farbe' from *Die schöne Mullerin*. The opera is primarily an exploration of personal relations and individual psychology in the form of a meditation on Shakespeare's *The Tempest*. Its whirling, fragmented and often abrasive idiom perfectly expresses the confusions and disturbances of its characters. As a psychological study in musical terms, it is brilliant. But even in the enclosed space of a formal garden Tippett does not insulate his characters from the wider political world. Faber, the work-oriented sexual playboy, is a close relative of King Fisher, while his wife Thea, withdrawn into herself and her garden, represents the opposite extreme, an impossible attempt to shut out the public world altogether.

Into this tangle comes Thea's sister, Denise, a political activist who has been tortured and disfigured as a result of her involvement in an unspecified liberation struggle. At first she has difficulty in relating to these self-absorbed individuals, but she is no model of pure responsibility. She has a confession:

The lust of violence has bred contamination in my blood.

So she is drawn into their interweaving patterns, and finally into a relationship with Mel, a black man. She tells her sister: Mel will uphold me as I am. But she soon discovers that her feelings for him are a new source of confusion and pain, a different kind of torture. She is attracted towards him first because he is black, rather than as an individual; he, of course, senses this. Tippett here begins to explore race relations, an issue that looms even larger in his next opera, *The Ice Breaks*.

The Knot Garden is a brief work (about eighty-five minutes) of exceptional coherence and intensity. If its final resolution, beautiful and truly earned as it is, is nevertheless not wholly convincing, this should be taken as mirroring an uncertainty about resolving such problems that is as much ours as the composer's. A conventional happy ending would be even less convincing.

The Ice Break is even shorter, but is generally judged to be less successful because it tries to encompass too much and so loses musical and dramatic coherence. But it is hard to be sure. *The Ice Break* has been the most neglected of Tippett's operas. Since its Covent Garden premiere in 1977 and a single revival in 1979, it has not been seen again in Britain, and it had to wait for a recording until 1992.

The Ice Break deals with three forms of conflict – between East and West, between black and white, and between generations – and it tentatively explores, with more hope than confidence, the possibilities of resolving these conflicts. Negatively, as always with Tippett, the message is absolutely clear. Such conflicts cannot be settled through violence, which is the product of hatred, and depends on the depersonalization and stereotyping of the group seen as 'the enemy'. So the black champion Olympion is killed in the fighting between blacks and whites, as is the white girl Gayle; Yuri, son of the refugees Lev and Nadia, is seriously injured. Yet out of this disaster Tippett sketches some possibilities of wisdom and reconciliation, represented in part by Hannah, Olympion's black girlfriend, who in her Act Two aria searches for some alternative to the anger of the black mob.

Part of the problem of the opera, though, is that the most moving and deeply felt music belongs to the older refugee pair, Lev and Nadia, and above all to Nadia's death scene at the opening of Act Three. Thus the emotional core of the music stands at an angle to its ostensible dramatic focus and narrative thread. Nevertheless Tippett here extends his investigation of conflict and aggression and their causes, and, in contrast, of what makes for personal wholeness and political harmony.

These preoccupations are still present in Tippett's fifth opera, *New Year*, whose central figure Jo Ann has to find the resources within herself and from others to face the world outside the room in which she hides away, the world of Terror Town. This she achieves partly through her commitment to her half-brother Donny, when she has to rescue him from a crowd that turns aggressive towards him on New Year's Eve, and partly through a visit from a space traveller, Pelegrin, who leads her through ritual tests similar to those of the last act of Strauss's *Die Frau ohne Schatten*. The opera ends with a slogan that Tippett borrowed from one of the concerts in honour of the then still imprisoned Nelson Mandela: 'One humanity, one justice'. Tippett clearly intends *New Year* to convey a political message, but it is not yet clear to me how effectively this message is woven into the fabric of the opera as a whole. Tippett is, and always has been, a political composer in the profoundest sense, exploring through both words and music the deepest and most perplexing challenges of the century he has lived through. His work reaffirms and renews the long and centrally important tradition of political opera.

Conclusion

There are a few moments in the history of opera when particular operas, or parts of them, have had a direct political impact. The inspirational effect of Auber's *La muette de Portici* on the patriots of Brussels in 1830 is probably the most celebrated instance. But *Guillaume Tell* at the Paris Opéra in the same year stirred up a comparable excitement, and Verdi's early patriotic operas helped to form the spirit of the Risorgimento. The sceptical, those who would prefer to believe that music, like poetry in Auden's view, 'makes nothing happen', would doubtless want to argue that these are the exceptions that prove the rule: that art reflects, refracts and meditates upon politics as upon other aspects of life, rather than directly influencing them or involving itself with them.

I am not persuaded of the validity of this distinction. Was Mussorgsky only reflecting upon Russian politics in his two great national epic operas, or did he not feel himself to be involved in the creation of a new, radical consciousness? Beethoven, it seems safe to say, hoped to instil in others the passion for freedom and justice that inspired *Fidelio*. Wagner certainly hoped that his operas would contribute to the shaping of a national spirit, which he believed was lacking in the Germany of his day. Smetana had the same hopes for his operas in Czechoslovakia. There can be no doubting the immediate political purpose in Prokofiev's *War and Peace*, even if difficulties in getting the work performed frustrated this intention. Tippett has always been a didactic composer. So is Hans Werner Henze. The notion that composers, or artists in general, are invariably or inherently detached from the public events and politics of their age is a fiction, one to which many people are strongly attached, but which obscures and distorts a proper and full understanding of their work.

As for the political impact of opera, we need to know more about contemporary audience responses to, let us say, *Boris Godunov*, or *Libuse*, or *Mahagonny*, or *Il prigioniero*, before we can confidently pronounce that none of these works, among many others, has made any direct political impact. These are difficult, subtle questions in any case, because what we are discussing is the formation of beliefs and opinions, the shaping of people's thoughts and imaginations. It is an area in which proof of influence, let alone decisive influence, is by its nature hard to come by. But it seems perverse rather than sensible to *start* from the assumption that people are unaffected in their beliefs, their view of the world, by what they see and hear in the opera house. If books and newspapers can influence our thinking, why not theatre and music?

Nevertheless, it may well be that the moments when a composer can speak for as well as to his immediate audience, in such a way as to become the voice of a great movement of feeling and opinion, are rare. Verdi achieved this at one time, and perhaps also Smetana. I doubt that the same can be said of Wagner or Mussorgsky, Weill or Tippett. Often it is only in retrospect that the specific political significance of a particular work may emerge. *Wozzeck*, for example, can been seen from one angle as one of those works that embody the experience of the ordinary soldier in World War One, as well as some of the radical lessons he might have drawn from that experience; but was it so understood in the 1920s? *War and Peace* certainly articulates the patriotic spirit of Russia at war with the Nazis, but by the time it was performed (in any form) that moment had passed. But deprived of topicality, it is not thereby emptied of its political meaning.

There are some regrettable gaps in my survey of political opera. I have said nothing about French grand opera and the work of Meyerbeer, for example. Berlioz has been similarly neglected. Among contemporary composers, for lack of recordings, I have not discussed the important body of work by Hans Werner Henze, in particular his collaborations with Edward Bond, *We Come to the River* and *The English Cat*. But enough has been said, I hope, to substantiate my basic, very simple contention: politics is not an obscure and destructive terrain into which the more foolish or over-zealous composers sometimes stray, at considerable and possibly mortal risk to their sacred calling. It is simply the realm of public and collective concerns and issues within which we all live, and which is likely to be of particular interest and importance to the composer of opera, because opera is essentially a public, large-scale form dealing with public events in public places, rather than merely private and domestic dramas. Those opera composers who, consciously or otherwise, have turned their backs on politics have narrowed the scope of opera and diminished its stature and excitement. If all opera had followed the path chosen by Richard Strauss, it would have declined into elegant insignificance. Fortunately, there were other composers, as we have seen, who sustained and renewed the operatic tradition by keeping it in touch with the central concerns of the twentieth century.

Recent years have witnessed something of an opera boom. Opera has become fashionable among the rich and the nouveau riche but, more important, it has also become more popular. In Britain three opera companies are now firmly established outside London and have built up regular audiences for opera in twenty towns and cities from Plymouth to Aberdeen, with subsidiary tours and smaller companies visiting many smaller and more remote centres. The standard repertory has been greatly expanded, and these days it is not necessarily the umpteenth revival of *La Bohème* that pulls in the biggest crowds. It may be Prokofiev's *The Love for Three Oranges* or Nielsen's *Maskarade* that provides the hit of the season. Audiences have become accustomed to radical and innovative stagings. Opera is no longer anticipated as 'concerts in costume'; nor is every new production of, say, *The Marriage of Figaro* or *Carmen* expected to be just the same as all the others that preceded it. And television has introduced Wagner's *Ring* and much else to tens of thousands of people for whom performances at Covent Garden or Glyndebourne are out of reach both geographically and financially.

It would be disingenuous to suggest that every member of this growing audience for opera is necessarily receptive of new operatic work, although some new works by Harrison Birtwistle, Philip Glass and John Adams, for example, have been warmly received. Nor can it be claimed that recent years have seen a renascence in the successful composition of opera to compare with the expansion of audience and repertory. But opera does seem to have shaken off some of its more frowsty associations for quite a number of today's leading composers, including Stockhausen and Berio as well as those already mentioned; and the tradition of political opera is being kept alive, by Tippett, Henze, Alexander Goehr and John Adams, among others. Indeed, among recent operas none has made a wider impact than John Adams's *Nixon in China*, which has been televised and recorded, and to which not even the most ingenious critic could plausibly deny the title of 'political opera'.

Nixon in China took as its subject the historic visit of the then American President and his wife to Beijing in February 1972, a visit that ended more than twenty years of United States ostracism of the most populous nation on earth. The opera benefits hugely from the excellent libretto of the poet Alice Goodman. The detail of the writing is, for the most part, apt and vivid, if occasionally too opaque to be ideal for a libretto; more important, it gives the opera a clear and strong dramatic structure. The three scenes of Act One in particular make a splendid sequence: from the arrival at the airport, with Nixon manically extolling the news value of his visit, to the first meeting with the aged and enigmatic Chairman Mao in his study, to the first evening's banquet in the Great Hall of the People.

Goodman recalled that she was adamant that 'it had to be an heroic opera. I would not write it as a satire'; the composer was of the same mind.[1] To see Nixon as an heroic figure would involve taking more than the usual librettist's liberties with history; but that is not quite what the opera does. What it does do is to take the episode seriously, as a momentous, though not un-comic, encounter between two radically different civilizations and their histories. Only Kissinger is treated as a basically absurd if sinister figure. Chiang Ch'ing is openly authoritarian. But the Nixons and the two veteran Communist leaders Mao and Chou En-lai are well-rounded, complex figures, neither ridiculous nor crudely wicked.

It is plain that *Nixon in China* is a further exploration of the theme of relations between the West and east Asia that has been a recurring preoccupation of twentieth-century composers from Puccini to

Richard Rodgers and Stephen Sondheim. But the balance of world power has changed since the days of Lieutenant B.F. Pinkerton, with his breezily exploitative attitude towards the Japanese. In John Adams's opera the situation is almost reversed. For all their power and status, the American President and his wife are palpably out of their depth in Beijing. Chinese manners and customs are bewildering, and cannot be brushed aside with Pinkertonian impatience. Nixon's attempts to talk straight politics are frustrated by Mao's taste for the elliptical and the philosophical. In her Act Two aria Pat Nixon returns in her mind to the homely America she loves, while in the final, meditative act, the exhausted President retreats into his recollections of selling burgers to American troops in the Pacific theatre of World War Two. In a strange world they clutch at the familiar.

Since *Nixon in China*, which had its premiere in 1987, the same team of John Adams, Alice Goodman and the producer Peter Sellars have gone on to tackle the even more difficult and topical subject of terrorism, in another opera based on recent events, *The Death of Klinghoffer*, which had its first performance in Brussels in March 1991. As I write, *Klinghoffer* has yet to be seen in Britain, but it is clear from the choruses, which have been performed separately, that Adam uses the chorus in the established operatic way, as the collective voice of the two peoples involved – the Palestinians and the Jews – and that Adams and Goodman have made great imaginative efforts to understand the conflicting griefs and grievances of these two nations, with their intertwined histories of suffering and injustice. Composer and librettist are to be admired, not only for their daring but also for their sensitivity in their treatment of contemporary issues of such importance and emotional potency.

Another recent political opera in which the chorus plays a leading role is Alexander Goehr's *Behold the Sun*, or *Die Wiedertäufer*. This was commissioned by Deutsche Oper am Rhein and had its premiere in Duisburg in 1985. Or rather it would be more accurate to say that a version of the opera, much cut and altered without the composer's permission, was performed there and elsewhere in Germany in 1985. Goehr's subject was the Anabaptist uprising and takeover of the city of Münster in 1534, and the utopian, millenarian Christianity that the Anabaptists professed and tried, for a brief revolutionary moment, to put into practice. As Goehr has said, 'The People are the protagonist

. . . and it is their choruses, the *turbae*, that are the central focus.'[2] Some commentators, including Andrew Clements, have suggested that the work fails as an opera for this very reason. The chorus, he argued 'cannot become a surrogate for personal characterization. When all is said and done, opera . . . is about individuals.' This is at least debatable, but although the opera has been broadcast by BBC Radio Three in its complete and intended form, Goehr's work requires a sympathetic staging before we can judge the validity or otherwise of Clements's criticism. It has yet to be seen in Goehr's own country.

Mention of these works is made not so much for the sake of an impossible completeness, but simply as a demonstration of the fact that the well-established tradition of political opera is still very much alive. Attempts to seal off opera from politics and reduce it to the level of an expensive but essentially frivolous enchantment are always likely to founder on the properly serious ambitions of composers and librettists, as well as on the conviction of most opera administrators and producers, that opera is a form of theatre with a range as great and as varied as spoken drama, capable of offering us a comparable experience and understanding of our history and our society. Opera as a substantial art form has always been involved with politics and will continue to be so in so far as it remains a living and important artistic experience. The alternative is charming, decorative triviality.

Notes

1 Mozart: Class Conflict and Enlightenment

1. Charles Rosen: 'Beaumarchais: the inventor of modern opera', *New York Review of Books*, 27 October 1988.
2. Ibid.
3. Beaumarchais, *The Barber of Seville, The Marriage of Figaro*, translated by John Wood, Harmondsworth 1964, p. 199.
4. Joseph Kerman, *Opera as Drama*, New York 1956, p. 107.
5. Basil Deane, 'A Musical Commentary', in *The Marriage of Figaro*, ENO Opera Guide 17, London 1983, p. 25.
6. Eric Blom (ed.), *Mozart's Letters*, Harmondsworth 1956, p. 158.
7. Ibid., p. 176.
8. Hugh Ottaway, *Mozart*, London 1979, p. 93.
9. Quoted in ibid., p. 70.
10. Kerman, p. 102. Performances figures are given by Michael Robinson in Tim Carter, *W.A. Mozart Le nozze di Figaro*, Cambridge 1987, p. 12.
11. See Stephen Oliver, 'Music and Comedy in *The Marriage of Figaro*', in *The Marriage of Figaro*, ENO Opera Guide 17, London 1983, p. 35; and Carter, pp. 140 and 145.
12. For information on Beaumarchais I made use of Frederic Grendel, *Beaumarchais, The Man Who Was Figaro*, London 1977. For da Ponte, see April FitzLyon, *Lorenzo da Ponte*, London 1982.
13. Blom, p. 184.
14. For example, Julian Rushton, *W.A. Mozart, Don Giovanni*, Cambridge 1981, p. 7.
15. See Antony Peattie, *Don Giovanni*, Welsh National Opera 1984, p. 21.
16. Rushton, footnote p. 140.
17. Dan H. Lawrence (ed.), *Shaw's Music*, Vol. III, London 1981, p. 196.

18. Edward Dent, 'The History of the Opera', in Eric Crozier (ed.), *Moart's Così fan tutte*, London 1945, p. 17. Sacheverell Sitwell is quoted in *Così fan tutte*, Welsh National Opera 1985, p. 31. Beecham is quoted in the Opera North programme, 1982.

19. H.C. Robbins Landon, 'A Commentary on the Score', in *Così fan tutte*, ENO Opera Guide 22, London 1983, p. 21.

20. Alfred Einstein, *Mozart*, London 1971, p. 481.

21. H.C. Robbins Landon, *Mozart's Last Year*, London 1988, p. 134.

22. Quoted in Katharine Thomson, *The Masonic Thread in Mozart*, London 1977, p. 13.

23. Robbins Landon, *Mozart's Last Year*, pp. 56–7.

24. Thomson, p. 14.

25. Thomas Bauman, *W.A. Mozart Die Entführung*, Cambridge 1987, pp. 34–5. See also Brigid Brophy, *Mozart the Dramatist*, London 1988, pp. 223–4.

26. Einstein, p. 481.

27. Thomas Paine, *Common Sense* (originally published 1776), Harmondsworth 1976, p. 120.

2 Opera and the Revolution

1. See Jean-Jacques Gabas, 'Opera in the French Revolution', *Opera Now*, June 1989.

2. Basil Deane, *Cherubini*, Oxford 1965, p. 5.

3. Christopher Headington, Roy Westbrook and Terry Barfoot, *Opera, A History*, London 1987, p. 116.

4. See Winton Dean, 'Beethoven and Opera', in Denis Arnold and Nigel Fortune (eds), *The Beethoven Companion*, London 1973, pp. 333–4.

5. Hugh Ottaway, 'The Enlightenment and the Revolution', in Alec Robertson and Denis Stevens (eds), *The Pelican History of Music*, Vol. 3, Harmondsworth 1968, p. 86.

6. Basil Deane, 'The Symphonies and Overtures', in Arnold and Fortune, p. 291.

7. Ibid., pp. 312–13.

8. Ottaway, pp. 94–5.

9. Quoted in Alec Harman and Wilfred Mellers, *Man and his Music*, London 1962, p. 632.

10. Quoted in Frida Knight, *Beethoven and the Age of Revolution*, London 1973, p. 20.

11. Lionel Trilling, *The Opposing Self*, London 1955, p. 53.

12. John Warrack, 'Bouilly and his "Fauvette"', *Opera*, June 1983, p. 596.

13. David Cairns, *Responses*, London 1973, p. 40.

14. Winton Dean, pp. 367 and 366.

15. Ibid., p. 380.

16. Otto Klemperer, *Minor Recollections*, London 1964, p. 99.

17. Peter Heyworth (ed.), *Conversations with Klemperer*, London 1973, p. 85.

18. For Schneider, see Antony Peattie, 'Perspectives of Freedom', in the Welsh National Opera's programme book for *Fidelio*, 1981.

19. Joachim Herz, 'Questions about *Fidelio*', *Opera*, May 1980, p. 436.

3 *Patria Oppressa:* Rossini, Bellini, Donizetti and the Risorgimento (Nationalism I)

1. Norman Stone in *Opera Now*, August 1989, p. 34.
2. Heine and Stendhal are quoted in the Welsh National Opera programme book for *The Barber of Seville*, 1986.
3. Stendhal, *Life of Rossini*, translated by Richard N. Coe, London 1985, pp. 457–8.
4. John Rosselli, *The Opera Industry in Italy from Cimarosa to Verdi*, Cambridge 1984, p. 82.
5. Ibid., p. 207.
6. Herbert Weinstock, *Rossini, A Biography*, Oxford 1968, p. 107.
7. Nicholas Till, *Rossini, His Life and Times*, New York 1983, pp. 85–6.
8. Richard Osborne, *Rossini*, London 1986, p. 3.
9. Francis Toye, *Rossini, A Study in Tragi-comedy*, London 1934, p. 200.
10. Rodolfo Celletti, cited by Rodney Milnes in *Opera*, March 1992, p. 272.
11. Stendhal, pp. 12 and 65.
12. Ibid., p. 87.
13. Philip Gossett, 'Rossini', in *The New Grove Masters of Italian Opera*, London 1983, p. 2.
14. Quoted in Pierluigi Petrobelli, 'Balzac, Stendhal, and Rossini's *Moses*', in *The Barber of Seville/Moses*, Opera Guide 36, London 1985, p. 106.
15. Stendhal, p. 319.
16. Osborne, p. 226.
17. Edward J. Dent, *The Rise of Romantic Opera*, Cambridge 1976, p. 116.
18. Winton Dean, 'Opera in France', in Gerald Abraham (ed.), *The Age of Beethoven 1790–1830*, London 1982, p. 105.
19. Dan H. Laurence (ed.), *Shaw's Music*, Vol. II, London 1981, p. 570.
20. See Alastair Macaulay, 'Tenor of the Three Glorious Days', *Opera*, August 1989, p. 922.
21. Lesley Orrey, *Bellini*, London 1969, pp. 39 and 42.
22. Simon Meecham Jones, 'Victims of the Sacrifice', in the Welsh National Opera programme book for *Norma*, 1985.
23. John Deathridge, 'Reminiscences of *Norma*', in the Royal Opera House programme for *Norma*, 1987.
24. For example, Simon Meecham Jones, and John Rosselli, p. 167.
25. Orrey, p. 48.
26. Peter Conrad, 'The Dramaturgy of Bel Canto', in the Welsh National Opera programme book for *I puritani*, 1982. See also Conrad's *A Song of Love and Death*, London 1987, pp. 119–22.
27. See Andrew Porter, 'Bellini's Last Opera', in Harold Rosenthal (ed.), *The Opera Bedside Book*, London 1965, p. 169.
28. Orrey, pp. 43–6.
29. Herbert Weinstock, *Vincenzo Bellini*, London 1972, pp. 146–7.
30. See ibid., pp. 18–20, and also p. 188.
31. William Ashbrook, 'Gaetano Donizetti', in *Masters of Italian Opera*, pp. 106–7.
32. William Ashbrook, *Donizetti and his Operas*, Cambridge 1982, pp. 67 and 630. For the Ruffini brothers, see p. 592.

4 Verdi: the Liberal Patriot

1. Dan H. Laurence (ed.), *Shaw's Music*, Vol. III, London 1981, pp. 583 and 570.

2. Quoted in William Weaver, *Verdi: A Documentary Study*, London 1977, p. 215.

3. Julian Budden, *Verdi*, London 1985, p. 53.

4. Charles Osborne, *Letters of Giuseppe Verdi*, London 1971, pp. 82–3 and 84. It is extraordinary that this brief selection, which predictably omits many of Verdi's more political letters, should be all that we have of Verdi's letters in English.

5. Ibid., pp. 161–2.

6. Quoted in Weaver, pp. 174–5.

7. Quoted in George Martin, *Verdi, His Music, Life and Times*, London 1965, p. 205.

8. Quoted in ibid., pp. 310 and 311.

9. Rudy Shackelford (trans. and ed.), *Dallapiccola on Opera*, London 1987, p. 134.

10. David Kimbell, Note to the Deutsche Grammophon (DG) recording of *Nabucco* (1983) conducted by Giuseppe Sinopoli.

11. Julian Budden, *The Operas of Verdi*, Vol. I, London 1973, p. 107.

12. Kimbell. See the same author's *Verdi in the Age of Italian Romanticism*, Cambridge 1981, pp. 456–7.

13. See Charles Osborne, *The Complete Operas of Verdi*, London 1973, p. 43.

14. Ibid., p. 58.

15. See George Martin, 'Verdi and the Risorgimento', in his *Aspects of Verdi*, London 1989, pp. 17–18.

16. Budden, *The Operas*, Vol. I, p. 163.

17. Julian Budden, Note for the Philips recording of *Attila* (1972) conducted by Lamberto Gardelli.

18. Budden, *The Operas*, Vol. I, p. 265.

19. Ibid., p. 414.

20. Quoted in Martin, *Verdi, His Music*, p. 214.

21. David Kimbell, Note to the DG recording of *Rigoletto* (1980) conducted by Carlo Maria Giulini.

22. Quoted in Andrew Porter, 'Giuseppe Verdi', in *The New Grove Masters of Italian Opera*, London 1983, p. 218.

23. Quoted in Budden, *The Operas*, Vol. II, London 1978, p. 173.

24. Quoted in ibid., p. 180.

25. Ibid., p. 209.

26. William Mann's essay was written for the DG recording of *Simon Boccanegra* (1977) conducted by Claudio Abbado.

27. Rodolfo Celletti, 'An Historical Perspective', in *Simon Boccanegra*, ENO Opera Guide 32, London 1985, p. 11.

28. Martin, *Aspects of Verdi*, pp. 79–91.

29. Peter Conrad, 'War and Peace', in *The Force of Destiny*, ENO Opera Guide 23, London 1983, p. 7. For the revision of the ending, see Bruce A. Brown's contribution to the same guide, 'That Damned Ending'.

30. Nicholas Payne, 'I Am What I Think', in the Welsh National Opera programme book for *La forza del destino* (1981).

31. Budden's remarks on Preziosilla and the end of Act Three are quoted from his Note for the EMI recording of *La forza del destino* (1988) conducted by Riccardo Muti.

32. Osborne, *Letters*, p. 122.

33. See Andrew Porter's Note to the EMI recording of *Don Carlos* (in Italian, 1971) conducted by Carlo Maria Giulini.

34. Budden, *Verdi*, p. 267.

35. Quoted in Martin, *Aspects of Verdi*, p. 98.

36. Budden, *Verdi*, p. 263.

37. Budden, *The Operas of Verdi*, Vol. III, London 1981, p. 125.

38. Ibid., footnote pp. 97–8.

39. Martin, *Aspects of Verdi*, p. 110. My information on the perceived anti-Catholicism of the opera is taken from the same source, Martin's essay 'Posa . . . The Flawed Hero'.

40. Budden, *The Operas*, Vol. III, p. 139, and *Verdi*, p. 268.

41. Weaver, p. 212.

42. Hans Busch (ed.), *Verdi's Aida*, Minneapolis 1978, p. 17.

43. Budden, *The Operas*, Vol. III, p. 258.

44. Quoted in ibid., p. 161.

45. Quoted in Martin, *Verdi, His Music*, p. 382.

46. Quoted in Michael Rose, 'Verdi's "Egyptian Business"', in *Aida*, Opera Guide 2, London 1980, p. 12.

47. Budden, *Verdi*, p. 272.

48. Martin, *Aspects of Verdi*, p. 27.

5 Wagner: from Revolution to Racism

1. John Deathridge and Carl Dahlhaus, *The New Grove Wagner*, London 1984, p. 95.

2. H.S. Chamberlain, Introduction to *Richard Wagner's Letters to August Roeckel*, Bristol n.d., p. 35.

3. Peter Burbidge, 'Richard Wagner: man and artist', in Peter Burbidge and Richard Sutton (eds), *The Wagner Companion*, London 1979, p. 21.

4. Curt von Westernhagen, *Wagner, A Biography*, Cambridge 1981, p. 133.

5. See Derek Watson, *Richard Wagner*, London 1979, pp. 32–3 and 50.

6. See Barry Millington, *Wagner*, London 1984, pp. 34–7.

7. Watson, p. 105.

8. Stewart Spencer and Barry Millington (eds), *Selected Letters of Richard Wagner*, London 1987, pp. 686 and 691–2.

9. Watson, p. 291.

10. John Deathridge, 'Rienzi . . . a Few of the Facts', *Musical Times*, September 1983. And see also his contribution to the English National Opera programme for *Rienzi*, 1983.

11. See Millington, pp. 157–60.

12. See John Deathridge, 'The "Authentic" Dutchman?', in the Royal Opera House programme for *Der fliegende Holländer*, 1986.

13. Timothy McFarland, 'Wagner's Most Medieval Opera', in *Tannhäuser*, Opera Guide 39, London 1988, pp. 26 and 28.

14. Quoted in Mike Ashman, *Tannhäuser* – an Obsession', in ibid., p. 12.

15. Carl Dahlhaus, *Richard Wagner's Music Dramas*, Cambridge 1979, p. 103.

16. *Sunday Times*, 7 August 1983.

17. Dan H. Laurence (ed.), *Shaw's Music*, Vol. II, London 1981, p. 663.

18. George Bernard Shaw, 'The Perfect Wagnerite', in *Major Critical Essays*, Harmondsworth 1986, p. 197.

19. I have throughout quoted from Andrew Porter's English translation of *The Ring*, London 1977.

20. Shaw, p. 208.

21. Quoted in Raymond Williams, *Cobbett*, Oxford 1983, p. 37.

22. Martin Gregor-Dellin and Dietrich Mack (eds), *Cosima Wagner's Diaries*, Vol. I, London 1978, p. 965.

23. Shaw, p. 247.

24. See Dahlhaus, p. 89.

25. Deryck Cooke, *I Saw the World End*, Oxford 1979, p. 312.

26. *Selected Letters*, p. 308.

27. Ibid., pp. 357 and 309.

28. Ibid., pp. 308–9.

29. Newman's phrase is quoted by Patrick McCreless, *Wagner's Siegfried: its drama, history, and music*, Ann Arbor 1982, p. 14. For Dahlhaus, see *Music Dramas*, pp. 114 and 65.

30. Robert Gutman, *Richard Wagner*, Harmondsworth 1971, p. 420. Theodor Adorno, *In Search of Wagner*, London 1981, p. 140.

31. *Selected Letters*, p. 307.

32. Ibid., pp. 219 and 184.

33. Ibid., p. 309.

34. Robert Donington, *Wagner's 'Ring' and its Symbols*, London 1974, p. 230.

35. Adorno, p. 94.

36. See Millington, p. 254.

37. Deryck Cooke, essay in the Decca recording of *Die Meistersinger* (1976) conducted by Sir Georg Solti.

38. Timothy McFarland, 'Wagner's Nuremberg', in *The Mastersingers of Nuremberg*, Opera Guide 19, London 1983, p. 27.

39. Ernest Newman, *Wagner Nights*, London 1977, pp. 300–2.

40. *Selected Letters*, pp. 701 and 708.

41. McFarland, p. 27.

42. See Barry Millington, 'Nuremberg Trial: is there anti-semitism in *Die Meistersinger?*', *Cambridge Opera Journal*, Vol. 3, No. 3, November 1991. I am very grateful to Barry Millington for making his article available to me in advance of its publication.

43. Dahlhaus, p. 65.

44. Deathridge and Dahlhaus, p. 158.

45. Robert Craft, *Current Convictions*, London 1978, p. 87; Gutman, pp. 603–4; Graham Bradshaw in the *London Review of Books*, 3 March 1983.

46. 'Nietzsche contra Wagner', in Walter Kaufmann (ed.), *The Portable Nietzsche*, Harmondsworth 1976, pp. 675 and 676.

47. *Selected Letters*, pp. 898–9.

48. Joachim Bergfeld (ed.), *The Diary of Richard Wagner 1865–1882*, London 1980, p. 202.

49. Quoted in Millington, p. 268.

50. Quoted in Watson, p. 291.

51. Bergfeld (ed.), p. 202.

52. Quoted in Gutman, p. 595.
53. Quoted in Millington, p. 105.
54. Curt von Westernhagen in *The New Grove Dictionary of Music and Musicians*, Vol. 20, London 1980, p. 113. Westernhagen's version of Wagner's life was replaced with a contribution by John Deathridge in the paperback *New Grove Wagner*.
55. See Craft, p. 96 and footnote p. 88.
56. Martin van Amerongen, *Wagner: A Case History*, London 1983, p. 147.
57. Pierre Boulez, *Orientations*, London 1986, pp. 276–7.
58. Debussy, 'Monsieur Croche the Dilettante Hater', in *Three Classics in the Aesthetic of Music*, New York 1962, pp. 48–9.

6 Russia, Czechoslovakia and England (Nationalism II)

1. Martin Cooper, *Russian Opera*, London 1951, p. 20.
2. Quoted in David Brown, *Mikhail Glinka*, London 1974, p. 73.
3. See David Brown, 'Mikhail Glinka', in *The New Grove Russian Masters*, Vol. 1, London 1986, p. 10.
4. Brown, p. 45.
5. Ibid., pp. 112–13.
6. John Bayley, *Pushkin: A Comparative Study*, Cambridge 1971, p. 169.
7. Letter of Vladimir Stasov quoted in the English National Opera programme for *Boris Godunov*, 1980.
8. See Laurel E. Fay, 'The Drama and Music of *Boris*', in *Boris Godunov*, Opera Guide 11, London 1982, p. 23.
9. Isaiah Berlin, in an essay in the Royal Opera House programme for *Khovanschina*, 1982. He also quotes Stasov's descriptions of the opera's leading characters.
10. David Lloyd-Jones, note for the RCA recording of Mussorgsky Orchestral Works, conducted by Claudio Abbado, 1980.
11. See M.D. Calvocoressi, *Mussorgsky*, London 1974, pp. 149–50.
12. See Israel V. Nestyev, *Prokofiev*, Oxford 1961, p. 327.
13. Colin Graham, interviewed in *3* magazine, November 1982.
14. See his letter of 11 March 1860, in Frantisek Bartos (ed.), *Bedrich Smetana – Letters and Reminiscences*, Prague 1955, pp. 59–60.
15. Quoted in the Welsh National Opera programme book for *The Bartered Bride*, 1982.
16. Quoted in John Tyrrell, *Czech Opera*, Cambridge 1988, p. 217.
17. John Clapham, *Smetana*, London 1972, p. 33.
18. See Pavel Eckstein's report from Czechoslovakia in *Opera*, September 1984.
19. Brian Large, *Smetana*, London 1970, p. 165.
20. In the Welsh National Opera programme book, 1982.
21. Tyrrell, pp. 8–9.
22. Quoted in Large, p. 239.
23. Ibid., p. 224; see also p. 212.
24. Quoted in Jan Smaczny, 'Dvořák and *Rusalka*', *Opera*, March 1983, p. 241.
25. Quoted in Alena Nemcova, 'The Premiere in Brno', in the Welsh National Opera programme book for *Jenufa*, 1984.
26. Quoted in Jaroslav Vogel, *Janáček*, London 1981, p. 232.

27. Jan Smaczny, 'Janáček and Czech Realism', in *Jenufa/Katya Kabanova*, Opera Guide 33, London 1985, p. 36.

28. See Vogel, p. 234.

29. Vaughan Williams's correspondence with his librettist is printed as an appendix to Ursula Vaughan Williams, *RVW*, Oxford 1988, p. 402.

30. Hubert Foss, *Ralph Vaughan Williams*, London 1950, p. 177.

31. Peter Pirie, *The English Musical Renaissance*, London 1979, p. 117.

7 Women in Opera

1. Catherine Clément, *Opera, or the Undoing of Women*, Minneapolis 1988.

2. Ibid., p. 11.

3. Ibid., p. 47.

4. Brigid Brophy, *Mozart the Dramatist*, London 1988, pp. 35, 37.

5. See Vincent Godefroy, *The Dramatic Genius of Verdi*, Vol. I, London 1975, pp. 252–2.

6. Julian Budden, *The Operas of Verdi*, Vol. II, London 1978, pp. 165–6.

7. David Kimbell, *Verdi in the Age of Italian Romanticism*, Cambridge 1981, pp. 648–9.

8. Rodney Milnes, 'Carmen', in Alan Blyth (ed.), *Opera on Record*, London 1979, p. 462.

9. Quoted in John Warrack, *Tchaikovsky*, London 1973, p. 138.

10. Clément, pp. 79 and 82.

11. Cynthia Marsh, 'Ostrovsky's play "The Thunderstorm"', in John Tyrrell (ed.), *Leos Janáček: Katja Kabanova*, Cambridge 1982, p. 44.

12. David Pountney, 'Producing "Kat'a Kabanova"', in ibid., p. 185.

13. Max Brod, '*Katja Kabanowa*', in ibid., p. 162.

14. George Steiner on *Lulu* in *The Listener*, 26 February 1981.

15. Pierre Boulez, *Orientations*, London 1986, p. 382.

16. See George Perle, 'Alban Berg', in *The New Grove Second Viennese School*, London 1983, p. 175; see also Douglas Jarman, 'Lulu: the Background', in the Royal Opera House programme for *Lulu*, 1981.

17. See Perle, p. 175.

18. Helene Berg (ed.), *Alban Berg: Letters to his Wife*, London 1971, p. 424.

8 Interlude – Opera without Politics: Puccini and Strauss

1. See Mosco Carner, *Puccini – A Critical Biography*, London 1974, p. 101.

2. Quoted in ibid., p. 104.

3. Bernard Williams, 'Manifest Artifice', in *Tosca*, Opera Guide 16, London 1982, p. 12.

4. Gaia Servadio, 'Tosca – 1944', in the English National Opera programme for *Tosca*, 1987.

5. Carner, p. 399.

6. Ibid., p. 399 and footnote.

7. Tom Sutcliffe, *The Guardian*, 29 September 1984.

8. John Louis DiGaetani, *Puccini the Thinker*, New York 1987, pp. 42–3. For Puccini's reactions to Mussolini and fascism, see Harvey Sachs, *Music in Fascist Italy*, London 1987, pp. 104–5.

9. Quoted in Michael Kennedy, *Strauss Tone Poems*, London 1984, p. 40.

10. Rollo Myers (ed.), *Richard Strauss and Romain Rolland, Correspondence*, London 1968, p. 132.

11. John Cox, 'Standing up for Strauss', *Opera*, June 1979, p. 533.

12. Quoted in Michael Kennedy, *Richard Strauss*, London 1976. p. 100.

13. William Mann, *Richard Strauss: a critical study of the operas*, London 1964, p. 305. Kennedy, *Richard Strauss*, p. 181.

14. Rodney Milnes, review in *Gramophone*, July 1986.

15. Luigi Illica's notes are printed in the text published by Welsh National Opera in *Andrea Chenier*, Preview No. 3, 1982.

9 Democratic Opera: Victims as Heroes

1. Quoted in John Warrack, *Tchaikovsky*, London 1973, p. 111.

2. Julian Budden, 'Puccini, Massenet and *Verismo*', *Opera*, May 1983, p. 477.

3. Ibid., p. 481.

4. Richard Mohr, sleevenote for the RCA recording of *Il tabarro*, conducted by Erich Leinsdorf (1972); Carner is quoted in John Louis DiGaetani, *Puccini the Thinker*, New York 1987, p. 122.

5. See David H. Greene and Edward M. Stephens, *J.M. Synge 1871–1909*, New York 1959, p. 61.

6. Peter Pirie, *The English Musical Renaissance*, London 1979, p. 155.

7. Raymond Williams, *Drama from Ibsen to Eliot*, Harmondsworth 1964, p. 177.

8. See Douglas Jarman, *The Music of Alban Berg*, London 1979, p. 66.

9. For an outline of Büchner's life and politics, see Julian Hilton, *Georg Büchner*, London 1982, Chapter 1.

10. Peter Gay, *Weimar Culture*, Harmondsworth 1974, p. 66.

11. George Perle, *The New Grove Second Viennese School*, London 1983, p. 152.

12. Helene Berg (ed.), *Alban Berg: Letters to his Wife*, London 1971, p. 229.

13. Quoted in Perle, p. 154.

14. Ibid., p. 161.

15. Mark deVoto, '*Wozzeck* in Context', in *Wozzeck*, ENO Opera Guide 42, London 1990, p. 11.

16. Jarman, p. 27.

17. Joseph Kerman, *Opera as Drama*, New York 1956, pp. 231–3.

18. Arnold Whittall, *Music since the First World War*, London 1977, p. 145.

19. Mirka Zemanova (ed.), *Janáček's Uncollected Essays on Music*, London 1989, p. 123.

20. See the Introduction to William E. Yuill (ed.), *The Soldiers*, Chicago 1972, pp. xii–xiii.

21. Quoted in *From the House of the Dead*, Welsh National Opera Companion, 1984, p. 52.

22. I have mislaid the source of this reflection by Janáček.

23. Quoted by Malcolm Jones in the Welsh National Opera programme book for *From the House of the Dead*, 1990.
24. Whittall, p. 189.
25. Luigi Dallapiccola, 'On the Twelve-Note Road', *Music Survey*, Vol. IV, No. 1, p. 330. Reprinted London 1981.
26. Rudy Shackleford (ed.), *Dallapiccola on Opera*, London 1987, p. 45.
27. Quoted by Douglas Jarman in Kim H. Kowalke (ed.), *A New Orpheus: essays on Kurt Weill*, New Haven 1986, p. 148.
28. See Douglas Jarman, *Kurt Weill*, London 1983, p. 136.
29. John Willett, Introduction to Bertolt Brecht, *The Threepenny Opera, Collected Plays* Vol. II, Part 2, London 1979, p. xvi.
30. See Note by Kurt Weill in ibid., p. 98.
31. Ronald Sanders, *The Days Grow Short*, London 1980, p. 156.
32. Jarman, *Kurt Weill*, p. 125.
33. Miles Kreuger, note for the EMI recording of *Show Boat*, 1988, conducted by John McGlinn.
34. Edward Jablonski and Laurence D. Stewart, *The Gershwin Years*, London 1974, p. 244.
35. Quoted in ibid., p. 222.
36. Quoted in the booklet for the recording of *West Side Story*, 1985, conducted by Leonard Bernstein.
37. Desmond Shawe-Taylor's review of the first performance of the opera is reprinted in Philip Brett, *Peter Grimes*, Cambridge 1983, p. 155.
38. See ibid., p. 190.
39. See Michael Kennedy, *Britten*, London 1981, pp. 123–4.
40. Tom Sutcliffe, *The Guardian*, 24 February 1988.
41. Quoted in P.N. Furbank, *E.M. Forster: a life*, Vol. 2, London 1978, p. 284.
42. E,M. Forster, 'What I Believe', in *Two Cheers for Democracy*, Harmondsworth 1965, p. 76.
43. Michael Tippett, *Moving into Aquarius*, St Albans 1974, p. 153.
44. Michael Tippett, *Music of the Angels*, London 1980, pp. 234 and 225.

Conclusion

1. Alice Goodman, 'Towards *Nixon in China*', printed with the libretto for the Nonesuch recording of the opera, 1988.
2. Alexander Goehr, 'Working on *Die Wiedertäufer*', *Opera*, April 1985, p. 384.

Index

References to the principal discussion of an opera are set in bold